Invitation to the Gospels

Donald Senior on Matthew,
Paul J. Achtemeier on Mark,
Robert J. Karris on Luke,
and
George W. MacRae, with Revision by Daniel J. Harrington, on John

Foreword by Lawrence Boadt

PAULIST PRESS

New York/Mahwah, New Jersey

Book design by Celine Allen
Cover design by Valerie Petro

Library of Congress Cataloging-in-Publication Data

Senior, Donald.
    Invitation to the Gospels / Donald Senior, Paul J. Achtemeier, Robert J. Karris;
foreword by Lawrence Boadt.
        p. cm.
Includes bibliographical references.
    ISBN 0-8091-4072-1
    1. Bible. N.T. Gospels—Commentaries. I. Achtemeier, Paul J. II. Karris, Robert J.
III. Title
    BS2555.53 .S46 2002
    226'.06—dc21

                                                                            2002005834

Published by Paulist Press
997 Macarthur Boulevard
Mahwah, New Jersey 07430

www.paulistpress.com

Printed and bound in the United States of America

CONTENTS

For Marie—she knows why
Paul J. Achtemeier

I dedicate this revised edition
to the memory of my only sister, Joanne M. Pritchett,
and to Joshua Elliott and Shawn Michael, sons of Samantha,
Joanne's daughter.
Robert J. Karris, O.F.M.

FOREWORD

In the enthusiastic beginnings of regular Bible study by Catholic parishes and schools in the 1980s, four of the leading New Testament scholars in North America joined together to put out four individual introductory study guides to the Gospels. It was published by Doubleday under the title of the *Invitation To...* series. It enjoyed great success as a simple and easy-to-understand first study of the riches of the individual Gospels.

That set of volumes has been long out of print, but under the inspiration of its original general editor, Robert Karris, O.F.M., the same premier scholars have revised and updated their introductions to the Gospels and have now combined them together in a single comprehensive study that makes available to every type of student or casual reader the same useful and easy introductory look at the individual four Gospels.

Since the original book, the author of the commentary on the Gospel of John, George MacRae, S.J., has died and so could not contribute to this new edition. But his fellow Boston Jesuit, New Testament teacher, close friend and leading American biblical scholar, Reverend Daniel Harrington, S.J., has undertaken to revise Father MacRae's work. No finer successor could be found for the task.

In a new century, biblical study in Catholic circles has come of age. It is actively encouraged by the bishops, priests and leading catechetical leaders; there are major biblical training programs for interested individuals throughout the country, such as the Denver Bible School Program, used in many dioceses. Hopefully, this excellent book will become a valuable tool in reaching still thousands more with the spiritual treasures of our Scriptures.

Lawrence Boadt, C.S.P.
Professor Emeritus of Biblical Studies
Washington Theological Union
President, Paulist Press

ABBREVIATIONS

Chr	Chronicles
Col	Colossians
Cor	Corinthians
Dan	Daniel
Deut	Deuteronomy
Eph	Ephesians
Exod	Exodus
Ezek	Ezekiel
Gal	Galatians
Gen	Genesis
Heb	Hebrews
Hos	Hosea
Isa	Isaiah
JB	Jerusalem Bible
Jer	Jeremiah
Judg	Judges
Kgs	Kings
Lev	Leviticus
Macc	Maccabees
Mal	Malachi
Matt	Matthew
Mic	Micah
NAB	New American Bible
NRSV	New Revised Standard Version
Num	Numbers
Pet	Peter
Phil	Philippians
Prov	Proverbs
Ps	Psalm

Pss	Psalms
Rom	Romans
Sam	Samuel
Sir	Sirach
Thess	Thessalonians
Tim	Timothy
Tob	Tobit
v.	verse
vv.	verses
Wis	Wisdom
Zech	Zechariah

Invitation to Matthew

Donald Senior, C.P.

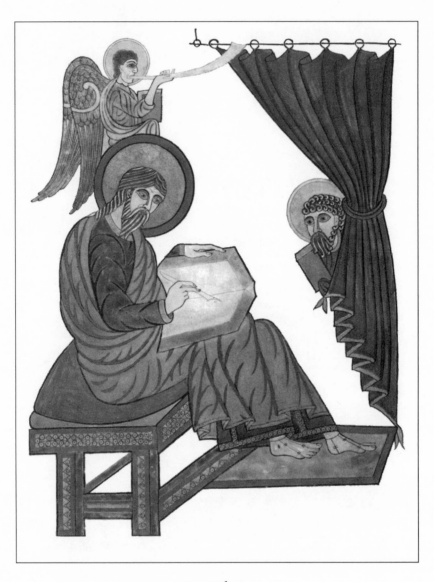

Matthew

Introduction to Matthew's Gospel

F ew Christians turn to the Gospels simply to brush up on their history or to solve theoretical problems. The believer seeks out the Gospels for inspiration and life. This instinctive estimate of the Gospels' purpose is corroborated by the results of modern biblical studies. The Gospels were not written to fill out Jesus' biographical dossier, nor are they abstract religious treatises. Each of the Gospels summons up an image of Jesus and his meaning for life designed to respond to the religious hopes and agonies of specific communities of Christians. The Gospels, like an effective sermon, tailor their message to a particular audience and a particular mood.

Matthew wrote his Gospel for a segment of the early church that desperately needed a sense of identity with the past and some direction for facing an uncertain future. The original recipients of the Gospel were, as far as can be detected, one or more communities of mainly Jewish Christians, probably living in Syria in the decade between A.D. 80 and 90.

The time and the place are significant. It was a time when those Christians whose roots were still in Judaism and its sacred history were experiencing, with other segments of the Jewish community, a tension that ultimately would lead to a wrenching separation, even alienation, from the religion of their ancestors. Prior to the Jewish revolt against Rome in A.D. 67, Jews and Jewish Christians seemed to have maintained relatively peaceful, if not cordial, relationships. The Book of Acts testifies that Palestinian Christians continued to worship in the Jerusalem Temple (Acts 2:46) and the ranks of the young church were swelled by an influx of Pharisees as well as Samaritans and Greek-speaking Jews. The early Christians considered themselves to be thoroughly Jewish and completely in tune with the religious history of

3

Israel; they were the people of the renewed covenant, of the Messianic
Age so longed for by the Hebrew Scriptures.

At the same time, those Jews who rejected the claims of Jesus and
his followers could still maintain enough tolerance for such fringe
groups as the Christians seemed to be. There were local harassments
and some degree of hostility and debate, but, in general, Jews who were
Christians and Jews who were not seemed able to share a live-and-let-
live attitude.

But as history moved to the decade of Matthew, A.D. 80 to 90,
some enormous changes engulfed both Judaism and Christianity and
led to the crisis atmosphere which helped trigger Matthew's Gospel. A
key event for both religious traditions was Rome's suppression of the
Jewish revolt of A.D. 67–70. When the armies of the Roman general
Titus pulverized the last fragments of resistance in Jerusalem and
destroyed the sacred city and its still more sacred temple, the destinies
of both Jews and Christians were profoundly altered.

For Judaism it meant the end of an era. The temple which had been
the unifying religious symbol of Israel was gone and so was the effective
influence of groups such as the priests and the Sadducees who had been
a major part of the nation's leadership. Gone, too, were the Zealots, who
had precipitated the revolt, and reform groups like the Essenes. The only
party resilient enough and astute enough to survive the war was the lay
reform movement of the Pharisees. Under the leadership of Yonahan
ben Zakkai, the sages of the Pharisee party gathered at the coastal town
of Jamnia and began to shape the future of an orthodox Judaism without temple or priesthood. Now the local synagogue, with its emphasis
on the teaching of the scriptures, and the home, where acts of piety and
devotion were sustained in family life, would be the focal points of Jewish identity. Israel's worship of Yahweh would not be the ancient ritual
of temple sacrifice but the "holocaust" of strict obedience to the law, the
law interpreted and taught by the rabbis.

The moral strength and leadership of the Pharisees enabled
Judaism to survive one of the most violent shocks of its long and often
tragic history. But, perhaps of necessity, it also meant an end to much of
the tolerance for religious diversity that had characterized pre-70
Judaism. The increasing numbers of Jewish Christians, and their claim
to be the inheritors of the promises of the Hebrew Scriptures, would
lead to a sharp and often bitter cleavage between this new minority
and the dominant majority of non-Christian Jews.

The destruction of Jerusalem and its temple also effected fundamental changes on early Christianity. Prior to A.D. 70, the religious center of Christianity had remained Jerusalem and the Jewish Christian leaders. But the sacking of Jerusalem put an effective end to this center of influence in the early church. For years prior to 70, Gentiles had been streaming into the community; soon they would be the dominant voice and culture in the young church. Christianity had accelerated its move to the west. As it did so, its distinction from Judaism would become more apparent and its debates with the Jewish leaders more heated.

Some sense of this complex history of the first century is necessary in order to fully appreciate Matthew's Gospel, for it was in response to this situation that the evangelist wrote his Gospel. The Christians of Matthew's community were witnesses to these turbulent years of transition and disruption. Most of them were Jews who had come to accept Jesus as the Messiah and Son of God. And they had seen their community grow with increasing numbers of new converts, including Greeks and other Gentiles from the mixed population centers of Syria. For the Jewish members of Matthew's community, faith in Jesus had never meant a repudiation of their Jewish past. Jesus was the Christ, the fulfillment of Israel's dream.

But now this continuity with their sacred past seemed threatened with rupture. Gentile converts brought strange customs, many of which contravened the Jewish law and were repugnant to refined Jewish moral sensitivities. And, with the destruction of Jerusalem and its impact on Judaism itself, these Jewish Christians had to contend with the growing hostility of their fellow Jews who had less tolerance for the kind of diversity represented by Jewish Christianity. Jewish Christians were accused of destroying the law and of forfeiting their claim on the Jewish scriptures. They were not to be part of the destiny of Israel promised by God and they were apparently banned from participation in Jewish synagogues.

It was a moment of religious crisis for Matthew's church. What had happened to the sense of kinship with the past? Was it right to launch out into a strange and untracked future? Matthew's church was infected with the perennial virus of people in transition: disunity and loss of perspective. This was the pastoral situation to which Matthew's Gospel attempted to respond. By editing the already written Gospel of Mark, by including precious materials about Jesus found in a collection of his sayings, and by incorporating a number of traditions known to

Matthew and his community, the evangelist would shape a story of Jesus' life that would have special meaning for his distraught Christians. The details of Matthew's pointed story will be spun out in the text and the commentary that follows. For the moment, we can simply alert the reader to Matthew's story line.

The framework of Matthew's message encompasses a full story of the life of Jesus.

A. Matthew's distinctive recital of this story begins with the remote origins of Jesus in the history of Israel and with the portent-laden traditions about his infancy (chapters 1 to 2). These events and the epic meeting of John the Baptist and Jesus (3:1 to 4:11) orient the reader to the dramatic beginning of Jesus' ministry as the Messiah.

B. The story quickens with Jesus' entry into Galilee. In this first great section of the public history of Jesus (4:12 to 10:42), Matthew portrays Jesus as the fulfillment of Israel's hope, as the Messiah who comes to teach genuine wisdom (chapters 5 to 7) and to bring deep healing (chapters 8 and 9) to God's people. His ministry of restoring life to Israel is one that is shared with his disciples and those who will take their place (9:35 to 10:42).

C. Another phase of the Gospel begins in chapter 11 (11:1 to 16:20). The mood turns sober as Matthew charts the varying responses to Jesus and his message. Jesus, like John, will be rejected by his own people. That rejection leads to the climax of Jesus' ministry in Jerusalem.

D. Matthew begins to orient the reader toward that fateful conclusion in a central section of the Gospel which opens in 16:21 with the first passion prediction and carries to the end of chapter 20 where Jesus and his frightened disciples stand before the capital city.

E. The most dramatic moments of Jesus' saga take place in the City of the Prophets (21:1 to 28:15). This is the setting for Matthew's recounting of Jesus' forceful presence in the temple, his last teaching, and the measured recital of his suffering and death. Jerusalem, too, will be the locale for the startling events which demonstrate that Jesus' death was no mere tragedy but a pivotal event in the history of the world.

F. Matthew closes his story back in Galilee (28:16–20). A new community born out of Jesus' resurrection is sent out on a world-wide mission.

This story line carries Matthew's Gospel from start to finish. But one of the distinctive elements of this Gospel is its concentration on the *words* of Jesus. At different stages in his narrative of Jesus' life, Matthew freezes the pace of the Gospel to include collections of the words of Jesus or "discourses" (cf. the Sermon on the Mount of chapters 5 to 7; the mission discourse of chapter 10; the parable discourse of chapter 13; the community discourse of chapter 18; and the judgment discourse of chapters 23 to 25). Matthew's use of so many sayings and parables of Jesus heightens his portrayal of Jesus as teacher, as one who reveals true wisdom to God's people.

By means of this narrative and its majestic portrait of Jesus, Matthew attempts to respond to the needs of his community. The very choice of this medium points to the dominant motif of Matthew's pastoral strategy. It is faith in Jesus Christ and a genuine commitment to his message that will give perspective to Matthew's suffering church. The reader of the Gospel should be alerted to some of the ways in which the evangelist goes about his task:

(1) He portrays *Jesus as the embodiment and fulfillment of all that Israel hoped for.* Matthew depicts Jesus as showing marked respect for the law, for Israel's institutions, and even for the leaders who ultimately oppose him (23:2–3). Jesus has come not to destroy but to fulfill (5:17–20). He is *the* Israelite, the obedient Son of Yahweh. This is a case Matthew will build steadily throughout his narrative and frequently linger over by explicit references to the Old Testament scriptures (cf. an explanation of the so-called "fulfillment" quotations in the commentary on 1:22).

By stressing that Jesus is the fulfillment of Israel, Matthew reminds his Christians that in following Jesus they are not abandoning their heritage but discovering its full meaning. Matthew's sharp critique of the religious leaders who oppose Jesus (and, by implication, the Christians who believe in him) also makes this case; the evangelist discredits the Jewish leaders as unfaithful and lacking integrity, as "blind guides" who lead their people astray.

(2) Matthew also interprets the events of Jesus' life, particularly *his death and resurrection, as the pivotal events in salvation history.* Jesus' roots go back to Abraham and David. He is the promised Messiah. And, in accord with God's promises, he comes first to Israel (10:5; 15:24). The tragic rejection of Jesus becomes a paradox of providence because God's plan of salvation will not be thwarted, even by Israel's infidelity. Now the invitation to the banquet of the kingdom is thrown open to the Gentiles as well. Thus the death and resurrection of Jesus begins a new and final age, an age in which the good news of the kingdom will be brought to the whole world, and an age in which the old order of the Mosaic law will be brought to fulfillment and its ultimate goal by the teaching and ministry of Jesus.

By viewing history through the lens of the Gospel, Matthew wanted to give his baffled Christians perspective on the disturbing changes they were experiencing and to counter the accusations coming from the synagogue. As Matthew stresses in his Infancy Narrative, the God of Israel had consistently used the unexpected and unassuming as instruments of his providence. The flood of Gentiles into God's vineyard was another of those marvelous surprises tucked into sacred history. One had to be open and ready for God's will.

By thus stressing continuity in the midst of the discontinuity his communities were experiencing, Matthew also hoped to retain the beauty and strength of his sacred Jewish heritage for the Christian community of the future that was to include both Jews and Gentiles.

(3) And, finally, Matthew sees *Jesus as a model of the inner life of the community* as it moves into its future. Jesus' teaching on love and reconciliation, his ministry of compassion, and, above all, his life-giving death, challenge the community to mold its own priorities on those of Jesus. Matthew's Christ is a doer who constantly censures the hypocrisy of words uncoupled from deeds. The Gospel's robust and even angry critique of the opponents of Jesus makes them a vivid example of what Christians ought *not* to be: insensitive legalists, blind leaders, and teachers who do not follow their own words.

Here again Matthew's ministry of continuity, of perspective, is at work. For through the teaching and example of Jesus he reminds his community that the only link with the past worth saving was Israel's call to fidelity. Obedience to the will of the Father was always the mark of a true Israelite, and that was the mark of Jesus and those who were his followers.

Matthew's church is a long distance from our own. Even though we know something about the agony of transition and discontinuity, the particular turbulence of the infant church in first-century Syria is not the kind we experience. But this does not make Matthew's Gospel a relic. Crisis has always triggered the best in Christian reflection. The experience of change, of suffering, of hopes uncertain can force us to dig deep into our tradition and to discover its power anew. So Matthew and his church must have done. His Gospel is "gospel" because it represents a Spirit-filled portrait of Jesus and his significance that is no longer local but universal, able to be "good news" for all those who believe in Jesus and hope to find perspective in him. The intention of the commentary that follows is to catch some of the beauty and power of Matthew's message.

I want to close this introduction on a personal note. Study of Matthew's Gospel has been a labor of love for me for more than thirty years. So I am grateful to Fr. Larry Boadt, C.S.P., and Paulist Press for the invitation to revise this commentary and to make it available once again to a wide audience. If it draws readers to discover the beauty and power of this Gospel, I will consider my work blessed. I want to dedicate this revision—as was the original version—to the students of Catholic Theological Union on whose shoulders will rest the future mission of the church.

Donald Senior, C.P.

EDITOR'S NOTE: Unless otherwise indicated, biblical citations are from the New American Bible.

I. Prologue:
The Gospel Begins
to Break into the World

Matthew 1:1 to 4:16

Matthew 1:1–17
JESUS' FAMILY TREE

The series of brief and colorful events that precede the beginning of Jesus' public ministry serve as a prologue to Matthew's Gospel. The first two chapters which recount the story of Jesus' infancy, begin Matthew's "ministry of continuity" (cf. Introduction): carefully making his case that Jesus is fully, faithfully Jewish, a Son of his Father, a model of fidelity, the very embodiment of God's presence among the people. The prologue also begins to highlight those aspects of the Gospel message which Matthew favors: a paradoxical sensitivity to things Jewish and to universalism, a close attention to the way people respond to Jesus and his message.

"The book of the genealogy of Jesus Christ, the son of David, the son of Abraham." These opening words serve as a title page for the prologue and seem to subtly hint at the entire span of the Gospel story. "Genealogy" translates the Greek term *genesis,* or literally, "origin." Matthew's opening phrase echoes Genesis 2:4 and 5:1 where the Bible speaks of the creation of the universe and the story of the descendants of Adam. By using this phrase, the evangelist hints that what will follow is not the account of an ordinary family tree, but the origin of one whose place in world history is cosmic and unparalleled.

The titles given to Jesus in this opening verse have been strategically chosen. He is the "Christ, the son of David," (cf. 1 Sam 8), thus the promised redeemer and king who would fulfill Israel's centuries of yearning for justice, peace, and freedom. He is the "son of Abraham." Jesus' Jewish roots sink deeper yet, back to the patriarch whose trusting pilgrimage from Ur had begun the long history of God's people (Gen 12).

The reference to Abraham is also the first of many signals that the final destiny of God's people would be more than they expected. As the New Testament writers were quick to note, Abraham predated the covenant and the law. He was, in a sense, the "father of a host of nations" (Gen 17:5), a solitary figure whose fidelity showed that ultimately it was not membership in a particular race or caste that made one righteous but one's integrity before God.

This dual track—firmly and faithfully Jewish and unexpectedly universal—leaves its mark on the carefully designed list of names which span the generations from Abraham to Jesus. The casual reader might consider this genealogical table a boring bit of obscure history, but tucked within these verses are important themes of Matthew's Gospel. Its function is not to provide clinching historical information. The list of names is partially borrowed from the long genealogical table of the first book of Chronicles and the Book of Ruth, but has been edited and clipped to fit the Gospel's purpose. That purpose is less archival than "theological"; it is a statement about Jesus' continuity with the past. His family history is bound up with those multiple generations of Jews who kept God's promise alive, from the beginning with the patriarch Abraham to the glory of David and the Jewish kings, through the wracking experience of exile, and down to the moment of Jesus' own entry into history.

However, the measured cadences of this genealogical list and its numerical symmetry (cf. v. 17) belie the note of the "unexpected," of *discontinuity*, which Matthew also subtly includes. In verses 3, 5, and 6 the names of four women break the rhythm of the list: Tamar, Rahab, Ruth, Bathsheba (referred to as "the wife of Uriah"). These, plus Mary, Jesus' mother, are the only women mentioned in the genealogy and each of them has a rather unusual niche in Jewish history: Tamar, the Canaanite woman who seduced her father-in-law Judah (Gen 38); Rahab, the prostitute of Jericho who aided the Israelite spies and helped ensure the conquest of the promised land (Josh 2:1–21); Ruth, the Moabite who with the help of Naomi snares Boaz as her husband (Ruth); Bathsheba, the wife of a Hittite and the mother of Solomon, a woman whose beauty kindles lust and murder in King David (2 Sam 11).

Some commentators speculate that these women are listed to offset hostile rumors about the circumstances of Jesus' own birth. But Matthew's purpose seems to be deeper than mere defense. These women were admired as heroines in Jewish folklore because of their astuteness and resourcefulness. And each of them is a foreigner who breaks completely unexpectedly into Jewish history and even into the lineage of the Messiah.

Thus, by reminding his readers of the extraordinary ways in which God has acted in the past, Matthew may intend not only to blunt hostile innuendoes against the tradition of Jesus' virginal conception (a tradition strongly affirmed by Matthew in 1:18–25), but also to send up another signal about the "outsiders." It had happened in Israel's past: God had incorporated non-Jews into the history of his people. Through the power of God's Spirit it could happen again.

STUDY QUESTION: The Gospel detects God at work in history, often in unexpected ways. Are we able to discover this same power in our own lives?

Matthew 1:18–25
NAMING GOD'S SON

The Gospel now focuses on the most important phase of the long genealogy, the birth of Jesus. Matthew is not concerned with picturesque details. The moment of birth itself is somewhat prosaically noted in verse 25. Instead, the evangelist stresses the divine origin of Jesus and, above all, his significance.

The narrative introduces us to Joseph, the husband of Mary and the hero of Matthew's infancy story. Joseph's Davidic bloodline makes Jesus legally a part of the royal family (v. 16), and by carrying out God's guiding commands Joseph protects Jesus for his future work. Joseph's description as a "righteous man" (v. 19), his many dreams (1:20; 2:13, 19), and his eventual forced journey to Egypt (2:14), suggest that the evangelist may be subtly casting Mary's husband along the lines of

another famous Joseph, the Old Testament patriarch who played such a
key role in the history of Israel (Gen 37 to 50).

When betrothed to Mary, Joseph discovers that she is with child.
The Gospel immediately informs the reader of Jesus' divine origin;
Mary is with child "through the holy Spirit" (v. 18). But Joseph will
learn of this only later. He is a "righteous" or "just" man, a quality
which seems to stress his compassion for Mary, because he decided to
waive his right (see Deut 24:1) to bring public charges against her. But
he also anticipates the quality of righteousness or faithful responsive-
ness to God's will that the adult Jesus will praise greatly and to which
Jesus himself is dedicated (see 3:15; 5:20).

The angel's message to Joseph brings us to the climax of Matthew's
opening chapter. The mission of God's Son is revealed in the names he
is given. He is to be called "Jesus," literally, "Yahweh is salvation."
Matthew will repeat this name in his Gospel more than any other
evangelist. The angel stresses its significance: "he will save his people
from their sins" (v. 21). The entire Gospel flashes by at this moment:
Jesus' words of compassion and forgiveness, his miraculous healings and
exorcisms, his graceful and wise teaching, above all, his death which
Matthew will call a covenant in blood "for the forgiveness of sins"
(26:28).

The evangelist himself breaks into the narrative in verse 22, and
introduces a style of Old Testament quotation which will be a special
feature of Matthew's Gospel. Twelve times Matthew applies an Old Testament citation to a specific incident of Jesus' life with an introductory
formula practically identical to the one in verse 22: "All this took place
to fulfill what the Lord had said through the prophet...." These quotations illustrate the Gospel's deep conviction that every detail of Jesus'
life fulfills the dreams and promises of the Old Testament (cf. 5:17–20).

The Gospel's first fulfillment quotation is one of its most striking.
Jesus' entry into human history fulfills the promise of Isaiah 7:14,
"Behold, the virgin shall be with child and bear a son, and they shall
name him Emmanuel." The original quotation was a promise of God
relayed to King Ahaz by Isaiah. If the king's faith were strong enough,
he would see that God's power would ensure the people's survival. The
new life begun in the womb of a young Jewish maiden was a precious
sign of this promise, a promise revealed in the name he was to bear,
"Emmanuel," "God is with us." For Matthew and his community, the
words of Isaiah perfectly describe the identity of Jesus and the signifi-

cance of his birth. They serve as testimony to the virginal conception of Jesus and thereby underline God's saving initiative in gifting creation with its most beautiful moment. And the name "Emmanuel" reveals a further dimension of Jesus' mission. He will save the people because he is "God with us." Jesus, God's Son, is Emmanuel because he will reveal the Father's will and establish his kingdom. The very shape of the title, "God with us," evokes the image of the covenant forged between Yahweh and Israel. Jesus is the embodiment of that covenant and its definitive renewal. The promise of abiding presence that begins Matthew's Gospel will be matched by the promise that ends it: "And behold, *I am* with *you* always, until the end of the age" (28:20).

STUDY QUESTION: The Gospel lavishes powerful names on Jesus: "Savior," "God with us." Do these names make sense to us? Do they express the meaning Jesus has for our lives?

Matthew 2:1–12
FIRST REACTIONS TO JESUS

Matthew's Gospel is especially concerned with *response* to Jesus and his message. This aspect of the Gospel will begin to be played out in the second chapter of Matthew's Infancy Narrative.

In this section of the Gospel, the reader will encounter a special type of literary technique. The stories about Herod and the wise men, about Jesus' journey from Bethlehem to Nazareth by way of Egypt, weave together Old Testament quotations, popular Jewish stories about Old Testament heroes, and basic elements of the Gospel tradition about Jesus into a rich and complex literary tapestry. The technique is reminiscent of an ancient Jewish literary craft called *midrash,* which was an artful combination of scriptural interpretation and reflection on contemporary events.

The story of Herod and the wise men contrasts the attitudes of two different groups of Jesus' contemporaries, one a faithless king and his Jerusalem court, and the other sincere searchers for the truth who come from afar.

Herod, the clever and ruthless Idumean who became king of Israel under Roman auspices, is joined by "all Jerusalem" (v. 3) in his disturbance at the news that an infant king of the Jews has been born. He has at his disposal the scriptures and learned men to interpret them (vv. 4–5). Although they correctly deduce that the Messiah is to be born in Bethlehem (cf. the quotation from Mic 5:1 which Matthew alters to read "by *no means* least" instead of the original "the least," thereby emphasizing the greatness that the birth of Jesus brings to this insignificant Judean village), the Jewish leaders begin to plot against Jesus' life. The first note of the passion story has already tolled.

The wise men, Gentile astrologists from the east, are guided only by a mysterious star. Their careful scrutiny of nature has led them to the threshold of belief. The information they seek from the Jews and their scriptures, as well as God's own guidance, leads them to Bethlehem where they are the first to pay Jesus the real homage he deserves (2:10–11). The Gospel's rejection by Israel and its acceptance by Gentiles has already been previewed in this opening chapter of the Messiah's life.

This clever story of a ruler's hostility, of honorable foreigners, of a guiding star, and of God's providence tips us off to the Old Testament tradition that provides the backdrop for this section of the Gospel. The Book of Numbers (chapters 22 to 24) narrates a curious event during the Exodus. Moses is threatened by the evil King Balak who calls on the services of a foreign sorcerer, Balaam "from the East" (Num 23:7). But Balaam refuses to deliver a curse as Balak desires and, instead, pronounces a prophetic blessing over Moses and the people, a blessing that predicts a great future for Israel and the emergence of a messianic king. The blessing includes these words which surely influenced the story of the Magi: "I see him, though not now; I behold him, though not near: A star shall advance from Jacob, and a staff shall rise from Israel" (Num 24:17). Later Jewish tradition understood the "star" to be a reference to the Messiah.

This Old Testament tradition beneath the surface of the Magi story allows the evangelist to transmit an almost subliminal message which helps interpret the history of Jesus. Herod is another Balak who will vainly try to stop God's salvific power. Jesus is a new Moses who will lead his people to freedom. The wise men, like Balaam, testify to the incredible vitality of God's providence. The exodus could not be thwarted; neither will the Gospel.

STUDY QUESTION: The wise men's search for truth and the blindness of Israel's leaders are the first of many sober warnings in Matthew's

Gospel. The "outsider's" sincerity can often be a jolting challenge to those within the warm confines of established churches.

Matthew 2:13–23
YOU CAN'T GO HOME AGAIN—
THE BEGINNING OF THE GOSPEL PILGRIMAGE

Two startlingly different characters, Herod and Joseph, provide the framework for the story of how the Messiah moves from Judea in the south to Galilee in the north (vv. 13–23). Herod's rage drives the Messiah's family into Egypt and keeps them there until his death. Fear of Herod's equally vicious son Archelaus (who would later be exiled to Gaul by the Romans because of his cruelty) causes Joseph to bring his wife and son to Galilee rather than Judea. Joseph's steadfast obedience is a counterpoint to Herod's hostility. The "righteous" is guided by dreams to protect the holy family and eventually to set the stage for the major events of the Gospel by bringing Jesus to Nazareth, in the northern district of Galilee where most of Jesus' ministry will take place.

Matthew's center of interest remains on Jesus. The entire episode of Herod's frustrated rage and his slaughter of the infants recalls events surrounding the birth of Moses. Moses was the object of Pharaoh's vengeance and had to remain in hiding until the death of the Egyptian leader (Exod 2:15 to 5:1). Josephus, a Jewish historian contemporary with the writer of the Gospel, retells the story and includes a slaughter of all male children and the detail that Moses' father received divine guidance in a dream. Moses gave the people God's law on Sinai and led them from slavery to freedom. This portrayal of Moses as lawgiver and savior forms the basic ingredient of his exceptional popularity in Jesus' own day. Matthew uses this image to shape his portrait of Jesus. One greater than Moses is here, one who will definitively reveal God's will and who will rescue his people from the shackles of death.

A series of Old Testament citations underwrites this Moses typology and carries the chapter to its finish. The fulfillment text of 2:15, a quotation from Hosea 11:1, punctuates the warning to Joseph and the subsequent flight into Egypt. The original passage in Hosea referred to the Exodus, the deliverance of the Jewish people from slavery. The quote is now applied by Matthew to Jesus ("my son") and not only refers to Jesus' eventual return from Egypt but subtly forecasts the definitive deliverance that a new Israel will experience through Jesus.

In verse 18, a fulfillment text of Jeremiah 31:15 provides a doleful commentary on Herod's slaughter of the Bethlehem children. This incident is not attested in any other records, but it does, in fact, accord with what is known of Herod's arbitrary and vicious character. The Old Testament quote referred to the exile in the sixth century B.C. Ramah was a town north of Jerusalem and was on the supposed route the Jewish deportees took as they left their homeland. Matthew's use of this text may suggest several layers of meaning. It identifies Jesus with the great Jewish experience of exile (note how this event has already been singled out in the genealogy, cf. 1:11–12, 17) and introduces the foreboding prophecy of Jeremiah, a prophet whose prediction of woe against a faithless Israel will serve Matthew's purpose more than once in his Gospel (cf. 27:9–10). Finally, the original context of this citation is one of eventual rescue and comforting hope (cf. Jer 31:15–20). Matthew may want to quietly remind his readers of Jesus' sure victory over pain and death.

The chapter closes with a somewhat puzzling citation that marks the arrival of Jesus and his family in Nazareth (v. 23). The precise identity of the Old Testament text is difficult to pinpoint. It may be a free rendition of Isaiah 11:1, "a shoot shall sprout from the stump of Jesse," which would involve a play on words between the Hebrew term for "shoot" (*nezir*) and the name of Jesus' home city. The Isaiah quotation was considered a prophecy defining the humble origins of the future Messiah, and this may have prompted Matthew's use of the text. Other commentators prefer a reference to Judges 13:5, "the boy is to be consecrated (*nazir*) to God from the womb." The text refers to Samson's vocation to be a *nazir*, an association of strict asceticism and dedication in ancient Israel. Matthew might have exploited the play on words to single out Jesus' own devotion to his messianic mission.

STUDY QUESTION: Matthew portrays Jesus as identified with the deepest experiences of his people: persecution, sorrow, exile, exodus. The Gospel invites us to reflect on our own life experience and to believe that the power of Christ is present there, too.

Matthew 3:1–12
JOHN: ELIJAH COME AGAIN

So close and yet so different—this is John the Baptist's role in the entire Gospel tradition. Like Jesus, John senses that a decisive moment is about to break over Israel (cf. 3:2 and 4:17). Again, like Jesus, John calls for repentance and the proof of repentance in good deeds (3:2, 8; and 4:17; 7:16). Both John and Jesus will suffer rejection, persecution, and even violent death (cf. 11:18–19).

But with equal insistence, the gospels stress the absolute superiority of Jesus to John. John is a forerunner, the promised Elijah who was expected to precede the Messianic Era (cf. Sir 48:10–11); Jesus *is* the Messiah. John announced the coming of the kingdom; Jesus inaugurated it. John's baptism was a ritual of repentance; Jesus would baptize with the Spirit and with fire, a gift that would forgive sins and quicken new life. John prepared the way; Jesus is the way.

This blend of comparison and contrast helps the reader prepare for the dramatic beginning of Jesus' public ministry.

Matthew gives particular attention to the reception John receives (3:5–11). Large crowds come to accept John's baptism and thereby declare their intention to reform their lives. The Pharisees and scribes are singled out (v. 7). These two Jewish groups—the Pharisees, lay reformers who stressed fidelity to the law, and the Sadducees, a conservative aristocracy from whose ranks the temple priests were chosen—become the chief opponents to Jesus in Matthew's Gospel. Although historically these two factions were often at loggerheads with each other, the evangelist lumps them together to typify the opposition of the Jewish leaders to the message of Jesus. John denounces them for the same type of failing that Jesus will accuse them of (cf. chapter 23). They are hypocritical, claiming to be repentant but failing to show the genuineness of their conversion by a life of good deeds. They smugly point to their membership in God's chosen race, but forget that fidelity, not race or class, is the only bond that binds one to God. The call to conversion involves responsibility. Those who respond will live a new life. Those who turn away or dissimulate will face judgment. The "ax lies at the root of the trees."

Throughout the Gospel, the perfect image of what a disciple ought *not* to be will remain the Sadducees and, particularly, the Pharisees. One should keep in mind that Matthew's purpose was not so much to excoriate these Jewish leaders but to warn his *Christian* readers against adopting the attitudes these Gospel characters exemplified.

STUDY QUESTION: Does the Gospel's indictment of the hypocrisy of the Sadducees and Pharisees have anything to say to me?

Matthew 3:13–17
JESUS COMES TO THE JORDAN

"Then Jesus came...." The waiting is over. The time of fulfillment is at hand. John has already stressed the pre-eminence of Jesus in his words to the Sadducees and Pharisees. Jesus is the "mightier one," the one who will baptize "with the holy Spirit and fire" (cf. vv. 11–12). Now when Jesus takes his place without pretense in the crowds who come forward to confess their sins, John is compelled to protest his unworthiness (v. 14).

For the first time in the Gospel Jesus speaks, and his words express a theme that Matthew will repeatedly emphasize: "...it is fitting for us to fulfill all righteousness" (v. 15). There are two key words in the sentence: to "fulfill" (the same Greek word Matthew so frequently uses regarding Jesus' fulfillment of Old Testament prophecies) and "righteousness" or "justice." The latter term has a double layer of meaning in biblical thought. God's "justice" is his saving activity on behalf of his people. *Human* "justice" or righteousness is the effort we make to respond to God's goodness by carrying out the divine will.

It is possible that both levels of meaning are present in this keynote statement of Jesus. God's "justice" or plan of salvation is fulfilled by the very presence of John and Jesus in world history. At the same time, Jesus is a model of *human* "righteousness" as well, because he carries out God's plan of salvation by his loving fidelity to his Father's will. This emphasis on obedience to the will of God, on obedience perfectly modeled by Jesus, is a hallmark of Matthew's portrait of Christ.

The scene closes with the moment of baptism. Jesus' dedication to his mission is rewarded in a dramatic revelatory moment. The heavens open, God's own animating and powerful Spirit is seen to rest on Jesus, and the Father himself (with typical Jewish reverence, referred to only obliquely as "a voice... from the heavens") reveals to the crowds: "This is my beloved Son, with whom I am well pleased." The words are a composite of Old Testament texts (cf. Ps 2:7; Isa 42:1; Gen 22:2) and their message is clear: Jesus is the one who will bring God's own kingdom to realization. He will demonstrate what loyal obedience to God and genuine service to humankind are all about. He is *the* Son.

STUDY QUESTION: The keynote of Jesus' life is the "fulfillment of all righteousness." The Gospel challenges us: How do we characterize the fundamental motivation of our own lives?

Matthew 4:1–11
THE TESTING OF GOD'S SON

The voice at the Jordan had publicly proclaimed Jesus as God's Son. Now the quality of that sonship is to be tested. The Spirit leads Jesus out into the desert, that hauntingly beautiful and quietly dangerous expanse of arid wasteland that wraps itself around the southern and eastern borders of Israel. The desert held many memories for the Israelites. For Moses and their ancestors it had been a sandy bridge of rescue from the slavery of Egypt to the possibilities of freedom in a new land. But that ominous desert landscape also held memories Israel might like to forget: constant murmuring against Moses and the God he obeyed; a willingness to abandon the march and return to Egypt; despair and infidelity which led to the idolatry of a calf of gold.

Those collective memories must be recalled in order to appreciate the point of this Gospel passage. Both Matthew and Luke present a version that greatly expands on a brief and cryptic scene in Mark (cf. 1:12–13). Their practically identical accounts (the order of the second and third temptations are switched) artfully exploit the Exodus memory. Jesus fasts forty days, just as Moses did (Deut 9:9–18). All of Jesus' replies to the temptation are taken verbatim from chapters 6 to 8 of the book of Deuteronomy, a key section where, at the end of the Exodus, Moses reminds his people of their covenant with Yahweh and the obedience this entails.

Each of the devil's attempts to subvert Jesus and his mission is turned away by a firm avowal of obedience. The sons and daughters of the ancient Exodus may have failed; this Son will not. He is asked to become a self-serving wonder worker, flexing his power for his own ends (4:3). But Jesus' food is the bread of his Father's will (cf. Deut 8:3). He is taken to a pinnacle of the temple and asked to probe the availability of God's provident care (cf. v. 6 where the devil quotes Ps 91). This temptation is shunted aside by a quotation of Deuteronomy 6:16, one should not "test" God since his care for his people is not in doubt. During the Exodus the Israelites had repeatedly challenged God's providence, as at Massah when they bluntly asked, "Is the LORD in our midst or not?" (cf. Exod 17:7).

These first two temptations were prefaced with the mocking phrase, "If you are the Son of God," a line that will have chilling echoes in the words of Jesus' mockers on Calvary (cf. 27:40). But the final temptation is the devil's naked plea for allegiance. Like a prospective buyer, Jesus is taken to a mountain and given a view of the kingdoms of this world. All of this might be his if he were to worship the right god. Jesus rejects the power of evil with the words of the first command of the Decalogue (Deut 6:13). There is only one power, only one God, and Jesus serves him alone. The Gospel will end with Jesus on another mountain (cf. 28:16–20). All power on heaven and earth is given to him, not by the prince of evil, but by the Father. Jesus' authority will be derived not from his control of this world's kingdoms, but from his absolute integrity and his life-giving service.

The devil slinks away defeated, and angels, signs of God's provident care, minister to Jesus (v. 11). God's Son has been tested and found worthy.

STUDY QUESTION: Jesus is faithful because he uses his gifts to serve others, thereby fulfilling God's will. To what or whom have I dedicated the gifts of my life? Am I a faithful son or daughter of God?

Matthew 4:12–16
DAWN IN GALILEE

Jesus, the faithful Son, is now ready to begin his life's work. This brief passage brings to a close the "prologue" which Matthew had carefully assembled since the beginning of chapter 1. The verses are crammed with geographical references and anchored with another "fulfillment" quotation (cf. above, p. 14), a combination reminiscent of the end of chapter 2 (cf. 2:13–23). There, as here, we are told of Jesus on the move. The threat of danger from Archelaus (cf. 2:22) caused Jesus to come to Nazareth. Now, with a possible hint of danger in the arrest of John (4:12), Jesus comes to Capernaum, a small village on the north-west shore of the Sea of Galilee, the base of operation for most of his ministry.

Matthew sees deep significance in this entry into Galilee. Here Jesus' words of wisdom and his acts of compassion would begin to heal a fractured world. Was it mere accident that it all began in Galilee, a district with an unusual proportion of Gentiles, and a part of Israel whose culture and orthodoxy were considered suspect by the Judeans to the south? No accident at all in Matthew's view. Even the setting of Jesus' ministry foretells the shape of the kingdom: The "outsiders" will heed the Gospel. A carefully edited citation from Isaiah (8:23 to 9:1) makes the point: "Galilee of the Gentiles, the people who sit in darkness have seen a great light, on those dwelling in a land overshadowed by death light has arisen." Isaiah's original words said "a light has shone." But for Matthew this is only the beginning of the Gospel, and the beginning of a new day is the dawn.

II. MATTHEW'S PORTRAIT OF JESUS: WISDOM TEACHER, COMPASSIONATE HEALER

Matthew 4:17 to 10:42

Matthew 4:17–25
THE KINGDOM OF HEAVEN IS AT HAND

Matthew used the words of Isaiah (4:16) to describe Jesus' ministry as "light" for those who live in darkness. The brilliance of that light will be displayed in a major section of the Gospel (chapters 5 to 9) for which Matthew now prepares us.

The theme of this section is sounded in verse 17 and Matthew stresses its introduction by an emphatic time formula which is peculiar to his Gospel (cf. 16:21; 26:16). *"From that time on"* Jesus begins his preaching: "Repent, for the kingdom of heaven is at hand." The coming of the kingdom of God was a traditional way the Jews expressed their dream of an Israel that would be truly free, whole, and clothed in justice. Such a state of affairs could only be the work of God, and of God's anointed one, the Messiah. The restorative work of bringing in the kingdom was the keynote of Jesus' own ministry. The things Jesus says and the acts he performs were understood as signs that at long last the promised age of the kingdom of God was about to break into the world.

Matthew will linger over Jesus' words and deeds in the five chapters that are to follow, thereby building up a portrait of Jesus in a way unique among the four Gospels.

The preparatory verses of 4:18–25 help frame that portrait. Jesus' first act is to call disciples. Their summons is highly formalized, not unlike the "call narratives" of the Old Testament in which prophet or king was swept into Yahweh's service. The crisp format indicates the meaning of "call." Discipleship is a gift of God and the proper response is willing obedience. Peter, who will play a prominent role in Matthew's Gospel, and Andrew, James, and John are called to share in Jesus' ministry, to be "fishers of people." Jesus' mission is not lingered over for its own sake. It is to be witnessed by the disciples, and, as will be spelled out in chapter 10, to be taken up by them and the community they represent.

Matthew's great portrait is previewed in verses 23–25, a sweeping summary of Jesus' ministry. Jesus' work is that of teaching and preaching the kingdom, of curing all kinds of diseases and sickness. Chapters 5 to 7, the famous Sermon on the Mount, will portray *Jesus the Teacher*. Chapters 8 and 9, a collection of miracle stories, will portray *Jesus the Healer*. The summary of the program cited in verse 23 will be repeated verbatim in 9:35, a clear indication of how deliberately Matthew constructs this crucial section of his Gospel.

Two final points should be noted about this summary passage. First, Matthew observes that Jesus teaches "in their synagogues" (v. 23). Although the Gospel will eventually surge beyond the borders of Israel and be accepted by Gentiles (cf. 28:19), it is first offered to Jews. They are the chosen people and Matthew has not lost his sense of continuity. Second, the target of Jesus' ministry is the vulnerable crowds who stream from all areas of Israel to hear him, "those who were possessed, lunatics, and paralytics" (v. 24). Jesus is not a detached dispenser of wisdom, nor a self-seeking wonder worker; what he says and what he does have one object—to make a suffering people whole.

Matthew 5:1–16
"JESUS BEGINS TO TEACH"—THE BEATITUDES

Matthew sets this scene with care. Seeing that suffering and searching crowd, Jesus climbs a mountainside, gathers his disciples about him, sits down, and begins to teach. The deliberate ascent, the mountain setting, and Jesus' position of authority (rabbis *sat* when teaching) once again summon up Moses' image (cf. Moses' ascent of Sinai to claim God's law for his people—Exod 19 and 20). A new Moses is here, and a new revelation of God's will is about to nourish that tattered flock of humanity.

The "Sermon on the Mount," the loosely linked sayings that Matthew has collected in chapters 5 to 7, begins with a series of "Beatitudes" or blessings. They form a "preamble" to Jesus' teaching, effectively distilling its essentials and pointing to the basic dispositions needed to understand Jesus' message. This style of speech was known from the Old Testament. Deuteronomy 27 and 28 string together "blessings" ("blessed are...") and "woes" ("cursed are...") which describe the good or ill fortune that follows from keeping or breaking the law. The books of Sirach (cf. 25:7–10) and some of the prophets have similar lists. In Luke's Gospel a more primitive listing of beatitudes is immediately followed by a series of woes (cf. Luke 6:20–26), but in Matthew the woes are reserved for chapter 23, a section of the Gospel that functions almost as a negative counterpart to the Sermon on the Mount.

The first four beatitudes might be considered together (vv. 3–6). The kinds of people declared "blessed" in this series recall the great prophecy of Isaiah 61:1–4 which foretells the Messiah's mission to the poor and afflicted (the text is used in Luke 4:18 and seems to be behind Matt 11:5). Each of these groups—the "poor in spirit," the gentle or "meek," those who mourn, those who hunger and thirst for what is right—are promised happiness or blessing *now* in view of a *future* reward. The disciples of Jesus can begin now to experience a life of blessing because their future is so assured that its promised gladness spills into the present. What keeps the beatitudes from being empty mockeries of human suffering is the authority of Jesus. Because Jesus is who he is, his promises of blessing become themselves the *cause* of blessing. Thus, at the very outset of the Sermon a fundamental theme of the Gospel has been sounded: Salvation is a gift, a gift whose creative power breaks into our world of pain and darkness to make us whole and blessed. The fullness of God's blessing will be experienced at the end of time, but even now such divine blessing belongs to those who follow Jesus' teaching. Although in the Gospel Matthew will repeatedly insist on the necessity of action, his even more fundamental insistence on salvation as a pure gift should not be overlooked.

Matthew's rendition of the beatitudes points to another side of the Gospel. Those singled out for blessing are not a particular social class, or mere inheritors of tragedy. Jesus' work with sinners and outcasts did not mean their poverty was a symptom of holiness. They were special objects of Jesus' mercy because they needed, and as God's people deserved, mercy. Their material and social deprivation also stood as vivid symbols of the absolute need and dependence that, in fact, describe the stance of all people before their God. But the poor and the outcasts could not presume on the gift of grace any more than the rich. To all, Jesus' message was two-edged. "The kingdom of God is at hand"—a promise of new life; but one must now live according to that gift, therefore, "repent."

Matthew's version brings out this attitudinal dimension of the beatitudes more clearly than Luke's version does (cf. Luke 6:20–22). It is not simply the poor, but "the poor *in spirit*," not simply those who hunger and thirst, but those "who hunger and thirst *for righteousness*." These phrases are not meant to blunt the reality of Jesus' mission of justice to the poor. Instead, they amplify an essential dimension of God's kingdom: To be gifted by God demands a change of heart.

The next four beatitudes (vv. 7–10)—all unique to Matthew—further illustrate the changed heart to which conversion leads. Each of the attitudes depicted becomes an important theme of Jesus' teaching in the Sermon and throughout the Gospel. Those who are merciful will receive mercy—a call for forgiveness and reconciliation that will be reflected in the Lord's prayer (cf. 6:12, 14–15) and in Jesus' teaching on the relationships and forgiveness that must bind the community together (cf. 5:23–24; 6:12, 14–15; 18:23–35). The "clean of heart," those whose actions are marked by absolute integrity, will see God—a call for sincerity Jesus will extend to one's word (5:37), one's judgments (7:1–5), and one's piety (6:1–6, 16–18). The peacemakers, those who do not perpetuate a cycle of violence (5:38–42), who refuse the sword (26:52–54), and who can accept the most radical of Jesus' commands, "love your enemy" (5:44–48), are promised the most breathtaking blessing of all: they shall be called "children of God" because such love fulfills God's ultimate command and creates the deepest kinship with the Father (cf. 5:45–48). Happy even those who suffer persecution "for the sake of righteousness," because like the poor in spirit—like Jesus himself—such giving and losing of life in the pursuit of the Father's will is, mysteriously, to find life (16:25–26).

The formation of true disciples is the purpose of Jesus' teaching. The remaining beatitudes (vv. 11–12) and two striking metaphors which complete the Sermon's preamble underline this. The address is no longer "they" but "you," Jesus' audience of would-be-followers. You are to rejoice in the sufferings you endure for the sake of the Gospel (v. 11). You are to be salt and light in a flat and dim world.

STUDY QUESTION: The beatitudes put a question to us: Can someone who is poor, gentle, suffering be truly "happy"? Much of our world would say "No." Jesus teaches that the only source of happiness worth yearning for is a heart renewed by the Gospel. Do we agree?

Matthew 5:17–20
JESUS AND THE LAW

As we noted in the Introduction, Matthew writes his Gospel for a Jewish Christian community that found itself in bitter tension with a majority of its fellow Jews, and adrift in a new and unexpected situation. This passage, found only in Matthew's Gospel and strategically placed at the very beginning of Jesus' own authoritative teaching, attempts to place Jesus and the law in a context of continuity. Verse 17 lays out the fundamental perspective: Jesus has come not to abolish or destroy "the law or the prophets" (the totality of the Jewish scriptures in which God's will was revealed) but to "fulfill" them. "Fulfill" translates the identical Greek word used by Matthew to introduce the Old Testament fulfillment texts (cf. above, p. 14), and the word used in Jesus' opening statement in the Gospel (cf. 3:15). In Matthew the word has the sense of completion, of accomplishing the purpose or goal God intended with the law.

The time frame for this "fulfillment" of the law is expressed in verse 18. In fact, two separate time references are given: "until heaven and earth pass away" and "until all things have taken place."

When will this be? At the definite end of the world? In that case, the entire Jewish law would still be in effect for Christians. But this does not seem possible, since in the course of the Gospel Jesus himself appears to abrogate some points of the law. The verse begins to make more sense when we grasp Matthew's sweeping view of history, a history that pivots around Jesus. The great drama of history in which God accomplishes the salvation of the world began with creation, quickened its pace in God's dealing with his chosen people and the gift of the law, and will bring down its curtain with the end of the world. But the most decisive moment of world history is Jesus and, even more specifically, the great act of salvation accomplished through his death and resurrection. Jesus is the beginning of the end. All that God intended to say through creation, through Israel, and through the law finds its ultimate expression in Jesus. All of God's plans for the future have clearly been expressed in the person and mission of his Son.

Thus for Matthew, the "passing away of heaven and earth" is, in a true sense, already here with Jesus. All things have been fulfilled, only Jesus and his teaching remain (cf. 24:35 where Matthew says precisely this). This is the reason for the vigorous demand of verse 20. The "righteousness" of Jesus' disciples must exceed that of the scribes and Pharisees, because the disciples are part of the new and final age of history. To come into contact with Jesus and his teaching is not only a privilege but also a responsibility. This bracing command in view of a radically new consciousness also explains the call for integrity in verse 19. The text originally may have referred to the Jewish law itself but now the "law" understood here is *Jesus'* "law," or the law as interpreted by him, which the Sermon and the rest of the Gospel will communicate. Matthew's Christians viewed Jesus not as abolishing their Jewish heritage, including that of fidelity to God's law, but as pointing the way to its full meaning. Another favorite Matthean theme is struck here: a call for sincerity that translates words into action. The one who carries out Jesus' commandments will be called greatest in the kingdom of Heaven.

STUDY QUESTION: Matthew insists that Jesus' teaching fulfills all that God commands. What exactly is this new "law" of Jesus? What demand does Jesus Christ make on a person's life? This is the question the Gospel poses.

Matthew 5:21–48
SYMPTOMS OF THE NEW HOLINESS

A deeper holiness is asked of the disciples of Jesus. This expectation was spelled out in verse 20. Now it will be forcefully illustrated by a series of six bold statements in which a command of the law as tradi-

tionally interpreted by others ("You have heard that it was said to your
ancestors...") is juxtaposed with the escalated and penetrating
demands of the Gospel ("But *I* say to you..."). A "new Moses" reveals
God's will to his people.

But it would be a mistake to conceive of Jesus as substituting one
law code (even a new and stricter one) for another. For Matthew's
Gospel, the Jewish law stands, but now its full meaning is understood
in the light of Jesus' authoritative teaching. The commands of Jesus as
presented in the Sermon are not some sort of law code but are forceful
and concrete illustrations of the kind of integrity and compassion
instinctively striven for by one who senses the meaning of Jesus' teaching. Each of these contrast statements deals with human relationships
and each makes clear that being a follower of Jesus calls for a radically
profound understanding of one's relationship to other people. Jesus
came to restore a people to wholeness, and the quality of his demands
illustrates how complete that restoration is to be.

The first statement (v. 21) cites the command of the Decalogue
against murder (cf. Exod 20:13; Deut 5:17), and refers to its legal sanction (cf. Exod 21:12). Jesus' teaching reinforces the intent of the law by
identifying anger and alienation as the *roots* of violence. Therefore, the
disciple must make reconciliation an urgent priority, whether one is
about to worship (vv. 23–24) or about to be embroiled in litigation (vv.
25–26).

The second antithesis also seeks to interiorize a command of the
law. It is not simply the overt act of infidelity that is destructive (cf.
Exod 20:14; Deut 5:18), but the lustful heart (v. 28). To look at a
woman as an object of lust is to violate the respect due a human person. The jolting series of warnings that emphasize the seriousness of
this demand (vv. 29–30) may have originally been used in another context (cf. Mark 9:43–48). Matthew may have appended these here
because the radical and obviously hyperbolic call to eradicate any
enticement to sin underlines the seriousness of mutual respect in Jesus'
teaching.

In the third contrast statement, the Jewish law (cf. Deut 24:1) gov-
erning the procedure for divorce (and thus presuming its possibility), is
directly countered by Jesus' own teaching (vv. 31–32). In the Gospels of
Mark (10:11–12) and Luke (16:18) Jesus' prohibition is without exception. The precise meaning of the apparent qualification ("unless the
marriage is unlawful") introduced in Matthew's version is difficult to

decipher. Jesus' teaching on divorce is repeated later in Matthew's Gospel and the reader is referred to that text for a fuller discussion (cf. 19:3–12).

The law permitted the taking of an oath in conjunction with a religious vow or to testify to the truth of one's statement (e.g., Num 30:3; Deut 23:22–24). A truly binding oath invoked God's name or a euphemism that obliquely referred to God (cf. the list Jesus cites in vv. 34–36). The rabbis had cautioned against the abuse of this practice, but Jesus' own command is still more stringent: "Do not swear at all" (v. 34). The sincerity and mutual respect that must characterize the disciples of Jesus make a simple "yes" or a simple "no" a sacred expression of truth.

The fifth contrast cites the famous "law of Talion" (cf. Exod 21:24), "an eye for an eye and a tooth for a tooth." The original intent of the law was to *limit* revenge by calling only for parity. But it was easily used as a quasi-requirement for retribution, even when in Jesus' own day that retribution would be primarily financial rather than physical. Jesus' own command once more "fulfills" a law by abrogating it, and insists that aggression is to be absorbed not returned. The illustration about going the "extra mile" in verse 41 probably refers to the highly resented capacity of the Roman occupation forces to requisition a private citizen to carry baggage or act as a guide. This contrast statement clearly distances Jesus from many of his contemporaries who considered it a sacred duty to openly resist the Romans. Here and in 26:52 violence is portrayed as alien to the Gospel.

This tone is amplified in the final and climactic antithesis of verses 43–48. The first portion of the traditional law quoted is from Leviticus 19:18, "You shall love your neighbor." The second half, "and hate your enemy," is not found in the Hebrew Bible. However, it does reflect the kind of particularistic thinking that defined the concept of "neighbor" in some sectarian factions of first-century Judaism. The members of the Jewish reform group at Qumran were urged "to love the children of light" (i.e., members of the community who observed the law) and "to hate the sons of darkness" (lawless Jews and Gentiles). In a society where fidelity to the law was not only a religious ideal but also a source of national identity against a powerful and oppressive occupant, it is easy enough to understand the stark terms in which the obligation to one's religion is put. This same social atmosphere reveals the incredible challenge of Jesus' own command: "Love your enemy." The "enemy" is not remote (and therefore easy for one to be noble about) but is as near and repugnant as the "persecutor."

These verses bring us to the heart of Jesus' teaching in the Gospel of Matthew. Almost all commentators agree that the command, "love your enemy," is the most uniquely characteristic saying of Jesus. It has no exact parallel in biblical or other Jewish literature of the period, although some texts advised about seeking revenge or retaliation for injury. The statements that follow this command (cf. vv. 45–48) amplify and confirm the centrality of this teaching of Jesus and reveal its fundamental motivation. To love an enemy is to demonstrate that we are "children of [our] heavenly Father." God's love is indiscriminate and gratuitous; his sun rises on good and bad, his rain falls on honest and dishonest. The traditional theme of imitation of God, used in biblical (cf. Lev 19:2) and pagan literature as well, is employed here to illustrate the importance of the love command. A person is most like the Father when that person does not confine love to a comfortable sphere of reciprocity (v. 46). The "tax collector" and "pagan," indicative of an "unconverted" person, can do as much. But the disciple is called to do more: to love even the enemy, and thus to be "perfect" as the heavenly Father is "perfect." The word "perfect" translates the Greek word *teleios* which has the connotation of "wholeness" or "completeness." The disciple experiences "wholeness" when he or she is animated by the kind of love that allows one to love even an enemy. Later in the Gospel, the same word "perfect" will be defined as "following Jesus" (cf. 19:21). That is really an alternate way of expressing the "love of enemy" command, because in the Gospel Jesus is portrayed as carrying out his own teaching with absolute integrity.

STUDY QUESTION: The core of Jesus' teaching is his command: "Love your enemy." Does this summarize our own understanding of what Christianity really means?

Matthew 6:1–18
ON DOING GOOD FOR YOUR FATHER TO SEE

Fulfilling God's commands is also the concern of this section of the Sermon. The opening verse spells out this theme. Our "righteous deeds" must not be an empty show but must proceed from an absolutely sincere heart. Matthew categorizes "righteous deeds" according to the three traditional works of Judaism: almsgiving, prayer, and fasting. A rigorous contrasting pattern (not unlike the contrasting statements in 5:21–48) decries the "righteous deeds" of the "hypocrites" which are done in public to attract attention and proposes Jesus' own teaching (note the authoritative "Amen, I say to you..." in 6:2, 5, 16) which insists that good works must be wholly dedicated to the Father.

Almsgiving (vv. 1–4) was a highly developed and admirable part of Jewish tradition. Jesus did not abrogate it but insisted that it not be accompanied by the trumpets of hypocrisy. Alms should be given in "secret," that is, as an expression of true love whose reward is assured by the Father. A patterned life of deep prayer was also a treasure of the Jewish heritage. Jesus' words, effectively contrasting the public arena of synagogue and street corner with the unpretentious privacy of a room in a house, call for a piety that does not keep one eye on the applause meter, but is a sincere and serious communication with the Father (vv. 5–6). Fasting, another traditional Jewish practice adopted by the Christians, is not to be an empty asceticism which attempts to cower others through subtle pride. Genuine fasting should free one to be of service (vv. 16–18), and to be even festive in the process.

Praying does not mean "babbling" (v. 7), the piling up of phrases and formulas to ensure a hearing, as some prayer forms from this period did. To do so is to subtly hope that one's language might control God. The same sincerity and straightforwardness that should rule almsgiving and fasting must guide the tone of one's prayer.

The "Lord's Prayer" (vv. 9–13) is offered as a pattern of authentic prayer. Some of its petitions are similar in content to a Jewish prayer, the Shemoneh Esreh, recited twice daily in the synagogue. But the bold directness of the Our Father bears the authoritative stamp of its ultimate author, Jesus.

The disciples are directed to address God as "Father," sharing in Jesus' own intimate filial relationship (cf. 11:25–31). Matthew's own community may have added the phrase "in heaven" (it is missing in Luke's version) to stress the sense of awe and reverence that must paradoxically co-exist with the Christian's unprecedented access to God. The first three petitions (vv. 9–10) state in alternate ways the same basic hope: a prayer that the Father's power would establish in the world of humankind the same network of peace, unity, and love that exists in God's own kingdom.

The same directness and instinct for the essential characterize the remaining three petitions (vv. 11–13) which shift from a future and outer-directed "your name," "your kingdom," "your will," to the palpable needs of the believer, "our bread," "our debts," "deliver us." Jesus' prayer is not utopian. The plea for "daily bread" is probably best understood as just that: a prayer for basic human sustenance. Because the unusual Greek word here for "daily" can also mean "future" or literally "tomorrow's bread," some believe that the bread referred to is symbolic of the kingdom and not just physical food. But the practical tones of the prayer and Jesus' own concern for feeding (cf. 14:13–21; 15:32–38) and healing (chapters 8 and 9) make the more prosaic interpretation the preferred one.

Another consuming concern of Jesus' ministry is expressed in a petition calling for forgiveness. This is the only petition that includes a *condition:* "as we forgive our debtors" (v. 12). The absolute centrality of reconciliation in Jesus' teaching and his insistence that genuine communion with the Father brings a new understanding of our relationship with each other is reinforced by the repetition of this theme at the end of the prayer (cf. 14–15) and at other key points in the Gospel (cf. 7:12; 18:21–22).

The prayer ends with a petition that we not be put to the "final test" and that we be delivered from the "evil one" (v. 13). Suffering and death can overwhelm us and therefore we ask the one in whose hands the ultimate destiny of the world rests not to "test us" beyond our strength. The tone of this petition (and the entire prayer) is not unlike the temptation scene of 4:1–11 where Jesus turned aside the enticements of Evil by affirming his total dedication to his Father. The prayer will be evoked again as Jesus faces his final test in Gethsemane (cf. 26:42).

STUDY QUESTION: As Christians we pray and give alms and even fast. The Gospel endorses these practices only if they derive from a free and sincere communion with God. How does our piety stand up to this standard?

Matthew 6:19–34
THE PERILS OF A DIVIDED HEART

This portion of the Sermon makes a connection between two important concerns: single hearted dedication to the kingdom and the practical needs of everyday living. The Gospel does not ignore the practical
necessities of food and clothing but places these cares in the perspective
of faith.

The evangelist brings together a series of originally independent
sayings and metaphors. The first (vv. 19–21) picks up the theme of a
heavenly reward for good deeds from the previous section (cf. 6:1–18)
and calls for a faith-wise use of possessions. Anxious padding of one's
own wealth is ultimately quite vulnerable to destruction (vv. 19–20).
Use of one's energy and resources for the kingdom is the only security
worth striving for.

The theme of dedicating one's life to the kingdom is restated (vv.
22–23) in the metaphor of a "sound eye" as a clear lens through which
God's light can flood the whole body. Like tasteless salt (another of
Jesus' arresting metaphors), inner light that turns out to be darkness
vividly portrays the futility of a life dedicated to an unworthy goal.

The third metaphor (v. 24) is more explicit. No one can attempt to
put priority on God and possessions without suffering from a divided
heart.

The section concludes with one of the Sermon's most lyrical passages (vv. 25–34). Since our bodies and the life that animates them are
gifts from God, we should not be concerned with the cares of food
and clothing as if God did not exist. Nature's own beauty challenges
the mentality which devotes anxious and all-consuming attention to
one's own material security. Such an attitude springs from "little faith,"
a quaint and effective characterization of imperfect discipleship that
Matthew will utilize repeatedly in his Gospel (cf. 8:26; 14:31; 16:8;
17:20). The follower of Jesus is to husband his or her energies and care
for doing God's will (v. 33). Thus this passage is not an invitation to
passivity, nor does it spring from a trivial romanticism about nature and
its beauty. These verses, and the entire section it concludes, are a call for
action—action that proceeds from commitment to the kingdom of
God. Such commitment frees one to live fully in the present and not to
be immobilized or diverted by anxiety about one's future (v. 34).

STUDY QUESTION: The Gospel again challenges us about the fundamental priorities of our lives. Are we "anxious" about the right things? Do we dedicate our lives to things that are worthy of us?

Matthew 7:1–12
THE BOND OF MERCY

The central section of the Sermon (6:1 to 7:12) now begins to slant to its conclusion. An exhortation not to "judge" a brother or sister (vv. 1–5) reminds the hearers of the principle of reciprocity: As we judge, so we will be judged. Awareness of our relationship to God should bring new understanding of our relationship to each other, a relationship that must be ruled by understanding and compassion, not the cold arrogance of judgment.

Verse 5 begins to move beyond the single emphasis of the prohibition against judging (v. 1). There is a difference between the hypocritical judgment of another and the genuine concern to correct or admonish an erring brother or sister. But self-deception can easily make "fraternal correction" a deft proclamation of one's own superiority. Only one whose eye is plank-free, who has admitted the need for repentance and conversion, is able to correct someone else with respect and compassion (v. 5).

The saying in verse 6 may have originally been used in the context of Jewish-Gentile tensions. "Dogs" and "pigs" were both used as disparaging terms for Gentiles. And this saying may have been contrived as a caution against sharing sacred laws and institutions with those who would not understand or respect them. But in the context of the Sermon, it seems to pick up the final admonition of verse 5. The call for compassion and understanding does not eliminate the need for discrimination and reverence. The *Didache,* a Christian writing almost contemporary with Matthew's Gospel, uses a similar saying to warn against sharing bread blessed at the agape meals with the "unholy."

The call for persevering prayer (vv. 7–11) seems at first glance to be dislocated from Matthew's earlier consideration of prayer (6:5–15). But, in fact, it blends into the conclusion of this section of the Sermon. The demand for absolute sincerity in our good deeds (6:1–18), for the single-minded dedication of our energies and our resources to God's will (6:19–34), and for compassionate (7:1–5) and prudent (7:6) dealings with our brethren revives one's sense of impotence before the exacting demands of the Gospel. Fidelity is a gift that should be sought with the same sense of need and trust as a child asks a parent for bread (vv. 9–10). Although Matthew continues to insist on action and good deeds as the touchstone of genuine fidelity, he is equally insistent that the ability to respond to the Gospel is also a gift.

The expository part of the Sermon concludes with the key saying of verse 12, the so-called "golden rule." This emphasis on the "love command" and its interpretation as the essence of "the law and the prophets" parallels the conclusion of the first major section of the Sermon (cf. 5:43–48). The climax of Jesus' own interpretation of the law is the command to "love your enemy." Loving one's enemy, doing to others "whatever you would have them do to you"—this is how Jesus' own teaching "fulfills" the purpose of the law (cf. 5:17). Matthew will repeat this crucial stance of the Gospel in 22:34–40.

STUDY QUESTION: Once again the teaching of Jesus slips into a single clear focus: "Do to others whatever you would have them do to you." Does my Christian life make a difference in the way I treat others?

Matthew 7:13–29
A CALL FOR FIDELITY

The Sermon on the Mount concludes with a string of paired images. There are two "gates," two "roads" (vv. 13–14), two kinds of trees and two kinds of fruit (vv. 15–20), two kinds of responses (vv. 21–23), two kinds of house builders (vv. 24–27). Each pair illustrates the need for decisive response to the teaching of Jesus and the consequences of such response. This theme of action and responsibility is a major motif of Matthew's Gospel.

The string begins with the image of the two roads or ways of life (vv. 13–14), a traditional metaphor in the Bible for one's life choice (cf. Deut 30:15–20). The narrowness of the road to life and the reference to the "few" who find it illustrates once again how fidelity is ultimately a gift of God. The test of good deeds is used to unmask "false prophets"

(vv. 15–20). Early Christianity brimmed with vitality and benefited from many prophetic types in its midst. These inspired preachers and healers apparently adopted Jesus' own itinerant life-style, preaching the Gospel from town to town. But such a freelance corps of missionaries also produced abuses, people whose miraculous powers were impressive credentials but whose brand of Christianity was, in fact, divisive and misleading. Matthew's community applied the same test of genuineness to the charismatic prophets as it did to all disciples: "By their fruits you will know them" (7:16, 20).

The following paragraph (vv. 21–23) probably refers to the same situation. Matthew's criterion is consistent. It is not enough to cry out in prayer "Lord, Lord," or even to prophesy or to work cures in Jesus' name. The ultimate test is the one that Jesus himself perfectly exemplifies: to do "the will of my Father in heaven" (v. 21). Those who are false disciples must bear the consequences. These "evildoers" will have no kinship with Jesus. This way (v. 23) of speaking about judgment is quite similar to the Matthean judgment scene of the sheep and the goats (cf. 25:31–46).

The concluding metaphor—the two ways of building a house (vv. 24–27)—illustrates Matthew's definition of a disciple: one who "listens to these words of [Jesus] and acts on them" (v. 24). The life constructed by such a truly sensible person will withstand the rigors of judgment.

The Sermon concludes with a formula ("When Jesus finished these words..." [v. 28]) that appears five times in the Gospel, each concluding a major discourse of Jesus and orienting the reader back to the flow of the narrative (cf. 11:1, after the mission discourse; 13:53, after the parable discourse; 19:1, after the discourse on community; and 26:1, at the end of Jesus' last discourse). In this case, the transitional formula is fortified by a reference to Jesus' impression on the crowd (v. 29). Jesus' "authority" derives not only from the impact of his penetrating wisdom, but from his identity. He is not a scribe of the old order but the Son whose teaching reveals the Father's will and whose own life is the perfect example of the fidelity he demands.

STUDY QUESTION: Matthew writes a Gospel for "doers," for those who do not simply say the right words or perform the proper gestures, but who really carry out the commands of Jesus in the practical decisions of their lives. The church still needs to listen soberly to the indictment of those who cry "Lord, Lord" but do not do the will of God.

Matthew 8:1–17
THE HEALING POWER OF JESUS

At the beginning of the Sermon on the Mount, Matthew had stressed that the crowds who swarmed around Jesus were wracked with suffering and disease (cf. 4:24–25). These same crowds who had thrilled to Jesus' teaching (7:28–29) will now witness the power of his compassion. Matthew completes his portrait of Jesus by using the next two chapters (8:1 to 9:35) to depict him as one who not only teaches with authority but heals with love.

Three crisp miracle stories form the first unit of this section. The unit's conclusion, a brief summary of Jesus' activity and a quotation from Isaiah 53:4 (cf. Matt 8:16–17), trumpets the theme: Jesus is God's Servant whose power to heal lifts the burden of sickness and sin from a suffering people. This is the savior Jesus announced in the infancy Gospel (cf. 1:21). This is the obedient Son who refused to use his power for self-aggrandizement in the desert test (cf. 4:3–4).

The trim lines of the stories of the leper's cure (8:1–4) and of the healing of Peter's mother-in-law (8:14–15) effectively stress Jesus' power. The leper reverences Jesus (literally "genuflects" before him) and addresses him as "Lord," using the Greek word *Kyrie,* a Christian title affirming the divine power of Jesus (cf. 8:2). The dialogue is terse, climaxing in Jesus' majestic "I will do it. Be made clean." In the third miracle, Jesus enters Peter's house and cures Peter's mother-in-law with a word.

The cure of the centurion's son (8:5–13), the only story in these two chapters not found in Mark, also emphasizes the power of Jesus. The centurion's deference to Jesus and their conversation about authority effectively make this point. The fact that the man is a Gentile also helps Matthew bring to the surface a strong undercurrent of the Gospel. The response of this Gentile to Jesus is a sign of the future when outsiders from the east and the west will share in the messianic banquet, while those who presume their right to be there will be turned away (vv. 10–13).

But Jesus has not rejected his own people. Even as he performs his acts of power, he abides by the Jewish law in reminding the leper to verify his cure with the temple priests and to make the prescribed offering demanded by the law (cf. Lev 14:2ff.).

STUDY QUESTION: Jesus has the power to heal. Is this a unique power unleashed only in the village of Capernaum, or does the Risen Christ still have the power to heal us and make us whole?

Matthew 8:18 to 9:17
FOLLOWING A HOMELESS JESUS

As Jesus is about to get into the boat (vv. 16–22), two would-be followers, a scribe and a disciple, provide the occasion for Jesus' warning about the rigors of discipleship, another major theme of the miracle section. The scribe's bold and apparently unconsidered declaration ("Teacher, I will follow you wherever you go") is brought up short by Jesus' reminder of the homelessness of the "Son of Man" (a title particularly associated in the Gospels with Jesus' death). The cost of the Christian mission will be spelled out further in 10:6–25. A disciple who begs leave to bury his father, an obvious sacred duty in Judaism, is met with Jesus' own unflinching demand that the Gospel, namely, "following Jesus," be put first above all things. Jesus is the way of life; anything less is to join ranks with the dead.

The story of the calming of the storm (vv. 23–27), the first of three miracles in this section, continues the "boat" motif. Matthew's rendition of this story will make a touching image of the church. The disciples "follow" (almost a technical term for discipleship) Jesus into the boat and, once at sea, begin to experience a violent storm (cf. v. 24, literally a giant "earthquake," a term often used to describe the troubles the community will encounter in the final age). Fear of the raging sea moves them to pray, "Lord, save us!" (again a title referring to Jesus' divine power). This is quite different from Mark's version where the disciples rebuke Jesus for being asleep (cf. Mark 4:38)! Jesus responds by asserting his majestic power over the chaos of the sea (the same power attributed to Yahweh in the Old Testament, cf. Pss 29:3; 65:8; 89:10; 93:4; 107:29) and by gently characterizing that frightened boat crew as men "of little faith" (cf. above, 6:30).

Two other miracles complete the trilogy. Matthew has radically shortened the colorful story of the Gadarene demoniacs (compare Mark 5:1–20), focusing on the demons' terrified recognition of what they face (v. 29). Jesus is the "Son of God" and his ministry of healing and teaching anticipates the final destruction of evil.

The cure of the paralytic (9:1–8) has also been clipped by Matthew, and again, the purpose is a sharper focus on Jesus' authority. This story may have originally combined a healing story with a controversy about Jesus' power to forgive sins. The latter has become the central point in Matthew's version (cf. 9:6). As in the stilling of the storm, so here the evangelist is dealing with the community's own experience as well as the history of Jesus. The reaction of the crowd (v. 8), praising God for giving "such authority to human beings," suggests that the controversy between Jesus and the scribes over the power to forgive sins now mirrors later tension between Matthew's church, which claimed such power, and the objection of the synagogue.

The theme of discipleship which began this section is strongly reasserted at its conclusion. The implicit rejection of Jesus in the protests of the scribes is countered by the instant discipleship of Matthew the tax collector (9:9), and Jesus' table-fellowship with sinners (v. 10) is opposed by the Pharisees. Jesus' citation of Hosea 6:6 in verse 13 (to be repeated in 12:7) stifles their murmurs against his ministry by reasserting the primacy of compassion over the less important stipulations of the law (the connotation of "sacrifice" in this context). Matthew presents Jesus as carrying out with rigorous integrity his own teaching (cf. 7:12) as well as continuing to reverence his Jewish heritage expressed in the law.

A final objection concludes this segment. John's disciples challenge the followers of Jesus on their failure to fast (vv. 14–17). The link with the previous material is the authority of Jesus and his ministry. Just as his teaching on love and his works of compassion radically fulfill the law and cause a renewed fellowship with sinners and outcasts, so his presence brings new meaning to the piety practiced by John and Judaism. The presence of the bridegroom at the messianic feast makes a piety of gloom impossible. Fasting will be observed in the church after Jesus' death, but, as 6:16–18 has already indicated, even then fasting must be done in a festive manner.

The metaphor of "new wine in fresh wineskins" returns to Matthew's theme of continuity and change. If the old order is willing to undergo radical conversion then it will be saved. If not, then it will find the new wine of the kingdom unbearable (v. 17). This plea for continuity and transformation will be sounded again in 13:52.

STUDY QUESTION: The Gospels never attempt to downplay the cost of discipleship. Following Jesus demands commitment and sacrifice. How costly is our own brand of discipleship?

Matthew 9:18–35
FAITH IN JESUS' POWER OVER SICKNESS AND DEATH

The final segment of the miracle section seems to concentrate on the question of faith. All of the Gospels stress the role of faith in Jesus' ministry of healing. The miracles were not considered random flexes of divine muscle, but vivid and effective signs of God's power to restore humanity to wholeness. It was not just one's sightless eyes or twisted limbs that needed restoration. The most searing wound is in the human heart. True healing would come when one responded by turning one's whole self toward God. Thus, if faith were not present, miracle was meaningless. At the same time, the emphasis on faith as a condition for healing does not mean that the fact that one is ill or has a disability is a sign of an inadequate faith. The Gospel does not endorse such a superficial litmus test. While not everyone has access to physical cure, all have access through faith to the more profound transformation of the heart and spirit that is the true concern of Jesus' mission.

Matthew affirms this basic Gospel notion through his editing of the miracle stories. The official trusts in Jesus' power to heal his daughter, even though she is already dead (contrast Mark 5:23). The woman with a hemorrhage is cured because her "faith has saved [her]" (v. 22). (In Mark's version [5:25–34] the reaction of the disciples and the presence of the crowd complicate the story, and the woman experiences healing before she confesses her faith. Matthew reverses the sequence in order to stress her faith). The two blind men (vv. 27–31) are able to see, also because of their "faith."

The cure of the mute which concludes the miracle section is hardly a miracle story at all, but merely a peg on which to hang the contrasting reactions of the crowd and the Pharisees (vv. 33–34). Here is the evangelist's prime concern: How does one respond to Jesus? The people are in awe at Jesus' works of mercy just as they were at his graceful words (7:28–29). But the Pharisees interpret Jesus' ministry as the work of Satan, not the work of God. Their reaction is one more muffled percussion which alerts the reader to the open rejection of Jesus that will soon explode.

STUDY QUESTION: Jesus was not a magician. Healing came only if the sick opened their entire person to God's saving power. Do we ask God for instant magic or for the transforming miracle of faith?

Matthew 9:36 to 10:42
THE DISCIPLES AND JESUS' MISSION

Chapter 10 will bring us to the second great discourse of Matthew's Gospel, Jesus' mission instruction to his twelve disciples. One should not expect a neat logical flow in this "discourse." As with the Sermon on the Mount, Matthew is content with a loose blend of materials from the sayings source and from Mark, tied together by his own reflections and conclusion.

Matthew 9:36 to 10:4
The Call
The preparation for Jesus' mission discourse recalls the introduction to the Sermon on the Mount (cf. 4:23–25). Jesus is moved to speak because of his compassion for the fractured humanity that encircles him. Matthew employs two traditional images to set the tone. The people are confused and dejected like the Old Testament image of "sheep without a shepherd" (on this Old Testament image, see Ezek 34:3ff; Jer 50:6). And they are expectant like a field of grain ready for an "abundant harvest," Jesus' own favored metaphor (cf. the parable of the sower, 13:3–9). But the mission of the Gospel is no mere response to need; it is a gift from God. Therefore the "master of the harvest" must be asked to send the harvesters (v. 38). The Beatitudes had asserted God's initiative at the beginning of the Sermon on the Mount, just as Jesus' call to prayer does here.

Matthew formalizes the call of the twelve disciples who will be "sent" on mission (thus earning the technical term "apostle," or "one sent"). The number is significant because it is the number of the original twelve tribes of Israel. This confirms Matthew's insistence that Jesus'

initial mission is to restore God's chosen people (10:5–6). The men
Jesus chooses themselves deserve the label "lost sheep": the awkward
and fearful Peter; Matthew the tax collector; Simon, probably a member of the hot-blooded Zealot revolutionaries; and the tragic Judas. The
Gospel will be proclaimed by the very ones who desperately need it.

Matthew 10:5–15
Instruction

This instruction details the identity between Jesus' own ministry and
that of the Twelve. They are to go only to the "lost sheep" of Israel. They
are to proclaim the dawn of the kingdom (4:17). They are to continue
the same works of compassion and reconciliation. Some of the practical
charges given probably reflect the style of the early Gospel preachers.
Like Jesus himself (cf. 8:20), the missionary is to travel light and is not to
expect a salary for his work (v. 8). He is to depend on the hospitality of
Christian households as he moves from town to town. An underlying
supposition of the discourse, and of other passages in Matthew (see discussion of 25:31–46), is that preaching the Gospel is a sacred task. The
missionary becomes the voice and presence of Jesus himself (cf. 10:40).
Therefore, welcoming or rejecting a missionary bears the same promise
and the same consequence as welcoming or rejecting Jesus (vv. 14–15).

There is one intriguing omission in the list of mission tasks shared
between Jesus and the disciples. Despite its centrality in Matthew's portrait of Jesus, "teaching" is not listed among the apostles' charges. That
seems reserved until the very end of the Gospel (28:20) where the
eleven apostles are given their commission to go to the whole world.
Does Matthew want to imply that the disciples are not yet ready to
"teach," because they have not yet confronted Jesus' passion and death?

Matthew 10:16–25
Warning

The discourse now turns sober. Jesus' own fate is a warning to the
church that following him will be costly. The Gospel's vibrant life is a
direct challenge to the forces of death. So the disciple is warned to be
open-eyed and prudent (v. 16).

Most of this section is taken from the apocalyptic discourse of
Mark's Gospel (cf. Mark 13:9–13), where Jesus' prophetic words alert

the community to the turmoil it must expect in the last days. In Matthew these same words are used in the mission discourse to help express the kind of wrenching experiences the early church had already had, and could continue to expect, as it carried out its mission. Persecution, rejection, family division: these were sometimes the cost of preaching the Gospel with integrity.

But pain is not the only sensation. Preaching the Gospel is ultimately to savor the joy and confidence Jesus himself experienced. The Spirit of the Father will give the disciples eloquence (v. 20) and their task will end with the "Son of Man's" victorious return (v. 23). This latter promise is difficult to interpret. The original intent of the saying may reflect primitive Christianity's hope that Jesus' victorious return was close at hand. But for Matthew's own church, "the towns of Israel" must now be understood as the far-flung villages of the world to which the Risen Lord has sent them (28:19).

Matthew 10:26–33
Encouragement

The hints of confidence in the previous section (10:19–20, 23) now break into full view. A series of metaphors not unlike the tone of the famous parable of the mustard seed (cf. 13:31–32) challenges the disciples to transmit the teaching of Jesus out loud and in the open (vv. 26–27). Paralyzing fear should not be an ingredient of Christian ministry. There is only one "fear" that should command a disciple and that is fear of the One who holds the power of life in his hands (v. 28). But such is not "fear" at all, but a consuming reverence and love for the Father whose providence carefully watches over these disciples who are more precious than many sparrows (v. 31).

Reference to the Father is now capped by reference to the Son who reveals him to the disciples (vv. 32–33). Fearlessly proclaiming the Gospel means fearlessly proclaiming Jesus. To fail at this is to sever one's access to the Father.

Matthew 10:34–42
The Costly Business of Being a Disciple

The discourse closes by lingering over the basic premise that began it. To preach the Gospel is to be identified with Jesus. The Messiah was expected to bring "peace," but Jesus' jolting words deflate any hope for a cheap or superficial peace (v. 34). Words taken from the prophet Micah (7:6) warn of family division (vv. 35–36). No allegiance can be allowed to shunt aside the Gospel and the Jesus it proclaims (vv. 37–38). Such commitment is not blind fanaticism, but the discovery of life itself (v. 39).

The final words of the discourse revert to the theme of hospitality. One who preaches the Gospel, whose life is genuinely identified with that of Jesus, has become a sacred presence. This sacredness might be masked by the weakness, the half-faith, the fear that Jesus' own disciples carry with them. But even a cup of water to one of these "little ones" (v. 42) will not go unrewarded (cf. 25:31–46).

STUDY QUESTION: The mission discourse pulls no punches: Anyone who preaches the Gospel with integrity will experience pain and joy. The discourse is directed to all who read the Gospel, not just a select few. How do I preach the Gospel? And in what ways do I experience the things Jesus speaks of in this instruction to his disciples?

III. "Are You the One Who Is to Come, or Should We Look for Another?"— Reactions to Jesus and His Message

Matthew 11:1 to 16:20

Matthew 11:1–15
"ARE YOU THE ONE?"

Matthew's transitional formula (cf. above, 7:28–29) signals a major turning point in the Gospel. Matthew has laid before us a portrait of Jesus, the Son of God, the Messiah of graceful word (chapters 5 to 7) and healing touch (chapters 8 and 9). Chapter 10 had claimed that Jesus' disciples and, through them, the church were to carry out the same mission. How will people respond? This question will dominate chapters 11 to 13 and its consequences will be played out in the rest of the Gospel story.

The figure of John the Baptist prefaced Matthew's account of the ministry of Jesus (cf. 3:1–15); now response to the Gospel will once more bind their fates together. A question of John's disciples enunciates the theme of the entire section: "Are you the one who is to come, or should we look for another?" (v. 3). Jesus' answer (vv. 4–5) uses the prophetic words of Isaiah (cf. 61:1; 35:5–6) to tick off the preaching and healing ministry described in the previous chapters of the Gospel. Jesus is the expected Messiah, the "one who is to come." And, as Matthew's additions to the words of Isaiah suggest ("lepers are cleansed . . . the dead are raised"), Jesus is more than Israel expected. A new beatitude reasserts the chapter's theme: blessed is the one who does not find Jesus an obstacle (v. 6).

The contrast between John and Jesus is again instructive (vv. 7–15). What did the people think of the desert prophet John? He was more than a prophet because he announced the arrival of Jesus. John is "Elijah," the great prophet hero of the Old Testament who was expected to reappear immediately before the Messianic Age (cf. Sir 48:10; Mal 3:23). But John, for all of his greatness, is still subordinate to Jesus. John represented the best of Israel; Jesus is the beginning of the new and decisive era of salvation. The saying about "violence" is obscure (v. 12), but it seems to capture the dramatic rush of life triggered by Jesus' arrival. The kingdom of God is being taken by storm because God's Son has brought the kingdom into the dusty squares of Galilee.

STUDY QUESTION: John's mysterious figure continues to haunt the Gospel story. His presence and his words prepare for Jesus' coming, but John does not get in Jesus' way. We might consider the figure of John as a model of Christian ministry.

Matthew 11:16–24
THIS GENERATION'S FAILURE

The Gospel has yet to describe the hostile resistance that will be thrown against Jesus and his message. But this passage is well aware of what lies ahead. "This generation"—indicative not only of Jesus' contemporaries but of the opponents of Matthew's own community— rejects John's prophetic message of repentance and Jesus' joyous ministry of the kingdom. The tragedy of Jesus' words is barely masked by an almost humorous comparison to the children of the marketplace who imitate the men who play the pipes at a wedding and the women who mourn at a funeral (vv. 16–17). The leaders of his own people will not join him. Their contemptuous label ironically confirms the Gospel's portrayal of Jesus' sensitive rapport with the outcasts: "a glutton and a drunkard, a friend of tax collectors and sinners." Yet "the works of the Messiah" (cf. v. 2) are truly the "works of wisdom" (v. 19). Jesus' compassion proves that he is the Son of his Father. This theme will re-emerge at the end of the chapter (cf. 11:25–30).

One of Matthew's most insistent messages is that confrontation with Jesus and the Gospel bears its own responsibility. To reject the

Gospel or to fail to take it seriously through repentance and good deeds is to invite judgment. The Galilean towns where Jesus will suffer rejection are promised such consequences: Chorazin, Bethsaida, Capernaum. This is Jesus' home region clustered around the northern end of the Sea of Galilee, but such proximity to Jesus is meaningless unless one takes his message to heart.

STUDY QUESTION: Jesus and his message cannot be toyed with. To hear the Gospel brings responsibility. What difference has the Gospel made in our lives, we who have heard it so often?

Matthew 11:25–30
"THE CHILDREN WHO SEE"

Acceptance or rejection of Jesus and his message is crucial because of who he is. These verses, which are supremely important in Matthew's Gospel, assert Jesus' identity in unmistakable terms.

The passage begins with a "thanksgiving," a prayer form common in Judaism and in early Christian liturgy. The lyrical cadence of the prayer and its emphasis on revelation causes many commentators to note its similarity to the style of John's Gospel. But these verses are completely at home in Matthew. Jesus' bond with his Father has been stressed from the beginning of the Gospel. The obedient Jesus is God's Son; not just *a* son, but *the* Son whose very presence is God's last and best word to Israel (v. 27). The context of this chapter and the wider framework of the Gospel will prove that the learned and self-righteous are blind to the beauty of the Gospel, while the outcasts and sinners— "the childlike"—respond with faith.

Themes of intimate revelation to a chosen few and the Son's privileged knowledge of his Father are found in the early chapters of the Book of Wisdom (cf. for example, 2:13, 16–18). Sirach (cf. 51:23–27; 24:18), another Old Testament wisdom book, also seems to be an influence on the beautiful words that conclude this chapter (vv. 28–30). The compassion of Jesus invites the weary and burdened to come to find rest. In Sirach, the Jewish law is personified and offers an almost identical invitation to those who seek God's will. Jesus is God's new "law." His "yoke" (another Jewish image for obedience to the law) is easy to those who accept it. His commands are not an oppressive burden but free one to be truly human and to find authentic happiness and peace.

STUDY QUESTION: Matthew portrays Jesus as the ultimate revelation of who God is. Does our own image of God harmonize with the compassionate and forgiving God that Jesus reveals?

Matthew 12:1–21
THE PRICE OF COMPASSION

The teaching of Jesus is an easy yoke and a light burden because his words and his ministry center on compassion and love. This was the final note of chapter 11. The two sabbath incidents that begin chapter 12 are examples of Jesus' teaching in action.

Deuteronomy 23:25–26 forbade "reaping" on the sabbath, part of the many laws that were intended to protect the sacred day of rest. Thus the Pharisees object when Jesus' disciples pick heads of grain (12:1–2). As Matthew presents the story, Jesus defends his disciples because they are hungry. Thus the sabbath law should be interpreted in the light of this clear human need. Two examples, one from history and one from the law itself, back up Jesus' interpretation. David looked after the needs of his own followers at the expense of the law (cf. 1 Sam 21:4–7) and the priests themselves have to bend some of the sabbath legislation in order to carry out their liturgical duties in the temple (cf. Num 28:9–10). But the final argument is Jesus' own authority (12:8). The primacy of compassion and mercy over all of the other demands of the law is at the heart of Jesus' definitive revelation of the Father's will. The words of Hosea 6:6 (cf. v. 7) are once again cited as an exquisite summary of Jesus' teaching: "I desire mercy, not sacrifice" (cf. also Matt 9:13).

Another sabbath incident (vv. 9–14) continues the illustration of Jesus' priorities. The hostility that now smolders between Jesus and his opponents is scarcely veiled. As Matthew notes (v. 9), Jesus goes to "*their* synagogue" and the question put to him is meant to be a trap: "Is it lawful to cure on the sabbath?" Jesus' interpretation is fearlessly proclaimed by word and action. Can one rescue an entrapped sheep on the sabbath (a point that was, in fact, hotly debated by the rabbis)? If one can show compassion to an animal, how much more should the deliverance of a human person become an urgent priority. Jesus' healing of the man with the withered hand is the final word. What Jesus teaches, he does; this has been the constant insistence of Matthew's Gospel (cf. 7:24). The Pharisees' hostility, which will eventually boil into total rejection of Jesus, begins now (v. 14).

Because of the leader's opposition, Jesus "withdrew from that place." A brief summary informs us that he quietly continues his ministry of compassion (v. 15). The words of Isaiah 42:1–4, thoroughly adapted by Matthew to fit his purpose, provide an interlude of quiet reflection on the significance of Jesus and his ministry as the din of opposition begins to build. Jesus is God's faithful "servant," and, in words reminiscent of Jesus' baptism (cf. 3:17), he is the beloved and Spirit-filled Son of God. The Greek word *pais* can mean servant or child (son) and Matthew may intend both senses here. Jesus' ministry is not a brawling display of power, a conception of messiahship Jesus rejected out of hand in the desert (cf. 4:1–4). This gentle, selfless servant comes to bring a decisive moment of judgment to his own people and to be a sign of hope to the "Gentiles."

STUDY QUESTION: Jesus is a model of integrity: what he teaches, he does. He carries out his mission resolutely and without fanfare. Sometimes our own good deeds are done with a side glance toward the approving crowd.

Matthew 12:22–50
WHAT KIND OF SPIRIT?

Matthew moves back to the theme of responsibility which dominates these chapters. An exorcism triggers contrasting reactions (12:22–24). The crowd is astounded and edges to the brink of recognizing Jesus: "Could this perhaps be the Son of David?" This messianic title had been given to Jesus in the first verse of the Gospel (cf. 1:1). But the Pharisees judge that Jesus' power is not from God but from "Beelzebul, the prince of demons."

Exorcisms pose in stark terms the ultimate significance of the Gospel. The power of God at work in Jesus' teaching and healing overwhelms the forces of darkness and death. For this reason, Matthew gives considerable attention to the Pharisees' accusation. Apparently playing on the popular etymology for the name "Beelzebul" as "Lord of the House," Jesus asks how Satan's household could be so divided that Jesus' actions which, in fact, destroy Satan's kingdom, can be construed as acting on behalf of Satan. Jesus' conclusion is inevitable and awesome: If Jesus acts through the power of God—as the Gospel testifies he does—then the longed-for reign of God has already begun to make its presence felt (v. 28). A mini "parable" restates Jesus' case in novel terms. Jesus is a "thief" who breaks into Satan's household, ties up that "strong man," and plunders his property (v. 29).

The stark cleavage between the Gospel's estimation of Jesus and the Pharisees' characterization of him as in league with Beelzebul forces a decision: one is either for or against Jesus (v. 30). In the difficult verses 31–32, the theme of response and the image of Jesus as Spirit-filled messenger (cf. the quote from Isaiah in v. 18) seem to converge. Ignorance might excuse one who rejects Jesus, the Son of Man. But to reject the Spirit of God which animates Jesus is equivalent to rejecting God himself and is therefore unforgivable. To reject forgiveness is to effectively place oneself in unpardonable circumstances.

A series of sayings continues Matthew's sober commentary on the rejection of Jesus (vv. 33–37). The familiar image of a tree and its fruits (cf. 7:16–20) is used again to illustrate the continuity between good deeds and a good heart, between bad deeds and an evil heart. The significant things we say or do have consequences because they reveal the basic values commanding our lives.

The chapter draws to a close with another gallery of contrasting attitudes. The scribes and Pharisees continue to reject Jesus by demanding a sign, thereby implying that the testimony of his own teaching and ministry is insufficient (vv. 38–45). Those who accept Jesus and thus have true kinship with him are his disciples who do the will of his Father (vv. 46–50).

The demand for some clinching guarantee that Jesus is the one will be honored only with the "sign of Jonah the prophet," a sign that turns out to be nothing other than Jesus' own life and ministry. Verse 40, which refers to Jonah's famous sojourn in the belly of the sea monster, alludes to Jesus' death and resurrection. Verse 41 recalls Jonah's preaching to the pagan Ninevites. Jesus' own mission is turned aside by Israel but is accepted as a sign of hope by Gentiles (cf. v. 21). This, too, should be a warning for those who turn a deaf ear to someone who is greater than Jonah and wiser than Solomon.

The pointed story of the return of the unclean spirit adds another warning to the list (vv. 43–45). Jesus' ministry is a cleansing purge of Israel. But if there is no response to his mission, the evil that has been driven out will come back to fill the void.

Early in the Gospel, John the Baptist had warned that descent from Abraham meant nothing unless it was coupled with genuine repentance (3:9). A similar atmosphere surrounds the story that closes chapter 12 (vv. 46–50). The family of Jesus has no claim on him. A bond of kinship is forged with Jesus only when one shares his dominating drive to do the will of his Father in heaven.

STUDY QUESTION: What do we perceive in Jesus? And what difference does our perception make in our lives? These are the probing questions Matthew's Gospel continues to place before the reader.

Matthew 13:1–58
MANY THINGS IN PARABLES

Matthew 13:1–2
Introduction
The third great discourse of Matthew's Gospel now begins. Like the previous two (cf. the Sermon of chapters 5 to 7 and the mission discourse of chapter 10), this "discourse" is really a composite of Jesus' words brought together by the evangelist from his various sources and designed to emphasize major themes of the Gospel.

We instinctively think of the parables as those pointed, colorful stories Jesus told in order to communicate with his audience. But Matthew views the parables from another perspective. As chapter 11 and 12 have demonstrated, some people were open to Jesus' teaching but others closed their minds and hearts to the Gospel. For this latter group, the parables are not provocative bearers of truth but puzzling riddles which they refuse to understand. The Hebrew word for parable, *mashal,* was broad enough in meaning to contain both nuances— explanatory metaphor or baffling riddle. In Matthew's Gospel, Jesus' teaching becomes "parable," an opaque riddle for those who refuse to understand, but revelation of the mystery of the kingdom for his disciples. Thus, the theme of response to Jesus which dominated chapters 11 and 12 is kept alive.

The evangelist has impressed a loose structure on this composite discourse. The first section (vv. 1–23) is dominated by a cleavage between the disciples who do understand and the crowds who do not. The second section of the discourse (vv. 24–50) is concerned with the judgment that will separate the sons of the kingdom from the sons of evil. Most of the material in the first section is adapted from Mark; most of the material in the second is unique to Matthew. And each section is dominated by a similar pattern: introductory parables to the crowds, comment on the reason for speaking in "parables," and, finally, private instruction for the disciples.

Matthew 13:3–23
On Being a Disciple or Being Part of the Crowd

The parable of the sower (vv. 3–9) begins the discourse. By itself, the story of the seed and its fate as it is scattered on so many kinds of soil seems to emphasize the inevitability of a rich crop (some a hundredfold, some sixty, some thirty) in spite of all obstacles. But the final phrase calling the listener to attention, and the explanation of the parable given by Jesus to his disciples (vv. 18–23), will shift the emphasis to the theme of *response*. This is where the focus of the discourse will remain.

Response is certainly the topic of the next segment (vv. 10–17) in which Jesus explains to the disciples his reason for speaking to the crowds in "parables." The followers of Jesus had been singled out at the end of chapter 12 because they were dedicated to the will of the Father. Here they are cited for being open to understanding the mysteries of the kingdom of Heaven revealed to them by Jesus. But for the crowds who have not yet committed themselves to Jesus and who eventually will turn against him (cf. 27:24–25), the teaching of Jesus is not revelation but "parable." Words adopted from Isaiah 6:9–10 (cf. vv. 13–14) spell out the reasons for the indictment: "they will hardly hear with their ears, they have closed their eyes, lest they see with their eyes and hear with their ears and understand with their heart and be converted...."

The first half of the discourse concludes with Jesus' explanation of the parable of the sower (vv. 18–23). The disciples do hear what Jesus says and thus they can understand the point of the story of the sower.

The early church loved to allegorize the parables of Jesus and it is likely that Matthew uses this technique here in order to continue the discourse's concentration on the theme of response. The different fates of the seed illustrate various reactions to the Gospel. In some people the Gospel takes no root at all because they are "without understanding." Others begin well but soon allow persecution or the lust for wealth to choke off the new life in them. Verse 23 defines the genuine disciple: "the one who hears the word and understands it, who indeed bears fruit and yields a hundred or sixty or thirtyfold."

STUDY QUESTION: This section's emphasis on perception and action, on hearing and doing, bears Matthew's unmistakable trademark. For the evangelist there is no genuine faith unless it is translated into decisive action. Do we agree?

Matthew 13:24–58
On Being a Subject of the Kingdom and a Subject of the Evil One
The pattern of the first half of the discourse is repeated. Parables to the crowds (vv. 24–33) will be followed by a comment on the reason for parables (vv. 34–35) and with private instructions to the disciples (vv. 36–50). The contrast between the disciples who understand and the crowds who do not dominated the earlier material. The surrounding context of chapters 11 and 12 leaves little doubt that this contrast is a reflection on Israel's rejection of Jesus. But the broader spectrum of images in the last half of the discourse (the "world," the "evildoers" and the "just," etc.) indicates that Matthew is not confining the challenge of the discourse only to this problem. *All* who hear the Gospel—Jew and Gentile—must decide whether it will be riddle or revelation.

A string of parables is now directed to the crowds. The parable of the weeds will receive its allegorical explanation later on (cf. vv. 36–43). The images of the mustard seed and the yeast (vv. 31–33) contrast unpretentious beginnings with glorious and powerful endings. They are a brisk warning to those who cannot perceive that in Jesus the kingdom is already at work (cf. 12:28).

A citation from Psalm 78:2 (13:35) verifies the fact that Jesus' teaching in "parables" (i.e., riddles) and the rejection of his mission which this implies are all within the scope of God's plan prophesied in the scriptures. Jesus now leaves the crowds outside and gathers his disciples inside a house (v. 36). The movement is a commentary on the closed hearts of those who refuse to understand Jesus.

Practically every detail of the parable of the weeds receives an explanation (vv. 37–43). The story becomes symbolic of judgment, a favored theme of Matthew. Those in the world will be called to responsibility at the great harvest. Another assortment of judgment parables, all of them unique to Matthew's Gospel, will be found in chapter 25.

The exquisite stories of the treasure in the field and the pearl merchant (vv. 44–46) play out the theme of responsibility in another key. Seeking the kingdom or, as Matthew puts it in other contexts, doing the will of the Father (12:50), calls for total commitment. One does not casually add this pearl to a collection or simply purchase one more parcel of land. *All* must be sold. An absolute fresh start is to be made.

The theme of judgment returns with the story of the dragnet (vv. 47–50). Its structure and message are practically identical to those of the parable of the weeds (cf. vv. 24–30). The Gospel cuts into one's life and one must decide. Jesus brings compassion and healing; he also brings a call to responsibility that is not without its consequences.

The parable discourse concludes as it began—with the theme of "understanding" (vv. 51–52). The disciples perceive the beauty and the truth of Jesus' words and the Gospel will document their struggle to make that understanding bear fruit. The discourse ends with a saying that practically defines the purpose of Matthew's Gospel. The scribe (i.e., one who understands the law) who becomes a disciple of the kingdom is one who is placed in authority over the household and is able to bring from his treasure house "both the new and the old." Jesus himself was such a "head of household," fulfilling the past by transforming the present. His disciples had to do the same by being faithful to the best of their Jewish heritage yet being open to the new realities God would reveal to them through Jesus' teaching.

Matthew's standard transitional formula (v. 53) signals that the discourse is over and the tempo of the narrative will resume. The scene flashes to Jesus' hometown of Nazareth (13:53–58). His own people hear his words and witness his power but they refuse to accept him. The chasm that separates Jesus and those who should have understood him recalls the scene at the end of chapter 12 (vv. 46–50). Kinship with Jesus cannot be presumed but must be exercised through obedience to God's will. The two stories pointedly frame Jesus' discourse on the urgency of "understanding."

STUDY QUESTION: Christians can sometimes speak too casually about "belonging to Christ" or "following Jesus." But the parable discourse warns us that kinship with Jesus should not be lightly presumed. A disciple of Jesus is one who has pondered his words and translated them into his or her life.

Matthew 14:1–12
PROPHETS WITHOUT HONOR

Herod's interest in Jesus and his speculation that Jesus might be John the Baptist brought back from the dead (14:1–2) occasion a flashback. At the beginning of Jesus' public ministry (4:12) we were told that John had been arrested. Later on, the imprisoned prophet had sent messengers to Jesus (11:2). Now John's tragic story is completed. Herod Antipas, son of Herod the Great and vassal of the Romans over the region of lower Galilee and Perea, had arrested John because the prophet had opposed Herod's incestuous marriage to Herodias, wife of his half-brother. Because of a frivolous oath, Herod submits to his wife's instigations and kills the prophet (thereby providing a negative example, as Peter will do at the trial, of Jesus' prohibition against oath-taking; cf. 5:33–37).

This flashback, and the warning transmitted to Jesus, bind John and Jesus together once again. At the beginning of chapter 11, Jesus had challenged the leaders for their rejection of himself and John. Now John's death as a prophet forecasts Jesus' own fate (cf. v. 5; compare 21:46 where the identical words are used of Jesus). The Gospel will speak openly of the passion in chapter 16 (cf. 16:21), but the end result of the mounting hostility against Jesus is already clear.

Matthew 14:13–36
JESUS AND HIS DISCIPLES—TWO GREAT SIGNS

The opposition to Jesus cannot stifle his ministry. Two great acts of power are now described. Jesus withdraws to a "deserted place" but the throngs pursue him and are waiting on the shore. Matthew continues

to highlight Jesus as the compassionate healer who cannot resist showing mercy to that tattered crowd (14:14). The first miracle of the loaves
(another will follow in chapter 15) demonstrates that compassion even
further. The act of feeding the multitudes triggers a number of biblical
images. Moses was involved in feeding the people with manna (Exod
16) and the great prophet Elisha multiplied food for the hungry (1 Kgs
19:21). Hopes for the messianic kingdom were painted as a lavish feast
with limitless food and drink (e.g., Isa 25:6). Thus, this miracle story
not only points to Jesus' compassion for the hunger of his people, but
also makes a strong biblical statement about Jesus' identity as one capable of satisfying that deep hunger.

Matthew's version of the story shows that the early community
continued to find new levels of symbolism in this miracle. The ritual
gestures of Jesus, the focus on the bread (rather than the fish), and the
careful collection of the fragments have strong eucharistic overtones.
And Matthew highlights the role of the disciples in the whole episode.
They do not rudely oppose Jesus (as they do in Mark 6:37) but are
important mediaries who distribute the bread (14:19) and gather the
leftovers. The disciples share in Jesus' ministry as he had promised them
(4:19).

The second miracle (14:22–33) is one of Matthew's most effective
passages. The basic details about Jesus' miraculous walking on the water
over an angry sea and his mysterious encounter with the disciples and
their battered boat are all borrowed from Mark (6:45–52). Both
Gospels make a profound assertion about the divine power of Jesus
who, like God depicted in the Hebrew Scriptures, treads upon the
crests of the sea (Job 9:8) and whose majestic words to the disciples,
"Take courage, it is I; do not be afraid," echo the revelatory words of
the God of Israel (cf. Isa 41:4, 10; 43:25, etc.).

But Matthew enriches the story with material not found in Mark.
Peter, the consistent spokesman for the disciples in this Gospel, asks to
duplicate Jesus' own dominance over the chaos of the sea (14:28). True to
the Gospel's assertion, the disciple is able to do the same as Jesus (cf.
10:1). But, as he will do throughout the Gospel, Matthew likes to pair
the disciples' glory with their flaws. Peter experiences the power of the
chaos, and fear begins to drag him down. His response is the best instinctive response of the believer: "Lord, save me!" Jesus instantly rescues Peter
and, when all are in the boat, the awed disciples worship Jesus with the
fullness of Christian faith: "Truly, you are the Son of God" (v. 33).

Mark's version of the story does not include the Peter incident and his portrait of the disciples presents them as completely lacking in understanding or faith. But for Matthew that boat crew images his own church: buffeted, frightened, but clinging to belief, a community "of little faith" (cf. 6:30).

The chapter closes with the boat at shore and the Gospel's repeated testimony to the healing power of Jesus (14:36).

STUDY QUESTION: The Gospel stresses the inclusion of the disciples in Jesus' power to feed and to heal. Only fear stands in the way of their ability to carry out their mission. Does our own story of Christian discipleship have any parallels to the experiences of Peter and the Twelve?

Matthew 15:1–20
WHAT MAKES A MAN CLEAN?

The angry drone of Jesus' opponents returns and once again the issue is interpretation of the law (cf. 12:1–14; 5:17–48). Scribes and Pharisees "from Jerusalem" (the city where Jesus will meet his death) challenge Jesus because his disciples do not wash their hands before eating, a practice not for purposes of hygiene but to prevent the ritual impurity caused by handling certain foods. The temple priests were bound to this by the Torah (Lev 22:4–7), but the obligation for others was debated.

Jesus counters that the Pharisees' tradition can be at odds with the very purpose of God's law, as when someone avoids supporting his parents by claiming that the money had been vowed for temple use. Many of the rabbis had opposed this kind of abuse. For Jesus it is a prime example of legalism gone sour. The searing quotation from Isaiah 29:13 indicts this wrongheaded perspective (vv. 8–9).

Jesus' teaching on the broader question of ritual purity is coupled with this dispute (vv. 10–20). It is likely that many of the early Christians in Matthew's community continued to respect their Jewish heritage by abstaining from certain foods declared "unclean" by the law and by rabbinic regulation. In Matthew's Gospel, Jesus stops short of nullifying this practice (note that Matthew omits Mark's verse, "Thus

he declared all foods clean" [Mark 7:19]). But Jesus continues to be the
great prophetic Teacher who "fulfills" the law by radically and unerr-
ingly pointing to its ultimate purpose. As Jesus' miniature "parable"
states (15:18), it is not the food one eats that taints a person, but what
comes "from the heart." The anger, the disrespect, the untruth that
breaks the bond between people and reveals the twisted intentions of
our heart—this is "impurity" worth our concern (15:19–20). Teachers
in Israel (or anywhere else) concerned about less would feel the lash of
Jesus' critique. They could pride themselves on being God's "vineyard"
(cf. Isa 5), but they would be jerked up by the roots. They may think
the wisdom of the law makes them a light to the nations, but they have
become sightless guides (15:12–14).

STUDY QUESTION: The Pharisees' concern for the peripheral and
the nonessential is a caution for contemporary Christians. Jesus' challenge comes to us: What really makes a person "unclean"?

Matthew 15:21–39
BREAD FOR THE OUTSIDERS

The argument with the scribes and Pharisees is broken off and Jesus
moves toward the northwest border region of Tyre and Sidon. A Gentile woman, a Canaanite (Matthew may have pointedly labeled the
woman with the Old Testament's most common term for the non-
Israelite) startles the disciples by recognizing Jesus and asking for a cure
for her daughter. The woman's faith—she calls Jesus "Lord" and "Son
of David" or Messiah—and Jesus' sharp reminder of his mission to
Israel (15:24) lean on the tension that the Gospel story has been building. Jesus has respected the destiny of the chosen people. He has come
to restore Israel. But the rejection of the Gospel by some of the Jews
and their leaders, and the openness of Gentiles, such as this woman, signal a startling future development in God's plan of salvation when the
mission of the community will extend beyond Israel to include Gentiles. The "dogs" (a contemptuous term for Gentiles) will eat the bits of
bread that fall from their master's table. The Gospel will promise even
more: the response of faith will become the only entry to the Lord's
banquet.

Jesus returns to "Galilee" ("Galilee of the Gentiles," as Matthew has named it, cf. 4:15). In terms hauntingly similar to the great opening scene of Jesus' ministry (4:23 to 5:1), the sick and the lame flow toward Israel's Messiah like a river of pain. He makes them whole. These same people are miraculously fed (15:32–39), a repeat of the multiplication of the loaves of chapter 14 (vv. 15–21).

Are these repetitions meant to foreshadow an eventual mission to the Gentiles? Jesus himself will not go beyond Israel. But after his death and resurrection, his disciples will bring the nourishment of his graceful words and his healing touch to all nations (cf. 28:16–20).

STUDY QUESTION: Matthew presents the tenacious faith of the Canaanite woman as a preview of the many "foreigners" who would eventually seek healing and nourishment in the message of Jesus. How much does our faith mean to us, the "children of the household"?

Matthew 16:1–12
BEWARE OF PHARISEE YEAST

Matthew continues to lace his account of Jesus' ministry with doses of opposition from the Jewish leaders. The Pharisees, now joined by the temple-based Sadducees, repeat their demands for a sign but once again their lack of faith is rebuffed (vv. 1–4). They will receive no sign but the "sign of Jonah," that is, Jesus' own ministry and his death and resurrection (cf. 12:38–42). The homespun verses about reading the "signs of the times" (vv. 2–3) are probably later additions to Matthew's text, since they are missing in most early manuscripts.

Matthew's unique perception of the disciples stands out in the brief discussion about "leaven" or yeast (vv. 5–12). In Mark's version (cf. 8:14–21) the disciples' chronic dullness and their abject inability to understand Jesus reach a new low. They are perplexed at Jesus' warning about the "leaven" of the Pharisees and Herodians (Matthew changes this to the more familiar grouping, Sadducees), and blink in confusion when he recalls the great messianic miracle of the loaves. In Matthew, the disciples' image is more even-keeled. They have faith, but only a "little," the designation consistently used by the evangelist (16:8; 6:30). They understand, but only gradually and with difficulty (16:12).

The sharp contrast between the disciples and the Jewish leaders (evident since chapter 11) helps prepare for a major development in the Gospel story. Peter's confession of Jesus as Messiah and Son of God (16:16) will prompt Jesus to begin instructing his disciples on the meaning of his death and resurrection. But such contrast does not tempt Matthew to idealize the disciples. Even in Peter's moment of prominence, he is evidently and painfully flawed.

STUDY QUESTION: The Gospel's portrayal of the disciples is honest and sympathetic: they are of "little faith." Can we recognize ourselves in the struggles and small triumphs of Jesus' followers?

Matthew 16:13–20
PETER: FOUNDING ROCK

In the northern Galilean city of Caesarea Philippi, Jesus poses a fundamental question: "Who do people say that the Son of Man is?" (16:13). The disciples play back the spectrum of popular opinion. When the question is put directly to the disciples, it is Peter, their constant spokesman (cf. 15:15; 17:4, 24; 18:21; 19:27), who comes back with an unflinching confession of Jesus as "the Messiah" and "Son of the Living God" (16:16). Unlike Mark's Gospel where Jesus' identity remains veiled until the passion, these titles come as no surprise in Matthew. Jesus has clearly been labeled as Messiah from his birth and the disciples had proclaimed him Son of God after his appearance on the lake (cf. 14:33). This brace of titles is important here because they are proclaimed now *by Peter*. Such fidelity to Jesus is the foundation of the community's identity.

Confirmation of Peter's act of faith comes in words found only in Matthew (16:17–18). Peter is blessed because he has been gifted with understanding by the Father (cf. 11:25). And this Simon, "son of Jonah," will be known by a new name that reveals his role within the community. The material Matthew incorporates here may actually be playing on the identity of the Aramaic words for rock (*kepa*) and Peter (*kepa*). But, beyond the word play, an intriguing symbol is at work. Jewish reflection on the origin of the world had led to the belief that the foundation of the entire universe had been laid at Mount Zion upon which stood the temple. This was the centerpoint of the world. Isaiah 28:16, a text that may have influenced Matthew 16:18, speaks of this "rock": "See, I am laying a stone in Zion, . . . a precious cornerstone as a sure foundation; he who puts his faith in it shall not be shaken." The image of a world foundation stone which is also the foundation of the temple points to the meaning of the "Peter" passage. On Peter, the leader of the disciples to whom will be entrusted Jesus' own ministry, a new "temple" and a new community is being built: "upon this rock I will build my *church*." Matthew is the only evangelist to use this technical term (cf. also 18:17) which derives from the Hebrew word *qahal* or "assembly" of the people of Israel. Against this foundation stone and the community built on it even the forces of death will be powerless (v. 18).

Peter's role as foundation rock brings with it new authority and, once again, the evangelist uses biblical and Jewish imagery to convey this. The disciple is given "the keys to the kingdom of heaven," a probable reference to Isaiah 22:22 where Eliakim is made prime minister of Judah in place of the faithless Shebna. Eliakim is given "the key of the House of David . . . when he opens, no one shall shut, when he shuts, no one shall open." And Peter, too, shall have such powers. He has the discretion of "binding" and "loosing," Jewish legal terms referring either to the power of interpreting the obligations of the law or to the power of excommunicating from the synagogue. It is not clear which of these is being confided to Peter here (note similar powers are given to the *community* in 18:18).

STUDY QUESTION: This passage is testimony to the continuity between Matthew's "church" and the life of Jesus. The community is distinctive because it follows Jesus and thus must share in the glory and the opposition that he himself experienced. Leadership in the community is validated if it is based on the kind of fidelity shown by Peter and the responsibility entrusted to him by Jesus.

IV. "Destined to Go to Jerusalem"— The Fateful Pilgrimage from Galilee to Judea

Matthew 16:21 to 20:34

Matthew 16:21–28
DESTINY IN JERUSALEM

Peter's confession and his designation as leader of a new elect community preface a major turn in the Gospel story. "From that time on"—the same deliberate phrase that marked the beginning of Jesus' ministry in Galilee (cf. 4:17)—signals a new phase of that ministry as Jesus openly speaks of his death in Jerusalem (16:21). This is the first of four such predictions in Matthew's Gospel (cf. 17:22–23; 20:17–19; 26:1–2) that project a sense of inevitable death yet certain vindication. This mood of vindication is implied in the time phrase taken from Hosea 6:2, a text which confidently asserts that "on the third day" Yahweh will "raise up" his beloved. A Jesus without the passion is simply incomprehensible from the Gospel's perspective. His selfless giving of life and the validation of that gift in resurrection are the clearest statements of his mission (20:28).

That is why Peter's resistance to the idea of Jesus' suffering is taken so seriously by the Gospel writers. In Matthew's account, the shock of Peter's obtuseness is deepened. The apostle is not only called "Satan," the tempter who seeks to subvert Jesus' purpose (as the prince of evil did in chapter 4), but he is also an "obstacle" or literally a "stumbling block" in Jesus' way. Matthew continues his calculated mix of the disciple's image. Peter, the "founding rock" on which the community is built, is also capable of being a "stumbling block," one who stands in the way by making judgments from the wrong perspective (cf. this alternate image of "rock" in Isa 8:14).

The right perspective, Jesus' own, is reiterated by a series of sayings calling for selfless dedication to the Gospel (vv. 24–26). Following Jesus has its cost: one must go to Jerusalem. But such fidelity also has its reward. The "Son of Man," a title for Jesus used in contexts both of suffering and judgment, will come to reward each one "according to his conduct" (v. 27), a constant refrain in Matthew. The saying in verse 28 may originally have referred to an immediate expectation of the Son's glorious return. But now within the context of Matthew's Gospel it probably refers to the triumphant enthronement of the Risen Jesus which concludes the Gospel (cf. 28:16–20).

STUDY QUESTION: Many of us might be tempted, as Peter was, to think of Christianity without the cross. But "giving of life" is at the heart of the Gospel and cannot be shunted aside.

Matthew 17:1–20
JESUS—SON AND LORD:
THE VISION OF TRANSFIGURATION

"After six days"—the words bind the haunting vision of the transfiguration to the preceding event of Peter's confession and Jesus' prediction of his fate in Jerusalem. Each of these episodes concentrates on the identity of Jesus and its implication for the disciples.

Matthew lingers over this scene's majestic portrait of Jesus. A number of details evoke the story of Sinai and seem to subtly reinforce the image of Jesus as the "New Moses": the incident takes place on a "mountain"; Jesus' transfigured face "shone like the sun" (cf. Exod 34:29, 35); he converses with "Moses and Elijah" (symbolic of the "law and the prophets," Matthew's typical way of speaking of the scriptures); a "bright cloud," a sign of the Lord's presence at Sinai and in the desert, overshadows them (cf. Exod 24:15–18).

Not only is Jesus the New Moses, the true lawgiver, but he is the "Son." Matthew repeats word for word the Father's declaration at the baptism (17:5). Jesus is the truly obedient Israelite who enjoys a unique relationship to the Father. He is the one who reveals the will of his Father to those he chooses (cf. 11:27). Thus, the believer must hear this voice: "listen to him." Jesus has already been to the "mountain" in Matthew's Gospel (cf. 5:1) and, brimming with authority, has brought the Mosaic law to its fulfillment. At the conclusion of the Gospel, the Risen Lord will stand once again on a mountaintop and his authoritative word will plunge his disciples into a new mission (28:16–20). But, before that time comes, Jesus must experience suffering and death. As this dark chapter of the Gospel begins to unfold, the transfiguration scene reminds us of Jesus' true identity.

Matthew also gives careful attention to the reaction of the disciples. In Mark, the transfiguration becomes another commercial for the disciples' ineptness. Peter is incoherent (9:6) and the rest gape in uncomprehending fear (9:6, 8, 10). Not so in Matthew. The reaction of the disciples corresponds to the majesty of Jesus. Peter addresses his transfigured master as "Lord," and his offer to set up commemorative booths is properly deferential ("if you wish"). At the sound of the voice from heaven, the disciples are gripped with reverential fear and fall prostrate in adoration (v. 6). The account ends with an exquisite detail found only in Matthew (v. 7). Jesus comes forward and soothes their terror with a healing touch: "Rise, and do not be afraid." In Jesus, divine majesty and gentle compassion meet.

As Jesus and his disciples descend the mountain, the gloom of opposition and impending death appears (vv. 9–13). Matthew uses the conversation about Elijah to return to a consideration of John, whose fate is a forecast of Jesus' own. John is that "Elijah" who was expected to herald the coming of the kingdom. But before the arrival of this glorious moment, both John and Jesus will experience rejection and death (v. 12).

The disciples have been able to absorb this warning of Jesus (v. 13) but their faith remains weak. Their "little faith" (v. 20) once again prevents them from carrying out the mission of life entrusted to them. Earlier, Peter had allowed fear and "little faith" to stifle his power over the chaos of the sea (cf. 14:30). The same things happen again. The "little faith" of the disciples has stopped them from curing a young man seized with the spirit of lunacy. But if a disciple allows the power of God to work through him, "nothing will be impossible."

STUDY QUESTION: The transfiguration confronts us with the full mystery of Christ: Jesus en route to his death, but the glory of his triumphant resurrection already putting that death into new perspective. Christian faith enables us to put our own experience of suffering and death in the perspective of Christ's resurrection.

Matthew 17:22–27
DEATH AND TAXES

In the following chapter we will come to the fourth of Matthew's major discourses (18:1–35), another composite of Jesus' sayings and parables dealing with the kind of relationship that should bind together those who belong to the kingdom of God. These few verses serve as a remote preparation for the discourse.

Jesus gathers his disciples together like a commander rallying his troops before a battle. A second time, he predicts the death and victory that await him in Jerusalem. Matthew's portrayal of the disciples continues to be distinctively different from Mark's. Matthew observes that the disciples are saddened by the prediction of death; in Mark we are told: "they did not understand the saying, and they were afraid to question him" (9:32).

The band now moves to the seaside town of Capernaum where an incident recorded only by Matthew takes place (vv. 24–27). Tax collectors approach Peter (confirming his leadership role blessed in 16:17–19) and ask if Jesus pays the "temple tax." Prior to 70 A.D. this half-shekel tax was levied by the Jews for the upkeep of the temple (cf. Exod 30:13). To pay it was a sign of solidarity with the Jewish people. Peter insists that his master does pay the tax, but once inside the house, Jesus uses the question as a teaching moment. Jesus and his followers are not "foreigners" but "sons" of the King. Therefore they are free from the obligation of any such tribute.

The story concludes with the decision to pay the tax "that we may not offend them" (v. 27). In a rather spectacular way, God's providence assures Peter the means of paying. This story was undoubtedly instruction for Matthew's church. Even though Christians were free, they might still observe some laws and customs out of consideration for Jewish sensitivities (cf. Introduction). Within the flow of the Gospel, this story has another function. The disciples are "children" of the King; what determines true greatness within this kingdom? This is the question that leads into the discourse of chapter 18.

STUDY QUESTION: The Gospel tradition, like Paul, proclaims that to be a Christian is to be truly free. But freedom must always be exercised with respect for the conscience of the less free. Such compassionate sensitivity is a hallmark of those who belong to the kingdom.

Matthew 18:1–35
DISCOURSE ON LIFE IN THE COMMUNITY OF JESUS

The fourth great discourse of the Gospel lifts up the essential qualities which should characterize those who belong to the community of Jesus.

The discourse, a composite of parables and sayings, can be divided into two main sections. The first half (vv. 1–14) deals with the church's responsibility to the "little ones," an affectionate term for the weak and straying members of the community. The second section (vv. 15–35) reflects on the ties that bind "brothers [and sisters]" together. Each section is molded by a similar pattern: a series of sayings is followed by a parable and sealed by a reference to the will of "your heavenly Father" (cf. 18:14, 35). Thus, two characteristic concerns of Matthew's Gospel are joined: the responsibilities of discipleship and the search for God's will. The whole is directed to the "disciples" and it is obvious that through these followers of Jesus the evangelist intends to strike home to the leaders and people of his own church.

Matthew 18:1–14
Concern for the "Little Ones"

The discourse opens with the thematic question of the disciples: "Who is the greatest in the kingdom of heaven?" Jesus jolts the disciples by placing a child before them. To even enter the kingdom (much less find rank within it) disciples must undergo a complete conversion (literally "turn around") and become "like children" (v. 3). The image of "becoming a child" is not an appeal for a romantic naiveté but a demand for genuine humility. The Christian must sense an utter dependence upon God for life and for every gift. Humility and lack of self-concern are appealing instincts in a child but hard-earned virtues for an adult. Jesus cites them as the fruits of genuine conversion and true greatness.

The image of a child begins to shift in verse 5. It now becomes a designation for a member of the community. Jesus identifies with a "child such as this" and, as the mission discourse had already proclaimed (10:40), to show hospitality to such a Christian is to receive the Lord who is always with them. Suddenly, in verse 6, the image of a "child" slides into that of "little ones." The same sense of humility and lack of pretense covers both terms, but "little ones" refers to the Christian not as a fresh example of a converted life, but as a member of a community that is weak and faltering in faith.

To "cause them to sin" (literally, "to be an obstacle to them," a good literal rendition of the Greek term *scandalon* which is used throughout this section) is a terrible crime against someone who, though weak, believes in Jesus (v. 6). The English word "scandal" can be restricted to doing something so enticingly evil that others are drawn into the sin (as the translation of the word "scandal" as "cause to sin" in vv. 8 and 9 implies). But the Greek word *scandalon* means a "stumbling block" (cf. 16:23) and thus could refer to a whole spectrum of obstacles thrown in the way of a weak person. It might be the allure of sin that pushes them farther away, or it might be the uncompassionate glare of the righteous that blocks their return. To be such an obstacle is a mortal break in the sensitive and compassionate response which the members of the community owe each other (vv. 5–7). To avoid being such an obstacle calls for dramatic decisive action (vv. 8–9).

As Matthew continues to emphasize, the Father's relentless love for his people is the ultimate source and model of Jesus' own compassion and of the mandate he gives his disciples (cf. 5:43–48). This dimension is introduced in verse 10. These "little ones" have their own angels before the Father in heaven. The Judaism of Jesus' and Matthew's day had become increasingly intrigued by angels, and some Jewish literature had spoken of individual protecting angels. But to speak of these angels as having constant access to Yahweh is unique and makes an eloquent testimony to the Father's particular concern for the weak.

That concern is amplified in Matthew's version of the parable of the lost sheep (vv. 12–14). In Luke's Gospel, the same parable (15:3–7) stresses the Father's joy over the repentance of one sinner, and is used by Jesus as a justification for his own ministry of forgiveness to the outcasts. Matthew shifts the focus of the parable by linking it to the theme of responsibility to the weak. The Gospel has already documented Jesus' own pastoral concern for "lost" and "confused" sheep (cf. 9:36; 10:6; 15:24). Now the disciples must accept this responsibility as their own. The refrain of the "Father's will" concludes this major section. Not one of these little ones should be lost. Since this is the Father's will, it must become an urgent priority of the community.

STUDY QUESTION: This section of the discourse emphasizes that a relentless compassion for the weak and the outcasts must be a central characteristic of the Christian community. How does our church or parish measure up to this Gospel demand?

Matthew 18:15–35
Forgiveness for the Brethren

The priority of compassion in the community does not mean permissiveness. The second half of the discourse opens with the outline of a procedure for dealing with a recalcitrant "brother" (18:15–18). Sensitivity demands that the fault be dealt with discreetly. But, if that fails, help should be sought from others (following the injunction of Deut 19:15, which called for two or three witnesses in major court proceedings). If even this step is rebuffed, then the brother is to be brought before the entire community (Matthew uses the technical term "church" as in 16:18. Here it probably refers to a local church). The community is invested with the power of "binding or loosing" (v. 18, cf. 16:19), which apparently refers to the authority of excommunication. The erring brother is to be considered as a "tax collector" or a "Gentile," that is, as an outsider in need of conversion. The use of these labels for the "outsider" might also subtly remind the community of the fact that Jesus had particular compassion for such as these (cf. 11:19).

This method is not unlike procedures used in some Jewish communities (such as the reform group at Qumran). Matthew's own church may have adapted similar methods for handling members whose behavior was seriously incompatible with the demands of the Gospel. But the setting in which this procedure is placed indicates that the priority of compassion is not forgotten. First of all, it is followed by a solemn saying of Jesus on the power of united prayer (v. 19). Presumably, one of the objects of such prayer would be to "win back" a brother or sister where all other efforts seem futile. The cohesive center of this praying community is ultimately the presence of Jesus. A Jewish saying promised that wherever two people discussed the laws the *Shekinah* or divine presence was with them. As Matthew has done before (cf. 11:28–30), sayings dealing with the law are transferred to Jesus. Fidelity to the words of Jesus ("God-with-us") brings his sustaining presence into the midst of the believers (cf. 1:23; 28:20).

Divisive wrongdoing calls for prudent action and sensitive correction. But even if radical discipline is necessary, compassion and forgiveness remain the only stance possible between members of the community. Peter's question (v. 21) swings the chapter fully back to this dominant theme. His words probe the limits of forgiveness. Jesus' reply appears to reverse the words of Lamech in Genesis (4:24), where this son of Adam called for blood vengeance seventy times seven. Now this becomes a number symbolic of limitless forgiveness.

The parable that concludes the chapter (18:23–35) is found only in Matthew and is typical of the scarcely veiled allegory that characterizes his style. The story of the king and his servant illustrates why forgiveness is so necessary. The servant owes a staggering debt to the king (literally, ten thousand talents, an astronomical figure in first-century economics) but is forgiven out of pity and the debt is completely canceled (v. 27). But this forgiven servant soon forgets his own situation and treats viciously a fellow servant who owes him a minor sum. The other servants can only be depressed at such blind behavior (v. 31) and the king is provoked to anger. Matthew's favorite theme of responsibility and judgment is played out again when the unforgiving servant is made to pay for his behavior (vv. 34–35).

The closing verse echoes Matthew's stress in the Lord's Prayer and the Sermon on the Mount (cf. 6:12, 14–15; 5:43–48). If we do not forgive "from the heart" then we simply do not recognize our own status as "forgiven servants" and we certainly do not know the Father revealed by Jesus.

STUDY QUESTION: Why does Matthew's Gospel make forgiveness such a pressing concern for the followers of Jesus? The answer to that question reveals the heart of the Gospel.

Matthew 19:1–15
NEW TEACHING IN JUDEA: DIVORCE

Matthew's standard transitional formula (cf. 7:28) signals another mile-stone in the Gospel story. With the discourse on community life now finished, Jesus moves from Galilee into Judea. According to Matthew's account, this is the first time Jesus has returned to the southern region since he and his parents escaped the tentacles of Herod (cf. 2:14, 22). Now Jesus is back, followed by large crowds and brandishing his heal-ing power (v. 2). Judea and its capital city Jerusalem will have another chance to lash out at this one "born King of the Jews."

As Jesus moves into Judean territory, he is confronted by some Pharisees who try to snare him with a question about the law: Is it per-mitted to divorce one's wife "for any cause whatever?" (v. 3). The ques-tion seems to reflect a first-century debate between two rabbinic schools on how to interpret Deuteronomy 24:1. The school of Sham-mai taught that divorce was permitted only on the grounds of adultery, while the school of Hillel allowed divorce virtually for any cause.

In Matthew's version of this story, Jesus refuses to accept the debate on these terms and immediately appeals to a text of the law he consid-ers most fundamental, and therefore binding, in this question. Jesus cites Genesis 1:27 and 2:24 to illustrate that the will of the "Creator" is that husband and wife enjoy intimate and unbreakable union (vv. 4–6). In typical rabbinic style, the Pharisees counter with the text of Deuteronomy 24:1 which supposes that divorce is permissible. But Jesus will not allow this as a decisive text. Moses permitted divorce only as a concession to the moral immaturity of the people.

In a solemn manner (v. 9), Jesus concludes the debate with his own authoritative interpretation of the law. "Whoever divorces his wife ... and marries another commits adultery." Embedded in this statement is an apparent qualification which continues to baffle interpreters. Lit-erally the phrase says, "except for uncleanness" (*porneia*, a general term in Greek). The New American Bible translation—"unless the marriage is unlawful"—reflects one solution that considers the phrase here, and in the other Matthean text of 5:32, as some sort of qualification or exception introduced into Jesus' originally unqualified prohibition (cf. Mark 10:11–12; Luke 16:18).

Two solutions seem most possible. One is to translate *porneia* as "adultery." Thus the saying of Jesus would prohibit divorce "except in the case of adultery." Matthew's Jewish-Christian community may have adapted the prohibition to their own circumstances. The weakness of this "solution" is that it makes Jesus' statement in verse 9 anticlimactic. He ends up accepting one side of a rabbinic debate that he initially had radically challenged! For this reason, some commentators prefer to understand *porneia* as referring to marriages that violated the strict Jewish laws of consanguinity (the word *porneia* is used this way in Acts 15:29). In this case, the adapted saying of Jesus would be directed to Gentiles who, prior to their conversion, were married to women within the restricted line of blood relationship. Before being accepted into the community, they would have to sever this illicit marriage bond; hence Jesus' prohibition against divorce allows this kind of "exception."

No solution can be definitive because there is no way of knowing exactly what the "exceptive clause" meant to Matthew's readers. But whatever the solution might be, it must be compatible with the demand for "deeper holiness" (cf. 5:20) that underlies so much of Jesus' teaching during this measured journey to Jerusalem. The reaction of the disciples (v. 10) confirms this. Jesus' demand for indissoluble unity in marriage and his prohibition of remarriage seem like impossible ideals. His reply offers no concession. The ability to respond to the Gospel is a gift (v. 11), but a gift that can move the disciple to a genuine holiness. He uses a startling image. Eunuchs were despised in Jewish society; Deuteronomy 23:2 forbade their participation in the assembly of Yahweh, although later rabbinic interpretation of that text permitted eunuchs entry. In Jesus' view there can be those who renounce the use of sex not because of impotence or accident but "for the sake of the kingdom of heaven." This may refer to both those who are unable to remarry (cf. 19:9) and celibates who forego marriage to free themselves for the Gospel mission.

As if to restate the need for radical response to the Gospel, the section concludes with the image of the child. People are bringing their children to Jesus to be blessed and he uses the moment to remind his disciples that the kingdom belongs to those who, like children, acknowledge their needs without pretense (cf. 18:2f.).

STUDY QUESTION: Each of the Synoptic Gospels testifies to Jesus' teaching on the indissolubility of marriage. What does this say about the meaning of marriage and the ideal of love and union the Gospel presumes between married Christians?

Matthew 19:16 to 20:16
THE DEMANDS AND REWARDS OF DISCIPLESHIP

This section continues the Gospel's concern with the cost of discipleship, a theme that has permeated Jesus' teaching on the road to Jerusalem.

A man approaches Jesus (19:16–22) and asks a question that has dominated Matthew's Gospel: "Teacher, what good must I do to gain eternal life?" It is not a question about frills; it is basic and practical. And it recognizes Jesus as the "teacher" capable of giving an answer. Jesus takes this question at face value: "If you wish to enter into life" keep the commandments where God's will has been made clear. Jesus ticks off the commands that deal with relationships, climaxing in the love command (as he did in 5:43–48). But the young man, again in tune with Matthew's Gospel, senses that Jesus' teaching calls for something more (19:20). To be "perfect," the young man must put aside his wealth and "follow Jesus."

"Perfect": the Greek word is exactly that used in 5:48 where Jesus capped his teaching on the fulfillment of the law. To be so animated by love that one can love an enemy—this is to be "complete" or "perfect" as the Heavenly Father is perfect.

In the Sermon on the Mount Jesus had defined "perfect" through his teaching on the love command. Here, in chapter 19, "perfection" is defined as putting aside everything in order to "follow Jesus." The two definitions are the same because Jesus carries out his own commands. To "follow him" is to fulfill the law of love. The invitations offered to the young man—"if you wish to enter into life," "if you wish to be perfect...," and "come, follow me"—make it clear that this passage is not an instruction for an elite, but the basic Gospel call for *all* those who would follow Jesus. Every obstacle to genuine discipleship must be put aside. For the young man, the cost is too high and he turns away with regret (19:22).

Jesus' teaching on marriage had staggered the disciples (19:10). His blunt words on the obstacle that wealth throws in the way of discipleship are no more digestible (vv. 23–26). Matthew does not present Jesus as an ideologue who opposes wealth on the basis of a particular social theory. Jesus is pragmatic: much wealth tends to demand total allegiance. So does God's kingdom. Jesus had already drawn the common-sense conclusion: "You cannot serve God and mammon" (6:24). Therefore a rich man is as likely to shed the encumbrances of wealth as a camel is to slip through the eye of a needle. Jesus' impossible hyperbole should not be diluted (the needle's eye was not a gate in the wall of Jerusalem at the time of Jesus, as some commentators have suggested).

The disciples' distraught question catches Jesus' point (v. 25) and enables him to restore their perspective: the ability to respond to the Gospel is never earned either by rich or poor. It is a gift (v. 26). The Twelve were given that gift and Peter, their spokesman, asks about the consequences. They are promised a place of authority at the moment of judgment (v. 28). They are the foundations of the new Israel Jesus has come to build. They and all who put aside any obstacle to following Jesus will inherit what the rich young man found too costly, "eternal life" (v. 29).

Discipleship as an interplay of gift and response is the focus of the thoughtful parable that concludes this section (20:1–15). Matthew frames it with two enigmatic proverbs that hint at presumption deflated, at expectation reversed: the first last, the last first (19:30; 20:16). And that, in fact, is the message of the parable. The kingdom is like a vineyard owner who hires from a labor pool at different hours of the day. When evening comes, all the laborers—even those hired at the last hour—are paid the same. Those first called protest such injustice. But the parable cleverly spears the listener on his own indignation. It is not a commentary on social justice, but on the unexpected generosity of God who gifts whom he will and when he will. Discipleship is never earned, only given. All that is asked of the one called is response, however and whenever the call comes.

STUDY QUESTION: The story of the rich young man invites us to search our own lives for the obstacles that stand in the way of following Jesus. The disciples' question and the parable of the vineyard laborers remind us that only God's power can truly free us enough to be disciples.

Matthew 20:17–34
UP TO JERUSALEM

"Jesus was going up to Jerusalem..."—for the first time the goal of this fateful trek is named. Jerusalem, "killer of prophets" (23:37), would be the arena for the remainder of Jesus' ministry. As the capital city looms

ahead, a passion prediction and a final instruction on discipleship conclude the journey.

The third prediction is the most detailed (20:17–19). Matthew
intensifies the anticipation of the passion events by explicitly using the
word "crucify" (contrast Mark's "kill," 9:31). The forecast of death leads
into the request of the mother of James and John (vv. 20–23). In Mark's
version, the two disciples do their own promotion; Matthew, perhaps to
soften the impression of raw ambition, has their mother intervene.
Their request to share in Jesus' glory "in his kingdom" is not rejected
but put into perspective. To share his glory one must be willing to share
his pain, to "drink his cup" (v. 22). This has been Jesus' constant message in the Gospel (cf. 10:24–25, 38; 16:24). If one seeks first the kingdom (accepting its pain and its price), then the Father will provide the
rest (6:33).

Neither Zebedee's sons nor the rest of the Twelve would learn
quickly to drink from Jesus' cup (26:39–41). So Jesus calls them all
together for a final instruction (vv. 24–28). True greatness in the community of Jesus is not to be determined by rank or by the flex of
power. Greatness is determined by how much one is willing to give in
the service of others. This is the kind of love that animated Jesus, the
Son of Man who came "to serve and to give his life as a ransom for
many" (v. 28). Jesus' death, as an act of loving service which brings life
to "many," is the ultimate model for genuine discipleship.

Jesus and his followers surge through Jericho, the oasis town a few
miles below Jerusalem (vv. 29–34). Galilee is far behind. Jesus' instructions to his disciples are practically concluded. His enemies are waiting.
It is as if the Gospel hesitates for a moment before plunging into the
turbulent events that will end Jesus' life. We are reminded of who he is
and why he has come. Two blind men sense his presence and cry out in
prayer: "Lord, Son of David, have pity on us!" (vv. 30, 31). Jesus, the
promised Messiah; Jesus, more than Israel had dared hope; Jesus, who
came to heal the blind and to draw believers in his wake.

STUDY QUESTION: Can we really accept the Gospel's criterion for
genuine greatness: "Whoever wishes to be great among you shall be
your servant"? It is the reverse of most of the world's way of calculating
greatness.

V. "Jerusalem, Jerusalem"— Final Days in David's City

Matthew 21:1 to 28:20

Matthew 21:1–17
JESUS IN JERUSALEM:
THE SON OF DAVID IN THE JERUSALEM TEMPLE

The march from Galilee is over. Jesus and his disciples halt at Bethphage, a village on the eastern crest of the Mount of Olives, the hill facing Jerusalem across the Kidron Valley. As Matthew will describe it, the entry into the capital city is to be dramatic and deliberate. Jesus is David's son; he is King and Messiah; and he comes back to his city with authority.

"Authority" is a key word in this section of the Gospel. The provocative march into the city, the prophetic gesture of cleansing the temple, the unflinching facedown with his opponents, and his final incisive teaching—all of this underlines Jesus' authority as Messiah and Lord. The forces of death are coiled for a strike against Jesus. But death will not erase an impression of absolute authority made in the final days in Jerusalem and its temple.

The entry into the city is planned (vv. 1–5). Two disciples are given crisp orders, and their exacting obedience of these begins to highlight the emphasis on Jesus' authority. The key to the scene is provided by the Old Testament fulfillment text which Matthew introduces into the account (vv. 4–5). A blend of Zechariah 9:9 and Isaiah 62:11, the quotation confronts Jerusalem, the "daughter Zion," with Jesus, her unexpected king. But this king continues to shatter the false expectations of his contemporaries. As the Gospel has consistently portrayed him, Jesus is not regal but humble, a servant of the poor and the outcasts (cf. 11:19). He is not enticed by the equipment of power, but rides on a donkey and a colt, signs of gentleness and peace (cf. Zech 9:10). The reference to *two* animals indicates how exactingly Matthew dresses these events in the authority of the Old Testament. In the original Hebrew quotation, the reference to a "donkey" and a "colt" were synonyms descriptive of a *single* animal. Here they are read as *two,* and Jesus is made to include both in his procession (vv. 2, 7).

The crowds, still intrigued by Jesus, are caught up in the triumph of the moment. They decorate the road and, using a verse of Psalm 118, explicitly acknowledge Jesus as "Son of David" (v. 9), the messianic title that prefaced the Gospel (cf. 1:1; 20:31). But the chilling hostility that greeted this Son of David at his birth has not been shaken off. Once again (cf. 2:3) Matthew notes that the "whole city" of Jerusalem is disturbed by the news of a king in its midst and they ask their disbelieving question, "Who is this?" (v. 10). Even the admiring answer of the crowds is not without its portent of death. "This is Jesus the prophet, from Nazareth in Galilee" (v. 11), and Jerusalem, as Jesus will remind his enemies, is a "killer of prophets" (23:37).

The unlikely royal procession ends at the temple (vv. 12–17). Matthew has thoroughly reworked the chain of events here. In Mark's account (11:11) Jesus enters the temple only for a brief inspection and then departs until the next day when he will return to purify it. But in Matthew, the purification of the temple is the final event of Jesus' assertive entry into the City of David.

Only a special currency was accepted for temple offerings, and for the convenience of pilgrims money changers were available. This commerce was strictly regulated, but the "prophet Jesus" sweeps it from the temple to make his point about genuine worship (cf. the quote from Isa 56:7), just as the prophets of the Old Testament had chosen dramatic signs to shake the conscience of the people. But in Matthew's account, Jesus does more. The blind and the lame come to him and he cures them (v. 14). King David had banned such people from entering the House of God (cf. 2 Sam 5:8). But now the temple is thrown open to the outcasts by one who is not only David's "son" but David's "Lord" (cf. 22:41–45) and "greater than the temple" (12:6).

Reactions once again put the reader of the Gospel on the alert. Children catch the wonder of Jesus (v. 15) and praise the "Son of David." But the religious leaders are "indignant" (vv. 15–16). Jesus squelches their protest with the words of Psalm 8:2. The poor and lowly sense God's power and are not afraid to give thanks for it. With that, Jesus turns and leaves the leaders and the city they think is theirs.

STUDY QUESTION: The presence of Jesus is like a purging fire, purifying and restoring the temple. We might place ourselves and our church in this scene. Are we open to renewal and reform, or do we react with indignation or indifference?

Matthew 21:18 to 22:14
PARABLES IN THE TEMPLE

The day after his triumphant march into Jerusalem, Jesus returns to the temple. Matthew will present this as a day filled with teaching and controversy. On the way into the city (vv. 18–22), Jesus and his disciples come across a fig tree that bears no fruit. In one of the Gospel's most bizarre miracles, Jesus curses the barren tree and it immediately withers. Mark's Gospel had used this story as a commentary on the fate of the temple (cf. 11:12–14, 20–26): on his way to the purification of the temple, Jesus curses the tree; on his return, the tree is found withered. Because Matthew had Jesus purify the temple during his first day in Jerusalem, the story of the fig tree has lost its clear connection to the fate of the temple. Now it is used as an example of the power of determined faith.

Once inside the temple, Jesus begins to *teach* (v. 23ff.). But the chief priests and the elders immediately challenge his authority to do "these things," presumably his bold action of the day before and his daring to teach on their home ground. Jesus' counter-question (v. 24) unmasks the insincerity of his interrogators and turns the focus of this entire section to the subject of recognizing Jesus as the herald of the kingdom. John the Baptist and Jesus are again paired (cf. 11:2ff.). The leaders failed to recognize John and, what is even more tragic, they look with sightless eyes on Jesus himself.

The three parables that follow pointedly illustrate the authority of Jesus and the consequences of failing to recognize it. Each is an easily deciphered allegory, a type of parable favored by our evangelist in which every detail is given a symbolic meaning. The parable of the two

sons (vv. 28–32) is found only in this Gospel and it repeats the demand
for repentance verified by action that is the hallmark of Matthew's
Jesus. The second son knows the right words ("Yes, sir"), but his
response is hollow. The sadder-but-wiser reaction of the first son is
more genuine. He repents and proves it by action. The point of this
parable was already made in the Sermon on the Mount: "Not everyone
who says to me, 'Lord, Lord,' will enter the kingdom of heaven" (7:21).
Jesus now blisters his opponents by turning the parable on them. They
did not hear John's call for repentance and they challenge Jesus. It is the
tax collectors and prostitutes, whose lives have been a "no" to God,
who now repent and enter the kingdom.

The parable of the "tenants" plays the same melody but with different words (vv. 33–46). Israel, the Lord's vineyard (cf. this traditional
image in Isa 5:1ff.) is tended by laborers who prove to be faithless. They
reject the servants of the landowner who come to claim his harvest.
Matthew gives heavy clues that these are the prophets rejected by Israel
by describing their fate as being "killed and stoned" (cf. 23:37). Finally
the landowner sends his son, the "heir." But the wicked tenants eject
him from the vineyard and kill him. What will be the fate of people so
blind that they kill the landowner's son? In the words of Psalm 118, a
favored text of the early Christians, the rejection of Jesus is a rejection
of the very cornerstone of God's kingdom. Matthew draws out the
consequences in a verse uniquely his: because the leaders of Israel have
not responded to Jesus and his Gospel, the kingdom is taken from their
charge and offered to the those who "will produce its fruit" (v. 43).

None of these parables is intended to be merely somber commentary on Israel's past failures. The last of the trilogy (22:1–14) makes it
clear that these lessons from history are meant to alert Matthew's own
Christian community to the consequences of failing to give full and
genuine response to the Gospel. The story of a wedding banquet,
another traditional biblical metaphor for the kingdom of God, plays
out its sad history of refusal. The feast is all prepared but the invited
guests are unimpressed. They refuse to come, some going calmly about
their business, while others turn ugly and kill the servants who
announce the feast. The king's reaction is ferocious. The invited guests
are punished and their town destroyed. And now the son's wedding
feast is thrown open to everyone, "bad and good alike."

To this point the parable seems to be another restatement of Israel's
failure to respond to Jesus. The consequences are judgment on Israel

(here Matthew may be alluding to the destruction of Jerusalem in A.D. 70, cf. 22:7) and the opening of the kingdom to the Gentiles. But the story is not over. The king comes into the banquet hall and finds a guest without a wedding garment (v. 11). Judgment falls on this man, too! He is thrown outside into the darkness. Matthew's message is clear. The Gospel makes the same demand on all, Jew and Gentile alike: a life that is "turned around" and given to good deeds. Anything less— an Israel without its harvest, a church without its wedding garment— will be cast into darkness.

STUDY QUESTION: Matthew seems to have a "Catch 22" view of the church: No person or group can be smug about their membership in the Christian community. The test of genuine conversion and a life of good deeds is applied to everyone; everyone can be moved from the "inside" to the "outside" darkness.

Matthew 22:15–46
"NO FURTHER QUESTIONS"

Stung by Jesus' parables (21:23 to 22:14), the opponents regroup for a final assault. Three times they attempt to ensnare Jesus with contrived questions. But the Messiah stands in the temple like an unbeatable champion and each question is turned back on his enemies until they dare say nothing more (v. 46).

The first wave comes from the Pharisees. They send their disciples and some supporters of King Herod to spear Jesus with a politically sensitive dilemma (vv. 15–22): "Is it lawful to pay the census tax to Caesar or not?" Jesus cuts through the hypocrisy of the flattering words with which they introduce the question and, by asking to see the "coin that pays the census tax," reminds them of the solution already adopted by many Jews. "Repay to Caesar what belongs to Caesar and to God what belongs to God." The reply jolts his questioners because it nimbly avoids their false dilemma and reasserts Jesus' own teaching. "What belongs to God," the Gospel has insisted, is one's whole self.

The Sadducees are the next to enter the ring and they, too, meet defeat (vv. 23–33). These members of the temple aristocracy were religious conservatives who opposed any idea not based strictly on the

written Torah. Thus, they attempt to ridicule the doctrine of bodily
resurrection, a relatively recent concept in Judaism, by citing Moses'
command about the practice of Levirite marriage (cf. Deut 25:5f. and
Gen 38:8), in which a man was obliged to have a child by his brother's
widow in order to assure the continuance of the clan. On the basis of
this law an absurd case about a woman with seven husbands is posed as
a "stopper" for Jesus. There is no hesitation in his answer. Resurrected
life is not "more of the same" but a new life which moves beyond the
expectations of the old. Even more serious than the Sadducees' misunderstanding of resurrection is the narrowness of their understanding of
God. Jesus matches their citation of Moses by referring to the words of
Yahweh himself (cf. vv. 31–32, quoting Exod 3:6). The God of Israel is
a "God of the living" whose fidelity is stronger than death.

The Pharisees huddle together for a last try (vv. 34–40) and a
spokesman poses a question about the greatest commandment of the
law. Jesus' reply is a summary of his entire teaching in Matthew's
Gospel. The "greatest" commandment is a fusion of two (cf. Deut 6:5
and Lev 19:18): total, selfless love of God and neighbor. On this command of love "depends" (literally, "hangs") the whole "law and the
prophets." Everything God intended in the scriptures and in Israel's
sacred history finds its fulfillment in this demand. This is what Jesus had
taught on the mountain in Galilee (cf. 5:17–20; 7:12). This is what his
life of obedience to his Father and gentle compassion to those in need
faithfully mirrored. And this is what he teaches again as he stands facing
his enemies in the temple, the religious heart of Israel.

They have hurled their questions at Jesus and they have been shat-
tered against his words. Now it is Jesus' turn: "What is your opinion
about the Messiah? Whose son is he?" (vv. 41–46). Their reply
endorses the title that has been applied to Jesus throughout this section of the Gospel: he is David's Son. But David's own psalm (Ps
110:1, a favored text of the early Christians) seems to imply something more. The Messiah is not only royal successor to the great
David, but he is David's "lord" (v. 44). Matthew's Gospel has made this
case all along. Jesus is the fulfillment of Israel's great messianic dream.
But he is more. The blind men of Jericho recognized this (20:30–31),
but the religious leaders, too smug in their own wisdom, do not. They
turn away discredited and defeated but smoldering with a rage that
will soon explode.

STUDY QUESTION: What does it mean to be truly wise? This is the question underlying the scene in the temple. Jesus is true wisdom because his divine teaching cuts through cloying complexities and false dilemmas to the heart of truth, truth summarized by faith in the God of the living and a firm grasp of his command to love.

Matthew 23:1–39
A PROPHET'S RAGE:
"WOE TO YOU, SCRIBES AND PHARISEES"

From the very beginning of the Gospel, Matthew has coupled his majestic portrait of Jesus with a somber record of rejection. Jesus' prophetic teaching in the temple (cf. 21:23 to 22:46) had brought the hostility of his enemies to a fast boil. Now Jesus would cauterize this tragic rupture with prophetic words of judgment, attacking the leaders of Israel for their hypocrisy, their blindness, and their narrow legalism. This is the most stark and bitter chapter in the entire Gospel and should be read attentively. Like the rest of the "speeches" of Matthew's Gospel, it is not a transcript of an actual discourse of Jesus, but a composite of sayings molded together by the evangelist. Some of the specific issues and the sharp polemical tone of the chapter may reflect not only the altercations between Jesus and his contemporaries, but also the later growing tensions between the early church and the synagogue (cf. Introduction).

The discourse is directed "to the crowds and to his disciples" (v. 1). This is an important clue for properly interpreting the chapter. Jesus' prophetic rage is not meant to be a broken record of accusation against Jewish leaders in the past, but a sober caution for the *Christians* of Matthew's own community about the kinds of attitudes that were fatal to genuine discipleship. Thus, this chapter becomes a negative version of the Sermon on the Mount.

Matthew 23:1–12
Genuine Teachers
Jesus' opening words reflect the respect for the law and the institutions of Judaism that has been characteristic of this Gospel (cf. 5:17–20;

10:5–6; 15:24). The scribes and Pharisees were commissioned to teach the law of Moses which Jesus came "not to abolish but to fulfill" (cf. 5:17–20). But the words of respect are only a preface to the real point of the chapter: a blistering judgment on religious leaders who are hypocritical. They are guilty of a fault that Matthew's Gospel has incessantly condemned: not practicing what they preach. Even what they manage to do comes not from the heart, but to catch the praise of others.

More is demanded of the disciples of Jesus (vv. 8–12). The example and teaching of Jesus and his absolute dedication to the will of the Father—these are the norms of true greatness in the community. Therefore, there should be no panting for title and rank. All are brothers and sisters and thus mutual service must be a hallmark of the Christian (cf. 20:24–28).

Matthew 23:13–32
A Prophet's Woes

The sins of the people had wrung from great prophets like Isaiah (cf. Isa 10) and Jeremiah (cf. Jer 20) strings of "woes" or predictions of doom. The blind conceit and twisted priorities of the religious leaders provoke Jesus to the same type of response. And once again, this list of indictments is not merely to pass judgment on past generations of Israel's leaders, but to scorch false leadership in the *Christian* community.

The first four woes (vv. 13–24) blister the scribes and Pharisees for their misguided teaching. Instead of leading people toward God's kingdom, they shut the gate (note the contrast to Peter who holds the keys of the kingdom, 16:19). For a brief time in the first century there was a robust Jewish missionary effort among the many pagans who admired the beauty of Judaism's ethic. The Gospel sourly predicts that if this mission disseminates the blindness of the leaders, it can only lead to darkness (v. 15). The next two woes specify their failure. The kind of legalism that smothers true religious experience is typified by rabbinic casuistry on oaths (vv. 16–22). Out of reverence for God's name, the taker of an oath could swear by something that obliquely referred to God: the temple, the altar, the heavens. But these euphemisms could be absurd if the oath-taker later denied he meant to swear on God's name. Thus the Gospel cites a number of rabbinic decisions that attempted to control this. But these minute regulations merely paper over a twisted notion of truth. The bond of trust among God's people must be such that a "yes" or a "no" is as firm as an oath (cf. 5:33–37). The leaders' most serious failure is their wrongheaded sense of priorities (vv. 23–24). The Jewish Jesus of Matthew's Gospel is not an iconoclast; even the law of tithing on one's garden vegetables should be respected. But such details must not be so picked over that they begin to crowd out the truly central and determining obligations of justice and faith. The unflinching demand of Jesus that all law be subordinate to the law of love breaks into the Gospel again (cf. 7:12; 22:34–40).

The remaining woes (vv. 25–32) settle on a familiar Matthean refrain: the condemning disparities between one's heart and one's action. The scribes and Pharisees who fret that a drop of wine on the outside of a sacred vessel might cause ritual impurity are themselves like dishes sparkling on the outside, soiled on the inside (vv. 25–26). Or they are like those Palestinian tombs whitewashed annually so no pilgrim will bump into them accidentally and incur an impurity; brilliant on the outside, full of death within (vv. 27–28). Purity that counts, Jesus has already insisted, comes from the heart (15:18).

The Jews of Jesus' day were intrigued by the prophets and had built tombs and monuments to honor those who had been mistreated by Israel. But respect for the still voices of the past was costless. Rejection of Jesus showed that the leaders could easily take their place with the generations who had rejected the prophets of old (vv. 29–32).

Matthew 23:33–39
Judgment
The scribes and Pharisees must bear responsibility for their failure to listen to God's good news. Jesus' words of judgment (v. 33) echo John's warning at the Jordan (3:7). Rejection of Jesus is a forecast of how his disciples will be treated. The mission discourse of chapter 10 has already spoken of this, and now this chapter, too, draws to a close with a sober glance to the future. Jesus will send "prophets and wise men and scribes"—characterizations that might describe Jesus himself. But this mission will be rejected too. So the long line of good people who have suffered in a just cause stretches on from Abel, the first to die in the Bible (Gen 4:10), to the last martyred prophet Zechariah (the rabbis tended to blend the figure of Zechariah the prophet with the

Zechariah of 2 Chr 24:20, the last book in the Hebrew Bible) and now to Jesus (cf. 27:4, 24) and into the future. The final words are Jesus' lament over Jerusalem, the city that Jesus, like all Jews, loved. As Yahweh had brooded over his people to protect them (cf. Isa 31:5; Deut 32:11), so this missionary of God longed to do. But refusal of his mission meant that from now on they would meet him only on the final day when they would greet him with an acclamation of faith (v. 39). Thus Matthew ends even this bitter chapter of judgment with a glimmer of future hope for reconciliation.

STUDY QUESTION: Jesus' prophetic anger as presented in Matthew's Gospel should be turned not on the Jews (as many Christians have been tempted to do) but on ourselves. The church must ask if it deserves indictment for hypocrisy, for blindness, for failure to recognize Jesus in the prophets, in the wise men, in the outcasts of our own day.

Matthew 24:1 to 25:46
THE CHURCH FACES ITS FUTURE

As Jesus leaves the temple the disciples ask about the fate of this great building. Jesus' blunt prediction of its destruction and further questions from the disciples (vv. 1–3) continue the theme of judgment already sounded in chapter 23.

Jesus is seated on the Mount of Olives, the broad-shouldered hill that overlooks the temple. Jewish tradition expected the final judgment to take place on this mountain (cf. Zech 14:4). Now it provides an apt setting for Jesus' prophetic words about the end of the world and the attitudes the Christian must take in order to be ready for it. As he has done throughout the Gospel, the evangelist assembles the discourse from a variety of materials, including Mark's version of Jesus' final speech (cf. Mark 13) and some fresh parables.

One of the special features of some sections of this discourse is its so-called "apocalyptic" style, a style popular in Judaism from the second century B.C. to the second century A.D. Because this period of history was so tense, religious writers used a bold and highly symbolic literary style to help steel their readers for a difficult future. As the term "apocalyptic" itself suggests (it comes from a Greek word meaning "reveal"), writing in this style often took the form of visions in which a hero or prophet from the past would forecast the future (the biblical book of Daniel is a good example). These great visions would include in their prediction some events that the readers would recognize as already having taken place! This was not meant as fakery, but was a literary device whereby the apocalyptic author could help his audience see this event as a part of an unfolding historical destiny. Only a few New Testament writings or passages use an apocalyptic style (cf., for example, the Book of Revelation), but these chapters from Matthew have some apocalyptic features. Jesus speaks of the "signs" that will precede the consummation of the world. Some of these things, for example the destruction of the temple and persecution, had already been experienced by Matthew's community. The reader must now see these traumatic events within the perspective of the Gospel. Nothing that will befall the community is outside of God's providence. But responsibility will also continue into the future. The community and its leaders are accountable for their fidelity or lack of fidelity to the teaching of Jesus.

The discourse, then, is not a clear timetable for the future. Many of its references to "signs" and significant events are highly symbolic and, for us at least, very obscure. And Jesus flatly states that no one can predict the day nor hour of the end (24:36). This discourse, like all the others, is "gospel," a call for conversion and fidelity as the disciples of Jesus move toward the final victory of God's kingdom.

Matthew 24:1–35
Signs of Final Victory
"Tell us, when will this happen [the destruction of the temple, cf. v. 2], and what sign will there be of your coming?" The way Matthew formulates this lead question (v. 3) indicates an awareness of an indefinite stretch of time before the final end. The temple's fate was in the past; the victorious final coming of Jesus was future. Much of the discourse's organization reflects this perspective on the end. First there will be remote signs of the end (vv. 4–14), then the beginning of the last days (vv. 15–28), and finally the coming of the Lord (vv. 29–31); in the meantime, the community is to be alert and faithful (the point of the judgment parables of 24:36 to 25:30).

The "beginning of the labor pains" (cf. vv. 4–14) will be marked by wars and persecutions. Even more disconcerting will be turmoil *within* the community. False prophets will deceive many, something that may have been a particular sore point for Matthew's church. And the teaching of Jesus will be neglected, especially his law of love (v. 12). But all of this must be seen as "labor pains," as part of the great drama of salvation which will end in triumph. Jesus' command to "make disciples of all nations" (cf. 28:16–20) will be carried out before the end can come (v. 14).

The beginning of the last days (vv. 15–28) will bring new portents. The scarring memory of the blasphemy committed in 168 B.C. by the Greek ruler Antiochus Ephiphanus is recalled (cf. 1 Mac 1:54; Dan 9:27; 11:31; 12:11). He had set up a statue in the temple sanctuary and this outrage ignited the Maccabean revolt. The mad Roman emperor Caligula had threatened the same kind of provocation in A.D. 40. This ultimate blasphemy becomes a sign of the agonies to be expected when the end is near. Further evidence of Jewish sensitivity lingers in the Gospel in the detail about the sabbath (v. 20). The community must pray that the end does not come in the winter or "on the sabbath," presumably so that escape from the turmoil will not have to violate sabbath regulations. Once again, false prophets are about their work of deception (vv. 23–25). Their enticing words and miraculous powers lead only to false Christs. But the final victory is not the preserve of a few. Nor is it something known by the private oracle of select prophets. The coming of the Lord will be as evident as a lightning bolt that flashes from east to west. It will be as inevitable as vultures around a corpse.

The end itself is described with typical apocalyptic imagery (vv. 26–35), much of it drawn directly from the Old Testament. The light of sun and moon is tapered and the stars fall from the heavens (cf. Amos 8:9). Like a victorious general, the "Son of Man" plants his ensign in the heavens and is greeted with a flourish of trumpets. Some commentators have speculated that the "sign of the Son of Man" might refer to the cross. But a vague military metaphor is more probable (cf. the same image in Isa 18:3; Jer 4:21; 51:27; it was also used in some Jewish liturgical texts). The moment of judgment is at hand. The Son of Man comes "upon the clouds of heaven with power and great glory," a description found in Daniel 7:13–14. And the people of the earth beat their breasts in repentance as they prepare for judgment (cf. Zech 12:10–14).

The use of these traditional metaphors shows that the Gospel does not attempt to provide detailed information about the end. Rather, it affirms its inevitability. The day of judgment will come as surely as the greening of the fig tree is a herald of summer (v. 32). Jesus' own word proclaims that the final days of victory will come. And that word is more sure and more enduring than heaven and earth (cf. 5:18).

Matthew 24:36 to 25:30
On Being Ready for the Lord

Only the Father, not the Son and surely not the disciples, knows the precise hour of the end (v. 36). More important than prediction about the future is how one intends to face it. This concern commands the rest of the discourse.

The story of Noah and the flood (vv. 37–41) illustrates how the end can come unexpectedly and find people unprepared. A string of four parables exemplifies the genuine Christian stance. The Christian must be "awake" (the parables of the householder, 24:42–44, and the ten virgins, 25:1–13), and "faithful" (the parable of the servant, 24: 45–51, and the parable of the talents, 25:14–30). By weaving these themes together Matthew shows that the two qualities are identical. The Christian keeps alert and ready by being faithful to Jesus' teaching. On this basis an unexpected future holds no terror.

The parable of the householder compares the coming of the Son of Man to a break-in (vv. 42–44). If the owner knew when the burglar was coming he would surely be on guard. The startling comparison is reminiscent of an earlier parable where Jesus compared himself to the thief who breaks into Satan's household and robs him of his captives (cf. 12:29). The servant parable (vv. 45–51) switches over to the theme of fidelity. The "faithful and prudent" servant will be rewarded at the master's return, if he is discovered carrying out his duty of caring for the household. But if the servant should fail in his role of compassion, then he will be punished with the hypocrites.

The parable of the ten virgins is found only in Matthew (25:1–13). Its story of two very different types of wedding attendants is an allegory on the need for alertness during the indefinite period of time before the end. The foolish bridesmaids are unprepared when the sudden arrival of the groom is announced and their lack of vigilance costs them access to the wedding celebration. The wise have diligently prepared and are ready for the call. There is some evidence in Jewish writings that "oil" was a symbol of good deeds. If Matthew intended that symbolism here, then he would have neatly blended the two dominant themes of this section. Five of the virgins are wise because their life has been filled with good deeds. The lives of the foolish are empty and thus they are "unknown" to the bridegroom.

The parable of the talents (vv. 14–30) continues the emphasis on good use of time, and shuttles back to the theme of fidelity. The "good and faithful" servants are those who are willing to risk their own security in using their gifts well. All are given generous gifts (even one talent is an enormous sum); but not all are willing to use them. The servant entrusted with one talent lets fear smother his initiative and he must stand accountable before his master. Fear had crippled the fate of the disciples in 8:26 and fear caused Peter to sink into the waves (14:30–31). Once again Matthew cites fear as the enemy of generous discipleship.

STUDY QUESTION: This section of the Gospel has drawn a lot of attention in recent times. On the basis of this discourse, some confidently forecast the end of the world, while others cite this text as proof of the Gospel's irrelevance. But careful reading of the Gospel challenges both attitudes: it discourages futile speculation about the time of the end and, instead, asks the believer to think seriously about his or her perspective on the destiny of the world. If the future is in God's hands, what should be our own attitude?

Matthew 25:31–46
Judgment of the Nations

We now come to the final phase of the Gospel's reflection on "judgment." The leaders of Israel have been judged on their rejection of Jesus (chapter 23); the community and its leaders are held accountable for their fidelity to Jesus' teaching (chapters 24 and 25). The "nations," those to whom the mission of the church is directed, will be judged on their instinctive response to the Gospel and to those who proclaim it (25:31–46).

This majestic picture of the Son of Man coming as king to judge the nations and sorting the sheep from goats is one of the Gospel's most vivid scenes. Not only does it portray the moment of judgment in a way that has stuck in Christian memory, but it also manages a clear distillation of the Gospel message. The righteous inherit the kingdom because they carry out the law of love that is the center of Jesus' teaching (5:1–48; 7:12; 22:34–40). But there is more. Jesus himself is identified with the hungry, the stranger, the poor, the sick, and the oppressed. Three times in Matthew's Gospel, there is a promise of Jesus' abiding presence with his church (1:23; 18:20; 28:20). Even more specifically, he sides with the "little ones" among the brethren who are entrusted with the ministry of preaching (10:40–42). Both sheep and goats are amazed to discover this. The judgment scene reaffirms in a startling way the criterion for genuine discipleship that has been the hallmark of the Gospel. It is not what one says but what one does that counts (cf. 7:21).

By describing the recipients of compassion or neglect as "these least brothers of mine" (vv. 40, 45), Matthew seems to nudge this judgment scene to another level of meaning. These are the kind of terms used to describe the missionaries. They are "brethren," members of the community (cf. 18:15, 21, 35) and "the little ones" who are sent to announce the Gospel (cf. 10:42). The "nations" or Gentiles will be judged on how they respond to this good news. Those who treat these lowly messengers with hospitality and compassion demonstrate that they instinctively grasp the meaning of the Gospel.

STUDY QUESTION: As was the case in previous sections of this discourse, the judgment of a specific group becomes a way of proclaiming the meaning of Christian responsibility to all. The question falls to us: How do we respond to the poor and "insignificant" people of our time? Do we recognize in them Jesus and his good news?

Matthew 26:1–16
PRELUDE TO THE PASSION STORY

The great drama of Jesus' passion begins with the same kind of transitional statement that occurred after each of the major discourses of the Gospel (cf. above, 7:28). But now Jesus has finished "all" of his speeches; the Passover, the moment of Jesus' final decisive action, has arrived. The first sixteen verses of the passion story serve as a "prelude" to the quick-paced narrative that will follow; the main protagonists are brought on stage, the issues are drawn, and the forces that will ultimately bring the story to its climax are set in motion.

Unlike Mark, whose passion story has an abrupt beginning, Matthew chooses to open with a rather formal scene. Jesus once more predicts his approaching death. The same Son of Man who will come in victorious judgment at the end of the world (25:31–46) must first experience the agony of defeat and death. Both dimensions—death and victory—are essential to the Gospel portrait of Jesus. The way Matthew shapes these opening verses is reminiscent of Deuteronomy 32:45, where Moses completes his instructions to the people of Israel and moves to his death on Mount Nebo. Jesus, the new Moses, has completed his teaching and now with measured assurance he confronts his death.

Throughout the Gospel and even here at a moment of humiliation and death, Matthew views Jesus through the lens of resurrection. Jesus, the suffering Son of Man, is also the Risen Lord of glory. This sets off a series of vivid contrasts that begins in the prelude and continues into the passion story. Jesus calmly predicts his impending death, while the chief priests furtively plot against him (vv. 3–5). Jesus welcomes the kindness of an unknown woman, while one of the Twelve barters away his master (vv. 6–13). Such counterpoints are designed to highlight Jesus' majesty and, at the same time, to offer forceful object lessons for the disciples.

The circumstances of Jesus' death would necessitate a hasty burial (cf. 27:57–61). But the kindness of an unknown woman at Bethany ensures that Jesus' body is not denied the loving respect that Judaism showed for its dead (vv. 6–13). Jesus interprets her action as his burial anointing. The disciples protest because they have not as yet fully comprehended Jesus' teaching. This woman's generous act of compassion in response to an immediate need is what the Gospel is all about, and Jesus praises her in an extraordinary way (26:13; cf. also 25:31–46).

The mood darkens. Judas, pointedly identified as "one of the Twelve," goes to the chief priests to betray Jesus. Throughout the passion story Matthew remains amazingly faithful to the text of Mark, but he does like to add snatches of dialogue as in this scene with Judas (cf. 26:15; contrast Mark 14:10). The counting out of thirty silver pieces is an evident allusion to Zechariah 11:12. The significance of this text for Matthew will be spelled out in 27:3–10 where the Judas story comes to its tragic finale. The frequent but subtle Old Testament allusions in the passion story signal to the readers that even these bleak moments have not escaped God's providence.

The prelude closes on a haunting note. "From that time on..."
(26:16, the same emphatic time phrase used in 4:17 and 16:21) Judas
looks for an "opportunity" to betray Jesus. In 26:18, the same root word
kairos, an "opportune time," is found on the lips of Jesus. Both men
move toward the *kairos:* one toward death but ultimate victory, the
other toward seeming victory but ultimate death.

STUDY QUESTION: Throughout the Gospel, the evangelist has
insisted on the role of suffering in Jesus' life. Now that drama will be
played out in detail. How does suffering and death fit into my life? Do
I face this fundamental question or do I try to avoid it?

Matthew 26:17–35
FELLOWSHIP AND BETRAYAL:
JESUS' LAST MEAL WITH HIS DISCIPLES

The passion story turns out to be a proving ground for fidelity. Jesus
himself is the model; he faces suffering and death with the same
integrity and obedience that marked his life. Other characters in the
passion account—the disciples, the Jewish leaders, the Romans—are far
less than model. Their infidelity demonstrates how fragile discipleship
can be. This concern becomes clear in the way the account of the Last
Supper unfolds. This moment of intense union between Jesus and the
Twelve is framed with predictions of Judas's betrayal, Peter's denial, and
the disciples' desertion.

Preparations for the Passover meal set the tone (vv. 17–19).
Matthew concentrates on Jesus' crisp commands and the disciples'
intent obedience. His "appointed time draws near" (v. 18): preparation
must begin. When everything is ready, Jesus and his twelve disciples
gather for the Passover meal. The prediction of Judas's treachery (vv.
20–25) turns the mood sober. Sharing the same dish, a gesture of
friendship, marks Judas as the betrayer. Judas's words (v. 25), "Surely, it is
not I, Rabbi?" use a title for Jesus that the Gospel has discouraged
(23:8) and stands in sharp contrast to the majestic title used by the rest
of the disciples, "Surely it is not I, Lord" (v. 22). Jesus' reply confirms
Judas's unwitting confession of guilt (v. 25).

The ritual of the supper is succinctly narrated. The concentration on Jesus' words over the bread and wine reflects the use of this text in the church's liturgy. In this fellowship meal shared by Jesus and his disciples, the church recognized the foundation of its Eucharist. Not only is Jesus' death an inauguration of the new covenant promised by Jeremiah (Jer 31:31–34), and not only is it a dying "on behalf of many," as Isaiah's Suffering Servant had prefigured (cf. Isa 53:12), but this death is "for the forgiveness of sins." This latter phrase added by Matthew recalls what the Gospel has previously affirmed about Jesus: He is the Savior who frees the people from their sins (1:21); he is the Servant who lifts the burden of pain and death from the helpless (8:17; 12:18) and who gives his life in service for the many (20:28). This Jesus is the very one whose death is proclaimed as the final act of love which forgives the world's sin and frees those trapped in the vice of death (cf. 27:51–54).

The account ends on a note of triumph (v. 29). The pledge of unity symbolized in the Eucharist cannot be broken, even by death. The next celebration between Jesus and his disciples will be with the new wine of the kingdom.

But the darkness of the passion story is only momentarily dissipated. Jesus uses the words of Zechariah 13:7 to predict of the disciples and Peter that "this night all of you will have your faith in me shaken" (literally, be "scandalized in me"; for the significance of the word, cf. above, commentary on 18:6). Ultimate reconciliation is promised after the resurrection (v. 32); but for now the disciples are not alert and they fail to take Jesus' warning to heart.

STUDY QUESTION: The Gospel surrounds Christianity's sacred celebration of unity and hope with examples of weakness and infidelity. What does this suggest about the meaning of the Eucharist?

Matthew 26:36–56
PRAYER AND ARREST IN THE GARDEN

The scene shifts to Gethsemane, a quiet grove on the slopes of the Mountain of Olives where the "handing over," that nightmare moment predicted four times in the Gospel (16:21; 17:22–23; 20:18–19; 26:2), is about to come true. The moment is preceded by a period of tense prayer (vv.

36–46), a scene that has made its impact on all four Gospels and even the Epistle to the Hebrews (cf. 5:7–9) and which reveals, in startling frankness, Jesus' humanity. He fears death and pleads to be delivered from it.

Jesus takes a select trio of disciples with him (v. 36). This opening verse seems to evoke Genesis 22:5 where Abraham leaves his servants behind and takes Isaac to the place of sacrifice. Once again the obedience of an Israelite will be tested, this time God's own Son. In Mark's account, emphasis falls on the failure of the disciples, as Jesus comes three times to find them asleep. Matthew shifts the focus to Jesus' threefold prayer (vv. 39, 42, 44), seeking even in the midst of fear and isolation to do the will of his Father. In 26:42, Matthew adds the phrase, "your will be done," a direct quotation from the Lord's prayer he had previously taught his disciples (6:10). Jesus does what he teaches.

His faithful prayer has its effect. Jesus rises up with renewed strength to face his "hour" (v. 46). The disciples, like the sluggish householder and unwise servants (cf. 24:42–51), are unprepared for this moment of truth. They will flee, but Jesus will stand fast.

That "moment" comes with Judas and an armed band. Judas had found the "opportune time" he had been seeking (26:16). Matthew's fascination with the fallen disciple continues, as once again he adds dialogue to the Markan story (cf. above 26:15, 25). The betrayer kisses Jesus and hails him once more with the inadequate title, "Rabbi" (cf. above, 26:25). Jesus' reply hints at the ultimate victory in which the Gospel views all of these events. He is well aware of Judas's intention and only after Jesus has thus signaled his "permission" can the armed band seize him (v. 50).

One of Jesus' followers (the Gospel of John identifies him as Peter) makes a futile attempt at resistance by striking the high priest's servant. Matthew makes this another opportunity for exemplifying Jesus' obedience. In the Sermon on the Mount, Jesus had demanded love of enemies (5:44) and eschewed all retaliation (5:39). He maintains that teaching now as violent hands lash out at him (vv. 52–54). No one—neither his tattered band of followers nor legions of angel warriors—can make Jesus swerve from his way of obedience. Jesus had rejected the seduction of miraculous intervention in the desert (cf. 4:1–11) and he rejects it here. God's will expressed in the scriptures must be fulfilled (26:54, 56).

The disciples flee and Jesus is abandoned to those who seek to destroy him (26:56). Now the passion story will run its swift course to the cross.

STUDY QUESTION: Jesus struggles to be faithful in the midst of suffering and confusion. What does this scene teach us about the meaning of genuine Christian prayer?

Matthew 26:57 to 27:10
THE VERDICT OF THE SANHEDRIN:
HE DESERVES TO DIE

Jesus, now a prisoner, is taken from the garden to the palace of Caiaphas, the high priest. Here the Jewish leaders will assemble to confront Jesus with their charges. None of the evangelists presents this scene with the precision of court transcripts. In fact, the historical details of these proceedings are almost impossible to reconstruct. For the Gospels, this moment is another opportunity to reflect on who Jesus is and what it means to be his disciple.

Matthew uses Mark's device of a dramatic pairing of Jesus and Peter (vv. 57–75). While Jesus unflinchingly proclaims his identity as Messiah, Son of God, and Son of Man, Peter recoils in fear and denies that he is a disciple of Jesus.

The hearing before the Sanhedrin, the official ruling body of Judaism, moves swiftly (vv. 59–68). A parade of false witnesses proves futile. But finally two witnesses (the number demanded for valid testimony according to Deut 19:15) accuse Jesus of proclaiming power over the Jerusalem Temple (v. 61). The Gospel does not brand this allegation as false because it knows that Jesus is indeed one "greater than the temple" and "Lord of the sabbath" (cf. Matt 12:6–8). Jesus' only answer is a majestic silence (a trait reminiscent of the Suffering Servant in Isa 53:7). Then the solemn moment comes. The high priest asks Jesus under oath if he is "the Messiah," the "Son of God" (v. 63). But the high priest is an unbelieving accuser, and thus Jesus' answer confirms the truth of Caiaphas's words while at the same time indicting his lack of faith. Jesus is the Messiah and the Son of God, but he is also the exalted "Son of Man" who will come in triumph to judge the world. Even *now* ("from now on"), in Jesus' impending death, God's victory has begun (cf. 27:51–54).

Reaction to Jesus' words is predictable. As the Gospel story has already demonstrated, Jesus is rejected by his own. He is judged deserving of death (v. 66) and, with blows and insults, the leaders mock Jesus' claim to be the "Messiah."

The scene now shifts to Peter (vv. 69–75) who at the beginning of the hearing had been standing at a fire and watching—as the Gospel story notes with gentle irony—"to see the outcome" (v. 58). Peter will not see the outcome because, as Jesus had predicted (26:31–35), the leader of the Twelve will fail. Matthew continues to make Peter an object lesson in discipleship. Fear forces Peter to escalate his denials from evasion to an oath (expressly forbidden by Jesus in 5:34) to cursing and swearing that he does "not know the man" (v. 74). But in spite of his denial, Peter the Galilean is one of those "with Jesus the Nazorean." And when the predicted cockcrow (cf. 26:34) pierces the night, Peter illustrates true conversion: he remembers the word of Jesus and weeps tears of repentance (v. 75).

The night-long session of the Sanhedrin concludes with a death verdict for Jesus and a resolution to take him to Pilate, the Roman governor of Judea and the only one empowered to carry out capital punishment (27:1–2). At this point Matthew interrupts the narrative to conclude the tragic history of another disciple, Judas (vv. 3–10). Matthew's version of Judas's death (cf. an alternate story in Acts 1:18) is an intricate blend of Old Testament allusions and some of the consistent themes of his Gospel. As predicted (26:20–25), Judas's betrayal leads to death. He is not moved to repentance but only to remorse and despair. Yet the responsibility of rejecting Jesus does not end with Judas. The chief priests pick up the "blood money" Judas had flung into the temple and thus symbolize that they too must bear responsibility for their lack of faith. Matthew views this entire episode from the viewpoint of the Old Testament. The words of Zechariah 11:12–13 (cf. 27:9–10) had predicted such betrayal. But it is Jeremiah whose symbol of the potter (Jer 18 and 32) and of a burial field (Jer 19) provide Matthew with the atmosphere of judgment cast over this tragic episode. As with all the fulfillment texts, Matthew affirms that these events fall within the context of God's mysterious providence.

STUDY QUESTION: Three Galileans face their moment of truth: Judas, Peter, Jesus. The Gospel subtly prods us—where do we stand?

Matthew 27:11–31
THE VERDICT OF PILATE AND THE PEOPLE:
"LET HIM BE CRUCIFIED"

It is now Pilate's turn to decide Jesus' fate. The Roman trial scene will closely parallel the account of the hearing before the Sanhedrin. The basic structure is the same: interrogation, verdict, mockery. And, as in the previous scene, the evangelist is more interested in significance than in detailed information.

Pilate's opening question, "Are you the king of the Jews?" (v. 11), strikes the theme of Jesus' messiahship sounded earlier by Caiaphas (26:63). The title "king of the Jews" emphasizes the political overtones of Jewish messianic hopes. Once again, Jesus' answer is deliberately enigmatic: he confirms the truth of Pilate's words but recognizes that the governor is unaware of what he has stated. The Jewish leaders add a chorus of accusations, but Jesus, God's Servant (cf. Isa 53:7), reverts to his eloquent silence.

Pilate is baffled by his prisoner and attempts to secure his release through a custom attested only in the Gospels, the freeing of a prisoner as a gesture of benevolence during the great Jewish season of Passover. Matthew uses the information already provided by Mark as a means of sharpening the underlying issue of the trial: one must accept or reject Jesus as the Messiah. The choice is posed in verse 17 and again in verse 21. The drama of the choice is heightened by preparation. Pilate's wife has been warned in a dream (always a medium of divine messages in Matthew's Gospel, cf. chapter 2) that Jesus is innocent and she pleads with her husband on his behalf (v. 19). Meanwhile the leaders sway the crowds for Barabbas. In some very ancient manuscripts, Barabbas's name is given as "*Jesus* Barabbas." If this were the original wording, then the choice is posed even more dramatically: "Which one do you want me to release to you, Jesus Barabbas, or Jesus called Messiah?" Crowd and leaders become one and demand that Jesus be crucified.

Matthew seals a dramatic choice with dramatic gestures (vv. 24–25). Pilate, the Roman governor, washes his hands, using an Old Testament ritual which declares one innocent of murdered blood (cf. Deut 21:6ff.). The crowds, now designated by the corporate title "the whole people" (v. 25), use another Old Testament formula which is a declaration of responsibility: "His blood be upon us and upon our children" (cf. 1 Kgs 2:32f.). For all of its solemnity, this passage should not be construed as a foundation for anti-Semitism. Matthew himself was most probably a Jew and his own church certainly included a substantial proportion of Jews. Thus, this Gospel incident could not be intended as a condemnation of the Jewish people. Matthew makes it a solemn declaration because he recognizes here a pivotal moment in salvation history. In the paradox of God's providence, the promise of salvation which had been confined to Israel was now, through the death and resurrection of Jesus, to break out into the whole world and include the Gentile nations. Those who rejected Jesus would have to bear responsibility for their choice. Matthew's church may have interpreted the destruction of the temple in A.D. 70 as fulfilling the time span of 27:25—"upon us and upon our children," i.e., on the contemporaries of Jesus and the following generation. From now on, the Gospel's promise of forgiveness and new life would be open to all who would respond (cf. Matt 21:43), Jew and Gentile.

Mockery and insult conclude the trial (vv. 26–31). Jesus' claim to kingship is cruelly parodied by the soldiers. Another moment of deep irony lies beneath the surface of the narrative. The reader knows that Jesus *is* king, a king who rejects the trappings of royalty ridiculed by the soldiers (cf. 21:5). This macabre coronation is unwitting preparation for Jesus' greatest act of service, and it is service that is the real basis of Jesus' power (cf. 20:26).

STUDY QUESTION: The evangelist searches history and discovers God's providence even in the midst of tragedy and failure. We should search the history of our own significant life choices, and place them in the perspective of faith.

Matthew 27:32–66
THE DEATH OF GOD'S SON
AND THE BEGINNING OF THE NEW AGE

With this scene, Matthew reaches the climax of the entire Gospel story. Jesus will die, but through that death astounding new life will begin.

At Golgotha, the execution site outside Jerusalem, Jesus is offered a mild sedative, stripped of his clothing, and crucified (vv. 32–38). The offering of wine and gall and the casting of lots for Jesus' garments contain allusions to Psalm 69:21 and Psalm 22:19, two biblical prayers that express the anguish of the believer who continues to trust in God even in the midst of pain and distress. The theme of these psalms will be the key to Matthew's interpretation of Jesus' death.

As Jesus is pinned to the cross between two malefactors, with a placard declaring the charge over his head, an amazing procession of mockery begins to file by. The taunts of the passers-by, of the Jewish leaders, and even of Jesus' fellow prisoners bring forward in ironic terms the Gospel's claims about Jesus: his authority over the temple, his ability to save others, his claim to be the Messiah, the king of Israel, and, above all, his abiding trust in his Father. That Jesus was the obedient and beloved Son of God has been the most insistent claim of Matthew's Gospel. Now, in words taken from Psalm 22 (cf. Ps 22:9; words repeated in Wis 2:18) and in a tone that echoes Satan's temptations at the beginning of the Gospel (cf. 4:3, 6), the ultimate challenge is hurled at the dying Jesus: "He trusted in God; let him deliver him now if he wants him. For he said, "I am the Son of God" (v. 43).

The finale is at hand. Darkness, a biblical sign of the end of the world (cf. Am 8:9), settles over the land. Jesus' last word is said (v. 46). He recites the opening verse of Psalm 22, a prayer of deepest agony and deepest faith. Even his prayer is mocked, as the Hebrew word *Eli* ("my God") is deliberately misunderstood as *Elijah,* the popular Old Testament figure called upon by Jews in distress, and who was expected to come before the Messiah (v. 47). And a last act of compassion is denied Jesus (v. 49). Finally, he cries out again in prayer and obediently returns to his Father the gift of life that had been his (v. 50; for this biblical way of describing death, cf. Gen 35:18; Eccl 12:7).

Jesus' death triggers an explosion of astounding signs (vv. 51–53). The great veil before the sanctuary of the temple is ripped in two, a quake splits the earth and breaks open the tombs of the dead, and the "saints" of Israel rise from their tombs and prepare to enter the Holy City of Jerusalem. This cataclysmic series of events, with the exception of the tearing of the veil, is unique to Matthew's Gospel and provides the evangelist's comment on the significance of Jesus' death. These kinds of "signs" were the very events that Judaism expected to take place at the end of the world when God would come to establish his kingdom. And this is precisely what Matthew intends to say. The tearing of the temple veil symbolizes that the old order has passed and now a new way to God is possible through the Risen Jesus. And further,

Jesus' ultimate act of love and obedience has ushered in a new age. Death has been defeated and a resurrected people march in triumph to Jerusalem. Matthew seems to allude in these verses to the haunting vision of the dry bones in the Book of Ezekiel where God breathes new life into a people without hope: "O my people, I will open your graves and have you rise from them, and bring you back to the land of Israel..." (37:12).

The centurion and his soldiers add the bottom line. Seeing the effect of Jesus' death, these Gentile witnesses answer the challenge of the mockers (cf. 27:43) with reverent awe: "Truly, this was the Son of God!" (27:54). Jesus' word is trustworthy. His compassion is no empty gesture. As he had pledged, he fulfilled all that was asked of him (cf. 3:15). He was indeed the beloved, obedient Son of God and in him the will of the Father was revealed.

The death scene ends on a muted note. The faithful women who stood by the cross (27:55–56) and who witness the burial signal the event that Matthew, in a sense, has already anticipated. They will be the Easter messengers who discover the empty tomb and who first meet the Risen Lord (28:1–10). But opposition continues to dog Jesus even after his death. By relating the story of the guards at the tomb (27:62–66), Matthew prepares a counterattack for an alternate explanation of the empty tomb that apparently still circulated in Jewish circles contemporaneous with Matthew (cf. below, 28:11–15).

STUDY QUESTION: The Gospel is not a private, personal story. Matthew insists that the implications of Jesus' death and resurrection are universal, even cosmic. Through his obedient death and the victory of his resurrection, Jesus has brought a new age of life to humanity. Does our faith stretch that far? Does it shape our view of history and of the ultimate meaning of human life?

Matthew 28:1–20
OUT INTO A NEW WORLD:
THE RISEN LORD COMMISSIONS HIS CHURCH

Matthew's description of the death of Jesus almost makes the Easter story anti-climactic. Signs of the resurrection break out (27:51–54) at the very moment of Jesus' obedient death. The former age symbolized by the temple has passed. Because of Jesus' death, the best hopes of God's people are revived and an unlikely community of Gentile soldiers acclaims Jesus as God's Son. But the Easter story is not superfluous, for it gives Matthew the chance to spell out in detail what is expected of those who live in the new age as disciples of the Risen Jesus.

The discovery of the empty tomb is quickly told (28:1–8). As in Mark's account (cf. 16:1–8), the women return to the tomb on Sunday. An incredible discovery awaits them. Matthew's version heightens the glory of this moment by adding the details about the earthquake, a resplendent "angel of the Lord," the rolling back of the rock, and the terror of the soldiers (vv. 2–4). These things, too, characterized Jewish expectations about the kind of events that would come at the end of the world. Matthew, then, continues to remind his readers that with the death and resurrection of Jesus a new and final age of history has begun.

The angel interprets the meaning of the empty tomb (an interpretation whose origin and substance is meant to stand in sharp contrast to the fabrication drawn up in 28:11–15). The Jesus who was crucified is not to be found among the dead. He is risen, just as he had promised. As in almost all of the Gospel resurrection stories, those who are privileged witnesses are given a "mission." The women are to alert the scattered disciples that Jesus will gather them together in Galilee. The women leave the tomb "fearful yet overjoyed."

That joy is compounded as they meet the Risen Lord himself (vv. 9–10). It is really Jesus who has risen; they are able to touch his feet. But he is also clearly the Risen Lord and so they do him homage. The mission given by the angel is reiterated. They are to tell Jesus' "brothers" to meet him in Galilee. "Brothers [and sisters]" is the very title of solidarity that Jesus had used in urging unlimited forgiveness and reconciliation among those who would enter the kingdom (cf. 18:19–20, 35).

Matthew's closing scene (28:16–20) weaves together into a breathtaking tapestry the brilliant threads that have run through his Gospel. Jesus, who had climbed a hill to proclaim words of grace and compassion to a sick humanity (chapters 5 to 7), Jesus the healer who had drawn the sick and disabled to him on a mountain to heal and empower them (15:29–31), Jesus who on another mountain had blinded his disciples with a glimpse of his future glory (chapter 17), now stands in majesty on a summit in Galilee. This Jesus, whose roots reach back to Abraham and David, whose words and works had identified him as the Messiah, as God's own Servant and Son, is now clearly recognized as the victorious Son of Man, that mysterious figure whom Daniel had prophesied would bear "all authority in heaven and on earth" (Dan 7:14). This same Jesus moves forward to heal and transform the "*eleven* disciples" whose truncated number testifies to the wounds of betrayal, of fear, "of little faith," of doubt (v. 17). But these "least brethren" will be the very ones to proclaim the Gospel and to build the community of the new age. Their mission is no longer confined to Israel (10:5) but must be to "all nations." They are to make disciples, to baptize, and to teach. The "law" of this new people is to be the law that has fulfilled the old law of Moses: Jesus' own teaching. Fidelity to that command of love would be the branding mark of those called into the kingdom.

To begin his Gospel, Matthew borrowed from the First Book of Chronicles (cf. Matt 1:1–17), whose panoramic history of the Jewish kings had attempted to give Israel perspective in a time of confusion and discontinuity. Matthew seems to turn to this book again in shaping the conclusion of his Gospel. The final chapter of the Book of Chronicles ends with a solemn decree of Cyrus, King of Persia (cf. 2 Chr 36:22). This unexpected instrument of God's providence had released the people of Israel from their exile and commanded them to build a new people and a new temple.

Now, centuries later, God's providence once again reaches out to bring his people back to life. But this time, the herald of the good news is no Persian king, but God's own Son, One whose infinite grace and startling power are revealed in the name he bears: "Emmanuel," "God-with-us." The revelation of this name stood at the beginning of Matthew's Gospel story (1:23). The promise of abiding presence which that same name inspires concludes the story: "And behold, I am with you always, until the end of the age."

STUDY QUESTION: Matthew's Gospel gives the church a breathtaking commission: to be a resurrection people, full of life and faith; to be a community founded in Christ's name and obedient to his command of love; to be believable witnesses of the presence of the Risen Lord in his world. The question lingers: Are we that people of the new age?

SUGGESTED FURTHER READINGS
ON MATTHEW'S GOSPEL

Raymond E. Brown and John P. Meier. *Antioch & Rome: New Testament Cradles of Christianity.* Mahwah, N.J.: Paulist Press, 1983. Provides background on the likely area (Antioch) in which Matthew's Gospel originated and was first received.

W. D. Davies and Dale C. Allison. *Matthew* (International Critical Commentary). 3 Vols. Edinburgh: T & T Clark, 1988–97. This massive commentary ranks as perhaps the best and most complete English language commentary on the Gospel. It is based on the Greek text of Matthew and provides exhaustive bibliographical references.

Daniel J. Harrington, S.J. *The Gospel of Matthew* (Sacra Pagina). Collegeville: Liturgical Press, 1991. A major commentary that emphasizes the Jewish background of Matthew's Gospel.

Ulrich Luz. *The Theology of the Gospel of Matthew* (New Testament Theology). Cambridge University Press, 1995. An analysis of the theology of Matthew's Gospel by one of the most interesting European interpreters of the Gospel.

J. Andrew Overman. *Matthew's Gospel and Formative Judaism.* Minneapolis: Fortress Press, 1990. Studies the context of Matthew's Gospel in relationship to first-century Judaism.

Mark Allan Powell. *God With Us: A Pastoral Theology of Matthew's Gospel.* Minneapolis: Fortress Press, 1995. As the subtitle indicates, this work explores some of the pastoral significance of Matthew's theology.

Anthony J. Saldarini. *Matthew's Christian-Jewish Community*. University of Chicago Press, 1994. Makes a forceful case that Matthew's community still considered itself to be thoroughly within the Jewish community.

Donald Senior, C.P. *The Passion of Jesus in the Gospel of Matthew* (Passion Series 1). Collegeville: Liturgical Press, 1985. A study of Matthew's passion narrative and its theological significance.

————. *What are They Saying About Matthew?* Revised ed. Mahwah, N.J.: Paulist Press, 1996. Provides an extensive review of current scholarship on all facets of Matthew's Gospel.

————. *The Gospel of Matthew* (Interpreting Biblical Texts). Nashville: Abingdon, 1997. Part of a series that provides the reader with background information important for the interpretation of Matthew's Gospel.

Graham N. Stanton. *A Gospel for a New People: Studies in Matthew*. Edinburgh: T & T Clark. Provides fine background analysis on some of the key theological and historical issues in Matthew's Gospel.

Invitation to Mark

Paul J. Achtemeier

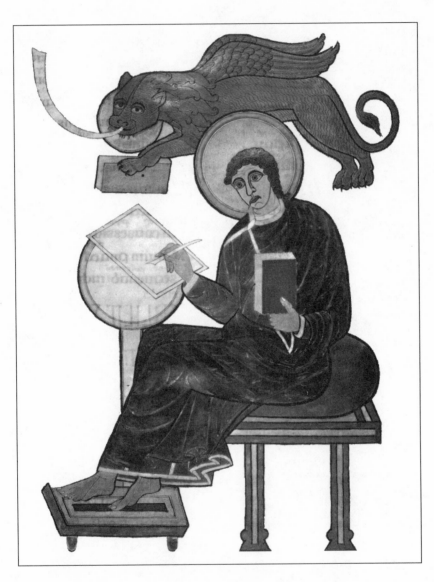

Mark

PREFACE

As in any commentary of this kind, my debt to fellow scripture scholars has remained unacknowledged in detail. One of the happier events of our age is the way in which study of the Bible has transcended not only national but also confessional boundaries. In many ways, as far as the study of scripture is concerned, the ecumenical problem has been solved, to the benefit of church and scholarship alike. I happily acknowledge here how greatly I have profited from such a state of affairs.

This commentary is characterized as much by what I have not been able to say as by what I have found room to say. I have left much unsaid, and many questions unanswered, partly for reasons of space, but partly because I am not convinced that reliable answers have yet been formulated. Much work has been done on this earliest of our Gospels, but much still remains to be done. Perhaps those who read these pages will find something of the excitement of a journey of discovery well begun, but as yet far from concluded.

The following pages are intended to be read within the context of the faith of Christ's church. When they are, they will be read within the context and intention of that early Christian who wrote the Gospel upon which this commentary is based.

Paul J. Achtemeier

EDITOR'S NOTE: Unless otherwise indicated, biblical citations are from the Jerusalem Bible.

Introduction to Mark's Gospel

Before the author of our Gospel of Mark set out to write an account of the sayings and deeds of Jesus, and of the climax of his career in his suffering, death, and resurrection, nothing comparable to it existed. The general impression one gets from a cursory reading of the first chapters of Acts is that the church, despite some opposition, was doing very well, both growing and thriving. Why, in that situation, would someone go to all the trouble of composing a Gospel, if the church apparently was doing quite well without it? In one sense, the very success of the early Christian enterprise may well have made some kind of "handbook" necessary, to help new converts learn more about their faith and to serve as a help for those who had not known Jesus, but who had now become evangelists of the faith rooted in him. As the church grew larger and more widespread, those people who had known Jesus could no longer keep in direct touch, and, to add a measure of urgency, as time passed those who had known and followed Jesus during his mission in Galilee and then in Judea would begin to die out. To whom could the church then appeal when differences in understandings of the faith arose? In addition to problems related to the spread of the church and the passage of time, there are indications both in Acts and in the Gospel of Mark that, in fact, there were aspects of the church's life where things were not going all that smoothly. The dispute about feeding widows in Acts 6, and the problem of admitting Gentiles as full-fledged Christians in Acts 15 are two examples.

The emphases one can discern in the way the Gospel of Mark is structured and the themes that are given special prominence give us some clues to the problems Mark may well have intended to resolve when he (or she!—we really don't know anything about the author, except from some later guesses) undertook to write his story of Jesus. If we follow those clues carefully, we can discover some of the problems that moved the author of Mark to invent a whole new kind of literature, in order to solve them. Careful attention to certain emphases in the Gospel narrative, for example, helps us to discern what appear to be at least three such problems. They are (1) the problem of the destruction of the temple when the Romans sacked Jerusalem and the relationship of that destruction to Jesus' return in glory (Mark 13); (2) the problem involved in following a crucified Lord, which appeared not to give much promise for a bright future for those who did; and (3) the related problem involved in understanding the significance of the fact that Jesus' life ended on a cross. A careful look at those problems will put us in a better position to understand some of the points the author of Mark was trying to make when he set out to write an account of the career of Jesus.

First, then, the destruction of the temple in Jerusalem. Palestine had never taken kindly to its Roman occupation, and ever since Herod the Great, with Rome's support and encouragement, forced himself on the Jews as their king in 37 B.C., the people had been looking for a way to dethrone Herod and drive out the hated enemies who supported him, namely the occupying Roman armies. The revolt that had long simmered broke out in A.D. 66, and, after mopping up in Galilee and in Judea east of Jerusalem to cut off all routes of escape, the Romans laid siege to Jerusalem. Once and for all, they intended to put down this rebellious people that had for so long given them so much trouble. The siege ended in 70 with the capture of Jerusalem and the subsequent burning of a large part of the city, including the temple. As in all such cases, looting and murder, pillage and rape accompanied the occupation.

Yet the question posed by the fall of Jerusalem and the destruction of the temple was this: were these events simply the result of Roman military policy, or were they God's way of punishing the Jews for their disobedience to his will in their continuing rejection of Jesus, as God had punished his people centuries earlier in the destruction of Jerusalem and the exile of the Jews to Babylonia? Such a question could not have been far from the minds of the Christians who had heard of, or even lived through, those events. If the center of Jewish worship had been destroyed, could that not mean that God was now preparing to bring history to a close by sending his Son, this time in visible and overpowering glory, to complete the judgment of all humanity? Could this destruction of Jerusalem not be the opening salvo in the final series of events that announced the end of the kingdoms of this world, and the coming of God's own kingdom? Then, as now, there were people who thought they had found evidence that Jesus would return very soon. Yet, if Christians came to believe this, what excesses of belief and action might be touched off? Incalculable harm could be done to the church if people were to take such a false notion seriously. Somehow, this event needed to be set in proper perspective, so that Christians would not take the kind of action that would be appropriate only for the time when Jesus actually did return with power to judge all the earth and establish in visible glory the kingdom of God.

Then there was the second problem. Ever since Jesus had been put to death as a political threat to the Romans and as a religious threat to the Jewish religious establishment, the danger had existed that his followers would be regarded in the same light. Obviously, those who claimed as their leader one who had died a criminal's death would be suspected of being criminals as well. That kind of attitude toward Christians was apparently on the increase in Mark's time, as Christians grew in numbers and their activities came to the attention of the Roman authorities. Some Christians were folding under the pressure. Yet if Jesus the Master had suffered, would that not also be the fate of those who saw in him God's final act of mercy for all humanity? If only the followers of Jesus could understand that such suffering, painful as it was, was not to be their final fate, as it had not been for Jesus. As Jesus, after his suffering, had risen from the dead to share in the glory of almighty God, so they, after their suffering, would find joy in God's kingdom. Yet somehow, Christians needed to be made aware of the fact that there was no safe and easy way in a hostile culture for true followers of Jesus. Before Jesus had been raised, he had suffered an agonizing death on a cross. The author of Mark was convinced that because that was the fate of Jesus, the way of the cross was the only path to glory for Christians as well. If that fact were overlooked, or forgotten, there would be no more true followers of Jesus. There would be no more church worthy of the name. Somehow that point had to be gotten across.

The third problem was closely related to the second. Not everyone who knew about Jesus was persuaded that he had to be understood so exclusively in the light of his passion. After all, hadn't he done some very miraculous things during his lifetime? Hadn't he attracted great crowds with his teaching in Galilee? Hadn't he risen from the dead, so that those who followed him could also expect to share in that resurrection and in heavenly glory? There were all kinds of stories about Jesus in circulation, telling about the things he had done and said. The difficulty was that everyone was interpreting these stories and sayings in a way that best suited their own opinions about Jesus. Such stories about Jesus were being used to justify what people wanted to believe and to do, rather than being used to teach people what they ought to believe, and how they ought to act. It was clear that these individual stories about Jesus, however valuable they might have been in themselves, were no longer sufficient to keep people from getting all kinds of strange ideas about the meaning of the career of Jesus.

We get a first-hand look at this problem in the letters of St. Paul. He had preached Jesus Christ, crucified and risen, to the people of the Greek city of Corinth. He had quoted some teachings of Jesus in that preaching, and he had told some stories about him too. Later on, when he wrote to the Christians there, he reminded them of some of those sayings and stories (1 Cor 7:10–11; 11:23–25; 15:1–7). The trouble was, those stories could easily be misunderstood. For example, the Corinthians had been told about the Eucharist. They had learned that the Eucharist celebrated Jesus whom God had raised from the dead. So they celebrated it, but they tended to convert it into one of the social banquets of which the Corinthians were so fond, imposing customs like seating the wealthy and important people in a special room, and serving them first and with better food than that given to the less important people. It thus became just another kind of wild party, with some people drinking so much they got drunk, while others got little if any food (1 Cor 11:21–22). Clearly, such behavior had nothing to do with the Eucharist, and St. Paul told them as much in no uncertain terms. Yet as long as those stories about Jesus were circulating by themselves, they were open to just such misunderstanding.

There are other examples of the problem of such stories about Jesus circulating as individual traditions. People who were interested in magic—and that included most of the Greco-Roman world of the first century—saw in Jesus' mighty acts evidence that he was a great magician. Maybe if they studied about him, they could gain some of that power for themselves (see Acts 8:9–19). People who were interested in philosophy heard some of the sayings of Jesus, and came to the conclusion that perhaps Jesus was another teacher of some philosophy, perhaps cleverer than the run-of-the-mill philosophers they ran into, so they tried to learn his philosophical doctrines (see Acts 17:18–21). How could these stories about Jesus be protected from such misuse and misunderstanding?

These were the kinds of problems that faced the author of the Gospel of Mark. How could they be solved? The solution our author hit upon was novel. He would put together a selection of these stories about Jesus in such a way that the order in which they were told would help to show how they were to be understood. He would arrange them in such a way that the climax of Jesus' life—cross and resurrection—became the climax of the story about Jesus. The author of Mark would write down the story of Jesus in such a way that everything that Jesus said and did led up to his passion, so that any interpretation of Jesus that left the passion out of account would be wrong. To do that, the author of Mark had to invent a whole new kind of literature. We have come to call that kind of literature a "gospel."

When our author wrote his Gospel, therefore, he set out to weave, from the familiar traditions, a tapestry of the career of Jesus that would give a perspective on the traditions the author used, and that would also give a perspective on the problems faced by Christians of his time and place.

What is quite remarkable is how faithful the author was to the traditions he had. Aside from providing links between the various stories (e.g., 2:1, 13; 4:1–2; 5:21; 6:1) and composing an occasional summary (e.g., 1:32–34; 3:7–12; 6:53–56), for the most part our author made his point by the way he arranged and juxtaposed the traditions. Sometimes he would sandwich one tradition into another (e.g., the two stories in 5:21–43, or in 11:12–25), so that when they were read together, they would help interpret each other. At other times, the author would make his point by the order in which he placed the stories (e.g., 3:20–35, followed by 4:1–12, so we see in family and Pharisees examples of those who observe but do not understand what Jesus is really about). In these and similar ways, the author of Mark seems to have wanted to preserve the traditions as he knew them, limiting his work to arranging them and putting them into a narrative that climaxed in Jesus' passion.

The author of Mark laid emphasis on the passion as the key to understanding Jesus in a variety of ways. It is clear throughout the

Gospel, for example, that the disciples simply did not understand who Jesus really was. Time and again, they betrayed their inability to grasp the meaning of what Jesus said, and what that meant for who he was. Yet it is also clear that this was due to more than simply their stupidity or to general human failings. They were not *meant* to understand who Jesus was during his time with them (cf. 6:52). Mark is dealing here not with human failure, but with God's plan for the salvation of humanity. The key to that plan is the death and resurrection of Jesus. Therefore, only *after* those events have occurred will Jesus be able to be understood for what he really is, and only then will anyone fully understand what he had to say. Mark 9:9 is a good example. There Jesus himself makes clear that his true nature (revealed in the story of the transfiguration, 9:2–8) is not to be revealed until after his resurrection.

The author of Mark makes that same point in other ways. For example, he makes it by the order in which he puts certain traditions. Thus, each of the passion predictions is followed by evidence that the disciples have understood neither what the prediction means for Jesus, nor what it means for them (chapters 8, 9, 10). Again, Jesus regularly forbade the demons to announce who he was. Our author tells us why that was so. The demons knew who Jesus was (1:34). For people without the supernatural knowledge possessed by demons, however, such knowledge could only really be possible after Jesus' passion.

The emphasis on Jesus' passion probably stems from the fact that people of that time were attempting to understand Jesus in ways that did not make clear that the passion was the key to the meaning of Jesus' career, as we mentioned earlier. The author of Mark was apparently trying to make it clear that no one, not even the disciples who lived and traveled with him for months on end, could understand Jesus apart from the passion. Mark's Gospel is therefore a warning. Any attempt to understand Jesus apart from his passion will inevitably fall into error. The mystery of who Jesus really was (scholars call it the "messianic secret") cannot be penetrated until God himself lifts the veil by raising the crucified Jesus from the dead.

The Gospel of Mark is therefore more than simply an attempt to tell the story of Jesus in a new format, namely as a story that climaxes in the passion. It is also an attempt to make the theological point that just as the passion was the climax of Jesus' historical career, so it is the climax and key to any attempt to understand him. If the path to glory leads through the vale of the cross, so does the path to knowledge about Jesus. He was not a magician, or a philosopher, or even primarily a teacher. He was God's Son who by his suffering and death redeemed humanity (10:45).

Our author solved the problem of the fall of Jerusalem and the destruction of the temple in a similar way. There were a number of stories in circulation about the meaning of the fall of Jerusalem. Perhaps someone had even written a short pamphlet about it. The author of Mark took those stories and interspersed comments on them in such a way that it becomes clearer that that cataclysm did not mean Jesus was about to return. In fact, it is impossible to figure out when Jesus will come, because that is known only to God. Christians are to remain alert in their faith, but because the time of Jesus' return cannot be calculated on the basis of historic events, they are not to assume that Jerusalem's fall means Jesus' return is now at hand.

Such interest in the fall of Jerusalem does not necessarily mean that Mark lived near that city, or that he was writing his Gospel solely for people of Jewish descent. The conquest of Jerusalem was so important that the Roman general who accomplished it, Titus (who later became an emperor of Rome), built a triumphal arch in Rome to commemorate that victory. Interest in that event was therefore spread far beyond the boundaries of Palestine. Again, the fact that Mark must translate Aramaic phrases in Greek (e.g., 5:41; 7:34) and explain Jewish customs to his readers (e.g., 7:3–4) indicates that he was writing to people who knew little if anything about either the language or the customs of Palestine. As we shall see in a moment, Mark's information about the geography of Palestine was so sketchy that it is hard to believe he grew up, or had ever lived, there. Although a later tradition says our Gospel was written in Rome by a Mark who was an interpreter of Peter, that seems to be little more than a guess intended to supply some missing information.

There are some other characteristics of the Gospel of Mark that are worth noting. The author was apparently so intent on pursuing theological goals when he composed his narrative that he did not pay attention to some of the historical details we would expect in a story about Jesus' career. But then, our author was not writing a "history," or even a "biography," of Jesus. His purpose in constructing the Gospel was to provide a framework within which individual traditions about Jesus could find their correct interpretation. As a result, he was not always careful about time sequences, such as when one day, or week, or month ended and another began. In most cases he simply put one tradition after another, with only the simplest kind of introductory phrases: "in those days," or "after some days," or simply "again." When he did give times of day, he did not always follow up on them. After telling us it was evening in 4:35, he does not mention any time again until 6:2, when we learn it was the sabbath. Obviously, not everything reported between 4:35 and 6:2 could have happened in one night. Several days must have passed, but Mark doesn't tell us how many. We can guess if we want, but then we can no longer say we are getting that information from the Gospel of Mark. So any attempt we make to write a "life of Jesus," one which seeks to give a day-by-day, or even month-by-month, account of his activities will for the most part be based on our guesses, rather than on information from Mark.

The same thing is true about the reports of Jesus' travels. The author of Mark occasionally tells us where Jesus was at a given time, or where he went, but, as in the case of time, these indications of geography are casual and intermittent. In some cases, they are all but unbelievable. For example, the geographical route outlined in Mark 7:31 is much more difficult in the Greek than most English translations are willing to acknowledge. Traveling from Tyre to the Sea of Galilee by way of Sidon and the Decapolis is roughly comparable to traveling from Philadelphia to Washington D.C. by way of New York city and central Pennsylvania. Even worse, the Greek says the Sea of Galilee is in the "middle of" the Decapolis, when in reality that body of water lies at the very northwest corner of that area. Either Mark was unfamiliar with the geography of Palestine (did you know Sidon is north of Tyre?) or he simply did not care much if his geography was accurate or not. In either case, we cannot use the geographical references he gave us to retrace the travels of Jesus. Again, if we try, most of the information will have to be based on guess-work.

Once Mark had achieved the theological breakthrough of arranging independent traditions about what Jesus said and did, and where he went, into the format of a story climaxing with the passion, those who followed him could then give more attention to individual details. If you compare Mark with Matthew and Luke, both of whose authors evidently used Mark as a source of material when they wrote their Gospels, you will see how, time and again, those two authors smoothed out the rough places in Mark, and gave the story a more even flow. But that is due in most cases to their desire to improve Mark's narrative, and not at all to any superior knowledge they had of the actual history of Jesus.

If we want to understand the Gospel of Mark, therefore, we will have to read it for what it is, namely a story that is meant to tell us about the religious meaning of Jesus. In doing that, it does not intend to give us what we would consider accurate historical information about the course of Jesus' life. What it wants us to learn is "gospel truth," not historical truth.

There are one or two other things we will also have to pay attention to if we want to understand the Gospel of Mark. For example, we must read Mark carefully, and all by itself, if we want to know what that Gospel is trying to tell us. We are so accustomed to having all four Gospels that we tend to read any one of them in light of the other three. Yet when Mark was written, there was no such thing as another Gospel. Matthew, Luke, and John were all written later. Therefore, we must resist the temptation to fill in Mark's narrative with some of the additional details furnished by one of the other Gospels. We will only confuse our attempt to understand what *Mark* is saying. Reading Mark by itself will take a real effort and close concentration, but it is the only way we can get at what Mark is trying to say, rather than what we think the Gospel ought to say. Only by concentrating on Mark, and in some cases limiting ourselves to the information Mark alone provides, will we really be able to understand this Gospel's message.

As is the case with most worthwhile things, the study of the Gospel of Mark, or of any book in the Bible, for that matter, is not always as easy as we might like. Yet it is surely worth the effort. It will demand careful reading, and hard thinking, but the rewards will be great. We have the chance, in reading Mark, to study the product of one of the towering figures in the history of religious literature. He not only created a new kind of literature—a "gospel"—but he put a stamp on the way the Christian faith is to be understood that endures to this day. We owe the fact that we think about Jesus in terms of a life that led to and climaxed in the passion to the theological genius of this unknown author, so modest that he did not even tell us who he was. In the pages that follow in this commentary, we will try to think that author's thoughts about Jesus after him, to see what they can teach us about our faith, and about ourselves. Any such exploration means high adventure, and hard work, and it is to such a task that this commentary invites you.

I. Jesus Appears, Preaching the Kingdom of God with Power

Mark 1:1 to 3:6

Mark 1:1–13
BEGINNINGS: JOHN THE BAPTIST

Mark 1:1–8
The Gospel Begins with John the Baptist

The opening words of this Gospel can appear a bit strange, because they announce that this is the beginning of the good news (Greek "gospel") of Jesus. Why announce that? Where else would the story begin but at the beginning? Mark had another intention with these words, however. For him, the story of Jesus must begin with John the Baptist if it is to be told correctly (cf. 11:30–33—how one understands Jesus is linked to how one understands John). That link is more than merely historical. It is grounded in the Old Testament, and in God's history of dealing with Israel, the chosen people; opening the story with an Old Testament quote makes that clear enough. The verses Mark quotes from Isaiah (actually the first two lines are from Mal 3:1; this may show that Mark got the whole quotation from an early Christian collection of appropriate Old Testament verses about Jesus) are intended to show that when John appeared, the long awaited final act of God for the salvation of humankind had begun. Later in his book, Malachi identified that last forerunner as Elijah (Mal 3:23; in some translations 4:5), and Mark is careful to make that identification too. The description of John in verse 6 closely parallels the description of Elijah in the early Greek version of 2 Kings 1:8, and later on, Mark will report that Jesus identified John as Elijah who was to come (9:13; cf. also Luke 1:17).

That John is a prophet is made clear by further details in this description of him. His message of repentance is the familiar prophetic call to return to faithfulness to God, a faithfulness that had characterized Israel's earlier time in the wilderness. Just as Israel had once been faithful in the desert (cf. Jer 2:2–3a), so Israel would finally return to the desert and to faithfulness to God in the last times (cf. Hos 2:16–19; in some translations 2:14–17). The desert is thus more important theologically than geographically. It makes the point about John that must be made, namely that in him the prophetic message about the final, redemptive times has begun its appearance. Yet John is no more than the beginning. He is not yet the fulfillment. John announced that someone would follow him who was so immeasurably greater that not even the most menial task John could do for him would be appropriate: slaves, not the host, removed the travel-worn guests' sandals. Thus John, in the desert, calls all Israel to repent and be washed clean of their sins, so they will be ready to greet the one who will come, who will be clothed in God's own Spirit.

STUDY QUESTION: Why is it necessary to understand Jesus in relation to the Old Testament, and the story of Israel as God's chosen people?

Mark 1:9–13
Baptized and Tempted

Jesus' baptism by John is almost surely based on a historical event. It created too many theological problems to have been invented; it makes Jesus look like a follower of John. Further, John's baptism was for the forgiveness of sins. Did Jesus need that? (See Matt 3:14–15 for further treatment of this.) Whether the individual details are historical, however, we cannot determine, but they are important for what Mark wants to tell us about Jesus.

The Jewish people of Jesus' time mourned the loss of prophets and the silence of God. Now, with Jesus' appearance, the heavens are again opened up (cf. Isa 63:19b [in some translations 64:1]; Ezek 1:1); God's Spirit comes once more (cf. Isa 11:1–2; 61:1; the meaning of the symbolism of the dove for God's Spirit remains unclear); and God's silence is broken. The voice from heaven draws on language from Psalm 2:7 and Isaiah 42:1 and announces that, like Israel (Exod 4:22; Hos 11:1) or Israel's kings (2 Sam 7:13–14; Ps 89:20, 26–27), Jesus is now commissioned to fulfill the task of being God's Son.

The Spirit then drove Jesus into the wilderness, the traditional abode of evil and demonic forces, for a test of strength with Satan. Mark thus lets us see the cosmic dimension of Jesus' earthly ministry. In Jesus, the final climactic battle between God and the powers of evil has been joined. The presence of animals (probably a sign of God's final peace; cf. Isa 11:6–9) and angels gives us a hint about who will emerge from the contest victorious, despite the apparent defeat on the cross.

STUDY QUESTION: Do you find evidence in our time that this cosmic battle continues? How does Satan oppose God in our world?

Mark 1:14–45
JESUS' MINISTRY INTRODUCED

Mark 1:14–20
The Time is Now

Mark begins his account of Jesus' public ministry in Galilee with a summary of Jesus' message: the time is now to accept God's good news and return to doing his will. The language of verses 14–15 reflects early Christian missionary terminology, showing how those early preachers summarized the message of Jesus that they were announcing. Mark puts such language here, along with the traditions about the calling of the first disciples, to make the point that everything that follows verses 14–15 illustrates the way the nearness of God's kingdom manifests itself in Jesus' ministry.

That God's rule over creation would one day become visible was known already in the Old Testament. What is new here is the statement that now is the time for that rule to begin. With Jesus' appearance, the kingdom begins to be visible. In Jesus' words and deeds, the contours of God's future take on concrete form, and our part in that future will be determined by how we react to Jesus. We will need to pay careful attention to the stories that follow immediately on verses 14–15 to see how Mark makes that point.

The four disciples whom Jesus called show how one must react to Jesus' summons. There is no hint in Mark that any of the four had known Jesus before the summons (contrast Luke 4:21 to 5:11) or had heard of him through John the Baptist (contrast John 1:35–42). Rather, in exemplary fashion, they respond immediately to Jesus' call, willing to abandon economic ties (v. 18; cf. 10:21) and even family (v. 20; cf. 10:28–29; Matt 10:37–38; and Luke 14:26–27) to follow Jesus. That is the way, Mark implies, that every person ought to respond to the summons of God's future. That is what it means to "repent and believe the good news."

STUDY QUESTION: We cannot imitate the way the first disciples followed the historical Jesus, since he is no longer present in that way. What are some appropriate ways we can respond to his summons?

Mark 1:21–28
What Kind of Teacher Is This?

The point we find in this story is very likely to be quite different from the point Mark intended to make with his original readers. We are most likely to dwell on the idea that Jesus had the power to cast out an "unclean spirit" or a "demon," and we will tend to think that this made Jesus unique in his time. Yet such activity was not at all unique to Jesus in his own world. Many wandering exorcists had such demon expulsions reported about them, and the telling of such stories had evolved into a regular pattern. That pattern is closely followed in our story (vv. 23–27a). After the demonic force made its presence felt, often with a formula to gain power over the exorcist (normally by pronouncing his name, and further indications by the demon that he knew who the exorcist really was), the exorcist replied with a counter formula, usually invoking the name of a god or demon more powerful than the one being dealt with, and then a command to the demon to leave. If the counter formula was successful, the demon was forced to leave, often with some visible or audible proof of its departure. The story often concluded with a description of the astonishment of the bystanders.

It is thus quite clear that our story had been told and retold often enough before it came to be placed in Mark's Gospel so that it had assumed that pattern. It is not the story itself, therefore, that is meant to carry Mark's point, but rather the framework into which Mark has put it. The framework emphasizes not so much Jesus' power over demonic beings, although of course Mark acknowledges that. Rather, the point is now Jesus' power as *teacher;* that is the point on which the crowd remarks (see also the introduction in vv. 21–22, which also emphasizes Jesus' teaching). The material Mark uses to bracket the story (vv. 21–22, 27–28) is designed to show us the kind of power and authority Jesus wielded when he taught. The same power that enabled Jesus to force the demonic powers to obey him was also present in his teaching.

It is also noteworthy that Mark chose to report the story in this form as the first of the many acts of power ("miracles") he would tell of Jesus. Mark seems to have wanted us to understand this miracle as providing the perspective from which all miracle stories of this kind are to be viewed, namely, that Jesus spoke with the same miraculous power by which he also acted. That means Jesus' power is available to many more people than Jesus could affect with his physical presence. Wherever his word is heard, his power is also present, to heal people from the evil forces that disrupt their lives. That is why Mark has identified the story of Jesus as "good news."

STUDY QUESTION: Is there any indication you find that Jesus' words still carry such healing power, even in our world?

Mark 1:29–34
Where Jesus Is, Healing Happens

The simple, straightforward story of the healing of Peter's mother-in-law is cast in the form the oral tradition gave to all such stories. It is noteworthy that in this story there is no mention of faith on the part of the woman or Peter or the other disciples. The faith of the recipient or even of friends is thus not a necessary element in Jesus' healing. The point of such stories is Jesus' divine power, not the attitude of the one afflicted. The story further confirms the importance of the first four disciples Jesus called. Peter, James, and John, sometimes with Andrew, were often present with Jesus when the remaining twelve were not (5:37; 9:2; 13:3). Yet the difficulties these most intimate disciples have in relating to Jesus (cf. 10:35–37; 14:66–72) show how hard it is to come to terms with Jesus as God's son.

Because verses 32–34 depend on their present context (the sabbath mentioned in v. 21 is now over, so people can gather around the door of the house mentioned in v. 29), the material contained in verses 23–34 either circulated as a unit before Mark wrote it down, or, as is more likely, verses 32–34 were composed by Mark as a summary of the kind of activity of Jesus he has been reporting. With these verses, Mark tells us that Jesus' healing ministry was far more extensive than he has space to report. Verse 34 has a further point, however. Jesus' command silencing the unclean spirit in verse 25, there simply part of the normal procedure in telling about an exorcism, here gains a new significance. That command is now understood to imply Jesus' desire during his ministry to keep his true identity unknown (cf. 3:11–12). But then why did Jesus do such things in public? There is obviously more to the command than simply Jesus' desire to avoid publicity. Mark points here for the first time to a dimension of mystery that will become increasingly important to his narrative. At this point, the nature of that mystery remains—a mystery!

STUDY QUESTION: Why would Jesus heal people in public and still not allow the demons to announce who he really was?

Mark 1:35–39
A Matter of Priorities

It is clear from the details in verse 35 that Mark intended us to link this story with the preceding accounts that told about a day's activity of Jesus in Capernaum. That activity had been enormously successful, and the crowds were clamoring for another day like it. Yet Jesus chose to withdraw, first for prayer, and then to go to other regions. He had been sent to announce the nearness of God's final rule, and success, or even human need, could not detain him from spreading that announcement. Jesus did not decide to give up healing for preaching. That is clear from verse 39. He simply could not stay in one place, for whatever reason, since his mission was to spread abroad the good news of God's coming kingdom. Yet verse 39 has further significance. Because Mark tells us Jesus not only preached but also overcame the demonic forces of evil, he will not let us lose the larger perspective against which we must understand the activities of Jesus as itinerant preacher and wonder worker. Jesus is part of God's final, cosmic battle against the powers of evil. To miss that point is to miss the meaning of Jesus.

STUDY QUESTION: Does Mark mean all disciples are to follow Jesus' model of being itinerant, or is the case of Jesus special? Is there a place for an ongoing announcement of God's coming rule in Jesus?

Mark 1:40–45
Jesus Conquers Leprosy

This is a puzzling story. There is a well-attested tradition in the ancient Greek manuscripts of Mark that instead of Jesus "feeling sorry for" the leper, Jesus is angered (perhaps at the demonic force that produces disease?). The word "sternly" in verse 43, furthermore, is the word used to describe the snorting of a war horse in battle; Jesus is portrayed as an ecstatic prophet. "Sent him away" in the same verse translates the word at the end of verse 39, used there to describe the expulsion of demons; it means "cast him out." What are we to make of that alternative picture of Jesus, snorting in anger and casting out the one suffering with leprosy?

Two points at least are clear. First, Jesus is a man possessed by God and is strange even in his own world. To reduce him to a sentimental "friend in the garden" borders on blasphemy. To confront him is to confront the living God. The only proper attitude is that of the leper, who says "If *you* want to, you can cure me." We are God's creatures, not his buddies. Second, this is a climactic act of Jesus. Leprosy made its victim a total outcast (see Lev 13:45–46) and religious Jews regarded the victims as the "living dead." To cure leprosy was equivalent to raising the dead.

It is small wonder that however hard he may have tried (v. 44, "say nothing to anyone"), Jesus could not keep from notoriety (v. 45). The problem is the very human desire to have God at our disposal so that we can use his power any time we want to. It is that human desire that hounded Jesus, and, frustrated, nailed him to a cross. God comes in his own way, and is not always welcomed in his world.

STUDY QUESTION: Does some of our piety conceal a desire to bend God to our will? What should be the Christian's attitude to God's power?

Mark 2:1 to 3:6
CONFLICT WITH RELIGIOUS AUTHORITIES

Mark 2:1–12
Who Does This Man Think He Is?

There is considerable evidence to indicate that at some point in the handing on of traditions about Jesus, two independent stories were combined into this one. This evidence includes the following. (1) The "all" (v. 12) who praised God are not likely to have included the opposing scribes (v. 6). (2) The conclusion in verse 12 has no reference at all to the dispute about forgiving sins. (3) There seems to be a break in the story between verses 10 and 11 where a phrase from verse 5 is repeated. (4) We can recover a formally complete miracle story in verses 3–4, 10b–12, which make no mention of the discussion in verses 5–10a.

It therefore appears that this combination of healing and discussion is the product of a combination of separate traditions, each of which, in itself, may in fact reflect an actual event. The use of the title "Son of Man" in verse 10 in a non-Markan sense (with only one other exception, that title refers to Jesus' death, and is used only in the second half of the Gospel), and the Markan language found in verses 1–2, but nowhere in the rest of the story, indicate it was combined when it came to Mark from his traditions. Mark then gave it an introduction, and put it here.

What does such a combination of miracle and dispute accomplish? Clearly, it demonstrates that Jesus' word is effective. Just as the lame walk when Jesus commands, so sins are forgiven when he forgives them. Perhaps it is easier to say "your sins are forgiven," because there is no way to check and see if that actually happened. To say "stand and walk," on the other hand, is to say something whose effects can actually be observed. In this story, the fact that the paralytic can walk is proof that Jesus' words are effective (we already saw the power-laden nature of Jesus' words in 1:21–28).

That combination also tells us something about Jesus. The scribes insist that only God can forgive sins (v. 6), something Jesus never disputes. Yet he then declares sins forgiven! Clearly, Jesus here was understood to be able to act for God. As we shall see, Mark understood the relationship of Jesus to God to be one of action, in which Jesus does what otherwise only God can do.

A further point is worth noting. Faith (v. 5) has nothing to do with the subjective state of the one to be healed, as though it were a necessary precondition to healing. Faith is ascribed to the four who brought the paralytic, and it describes faith as something that translates itself into action. Those four let nothing hinder them from bringing the paralytic to Jesus. That is what "faith" means in this story.

Finally, if healing and forgiveness of sin are so closely related, then Mark may want us to understand that all healings are illustrative of Jesus' restoration of the fellowship between God and humankind which is ruptured by our rebellion against God, with its resulting separation from him. Jesus' "authority" to heal and forgive means that, in him, the grace-filled nearness of God's kingdom makes itself felt.

STUDY QUESTION: Does Mark mean healing will *always* follow the forgiveness of sin? Can a sick person still believe God has forgiven his or her sins?

Mark 2:13–17
Jesus Offends Some Religious People
These two stories, perhaps combined and given an introduction by Mark (v. 13), are meant to illustrate Jesus' saying found in verse 17. The story is not really about Levi, who is so unimportant that Mark never mentions him again.

Tax collectors were "sinners" in the eyes of religious Jews, not only because they served the occupying Roman government but also because their business required association with ritually impure people. Tax collectors and all others who did not scrupulously follow the priestly laws of ceremonial purity were avoided by the Pharisees. Those Pharisees have often suffered from bad press in our day. They were not bad. Their problem was that they were too religious! They tried to realize the divine command that Israel become "a kingdom of priests" (Exod 19:6) and they were so single-minded about it that they put this ahead of everything else in life. Whoever didn't put those rules about being as pure as a priest above everything else, they automatically branded as sinners. That is why they could only react with disgust when Jesus wouldn't also keep those rules. He actually associated with sinners! Worse yet, he sought them out, and even ate with them. When the Pharisees challenged him, he said his task was to seek out the sinners, not associate with the virtuous.

That sounds as though there are people virtuous enough not to
need Jesus. Yet who is so well as to not need a physician if the physician
is God himself? Who is so good as to be able to tell God that he or she
does not need his forgiveness? Jesus here acted out God's forgiving attitude to sinners. God comes to them! Those who think they are not
sinners thus exclude themselves when God comes to call, and to be
separated from God is to be a sinner. Thus the very righteousness of
the self-righteous makes them sinners! That is the price the Pharisees
paid for being so religious.

STUDY QUESTION: How is it possible to be "too religious"? Doesn't
God like religious people better than sinners?

Mark 2:18–22
Now What about Fasting?

One of the major problems with Jesus was that he did not act like a
religious person should. His refusal to fast caused problems for all law-
abiding Jews. In fact, he may have even caused difficulties for later
Christians as well, since verses 18–19a seem to mean no fasting at all,
while verses 19b–20 seem to mean no fasting only while Jesus is physi-
cally present. These latter verses almost look like they were put there to
justify the later Christian practice of fasting. Yet the passage closes with
verses 21–22, which again seem to imply that if you combine the new
things Jesus brings with old religious customs (like fasting!), you
destroy both. That seems to mean the same as verses 18–19a, namely,
that the old custom of fasting is no longer appropriate, now that Jesus
has come. Perhaps verses 19b–20 are only meant to hint at the sadness
Jesus' followers will feel when he goes to the cross.

Despite such problems, the main point of these verses is clear. With
Jesus something so decisively new has happened that there is no chance
to remain unchanged by it. With his presence, only joy is appropriate, a
joy that can be compared only to a wedding time, the happiest of times
for Jews of that period. The joy will be marred by sorrow at Jesus'
absence. There is still a cross in his future. Yet, this much is certain: with
Jesus in our midst, the only appropriate reaction is joy.

STUDY QUESTION: What effect does Jesus' resurrection from the
dead have on the way we understand this story?

Mark 2:23–28
Don't Sabbath Rules Mean Anything?

The Gospels make it abundantly clear that Jesus often disregarded the multitude of Jewish laws limiting activity on the sabbath (our Saturday). This story presents one reason for, and defense of, that disregard.

The way Mark tells the story, it is plain that the reason the disciples plucked grain was not to eat it—there is no mention that they were hungry—but to clear their path through the field. Matthew and Luke later add the detail about hunger to conform to a detail about David's followers (v. 25). Jesus' defense is therefore not to enunciate a different law, namely, "human necessity supersedes sabbath legalisms," the necessity here being hunger. Rather, as verse 28 makes clear, the defense is based on who Jesus is. The comparison Jesus draws in verses 25–26 is between himself and David, not between the hunger of his followers and those of David. Jesus, the lowly carpenter of Nazareth (so he appeared to the Pharisees), here put himself on a par with King David. What David, as God's anointed, could do, Jesus may also do.

The final two verses confirm this point. They apparently circulated independently of this story as a saying of Jesus, and were put here by Mark, who used his characteristic phrase "and he said to them" to connect it. These last two verses make the point that because "man," that is, a human being, is more important than the sabbath, Jesus is free to act as he sees fit (for the parallel of "man" and "son of man," see Ps 8:4; both lines make the same point there as they do here). In this context, however, the verses point to the importance of Jesus. He, as the Son of Man, is (like God), Lord of the sabbath; for that reason he is free to act as he sees fit. The story in this Gospel shows Mark's high Christology.

STUDY QUESTION: Do we, as followers of Jesus, have the same freedom in regard to rules about Sunday?

Mark 3:1–6
Jesus, the Law-breaker, Heals

This is the fifth story that details mounting opposition to Jesus (the stories began with 2:1). It is once more the sabbath, Jesus is faced with a potential healing, and his opponents wait, ready to pounce. In cases of mortal danger, even Pharisees allowed appropriate rescue operations on the sabbath, but this was not such a situation. The man was in no mor-

tal danger; Jesus could easily wait until the sabbath was over to restore
the hand. Yet, as Jesus' question shows (v. 4), the real issue was, can it
really be unlawful to do good on the sabbath? His opponents, by their
spying presence, indicate they would have to answer "yes" to that question. Even more, as verse 6 indicates, they are seeking a reason, on the
sabbath, to kill Jesus. Thus their actions show they would also have to
answer "yes" to the question: Is it lawful to do evil on the sabbath?
Thus the law, as it is here applied by the Pharisees, forbids doing good
and allows doing evil on the sabbath! What a perversion of God's law!
By this confrontation, and by his act of healing, Jesus makes clear that
the Pharisaic interpretation of the law has negated God's will as it is
expressed in that very law. That is the whole problem with the ultra-
religious Pharisees. In the name of religion, they pervert the goal of
religion.

In this incident, Jesus offered the Pharisees a chance to see the box
into which they had placed themselves, using the law to defeat the
intention of the law. They did not take it. Faced with the choice
between their interpretation of the law and Jesus, they chose their
interpretation, and sought to put mercy to death.

STUDY QUESTION: Do all religious rules eventually eliminate a
place for mercy? Can rules and mercy ever exist side by side?

II. Jesus' Ministry in Galilee, and His Rejection by His Own

Mark 3:7 to 6:6

Mark 3:7–35
TRUE FOLLOWERS OF JESUS

Mark 3:7–12
The Crowds Respond

Style and language make it clear that Mark is largely responsible for the present shape of these verses. With this summary, a new segment begins which reaches to 6:6, where, like the previous segment (1:1 to 3:6) it ends with rejection of Jesus. Placed directly after 3:6, these verses contrast the reaction of official Judaism (3:6) with that of the common people from a wide area.

It is clear that Mark understands the popularity of Jesus to be due to his reputation as a wonder worker. The crowds were attracted by "all he was doing," they threaten to crush him in reaction to the healing he continued to do, and he faced again the problem of unclean spirits identifying him (cf. 1:34). Verses 11–12 do constitute a problem. Jesus' unwillingness to let unclean spirits "make him known" can have nothing to do with any notion Mark may have had that Jesus didn't want to be known as a miracle worker. Verse 10 makes that impossible, since in fact it reports Jesus continued to heal. Nor can it be due to any supposed desire by Jesus to avoid publicity. He made no effort here to escape the crowds, only to keep them from crushing him. Perhaps the problem is that it is not appropriate for demons to announce who Jesus really is, namely not just another wonder worker, but God's Son. Or perhaps the time had not yet come when people would understand correctly what "Son of God" truly meant.

STUDY QUESTION: Why would it be inappropriate for unclean spirits to make Jesus known as Son of God? Can a correct identification of Jesus ever be out of place?

Mark 3:13–19
Twelve Are Appointed
The order of stories here in Mark implies that Jesus' response to his rejection by religious authorities and his popularity as wonder worker was the creation of an inner circle of twelve, who were to accompany him and share his ministry (vv. 14–15; cf. 1:39). The location (Greek: "the mountain") has theological rather than geographic significance. Just as God on Mt. Sinai made the twelve tribes of Israel his people, so now Jesus on a mountain constituted, through these twelve, the new Israel. That the number, not the men themselves, is important is shown by the fact that while the number twelve is constant throughout the New Testament, the names of the men vary among the Gospels (cf. Matt 10:2–3 and Mark 3:16–19 with Luke 6:14–16 and Acts 1:13; John has names mentioned in no other Gospel). Similarly, the first three men in the list are given new names, not because of their personal character (for Peter, see 8:33; 14:66–72; for James and John, see 10:35–37), but because they will now play a significant role in God's plan of salvation (cf. Abram/Abraham, Gen 17:5; Jacob/Israel, Gen 32:29 [in some translations 32:28]; 35:10, for similar instances of a change of name). Peter's importance in all such lists may rest on remembrance that he was the first of the twelve disciples to see the Risen Jesus (1 Cor 15:5). Perhaps for that reason, his calling as disciple is also recorded first (1:16; cf. Luke 5:1–11). Finally, the fact that many of those named here played no role recorded in the New Testament in the subsequent life of the church, and the fact that the betrayer is included in their number, points to the fact that the choice of the Twelve did originate with Jesus, rather than with the later church as an attempt to justify those who led it after Jesus' ascension.

STUDY QUESTION: If the number twelve implies that the followers of Jesus constitute the new Israel, what does that say about the ongoing relationship between the church and the people of Israel?

Mark 3:20–30
Jesus Is a Source of Confusion

Mark describes again the contrast between the masses who respond to Jesus and the small groups who reject him. The irony is that precisely those who ought to have recognized his importance, his family and the religious authorities, not only failed to recognize it, but instead openly rejected it. If, as seems likely, Mark has put these traditions into their present order, he has pronounced a hard judgment on Jesus' family, namely that their attitude to Jesus is comparable to that of the scribes. This is evidence that members of Jesus' family were not among those who followed him prior to his resurrection (cf. John 7:5).

Although Mark begins with the relatives, the objections of the scribes are detailed first. The discussion of the family is then completed in verses 31–35, thus bracketing the material about the scribes with material about Jesus' relatives. Jesus' response to the accusation that he controls devils through devilish power is given in "parables." This is the first occurrence of that word in Mark. He will given extended examples of parables in chapter 4. Parables require some commonality between speaker and listener to be understood. To those who have no sympathy for Jesus or his claims, Jesus' parables make little sense (cf. 4:10–12). Characteristically, these parables do not illustrate timeless moral truths. Rather, they explain the kind of conflict in which Jesus is engaged. We may thus expect subsequent parables to pursue the same goal of giving perspective on Jesus and his mission.

The point of verses 23–26 is not entirely clear. Perhaps they are meant to say that if Jesus operates as the prince of devils in casting other devils out, Satan is shown to be divided and powerless, something patently false. Or perhaps they are meant to say that whatever you think of the source of Jesus' power, what he does shows that Satan no longer has the upper hand. The climax in verse 27 is clear enough, however. Jesus is the stronger one, who controls devils not as their prince but as their conqueror (cf. Isa 49:24–25, where the stronger one is God himself).

Verse 30 is the key to the meaning of verses 28–29. The one limitation on God's limitless forgiveness of sin is to insist that Jesus' authority is from Satan rather than from God, as the scribes had just done. This means that if Jesus incarnates God's forgiveness of sin (cf. 2:17; 10:45), then the unforgivable sin is to reject that forgiveness by rejecting Jesus. To refuse Jesus is to refuse God's forgiveness that Jesus embodies. For such a refusal of the source of forgiveness, no further forgiveness remains. The key, therefore, is Jesus. To accept him is to be accepted (forgiven) by God. To reject him is to reject God (and his forgiveness) as well.

STUDY QUESTION: Is there any modern equivalent to the claim that it is Satan, not God's Spirit, that is at work in Jesus? Is the emphasis here more on a sin that can't be forgiven (v. 29), or on the overwhelming grace that forgives "all people's sins" (v. 28)?

Mark 3:31–35
Who Belongs to Jesus' True Family?

These verses constitute the conclusion of the passage that begins with 3:20, and by so bracketing the attitude of the scribes to Jesus, they show that Jesus' own family joined in such rejection at this point in his ministry.

The form of this story indicates that it circulated in the tradition as an independent unit before Mark put it in his Gospel. Its point is not so much the exclusion of his relatives as the wider inclusion into his family of all who willingly follow him. Blood descent is no longer enough to qualify one for inclusion in God's redemptive family. Perhaps that is a hint that inclusion among those favored by God no longer depends on racial descent, as it did in Judaism. The placing of verse 35 after verse 34 makes it clear that they do God's will who hear Jesus. That kind of claim was bound to offend pious people who found little in Jesus to fit their expectation of the final divine redeemer of Israel.

It is that offense inherent in Jesus that Mark has emphasized by placing this originally independent story into this context. By placing accounts of Jesus' relatives before and after the scribes' negative judgment on Jesus, Mark gives the attitude of Jesus' family a similarly negative interpretation. Jesus is so unexpected, so strange in his own world, that even those in a position to know the most about him (his family) and his religious claims (scribes) are offended by him.

STUDY QUESTION: Are there elements in Jesus' actions and words that continue to be offensive to those who think they know him best?

Mark 4:1–34
AND HE TAUGHT THEM MANY THINGS IN PARABLES

Mark 4:1–20
Parables and the Meaning of Jesus

A preliminary consideration may help to dispel some of the problems regularly encountered in attempts to understand these verses. We are dealing here with parables, not allegories. In an allegory, something already known is put into a kind of code, and every element in the allegory stands for something. Revelation 17:1–6 is a good example of an allegory. It is really a description of ancient Rome, but it is disguised as the description of a woman. An allegory therefore tells familiar things in a strange, coded form. A parable, on the other hand, is a story about familiar things, designed to get the listener to perceive something new. The point of the story as a whole, not its individual details, is intended to apply to the current situation and illumine it. The parable is therefore a story about familiar things that seeks to open a new perspective on the situation of the listener.

Mark's language makes it evident that he has assembled these stories and sayings contained in 4:1–34 from his traditions. His introduction (vv. 1–2) makes it clear that though the parable of the sower is only one example of the parables Jesus spoke (v. 2), it is clearly the key example (v. 13). Misunderstanding here means misunderstanding of all Jesus' parables. Mark framed the parable with two commands to pay attention (v. 9, and the "listen" of v. 3), provided from his tradition two explanations for it (vv. 11–12, 13–20), and then illustrated its point with sayings (vv. 21–25) and further parables (vv. 26–32). All that shows how important Mark took this first parable to be.

The agricultural procedure described in the parable is normal enough. Palestinian farmers plowed only after sowing, so seed on paths in the field and among thorns would be plowed under with the rest, and one cannot always tell where the soil lies thin over the limestone shelves common in Galilee (the "rocky ground" of v. 5). The harvest, however, seems to be quite beyond normal expectations. What began as a normal, even somewhat unpromising event results in something astounding. Who could have known, observing the farmer in his ordinary activity, that this time the results would surpass all expectations? The parable contains an implicit warning. To think that this sower was an ordinary sower was proved wrong by the harvest. Don't make the same mistake with Jesus. To account for Jesus in ordinary terms will be proved wrong by God's coming kingdom.

Mark reinforces that point in verses 11–12. The parable points to the mystery of the kingdom of God. Note well that it does not give us further information about the kingdom. Matthew and Luke interpreted Mark that way (see Matt 13:11; Luke 8:10), but Mark does not say the parable provides us with information about myster*ies*. Rather the parable points to one mystery, without which there is only confusion and inability to repent (v. 12).

What is that mystery, given to those who "formed his company"? It is the link of Jesus to the kingdom. It is to see in Jesus one in whose words and acts God himself is at work, and then to follow him. Without such a perspective on Jesus, one will miss the importance of the events surrounding him, as scribes and family have just demonstrated (3:20–35). Those who accept Jesus as potent herald of God's coming kingdom ("you" in v. 11, i.e., those who follow Jesus, v. 10) see in Jesus the key to those events. Those who do not, find only confusion worse confounded (v. 12). Explanation and parable point to the same thing: to Jesus' actions are attached the astonishing results of God's kingdom. Failure to recognize the importance of Jesus means failure to understand anything about him at all.

That is the situation faced by those who hear and see Jesus. If they accept him as God's sign, they are able to understand what he does and says. If they reject him, they find what he says confusing, and what he does objectionable (again see 3:20–35; it is not accidental that Mark has chapter 4 follow that passage!).

Mark appends a second explanation (vv. 13–20), which by vocabulary and content shows it originated as an early commentary by the Christian community on this parable. The allegory is not consistent. In verse 14, the seed is the word, in verse 17 it is the people who receive it. Even here, therefore, the intention is not the allegory as such, but the attempt to make the parable meaningful for a time when the problems outlined in verses 15–19 had become acute. Marks uses this explanation to reinforce his point once more: those who see and hear everything Jesus does and says, yet refuse to accept Jesus for what he is, soon become the "outsiders" described in verse 11. Only those who accept Jesus (the "good soil" of v. 20) profit from what he says.

In this chapter, then, Mark gives the reason why some who had seen what Jesus did and said—family and scribes—still misunderstood him so completely: they had not recognized his importance for God's kingdom. One faces in Jesus the reality of God's rule. That is the situation the parables seek to illumine.

STUDY QUESTION: Can reports of what Jesus said and did still cause confusion in our day? Can modern parables be found to help illumine our situation vis-à-vis Jesus?

Mark 4:21–25
Sayings on the Parable's Point
Mark continues here to assemble material from his traditions. That is shown by the repeated Markan formula "He also said to them (vv. 21, 24), the phrase about listening (v. 23; cf. v. 9), and the fact that though both Matthew and Luke repeat all these sayings, they put them into other contexts, perhaps because they knew they were originally unattached to one another. We can only guess what they meant originally, but Mark makes his intention clear. Like the parable, they warn the listener not to ignore the kingdom's first rays of dawn in Jesus, however unpromising this may seem. The strange Greek of verse 21 shows that. Literally, it reads: "Does a lamp come, in order to be put under a bushel or under a bed?" But what "lamp" is thus able to "come"? Clearly, it refers to Jesus. Though the light of the kingdom he brings now seems dim or even hidden, it will yet, in its time, become manifest (v. 22). For that reason, special attention must be given to Jesus (v. 23), since one's final reward depends on how one reacts now to Jesus (v. 24; cf. 8:38). Not to recognize in Jesus the potent herald of God's kingdom means Jesus' future words and deeds will only increase confusion about him (v. 25). We have had an example of that already in scribes and family (3:20–35).

STUDY QUESTION: Do these verses suggest parables are told in order to confuse people, or to increase their understanding of their own situation? How do the parables accomplish that purpose?

Mark 4:26–34
Two More Parables, and Some Closing Remarks
Mark returns in these verses to two final parables about seeds, which, along with the parable of the sower, he means us to understand as

examples of the many other parables Jesus told, but which Mark does not report (v. 33a). God's kingdom is so new, and its coming so unexpected, that it cannot be described directly, but only in word-pictures. Only in that way can we gain some understanding of it (v. 33b). Yet we must remember that these are parables. They are meant to illumine the listener's situation. People in the early church may have seen similarities here to their own situation. Verses 27–28 may have been seen as encouragement in the time of waiting between Jesus' resurrection and his return. Despite God's seeming inactivity, the kingdom will come. Verse 32 may have been seen as a reference to the universality of the church's mission. All peoples find "shelter" in the church. But such allegorical elements are foreign to the true parable.

All three parables in Mark make clear, each in a different way, that if one judges by present appearances—the ordinary activity of the sower, the routine activity of the farmer while his crop grows, the tiny size of the mustard seed—the results will prove one wrong. From the ordinary activity of the sower, a great harvest results. From the ordinary routine of the farmer's life, the harvest surely results. From the tiny mustard seed, a great bush results. But unless one is told that at the beginning, who would anticipate such tremendous results? Such telling is the point of these parables.

The parables thus shed light on the situation of one who observes Jesus' activities. In facing Jesus, one does not confront an ordinary person, and thus one is not in an ordinary situation, however much it may appear to be so. Normal explanations (e.g., vv. 3:21–22) are false when applied to Jesus. Those who persist in them will be proved wrong.

Verses 33–34 summarize Mark's view of the purpose of the parables. Only by them can people be shaken loose from an ordinary way of viewing events, specifically the words and deeds of Jesus, which are a prelude to the coming of God's kingdom in power. That is why Jesus told parables, in order to provide his listeners a new perspective from which to view their situation vis-à-vis Jesus. Only by recognizing Jesus as the potent herald of God's coming kingdom will one understand one's present situation correctly. Only those who are committed to Jesus, that is, his disciples, can understand that!

STUDY QUESTION: Can parables still say something to us who recognize Jesus' relation to God's kingdom, or can we safely ignore their call to see our situation in extraordinary terms?

Mark 4:35 to 5:43
HE DID WONDROUS THINGS

Mark 4:35–41
Master of Wind and Sea

With this account Mark begins a series of miracle stories that may already have been collected before he received them. Although the reference to Jesus being in the boat ("just as he was, in the boat," v. 36) connects the story to 4:1, a detail forgotten in the rest of chapter 4 (see v. 10), the reference to "other boats with him" suggests an earlier context, since we hear no more about these "other boats."

Although this narrative is told in the common form of Hellenistic miracle stories, it has dimensions that point beyond an ordinary miracle account. Words used in v. 39 ("rebuke," "be quiet!") are identical to words used in 1:25 in the story of the expulsion of a devil. This hint of devilish power behind the storm points the reader to elements of the Old Testament story of creation. In common with other ancient Near-Eastern peoples, the Israelites knew a story that pictured creation as a battle between God and a sea-monster. Creation resulted when God subdued this monster (see Isa 51:9–10; Pss 74:13–14; 89:10; Job 9:8, 13; "Rahab" and "Leviathan" are names for it), and forced the chaotic waters to remain within their allotted bounds (see Pss 33:7; 104:9; Job 38:8–11). Behind our miracle story there lurks therefore the awareness that only God has the power to order and sustain his creation. The disciples' final question shows that, despite their lack of confidence in Jesus' care for them (v. 39a; their lack of faith, v. 40), they recognize this point, namely that Jesus here does what the Old Testament knew God alone could do (see Pss 89:9; 107:28–29). God's power is now a work in Jesus.

STUDY QUESTION: Is it still important for us that Jesus acted with God's power, or is this just an ancient and irrelevant, if interesting, story?

Mark 5:1–20
Jesus Heals a Demoniac in Gerasa

The present shape of this story attests to the many changes it underwent as it was told and retold in the primitive church. Some of the elements in the story do not always fit well into the present shape of the narrative and there is considerable repetition of detail. The attempts to bind and control the demoniac are told twice over (vv. 3, 4), two meetings with Jesus are described (vv. 2, 6), and we are told twice how people found out about these events (vv. 14, 16). In addition, the response to Jesus' command to the demon to leave (v. 7) comes before the command is mentioned (v. 8), it is not clear whether there is only one demon (v. 8) or there are many (vv. 9, 10, 12), and the detail about the herd of pigs, though interesting, is really not essential to the story (vv. 11–13). All of this, together with the rambling nature of the narrative, may indicate that originally there were two versions of this incident in circulation, much as there are in Mark two versions of Jesus' wondrous feeding of the multitudes, and that at some point before Mark received the tradition, the two stories about the Gerasene demoniac had been combined.

Yet, however this narrative got its present form, one point emerges with clarity, namely the great, even incontestable power Jesus had at his command. Jesus was confronted with a demoniac so powerful that no one had yet found a way to control it (vv. 3–5). The unclean spirits are so powerful that they are able to resist Jesus' initial command to go out from the man (v. 8), yet they are reduced to begging to be allowed to inhabit pigs, where once they had inhabited a man (vv. 10–13). The demons know Jesus' identity (v. 7) and use a common formula designed to gain control over another person ("swear by God" or "I adjure you by God," v. 7), both indications for Jesus' contemporaries that the one uttering them had control over his opponent. Yet despite that, Jesus forced the demons to name themselves, and then, unaffected by the demons' initial advantage, overcame them. Even the inordinately large number of pigs in the heard (two thousand, v. 13) attests to the enormous number of devils in combat with Jesus. The inference seems to be that only such a large number of pigs would be sufficient for all of them to find a new dwelling place.

This story makes another point that we have already found in Mark, namely that miracles as such do not lead to faith in Jesus (e.g., 3:22). In this story, the reaction to the curing of the demoniac is not faith in Jesus, but fear (v. 15) and the desire to be rid of him (v. 17). There is no hint that those who told and retold this story connected the desire that Jesus leave to the economic loss represented by the destruction of so many swine. Rather, this reaction is clearly designed to show that seeing miracles of Jesus, even being convinced he could do them, as these people clearly were, is not enough to awaken faith in Jesus. Such faith, Mark knew, is possible only after cross and resurrection. In light of that final fate of Jesus, these stories can be understood (that is why Mark put them into the longer narrative of his Gospel that climaxes in cross and resurrection). Prior to Jesus' final fate, events like this only awakened fear and mistrust.

The story ends with another surprise. Instead of being told to keep silent about this event (cf. 1:34, 44; 3:12), the demoniac is told to spread news of it throughout the Decapolis (a region of ten cities under direct Roman rule to the east and south of the Sea of Galilee). Further, instead of being asked to give up family and friends for Jesus (cf. 10:29), this man is forbidden to accompany Jesus, and is told to return to his own people (v. 19). There is apparently no set formula for discipleship. In each instance, the circumstances determine what is appropriate for one who wants to obey Jesus.

This story was told, therefore, to make theological points, not to satisfy our historical curiosity. Even the location is wrong for that, since Gerasa is located thirty miles from the shore of the Sea of Galilee. The story is not meant to make us wonder about the pigs, or try to determine what may have excited them to their destruction, or to wonder how so many demons could inhabit one human being.

Rather, this story, like the one before it, is intended to show the incontestable power by which Jesus spoke and acted during his earthly career. It was to make that point that the many details were included in the story, and it is that point that still stands out for those who read it with eyes to see what Mark wants to tell us. In Jesus, God's own power is at work among his people, Jew and, here, Gentile alike. Therefore his words about God's coming kingdom *must* be taken with utmost seriousness.

STUDY QUESTION: Is there any evidence in our day that Jesus continues to use such power for his people?

Mark 5:21–43
Jesus Is Master over Sickness and Death

This is the third account that demonstrates the extent of Jesus' lordship: over nature (4:35–41), over demons (5:1–20), and over sickness and death (5:21–43). A careful study of the style of these two stories reveals differences significant enough to allow us to conclude that they were composed independently of one another, probably by two different people. Various similarities of detail probably account for their association with one another. Both tell about females helped, both concern situations of a desperate nature, both use the number twelve (the duration of the woman's illness, the little girl's age), and, perhaps most important, both stories tell of faith in connection with healings. We cannot rule out the possibility that the two stories were already associated when Mark received them, but Mark's fondness for inserting one story into another (e.g., 11:12–28; see also 3:20–35; 6:7–32) makes it likely that he is responsible for their present combination. Normally, when two accounts are thus "sandwiched," one story comments in some way on the other. In this instance, perhaps the story of the healing of the woman gains in seriousness by its association with a story in which someone is raised from the dead.

The story of the woman contains a description of the incurable nature of her affliction (vv. 25–26). That makes her cure all the more remarkable, and such emphasis on the seriousness of the malady is common in secular miracle stories of this time. Nor is the flow of healing power from someone's clothing unique to this account (cf. Acts 19:11–12). What is important here is that the desire to touch Jesus' garments in full expectation of healing (v. 28) is identified as faith (v. 34). Indeed, it is that faith, as Jesus remarks, rather than the touch alone that has restored her to health (v. 34). That Jesus could perceive her touch in the midst of a jostling crowd (vv. 30–31) shows that her intention in touching him made her touch unique. Faith seems to mean here, as it did in 2:4–5, letting nothing hinder one from seeking out Jesus' help.

Perhaps most remarkable of all, however, the word used for "healing" in this story is not the usual one. The word used here had the basic meaning "to save." In verse 28, the woman says to herself: "If I can touch him, I will be saved," and verse 34 can similarly be translated: "your faith has saved you." That meaning is reinforced in verse 34 by Jesus' use of the word "peace," which has clear overtones, in its Old Testament use, of salvation as wholeness and restoration. Further, when Jesus addresses the woman as "daughter," he is including her in the messianic family of those who find in Jesus their way to God (cf. 3:33–35). There is therefore reflected in this story of a hemorrhage stanched the clear indication that faithful expectancy of God's help in Jesus brings one into the orbit of salvation.

Reflections of a deeper meaning are also present in the story of the little girl raised from the dead. Her death has put her beyond Jesus' power to help; so at least the messengers think. Jesus' response reveals the deeper dimension in this story. The phrase "Do not be afraid" is a regular formula used when God appears (it is a "theophanic formula": see Gen 15:1; 21:17; 26:24; 46:3; Judg 6:23; Dan 10:12, 19). The verse is thus more than encouragement to a saddened father. It provides a clue as to who this Jesus really is.

That the little girl is dead is shown by the presence of mourners, customarily hired to lament the deceased. Jesus' words about sleep, therefore, in verse 39 do not constitute a medical diagnosis. They are the confident assertion by one who acts with God's power that death itself cannot thwart him. In God's presence, death is no more threatening than sleep. That is demonstrated when, with a touch and a word, the sovereign Jesus restores life to the dead girl.

Both stories are told in a form familiar to Mark's Hellenistic contemporaries. The desperate nature of the malady, the effectiveness of the cure, the inclusion of a phrase in a foreign tongue (v. 41), all belong to the usual miracle story common in Mark's world. The unique point of our narratives is thus not to be sought in such details. Rather, it is those elements in the story which point beyond an interest in a miracle as such that reveal to us the point Mark is seeking to make by using these stories.

Such elements in these stories tell of one who worked by God's own power, and who, by awakening faith in those who heard of him and then sought him out (vv. 22, 27), bestowed on them the gifts of God's own salvation, namely wholeness and life. Yet those elements tell us even more. Who would not see Jesus' own resurrection prefigured, however dimly, in the command to the little girl to arise (the same word from which, in Greek, the word "resurrection" is derived)? The stories thus contain hints, for those with eyes to see them, about who this Jesus is. He can pronounce God's salvation (v. 34), he can use the theophanic formula that announces the divine presence (v. 36), he can wield God's sovereign power over death itself, as he will one day become the one by whom death is conquered for all humanity.

The hints remain veiled, however, for us who read the stories as for those who saw and heard Jesus. It was still all too possible to see in Jesus simply a worker of wonders, in total disregard of his own announced connection to God's coming kingdom. Until cross and empty tomb, that possibility of misconstruing Jesus remains. Indeed, it predominates even among the disciples who in the end forsake him and flee. For that reason, Mark pictures Jesus as insisting that information about his wondrous deeds not be spread abroad (v. 43a). That insistence reflects a theological, not a historical point. Too many people knew the little girl had died to keep her resurrection a secret for long. Rather, such insistence points to Mark's awareness that only in light of cross and resurrection can Jesus finally and fully be understood.

STUDY QUESTION: What other hints can you find in Mark's Gospel that point to his belief that only the cross and resurrection reveal the true meaning of Jesus?

Mark 6:1–6
THE CROSS FORESHADOWED:
JESUS IS REJECTED BY HIS OWN

In stark contrast to the triumphant lordship displayed in the preceding accounts (4:35 to 5:43), Jesus is here ridiculed and rejected in his own hometown. The place Mark put this story, and the part he played in shaping it (shown by Markan vocabulary and style) show that Mark intended that contrast.

Contrary to normal Jewish practice, Jesus is identified by his mother rather than his father, although some ancient manuscripts read "son of the carpenter and Mary." Yet Mark nowhere in his Gospel mentions Joseph, perhaps because he had long since died, perhaps because Jesus' true father is God. Later church disputes over whether Mary remained a virgin after Jesus' birth raised problems about how "brothers" and "sisters" are to be understood here. In Mark's context, their mention is merely intended to show that the villagers perceived Jesus as no different from any of them. His family was known, including his brothers and sisters. The problem of Mary's virginity is simply absent from Mark's Gospel.

The point of this passage is not the nature of Jesus' family relationships, however. It is his rejection by his own people. Incredible though it be, it is surely intended by Mark to foreshadow the ultimate fate

Jesus will experience at the hands of "his own people," that is, disciples, Jews, indeed, all humanity.

Verse 5 is not meant to say that miracles are possible only where faith is present; some are accomplished despite faith's absence (e.g., 4:35–41), but lack of faith will prevent those needing help from coming to Jesus in the first place. Yet verse 5 does show that, for Mark, the meaning of Jesus' miracles is not grasped except through faith in him. Awe at Jesus the wonder worker is an inadequate response for Mark. Only faith-filled following will do.

STUDY QUESTION: Can you find other places in this Gospel where Mark hints at Jesus' final rejection by "his own?" If we understand "his own" to be those who ought to know him best, is such rejection still a problem?

III. JESUS BEGINS HIS FINAL JOURNEY— MISSION AND MIRACLES

Mark 6:7 to 8:21

Mark 6:7–29
JOURNEY FOR MISSION AND THE DEATH OF JESUS

Mark 6:7–13
The Twelve Sent Out on Mission
With this story, shaped again in large part by Mark as style and vocabulary show, a new segment of the Gospel begins which will reach to 8:21, and will end, as did the first two segments (3:1–6; 6:1–6) with Jesus being misunderstood. Similarly, as the second segment began with stories that implied Jesus responded to rejection with the choice of the Twelve to "be with him" and to engage in missionary activity (3:7–19), so this third segment begins with an account of Jesus sending out the Twelve on a mission to preach and heal, on the heels of Jesus' rejection in his hometown. Since in each case the segment begins with a story displaying signs of Markan literary activity, it is clear that this repeated pattern reflects Mark's own design. Perhaps it was meant as encouragement for later missionaries who similarly suffered rejection.

The instructions to the Twelve (vv. 8–9) probably indicate they are to rely on God for all their needs. Missionaries who provide against every anticipated adversity (money, extra clothing, and the like) are scarcely believable when they announce the nearness of God's kingdom. The authority to cast out devils (or unclean spirits—they are the same) shows that God's victory over Satan, already visible in Jesus, continues in the activity of those Jesus sends out.

The missionaries are not to move from house to house seeking better accommodations (v. 10), but when they do meet refusal, they are to symbolize God's judgment against such an act by separating themselves completely from that region, even to ridding themselves of the dust that clings to their sandals.

STUDY QUESTION: Are there any activities of modern missionaries, here or abroad, that render unbelievable their message of God's forgiving love in Christ?

Mark 6:14–29
The Cross Foreshadowed: Herod and John the Baptist

This story, set between the sending out of the Twelve (6:7) and their return (6:30), is a rather fanciful account of the fate of John the Baptist, told long after the fact (see 1:14: John's arrest came before Jesus began his public ministry, according to Mark), with the apparent purpose of displaying John as the forerunner of Jesus not only by what he said, but also by the fate he suffered. We have here intimations that when Jesus left his hometown, he began a journey that would end with the cross.

The attempts to explain who Jesus was (vv. 14–16) show that the impression he made was as a wonder worker. They also show the variety of interpretations possible to account for such a person. While Elijah was expected to return before the last days (see Mal 3:23 [in some translations 4:5]; Sir 48:10–11), he was also famous for his miracles (see 1 Kgs 17:10–24). Herod's recollection of John's death (v. 16) gives Mark the narrative opportunity to include a tale about that event.

The account of John's beheading, written prior to Mark's Gospel as its language and style show, is characterized more by its lurid detail than by its historical reliability. Herod did not marry Philips's wife; Herodias had been the wife of Herod's half-brother, also named Herod (v. 17). Philip later married Herodias's daughter, Salome. Herod was a tetrarch, not a king, who ruled at the pleasure of Rome; he could not give up an acre without Rome's permission (vv. 22–23). Nor did a king's daughter provide entertainment as a dancing girl at the kind of party Herod gave (vv. 21–22).

The enmity between Herodias and John the Baptist is confirmed by another contemporary writer, however. Herod did in fact divorce his wife, a Nabatean princess, to marry Herodias, and John denounced that action. The father of the Nabatean princess later avenged the dishonor of her divorce by crushing Herod's army, and would have overrun his territory had not Rome intervened to restore the balance of power.

The account in Mark thus has a historical basis, but it has been filled out with a variety of details. While some of those details seem little more than gossip, others have a more serious intent. Some influence on the story seems to have come from the accounts in 1 Kings 18–19 (see esp. 19:1–2) of the hostility between Jezebel and Elijah. Since John will later be identified as the returned Elijah (Mark 9:13), such influence accords with Mark's own understanding of John. Perhaps most important of all, this story gives us a hint of Jesus' own fate. He, like John, will be put to death with the conspiratorial connivance of prominent people. It was probably for that reason that Mark found a place for this strange story, the only one in his Gospel where Jesus plays no part at all; he isn't even mentioned. John, the promised Elijah who was to herald the last times, is forerunner to Jesus in his manner of death as well as in his message.

STUDY QUESTION: Are there modern attempts to come to terms with Jesus, attempts similar to those we find in verses 14–16? Why are there so many different attempts to explain him?

Mark 6:30 to 8:21
MIGHTY ACTS AND MANY ARGUMENTS

Mark 6:30–44
Jesus Feeds Many with Little
These verses present quite clearly a story cast in the traditional miracle form (vv. 35–44), with an introduction provided by Mark to fit it into its present context (vv. 30–33). Many of the details are thus dictated by the form of the story and are not expressions of any theological intention (e.g., the disciples distribute the food, v. 41, because the crowd is so great, not as an intentional prefigurement of the later services of the diaconate).

The story of the return of the disciples from their mission (cf. 6:7) bears enough signs of Markan composition to allow us to conclude that he is responsible for its present form, even if there is some tradition underlying it. We learn nothing of the missionary journey, save that it was completed in accordance with instructions (cf. v. 30, with vv. 7, 12–13).

The phrase that begins verse 34 (Greek: "And when he came out, he saw...") is more appropriate for coming out of a house (see the same verb used in 1:29, 35; 2:13), indicating an earlier context for this story in Mark's source. As verse 36 shows, a totally deserted area is not envisioned by the story. There are farms and villages where food would be available. The problem, similarly, in verse 37 is lack of enough money to buy sufficient bread, not the unavailability of any bread in that location. When a deserted area is envisioned, as in 8:1–10, such details are changed (see esp. 8:3–4). Mark is therefore the one responsible, through his introduction, for locating this story in a place where Jesus and the Twelve would be free from crowds (v. 31). Nevertheless, Jesus cannot escape those crowds, again a typical Markan motif (cf. 2:13; 3:7).

Because the story of the feeding (vv. 35–44) is cast in miracle form, there is no foundation for the notion that it was originally simply intended to tell of the way Jesus' loving spirit induced a great crowd of people to share food with one another. The emphasis on the enormity of the problem (vv. 35–38: no food, insufficient money, insignificant resources in only five loaves and two fish) and the details provided to prove a miracle had occurred (vv. 42–44: all had enough, with a large amount left over; the great number fed) make it clear that, from its inception, this story was meant to tell of a wondrous deed of Jesus.

The story is, however, evocative of other events told in the Bible: the children of Israel fed with manna in the wilderness (Exod 16), Elijah feeding a hundred men with few provisions (2 Kgs 4:42–44; John 6:9 makes such an evocation explicit with mention of "barley loaves"), even the institution of the Eucharist (cf. v. 41 with 14:22). Yet later references to this story by Mark (6:52; 8:17–21) make it clear that he saw this story as an example of the inability of the disciples to understand Jesus, even after their experience of an act as spectacular as this. If the reference to the Eucharist was intentional in the pre-Markan tradition of this story, Mark may deliberately have tried to disassociate the two, since for Mark, the Eucharist is based not on Jesus' miraculous deeds, but rather on his sacrifice on the cross, as his account of the words of institution makes clear (cf. 14:22–25 with the context of 14:17–31, and indeed, the passion account as a whole). Perhaps Mark wants to emphasize that Jesus cannot be understood apart from the cross, even when the disciples share in an event that so clearly points to who Jesus is: like Elijah, he can feed multitudes from little. Indeed, like God himself, Jesus can provide in the wilderness.

STUDY QUESTION: Why do you think Mark wanted to emphasize so strongly that one cannot rightly understand Jesus until one knows he was crucified and risen?

Mark 6:45–52
Jesus Walks a Stormy Sea

By any measure, this is a perplexing story. A number of details within the narrative stand in tension to one another, and to the larger context in which the narrative is found. There are two reasons given for dismissing the disciples: to permit Jesus to send away the crowd (v. 45) and to give Jesus solitude to pray (v. 46). Although Jesus sees the boat in difficulty "when evening came" (v. 47), he does not go to them until the "fourth watch," that is, between 3:00 and 6:00 A.M. And when he does reach them, it is not to help after all; he "was going to pass them by" (v. 48). Jesus compels the disciples to set sail for a destination (Bethsaida, v. 45) which they do not reach (see v. 53); the dismissal and the disciples' trip "far out on the lake" take place before evening came, yet in verse 35 it was already "very late."

Such narrative problems make it clear that Mark put this story here, and adapted it to this context (vv. 45 and 52 almost surely are due to Mark), for reasons other than a desire to give us accurate historical or geographical information. If, as seems very likely, Mark appended verse 52, that provides the reason why he included the story here. The reason is the disciples are still totally unable to understand Jesus, even after he fed a multitude with little and walked on the sea (in the Old Testament, this latter act is attributed to God, Job 9:8; Ps 77:19; Isa 43:16; Greco-Roman authors also regularly attributed it to various gods and heroes). Had they perceived the meaning of Jesus (i.e., his divine status and mission) from the feeding, Mark implies, their terror (v. 50) and confusion (v. 51) would not have occurred. Yet their inability to understand seems beyond their control. The language of verse 52 clearly implies that.

What the story may originally have meant—a manifestation of Jesus' true status, comparable to the transfiguration; a stormy sea calmed, comparable to the story in 4:35–41—can only be speculated. What it means here in Mark's context seems clear enough: seeing the miraculous power Jesus manifested during his earthly career is not enough to enable one to understand him. In Mark's view, such understanding awaits a final event: the cross.

STUDY QUESTION: What value does a story like this still have for us, who know about the cross, and can thus, in part at least, understand Jesus?

Mark 6:53–56
People Flock to Jesus

Although language and style indicate that Mark had a hand in shaping these verses, the reference to the landing at Gennesaret, contrary to Jesus' instruction in verse 45, and to the fringes on Jesus' garment (cf. Num 15:38–39—Mark nowhere else mentions such details) point to underlying tradition. Attempts to account for the change in destination (blown off course by the wind; Jesus changed instructions after getting into the boat) remain pure speculation, and add nothing to our understanding of Mark.

The point made in these verses is common enough in Mark. Crowds press in on Jesus (cf. 3:7–8, 20; 4:1; 5:21), frequently to take advantage of his healing powers (1:32; 3:10). Verse 56 indicates that the woman healed by touching Jesus' garment (5:27–28) was not unique. In fact, these summaries seem intent on saying that the narratives of healing Mark recites are simply examples of an activity repeated many times over.

The contrast between the attitude of these people toward Jesus and that of the religious leaders in the following story is striking, and may account for this summary being placed here. Common people flock to Jesus to be healed (the verb can also mean "to be saved"). Pharisees and scribes pick at any point they can find to discredit and reject him (7:1–2).

STUDY QUESTION: How do you account for the difference between these people, who seek Jesus out because of his miracles, and the disciples, who were "dumbfounded" by a miracle (v. 51)?

Mark 7:1–13
Good Rules and Bad Results

There are indications that Mark assembled this passage from individual traditions he knew from his sources. Verses 3–4 interrupt the sentence in which they occur (vv. 2–5; the English has smoothed the rougher Greek text), and seem to be an explanation Mark inserted. The phrase introducing verse 9 is often used by Mark when he connects independent traditions. The repetition of the point in verses 8 and 9 may be the reason Mark felt it appropriate to connect them.

This is the last incident Mark reports of Jesus' Galilean ministry. Perhaps he chose these passages to show the kind of mounting opposition Jesus faced in Galilee because of the activity of religious leaders "from Jerusalem" (v. 1). It was that opposition that brought his Galilean ministry to an end, as it would be instrumental in bringing his career to an end, on a cross in Jerusalem.

At issue is not hygienic, but ritual purity (cf. Lev 22:1–16). While verses 3–4 describe acts not universally observed by Palestinian Jews in Jesus' time, they may reflect practices of Jews living outside of Palestine in Mark's time. In any case, the problem centers on the "traditions of the elders," that is, the oral law. These traditions were developed in an attempt to clarify certain provisions of the written law (the "Torah"— the first five books of the Old Testament), to apply them to changing situations, and to see that major provisions remained unbroken. This latter activity, called "building a fence around the law," set up many lesser regulations designed to protect a major law. For example, if labor is forbidden on the sabbath (Exod 20:8–11), provisions to forbid carrying any burden or doing any traveling will make sure no one can carry tools or travel to a place where labor can be performed.

The question here is thus not so much the validity of the law as it is the validity of the Pharisaic interpretation of that law. This was a problem not only for Jesus, but for the early church as well (note that the question concerns Jesus' disciples, i.e., his followers, in vv. 2, 5). Verse 6 shows the real issue: hypocrisy. Yet this hypocrisy does not refer simply to personal insincerity. It means here substituting legalisms for obedience to the true intention of the law. Thus, the very sincerity with which the Pharisees follow their religious traditions has led them into the hypocrisy of ignoring the true intention of the law. The Pharisees' problem is not lack of sincere religious zeal. Rather, it is a problem of misdirected religious zeal (cf. Rom 10:2–3) which leads them away from God and his will. The more sincere the Pharisees were about their traditions, the more they were led by them to oppose God's will, and to oppose Jesus as well.

The example of such "hypocrisy" in verses 10–12 does not reflect official Pharisaic Judaism of any period we know. It may refer to an individual case, or to the practice in some isolated area. The point, however, still stands. Reverence for Pharisaic traditions leads inevitably to opposition to what God really wants (vv. 7, 8, 13). This is most clearly illustrated in Pharisaic opposition to Jesus. Their zeal for their understanding of God's will led them to oppose God's own Son. That is the irony and the tragedy of Jewish opposition to Jesus.

STUDY QUESTION: Do we run any danger of allowing religious rules to get in the way of our doing God's will? Can the pure intentions of those who make those rules guarantee such a thing won't happen?

Mark 7:14–23
What Makes a Person Unacceptable to God?
In this continuation of 7:1–13, Jesus turns from remarks about Pharisaic interpretation of the law to an attack on the basic premise of the whole Jewish legal code: the difference between clean and unclean foods. The point of these verses is unmistakable. No food can render a person unclean, that is, unacceptable to God. Consequently, all rules forbidding those who observe dietary laws from eating with those who do not are also abrogated. Such a statement is revolutionary, not only for Jews, but for all who by some form of asceticism think to render themselves acceptable to God. Perhaps because of its radical nature it is called a "parable," that is, a potentially confusing saying (cf. 3:23), and is given further explanation (vv. 17–23). As the concluding remark of verse 19 makes clear, however, the intent of this passage is to abolish all differentiation between foods for religious reasons.

Yet if Jesus stated this as clearly as this passage indicates, it is difficult to imagine how attitudes toward food could have been so divisive in the primitive church. There was in fact considerable dispute about the issue (cf. Acts 11:1–3; 15:1–2, 5; Gal 2:11–13; Col 2:20–22) and a compromise seems to have been the best solution that could be reached (Acts 15:23–29). In light of that, can Jesus have made statements as clear as the ones contained in these verses? Or do these verses reflect a later attempt by the Gentile church to justify its repudiation of Jewish dietary laws (cf. Rom 14:14)?

If the signs of Markan composition are unmistakable—the typical transition in verse 14; the Markan exhoratation in verse 16 (cf. 4:9, 23); the private instruction of the disciples in verse 17a (cf. 4:10; 9:28; 10:10), and the Markan formulation of 17b (the same language appears in 4:10); the Markan attachment formula in verse 18—and if the list of vices in verses 21–22 is more characteristic of Hellenistic than of Palestinian Jewish writing and points to a time later than Jesus (for other, similar lists, cf. Rom 1:29–31; Gal 5:19–21a; 1 Tim 1:9–10; 2 Tim 3:2–4), nevertheless, it was just such a radical attitude toward the Jewish law that got Jesus into trouble with Jewish religious authorities (e.g., 3:1–6) and that provoked precisely those disputes with them which are pictured throughout the Gospel traditions. If these words themselves do not go back to Jesus, the sentiment about the Jewish law surely does, and we are justified in finding in them an accurate reflection of the mind of Jesus.

STUDY QUESTION: If the distinction sacred/profane is eliminated in respect to foods, but not actions (vv. 21–22), are there other aspects of our life where that distinction is to be eliminated? Where it is to be applied?

Mark 7:24–30
Can Gentiles also Come to Jesus?

The occurrence of this story immediately following the dispute about Jewish legalism contrasts clearly the reception Jesus found among Jewish religious authorities on the one hand and Gentiles on the other. The point of the story is the dialogue in verses 27–28, where the woman's persistence in the face of Jesus' sense of priority (Jews first, only then Gentiles, cf. Rom 1:16; 2:9–10; Acts 19:8–9) finds its reward. Her persistence is surely to be understood as faith (Matthew makes that explicit, cf. Matt 15:28). She is confident that Jesus not only can, but will help her. Such confidence in Jesus overcomes all barriers of race, a point the later acceptance of the Gospel by other Gentiles will confirm (see Acts 10:34–35; 15:6–9).

Mark is responsible for giving the story that explicit point, by locating it in the region around Tyre (v. 24). The original locus of the story was probably Galilee. The careful identification of the woman as a Syrophoenician Gentile would be more appropriate if that nationality were unexpected (as it would be in Galilee) rather than what one would expect (as in the area of Syrophoenicia). Indeed, if Jesus was in the region of Tyre, a non-Jewish land, then he himself was not restricting the "food" (Gospel) to the "children" (Jews) as he claims is proper (v. 27). By placing this story within the framework of Jesus' journey to non-Jewish territory, Mark has made explicit what was already implicit in the story, namely that Gentiles who come to Jesus in faith find acceptance. Thus, the possibility of a mission to the Gentiles, already implicit in the original story (vv. 25–30), was carried a step further by Mark. His point is clear. The later Gentile mission can legitimately trace its roots right back to Jesus.

STUDY QUESTION: Does the miracle-story context have any significance, or add any weight, to the point Mark is making by his use of this account?

Mark 7:31–37
Jesus Heals a Deaf-mute

As we noted in the Introduction, the geographical route described in verse 31 is at best confused (the English has "improved" Mark's Greek here), and probably is intended simply to return Jesus from the area of Tyre.

Mark's Greek gives a different flavor from the English at some other points as well. In verse 33, the Greek simply states "Jesus spat and touched his tongue." Saliva is not mentioned. In verse 35, the Greek says that the "bond" of his tongue was released, using a word (bond) that is associated with demonic impediments. The implication is that Jesus freed his tongue from unnatural bondage, rather than from some natural restriction. The presence of a word in a foreign language ("*ephphatha*") and the mention of Jesus' sighing (v. 34) similarly belong to the common description of healings from demonic possession. The story may thus originally have been intended as a further example of Jesus' power over the minions of Satan.

There is a distinct flavor of the Old Testament about the story as well. The word describing the speech impediment is found in only one other place in the Greek Bible, Isaiah 35:6, a passage to which our verse 37 may also point (i.e., Isa 35:5–6). In Isaiah, these verses point to the final times and God's salvific restoration of Israel. Jesus is thus pictured here as an agent of God's final deliverance.

Mark may also be responsible for verse 36, which shows that despite Jesus' apparent desire not to be known as a miracle worker, his fame nevertheless spread widely (cf. 5:42, where the same idea is implied).

STUDY QUESTION: How important for our understanding of Jesus' act in this story is it to understand him in terms of Isaiah 35:5–6?

Mark 8:1–10
Jesus Feeds Many with Little—Again!

The remarks by Jesus (vv. 2–3) and the reply by the disciples (v. 4), unimaginable if the events recorded in 6:35–44 had in fact already occurred (would no one have remembered that remarkable event in such similar circumstances?), make it clear that this is another account of the same event recorded there. While there are similarities, striking at times, between the two stories, there are also a number of differences in detail. Here the problem is a deserted location (v. 4), whereas in chapter 6 the problem was lack of money (6:37); here people have been with Jesus a long time (v. 2), there it was late in the day (6:35); here Jesus begins the discussion about food (v. 2), there the disciples began it (6:35); here there are seven loaves and a "few" fish (vv. 5, 7), there five loaves and two fish (6:38); here seven baskets of fragments are collected (v. 8), there twelve (6:43), and the words used for "basket" differ; here four thousand are fed (v. 9), there five thousand (6:44). Yet, despite such differences, the overall impression left by the two stories is so similar one must wonder why Mark would choose to include both in his Gospel, even if both were present in his sources.

The absence of any indication of place in verse 1 makes it unlikely that Mark intended this feeding to be understood as occurring on Gentile soil, thus showing Jesus feeding the Gentiles, with the earlier incident then understood as occurring on Jewish soil, showing Jesus feeding the Jews and in that way having Jesus bring the "bread of life" (a phrase nowhere used in Mark) to all peoples. Rather, as 8:17–21 will show, Mark uses both feedings as prime examples of the stunning inability of the disciples to grasp the significance of Jesus on the basis

of the wondrous acts they have seen him perform. As later parts of the
Gospel will make clear, only knowledge of Jesus' suffering, and the
resolve to endure if necessary the same fate in one's own life, enable
one fully to understand the meaning of Jesus. Mark found in these two
stories an occasion to emphasize that point.

It is worth noting that had we only one of these stories, we would
be tempted to account for the vivid detail by attributing it to an eye-
witness description. The equally vivid yet different details in the two
stories, coupled with the psychologically unimaginable reaction in
verse 4 if this latter account were the second such historical occurrence, show that such details belong not to historical reminiscence but
rather to the storyteller's art. That probably applies also to verse 10:
there is no other record anywhere of a place called "Dalmanutha."

STUDY QUESTION: Compare both feedings with John 6:1–15.
What can you say on the basis of such a comparison about the different point each story seems intent on making?

Mark 8:11–21
Jesus in the Midst of Misunderstanding

This episode, for which the signs of Markan editorial activity are abundant, is one of the more difficult passages in the whole Gospel. The
context is not always smooth (v. 15 disturbs the flow of thought from v.
14 to v. 16) and the meaning is difficult (what does "sign from heaven"
mean? to what does "leaven" refer? what is it that the disciples should
have understood from the two feedings?). The changes Matthew and
Luke made to this passage show that even they found it hard to understand in its present form (cf. Matt 16:1–12; Luke 12:1, 54–56).

The Pharisees' request for a "sign from heaven" probably meant
Jesus was required to say beforehand what he would do, or was asked
to predict some future event, so that the divine origin of the results
could then be verified (cf. Deut 18:21–22). This is clearly counter to all
Jesus intends to do. He does all he can to avoid being understood as
wonder worker or soothsayer, as his response makes clear. Jesus will not
give the impression that God stands ready to do his bidding.

The saying in verse 15 is probably to be understood in relation to
the Pharisees' question. Such a temptation to Jesus to act the part of a
wonder worker is perhaps the "leaven" (in Jewish references, leaven vir-

tually always has an evil connotation) his followers are to avoid (for
other interpretations, cf. Luke 11:29–30; Matt 12:39–40). Mark has
included this warning in the discussion about lack of bread. How the
disciples could worry about a shortage of bread in light of the two
wondrous feedings is all but incomprehensible. That appears to be
Mark's point, however, and it becomes abundantly clear through the
questions Jesus asks in verses 19–20. In light of all the bread provided,
eaten, and left over, how can they still be preoccupied with arguments
about lack of food? By thus failing to understand who the Jesus is
whom they accompany, they have put themselves into the ranks of
those "outside," to whom all things appear confused and misleading
(the language of v. 18 is clearly reminiscent of 4:11–12). This episode
confirms what was said in 6:52. Not even Jesus' closest companions
have understood who he really is.

These verses end the third segment of Mark's Gospel. As in the
case of the first (1:1 to 3:6) and second (3:7 to 6:6) segments, this one
too ends on a negative note. Just as the Pharisees (3:1–6) and Jesus'
own people (6:1–6) failed to understand, so the disciples now include
themselves in the same group. The career of Jesus is clearly headed for
tragedy. Only divine intervention, it would seem, can rescue his life
from failure. That is exactly the point toward which Mark is moving
his narrative.

STUDY QUESTION: If there were some symbolic meaning to
"bread" in this segment, what do you think it would be? Can you find
in Mark's narrative thus far anything that would justify finding here a
symbolic meaning? Can you find anything to argue against such a
meaning?

IV. JESUS OPENS BLIND EYES: TEACHINGS ON THE LIFE OF DISCIPLESHIP

Mark 8:22 to 10:52

Mark 8:22–26
OPENING EVENT: JESUS HEALS BLIND EYES

With this story, Mark begins the fourth segment of his Gospel, a segment which is also concluded with an account of curing blindness (10:46–52). The content of this segment centers on instructions to Jesus' disciples and is organized around the three passion predictions (8:31; 9:31; 10:33–34). This story therefore begins a segment where the disciples, who have just shown themselves blind to the events in which they have participated (see esp. 8:11–21), have made clear to them who Jesus is, and what their response as disciples must be.

The significance of this story must be derived from its placement in Mark's narrative, rather than from any hints in the content. There is no mention of faith, nor any wondering assessment of Jesus. It could be told of any other wonder worker of the Greco-Roman world with only a change of the name. The two-fold attempt to effect the cure simply emphasizes the difficulty faced by Jesus in this healing, and is not unusual in Hellenistic miracle stories.

In its present context, however, it may well point to the difficulty Jesus experienced in curing the "blindness" of his disciples about who Jesus was and what they had to become as his true followers. Equating their life with him during his earthly career as the first attempt to "cure" their "blindness" and the resurrection as the second and successful attempt is perhaps too fanciful. Yet surely Mark felt it appropriate to

161

place this story at this point in his narrative because it did show how hard it was for Jesus, at this juncture, to cure this stubborn case of blindness.

STUDY QUESTION: Neither Matthew nor Luke used this story in their Gospels. Why do you suppose they omitted it?

Mark 8:27 to 9:29
FIRST PASSION PREDICTION
AND ATTENDANT EVENTS

Mark 8:27–33
Who Understands Jesus Correctly?

This passage is the first in Mark's Gospel that deals directly and openly with Jesus' final fate, but it also shows how blind the disciples still are (cf. 8:22–26). Though Peter, here as so often spokesman-representative for the Twelve, is able to answer Jesus' question about his identity with an affirmation more appropriate than that accorded to Jesus by other people (vv. 27–28; cf. 6:14–15), his reaction to the announcement that Jesus must suffer betrays the position he occupies: satanic opposition to God's will (v. 33).

Verse 30 by its content and verses 31–32 by their language show Markan editorial activity. If verse 33 originally followed verse 29, it showed a more negative reaction to the title "Christ" than is evident in the present context. Yet verse 30, with its typical Markan injunction to silence, makes clear that that title can only be misleading until after Easter, when cross and resurrection have made it evident that national, even military, aspirations, so often associated with that title, are no longer appropriate when applied to Jesus. Only when "Christ" (literally "anointed one," long expected by the Jews as glorious king) is interpreted as the "Son of Man" who must suffer, can it be appropriate.

The prediction of Jesus' suffering and resurrection (v. 31) probably has been influenced in its language by memories of Jesus' actual fate, and by theological reflection on it by early Christians. While Jesus may well have intimated to his disciples that his fate included violent death at the hands of Jewish religious and legal authorities, the confusion of the disciples on Good Friday, and their disbelief at the news on Easter morning, would be all but incomprehensible if Jesus had foretold his fate as clearly as this.

The title "Son of Man," used only by Jesus of himself in Mark's Gospel, is of uncertain origin and meaning. Some earlier uses indicate humility (e.g., Ps 8:4; Ezek 2:1), some grandeur (e.g., Dan 7:13–14). Whatever its original meaning may have been, in Jesus' mouth in the Gospels it is regularly associated with Jesus' death, his resurrection, and his future coming as judge. Scholars have reached no agreement on whether, or in what sense, the title was used by Jesus himself. But on one point there is clarity. In Mark, it is a key to the true meaning of Jesus. For that reason, this passage is the first in a longer segment of Mark's Gospel that is designed to make clear to the reader who Jesus is and how we are to respond to him.

STUDY QUESTION: Verse 33 employs language often used in stories of expulsion of demons. Do you think Mark understood Peter's rebuke of Jesus (v. 32) to be demonic in origin? Are there other instances where disciples' misunderstanding could have been thought to be demonic?

Mark 8:34 to 9:1
Discipleship Means Losing to Win

If "nothing succeeds like success," what is left over for failure? Peter, representing all humanity, made the answer plain: avoid it (8:32)! Follow a man headed for disgrace on a cross? Unimaginable! Yet these verses make equally plain that anyone who would follow Jesus must also be prepared to share his fate. What that means these verses set out to explore.

In the first instance, it means living a life of giving, not getting (v. 34; cf. 10:45). The opposite of such a life is preoccupation with ourselves (v. 35), and such preoccupation, in whatever form, religious or psychological, means closing ourselves off from the needs of others. That, says Jesus, is to lose the point of life (v. 36). Even gaining the world at the price of losing one's life is a poor bargain (v. 37). Yet our whole culture so urges us on to become the "one who has everything" that these words represent a total reversal of our values (cf. Phil 3:7–8). Such a deliberate reversal is what "repentance" is all about. It means turning away from one set of values and accepting another. These verses thus make concrete what Mark began with as a summary of Jesus' message: "Repent, and believe in the Good News" (1:15). This reversal of values which occurs when we follow Christ is not a matter of indifference. One's eternal fate hangs in the balance (v. 38). When God in Christ hangs on a cross, it brings the whole world to that decision: for him or against him.

Mark, who has assembled these verses, adds 9:1 to emphasize the urgency. In foreshortened prophetic expectation, Jesus announced the visible rule of God (the "kingdom of God come with power") within the lifetime of his generation. Like the prophets before him, Jesus saw the future, but misinterpreted the speed at which it was coming. If that means he did not know when the kingdom was coming, it is no more than he himself admitted (13:32). Whatever the timetable, however, Christ crucified and risen is the key to God's future, and following him is the only way to have a share in it.

STUDY QUESTION: In what concrete ways is it possible for us to renounce ourselves and follow our crucified Lord?

Mark 9:2–8
A Glimpse into the Future

By his placement of this story, Mark portrays divine confirmation of Jesus' statement of his future (8:31). His suffering is in accord with God's will, and its result will be heavenly glory for Jesus.

Speculation about where the "high mountain" is located is pointless. A mountain is the traditional place where divine revelations take place (cf. Exod 24:12; 1 Kgs 19:11). The reference to "six days" is also unclear. The point of the story is to be found in verse 3, where, in details borrowed from expectations associated with the last times, Jesus' final glory is seen, and in verse 7, where God himself confirms that this Jesus must be listened to when he speaks of his own fate (8:31) and that of his followers (8:34–38). Elijah and Moses may be intended to show that the law (Moses) and prophets (Elijah) bear witness to Jesus, but they too are more likely intended to point to final times (cf. Mal 3:23 [in some translations 4:5]; Deut 18:15).

Peter, again spokesman (this time for the "inner three": cf. 5:37; 13:3; 14:33), suggests action probably intended to prolong this experience of heavenly glory. That it is as inappropriate as his previous reaction (8:32) is shown by the negative interpretation of the suggestion (v. 6).

The cloud, typically associated in the Bible with God's presence, is also a divine vehicle in the final events (cf. 13:26; 14:62) and continues the imagery of ultimate glory. The abrupt ending following God's declaration (addressed this time not to Jesus, as in 1:11, but to the disciples) shows this to be the climax. Until the end, Jesus' words (v. 7: "listen to him") are all we have of such glory.

STUDY QUESTION: Do you think Mark intended this as a glimpse of Jesus' coming resurrection, or of his final coming at the end of time?

Mark 9:9–13
Elijah and the Coming Cross

The logical sequence, as indeed, the wording itself, is not entirely clear. The better connection of verse 11 following immediately after 9:1 has led some to suggest that it was an original sequence, which Mark interrupted by inserting the story of Jesus transfigured. Verses 9–10 clearly bear a Markan message: only after the resurrection can the true nature of Jesus, and his full glory, be understood. Until that time, events like the transfiguration are not to be discussed publicly. That the disciples persist in their inability to understand Jesus prior to that time is emphasized in verse 10.

If the connection between vv. 9–10 and 11–13 is not entirely clear, the point of those latter verses is. If, as Malachi 3:23 (in some translations 4:4–5) says, Elijah comes before the final times, how could Jesus be the Messiah if Elijah has not yet come? The answer: Elijah has already appeared in John the Baptist. But John/Elijah suffered and died at the hands of violent men, as scripture had said. If, then, scripture also says the Son of Man will suffer, how can that be doubted? Mark has shaped here yet another prediction of the suffering of Jesus.

The point that emerges from these verses is that Jesus' glory, just seen, cannot be understood until after the Son of Man has fulfilled the suffering written of him, and risen from the dead. That is a point Mark never tires of making.

STUDY QUESTION: Why do you think Mark felt it so important to connect Jesus' glory with his suffering?

Mark 9:14–29
Jesus Cures a Boy Possessed

Some of the details in this complex story are common to accounts of exorcisms that circulated in the Greco-Roman world: the demonic aberrations in behavior, sometimes self-destructive; the command to the demon to leave and not return; the evidence of the violent exit of the demon. Some other details, however, which are confusing and even self-contradictory, cannot be explained in that way. There are, for example, two descriptions of the illness (vv. 17–18 and v. 22); the crowd is present (v. 14) but later assembles (v. 25—the English translations obscure the problem present in the Greek); the symptoms of the illness (vv. 18, 20, 22) have nothing to do with deafness (v. 25) or dumbness (vv. 17, 25); and the disciples who figure so prominently in verses 14–19 disappear completely in verses 20–27. Such confusions have led scholars to think this may be an early combination of two similar miracle stories, one contrasting the disciples' impotence with Jesus' power and the other contrasting the father's imperfect faith with Jesus' healing response.

There are some other unclear details—the reason for the amazement of the crowd (v. 15) is not given, and it is not clear to whom the words about the "faithless generation" (v. 19) refer (disciples? bystanders? the father?)—but in its present shape, the story deals with faith, and primarily with Jesus' ability to perform his healing deeds despite its absence. Not only the disciples but even the father lacks the kind of faith Jesus seeks (the Greek of v. 24 is sometimes distorted in English translations; "help my unfaith" or "lack of faith" is closer to its intent). Nowhere is there any hint that the father finally did achieve sufficient faith. The point is rather that God's power at work in Jesus is so strong that neither imperfect (v. 24) or even absent (v. 19) faith can thwart it.

Perhaps that is the reason Mark gave the combined story an introduction (v. 14) and a conclusion (vv. 28–29) and put it in this section of his Gospel that deals with instructions to the disciples. That final reference to prayer tells us that the only appropriate response to Jesus is total, trusting reliance on God's power, which is the attitude of prayer as well as of faith. Yet the story also assures us that, however imperfect our faith may be, Jesus is nevertheless able to overcome the evil forces at work within our lives.

STUDY QUESTION: Why do you suppose Mark thought this was an appropriate story to place after the account of the transfiguration?

Mark 9:30 to 10:31
SECOND PASSION PREDICTION
AND ATTENDANT EVENTS

Mark 9:30–32
A Second Formal Passion Prediction
Mark continues here the pattern he set with the first prediction of the passion and that he will continue with the third. After the prediction (8:31; 9:31; 10:33–34) there is a problem of misunderstanding (8:32–33; 9:33–34; 10:35–41) followed by instruction on the nature of discipleship (8:34–38; 9:35–37; 10:42–45). Interspersed are stories that reveal Jesus' true nature (9:2–8) and power (9:14–29; 38–41) and additional teachings.

The details in this prediction show that even the most careful concentration on teaching the disciples (v. 31) fails to achieve that goal (v. 32). How difficult it was for the disciples to understand what it meant to follow Jesus! How difficult it remains for us to understand that!

STUDY QUESTION: The enemies of the Son of Man are men (i.e., human beings, v. 31). What does that irony say about the way people relate to God?

Mark 9:33–37
True Greatness in Humility
Unlike contemporary American culture, the Greco-Roman world saw no particular virtue in being a child, or in children as such. Powerless and helpless, a child was entirely at the mercy of the head of its family. It is in that context that these verses must be understood. As a correction to the disciples' dispute about which of them was greatest, a dispute that betrayed their total incomprehension of all Jesus had thus far said about his fate and about the proper acts and attitudes of those who would follow him, Jesus uses a child to illustrate the necessity of being

concerned for the powerless, not the great. In an act that figures forth his point, he embraces a child, as he will later figure forth that point by embracing a cross.

Although this combination in Mark of originally independent sayings of Jesus is not without its difficulties (Jesus summons in v. 35 those who are already with him in the house, v. 33), the common point clearly has to do with the proper stance of a follower of Jesus. That proper stance is humility, not pride, a hard lesson for disciples to learn.

STUDY QUESTION: "Child" and "little one" are sometimes used for followers of Jesus (e.g., 9:42). In that light, what would verse 37 say about the attitudes Christians should have toward one another?

Mark 9:38–41
Who Belongs to the "In-group"?
Mark continues to assemble the sayings of Jesus he found in his tradition (Matthew and Luke also used them, but put them into other contexts they apparently thought more appropriate). Verses 38–40 point to a phenomenon known in the time of the early church (see Acts 19:13–14), and perhaps equally likely to have occurred during Jesus' lifetime. The astonishing thing here is the open and tolerant attitude Jesus displays. Like the warning against personal arrogance (vv. 33–37), these verses speak against any kind of group arrogance. Even a minor helpful gesture toward one who follows Jesus will be favorably noted by God (v. 41). Thus, no one who takes Jesus seriously is to be despised, as nothing positive done in his name is to be forbidden by those who follow him.

STUDY QUESTION: Do these verses have any application to contemporary definitions of "Christian" and "church"?

Mark 9:42–50
Above All Else, God's Will
Whether Mark or his tradition combined these verses, the reasons for their combination are not always clear. Verses 42–48 center around the phrase "cause to sin." Verse 49 seems connected through the word "fire" to verse 48, and verse 50 by the word "salt" to verse 49. Such

word associations were probably an aid in memorizing such groups of sayings. From verse 42 we also learn that the "little ones" who are so utterly dependent (see comments on vv. 33–37) are those who depend as much on God in faith as little children depend on their fathers.

The figure of a millstone around the neck is a poetic exaggeration to make a point. Such exaggeration is then continued in the following verses (for other examples, see 10:25; Matt 7:4–5, 9; 23:24). The point is not advice on self-mutilation, as though such extraordinary deeds would earn extraordinary rewards. Rather, this is a radical way of making the point that obeying God, and thus remaining in fellowship with him, is so important that nothing, even what we might otherwise regard as indispensable, is to stand in its way.

The word for "hell" is derived from the Hebrew word for "Valley of Hinnom," a place south of Jerusalem where human sacrifices had once been offered to the God Moloch (2 Kgs 23:10; Jer 32:35). Desecrated by King Josiah, it became the city dump for Jerusalem, and a figure for the place of final judgment (see Jer 7:32; 19:6). The final phrase of verse 47, drawn from Isaiah 66:24, also reflects such an image, which again points to the seriousness which attaches to obeying and disobeying God.

The references to salt in verses 49–50 are unclear, precisely because salt had so many symbolic meanings, among them sacrifice, preservation, purification, and fellowship. Verse 49 could refer to trials Christians would have to undergo, even to the point of self-sacrifice (cf. Luke 14:26–27; Mark 8:34). Another form of verse 50a is found in Matthew 5:13. Perhaps the point of both is a warning against laxity in discipleship. If salt means fellowship in verse 50b, it could be advice on maintaining a peaceful community. But we simply cannot be sure what meaning was intended.

STUDY QUESTION: Can you think of figurative images other than those used in verses 43–47 by means of which to describe in more contemporary terms the importance of obeying God?

Mark 10:1-12
The Importance of Marriage
This section of Mark's Gospel (10:1–27) appears to be a collection of instructions to Jesus' followers on how they are to live in regard to

marriage (vv. 1–12), children (vv. 13–16), and wealth (17–27). This and the sections that follow show that Jesus is not being forced to travel to Jerusalem. He moves willingly to the fate that awaits him there (cf. 8:31; 9:31).

There was considerable dispute among lawyers in the Judaism of Jesus' time about valid reasons for divorce. Should it be entered into only for the most serious causes (e.g., unchastity, adultery), or is it allowed for any reason at all (e.g., too much salt in the food the wife prepared)? That divorce was permitted to the husband (though not to the wife) was assumed on the basis of Deuteronomy 24:1–4. Whether the Pharisees wanted Jesus' opinion on this dispute or wanted to test whether he would set himself against the law of Moses (v. 2) is not clear.

Jesus answered by setting one part of the Jewish Scripture (Gen 1:27; 2:24) above another (Deut 24:1). The import of Jesus' words is clear. The sexual union sanctified in the marriage bond is grounded in creation, and hence is not sinful, but rather reflects God merciful will for his creatures. That bond, once entered into, is not lightly to be cast aside.

To the Pharisees' question, therefore, of what is *allowed* (v. 4, implied in v. 2), Jesus responds in terms of what God has *commanded* (v. 3, implied in v. 7). To a question designed to find the outer limits of activity that could still be considered lawful, Jesus answered in terms of the true intention of God.

To this dispute, Mark has appended in verses 10–12 another saying that makes the same point. The situation envisioned in verse 12 is possible only under Roman law, where, unlike Jewish legal practice, a woman could also initiate a divorce. St. Paul quoted a similarly adapted form of this saying of Jesus (1 Cor 7:10–11). Clearly, then, when the early Christian community faced a new legal situation as it carried its mission to the Gentiles, it felt this saying about marriage was so important that it had to be adapted, so its original intention would not be lost. Thus, verses 11–12 simply reinforce the point of verses 2–9. Marriage is willed by God, and neither husband nor wife may be exempted from the seriousness of maintaining the marriage bond intact.

In a society like ours which is disturbed to the point of psychosis by the problem of divorce, these words of Jesus help us see the root of the problem. Marriages entered into hastily and for frivolous reasons, which mock the serious, even sacred nature of the marriage union, are the cause of many of our problems. The question for us can never be:

"How much can we get away with?" The question must always be: "What is God's gracious and merciful will for his creation?" Only that question will allow us to formulate answers that do not go counter to God's mercy to us and to all creation.

STUDY QUESTION: Perhaps more sharply in this passage than in any other the words of Jesus stand in judgment on the easy moral solutions embodied in our culture, in this case concerning divorce. Do you think more stringent civil laws will solve the problem?

Mark 10:13–16
As a Child, or Not at All

Contrary to a rabbinic saying, which saw attention to children, like drinking too much wine or associating with the ignorant, as a pernicious waste of time, Jesus rebuked his disciples for driving off (English translations regularly soften their act) some children. Rather, says Jesus, they are models for the way into the kingdom. At issue is not a child's natural innocence or purity, let alone its intellectual docility or even ignorance. A child in Jesus' culture "deserved" nothing, and had no claim on anyone for wages or reward. If a child was well-treated, it was because of the love and generosity of the parent. So we receive the kingdom of God, Jesus says, as a gift of grace, not as something fully deserved or clearly earned, or we don't receive it, or enter it, at all. The blessing by Jesus that follows shows that acceptance by him is tantamount to such entry.

STUDY QUESTION: Who occupies the place in our culture that children did in the culture of Jesus? People on welfare? the handicapped? the aged? some other group?

Mark 10:17–22
A Rich Man in Trouble

By his question, the man (no hint in Mark that he was either young or a ruler) shows his awareness that more is necessary before God than just following the rules. Otherwise, since he had done that all his life, he would not have asked Jesus how to gain eternal life. Jesus' response is difficult for those who know him as Risen Savior. Surely he is good!

Yet Jesus during his earthly life never confused himself with the Father
(v. 18b), and when Jesus here, as he so often did, spoke and acted for
God (cf. 2:1–12; 4:35–41; 10:13–16), he nevertheless did it in the consciousness that he was the Father's agent, not the Father himself.

The command to sell all and give to the poor is not intended to be
one more rule, one which everyone must follow. Jesus did not always
require that everything be sold to benefit the poor (cf. 14:3–9), nor
that one had to leave all to follow him (cf. 5:18–19). Rather, for *this*
man at *this* time, wealth was what hindered him from becoming a follower of Jesus, and he was to be rid of it, as anyone must be rid of anything which hinders him or her from taking Jesus seriously. The intent
of this story is not to say that poverty is more blessed than wealth, or
that only the economically poor can be saved. What it does say is that
nothing, including wealth, dare stand in the way of our becoming followers of Jesus.

STUDY QUESTION: What are some other hindrances besides wealth
that can keep us from becoming followers of Jesus?

Mark 10:23–27
Riches Won't Help with God

If the kind of achievement that brings riches will not qualify a person
for entry into God's kingdom, neither will any other kind of human
achievement. That is the point of verse 27, which climaxes this passage.
Entry into God's kingdom is by his grace, or it does not occur. We may
well share the disciples' astonishment at that, but the two sayings of
Jesus, the one in verse 24 without the qualification about riches, make it
impossible to ignore. We have about as much chance of achieving
acceptance with God because of our accomplishments as a camel has of
getting through a needle's eye. The comparison is meant to picture
impossibility. The suggestion that in Jesus' language, "camel" (*camelos*)
could be, and was here, mistaken for "hawser" (*camilos*) helps little. A
hawser won't go through a needle's eye either. The fable about a narrow
gate in the wall around Jerusalem called "Needle's Eye" which a camel
had great difficulty passing through is not recorded until the ninth century. In their own way, such attempts to get around this saying show its
correctness. How difficult it is to accept that only by God's grace, not by
our own virtues, do we have access to him and his kingdom.

STUDY QUESTION: In Genesis 18:14, a phrase similar to verse 27 describes a miracle. Is our salvation to be understood similarly as a miracle?

Mark 10:28–31
True Wealth and God's Kingdom

If riches won't qualify one for the kingdom, following Jesus does not mean impoverishment. Verses 29–30 probably reflect, in their present working, the experience of Christian fellowship present in the primitive church; what one had, all had (cf. Acts 2:43–47; 4:32). What one therefore lost in order to follow Jesus would likewise be gained by following him. The addition of the phrase about persecution (v. 30), and the saying about the final reversal of values (v. 31) nevertheless make clear that one must follow Jesus for his sake, not for the sake of any material reward. The absence of "wives" from verses 29–30 has caused much speculation. The omission is perhaps intentional. While the figure of many parents (father, v. 29; mother, v. 30) is tolerable, the idea of many wives could only give rise to misunderstanding.

STUDY QUESTION: Is verse 31 appropriate as a concluding word for the whole section (9:30 to 10:30), or did Mark intent to restrict it just to these verses?

Mark 10:32–45
THIRD PASSION PREDICTION
AND ATTENDANT EVENTS

Mark 10:32–34
Yet Once More, the Passion is Predicted

With this third prediction of the passion, Mark begins once more his cycle of traditions: prediction, misunderstanding, and instructions about discipleship (the other two sections begin at 8:31 and 9:30). The detailed prediction (vv. 33–34) appears influenced by knowledge of the actual events, at least as they are described in Mark's own passion narrative; the form of this prediction may have been shaped by liturgical or catechetical use. The word describing the state of the disciples in some translations is "daze" (Jerusalem Bible: "they were in a daze"), but even that translation renders the same word in 1:27 as "astonished" and in 10:24 as "astounded." Either of those would be preferable here, since Mark's point appears to be the fear inspired by Jesus' resolute action in taking the way to Jerusalem, which must lead to his passion. Fear and astonishment regularly accompany the reception of divine revelation in biblical narratives, and Mark may want to give further notice that Jesus' fate accords with God's will.

STUDY QUESTION: Is there special significance in the fact that Jesus goes "ahead" of his disciples on the way to Jerusalem (cf. 14:28; 16:7)?

Mark 10:35–45
On "Looking Out for Number One"
Once again, Mark has followed Jesus' prediction of his coming death and resurrection with traditions that show the inability of the disciples to understand what that means, and some further sayings of Jesus about true discipleship (cf. 8:31–9:1; 9:31–37). It was apparently an important sequence for Mark.

The request from James and John for places of special honor receives several answers in the verses that follow it. Honor comes only after suffering (vv. 38–39). God, not Jesus, will determine such rankings (the intention of v. 40). True honor means serving, not ruling (vv. 42–44). Entry into Jesus' "glory" is by the same path for all: Christ's suffering on our behalf (v. 45). It is thus apparent that our present passage represents a collection of sayings on this theme, rather than a verbatim historical record, although the request of the Zebedees may well rest on accurate memory.

It is also clear that Mark has shaped this passage in light of its nearness to the account of Jesus' passion. The reference to Jesus' glory is echoed in a saying of Jesus during his trial (14:62), and the figure of "cup" is used again by Jesus in his prayer in Gethsemane (14:36; that shows that vv. 38–39 also refer to suffering here). The final verse, a kind of capsule summary of Mark's understanding of Jesus, shared by other New Testament authors (cf. Rom 3:24–25; 1 Col 6:20; Gal 1:4; 3:13–14; Heb 2:17–18; 1 Pet 2:21, 24), is a fitting introduction to the story of Jesus' final days.

Perhaps these verses are mainly intended to say something about proper behavior within the church. We are to deal with one another (vv. 42–44) as God has dealt with us in Christ (v. 45). That is what "following Christ" means. Rule in the church is therefore accomplished only by serving. That is especially significant in the light of the request made by James and John. High rank in the church is not a matter of glory and power, it is a matter of service, perhaps even of suffering, because that was the fate of the master of the church. In political life, rule goes to the powerful, and they use it for their own enrichment and comfort. "This is not to happen among you," Jesus says. Those who follow Christ must let that fact shape their total lives, in and out of church.

STUDY QUESTION: In the light of this passage, were the other ten disciples justified in being indignant with James and John? What is the proper way of dealing with people who insist on putting their own interests first?

Mark 10:46–52
CONCLUDING EVENT: BLIND EYES HEALED

Mark 10:46–52
Faith Cures Blindness

The awkward language of the first verse, more apparent in the Greek original than in our English translations (the references to disciples and crowd are ungrammatically tacked on, and the entry and immediate departure from Jericho seem artificial), make it clear that Mark has adapted this story to its present context. The story is unique in Mark in several respects. It is the only miracle whose beneficiary is named, it is the only story where Jesus is called "Son of David" (in Jewish tradition, a descendant of David would be the Messiah), and it is the only story where the one healed follows Jesus. The final act of this kind to be reported in Mark, it serves as the climax of Jesus' ministry of healing and teaching, and as the transition to the account of Jesus' fate in Jerusalem.

It is with this story, then, that Mark concludes the fourth major segment of his Gospel. The segment ends, as it began (8:22–26), with a story of blindness healed. Since the segment contains the major portion of instruction to the disciples included in this Gospel, Mark probably intends the symbolism, namely, that only those who experience the miracle of Jesus' power (most clearly expressed, for Mark, in cross and resurrection—hence the three predictions of the passion) have their eyes opened to his importance. The story adds another dimension to the reception of that "miracle." It is faith (v. 52). Such faith means to persist in calling upon Jesus, despite any hindrance (vv. 47–48), and then to follow him, despite any threat ("in the way" in v. 52 is used by Mark to mean the way to Jerusalem, and suffering).

STUDY QUESTION: What element in this story, do you think, made Mark deem it appropriate for use as the bridge between disciples' instruction and Jesus' passion?

V. JESUS IN JERUSALEM

Mark 11:1 to 16:20

Mark 11:1 to 12:44
JESUS IN THE TEMPLE: ACTION AND REACTION

Mark 11:1–11
Jesus Comes to Jerusalem

We must be careful to read this story as Mark wrote it, not as we know it from other Gospels, if we want to see the point Mark intended to make with it. It is not a triumphal entry into Jerusalem here in Mark (cf. v. 11), nor is there any indication people from Jerusalem came out to take part in the procession. The people involved are Jesus' followers. They don't call Jesus "king," but refer to the coming of David's final kingdom (v. 10). Even the palm branches are missing in Mark's story. Rather, the people scatter their garments, along with leaves and rushes from the fields in Jesus' path (v. 8).

Though the two villages named do not have any particular significance (they lie about one and a half miles apart on the road up to Jerusalem), the reference to the Mount of Olives does, since there was a tradition, based on Zechariah 14:4, that the Messiah would appear there in the last times. That, coupled with the explicit references to the "colt," which recalled Zechariah 9:9, shows that Mark did see messianic significance in this story. It is the appearance of the Messiah, but, typically for Mark, in such a form that even those who saw it did not really understand it.

The directions Jesus gave his disciples, unless they are intended to demonstrate Jesus' prophetic powers, indicate that Jesus was more familiar with this area than Mark's narrative would have led us to believe. Either way, the impression is clear that what happens is not accidental. It happens as planned, a theme Mark has continually emphasized with regard to Jesus' passion (e.g., the repeated predictions of it).

The gesture of scattering garments and rushes in the road announces Jesus as King (cf. 2 Kgs 9:13), as does his gesture of riding on a colt never before ridden, yet it is also clear that he comes not as a military hero mounted on a horse of war, but on a colt, as a messenger of God's peace (cf. Zech 9:9–10). The cry of the people is taken from Psalm 118:25–26, verses that belong to scripture passages read by festival pilgrims during their morning prayers. But again, in Mark's perspective, "Hosanna" (Heb.: "Help us!" cf. Ps 118:25) addressed to Jesus has it ironic overtones. Jesus will do just that, but in a way that will cause those who now celebrate his coming to Jerusalem to fall away (see 14:50) in the very moment when the events that make such help possible (Jesus' death; cf. 10:45) begin to unfold. The story thus continues Mark's narrative of the career of Jesus who came as Messiah in such a way that, prior to his passion, he simply could not be fully understood.

STUDY QUESTION: Why would God's Messiah come in such a way as to remain hidden until his resurrection?

Mark 11:12–25
From the Fig Tree Learn a Lesson: Jesus and the Temple

By inserting one tradition (temple cleansing, vv. 15–19) into another (fig tree cursed, vv. 12–14, 20–25), it is clear Mark means us to see them as interpreting one another (cf. 5:21–43 for a similar combination of traditions). That means the fate of the fig tree, and of the temple, are the same. Jesus' "curse" means they will "die." That the fig tree did so the next day (v. 20) means the destruction of the temple (cf. 13:2) is similarly certain.

The reason for the symbolic "destruction" of the temple (vv. 15–16) is given in verse 17. The reference to "a robbers' den" does not mean Jesus was irked at dishonest business practices by those who sold animals and changed money. He drove out the buyers as well (v. 15).

More important, that phrase comes from Jeremiah 7:11, where it refers to the place where robbers retreat for safety *after* they have done their evil deeds. Jesus' accusation is directed not against sharp business practices, but against the idea that no matter what people do, they are safe from punishment in the temple, or more broadly, because of the sacrifices regularly offered in the temple (cf. Jer 7:9–15). Nor does Jesus have in mind merely a reform of temple practices. Animals were necessary for cultic sacrifices, and only coins with no image, human or animal (cf. Exod 20:4) could be used to pay temple taxes. Both were present to aid temple worshipers, but if no animals were available for sacrifice and if no money could be paid to support the temple, the temple could no longer function. With this act of prophetic protest, therefore, Jesus fulfilled the Old Testament predictions of the temple's end because of the faithlessness of the chosen people (cf. Jer 7:12–15; Hos 9:15).

What the temple was supposed to be was a house of worship "for the peoples" (v. 17; cf. Isa 56:7). It had not become that instrument of salvation, and so had outlived its usefulness. Indeed, in God's plan, Jesus, not the temple, is that "instrument." He is the one through whom salvation will be offered to Gentiles, as his travels in their lands have already indicated (7:24, 31; 8:27). Thus, in God's plan, salvation through Jesus will be offered to all Gentiles (or "nations"; the Greek word is the same) before God's kingdom comes (13:10; cf. Rom 11:25–26a). The temple no longer has a role in that plan.

That is probably the explanation of that strange phrase: "it was not the season for figs" (v. 13). The fig tree, symbolic of the temple in their common curse and destruction (it is total; cf. "from its roots" in v. 20), here also symbolizes the place of the temple in God's plan. There is no fruit on the fig tree because it is not the tree's proper time for that. Similarly, there is no fruit of salvation in the temple, that is, all nations worshiping there, because it is no longer the temple's proper time for that either. The "place" of salvation has been shifted from temple to Jesus. Thus, in God's plan, the temple is barren. This the barren fig tree also shows us symbolically. The "curse" (v. 14) is not due to Jesus' unreasonable expectations about figs. Mark means it to tell us more about the fate of the temple.

That is probably also the reason for the final words about faith (vv. 22–25). For Mark, faith is always linked to Jesus. Hence, faith-filled prayer is now related to Jesus, not the temple. If we would find God in any effective way, it must be through Jesus who now teaches us about prayer, not through a temple whose time has passed. These verses show us how in God's plan God is to be found: in faithful prayer, prayer so powerful that not even mountains can stand against it (vv. 22–24), and in enacting God's loving forgiveness of us in our treatment of our fellow human beings (v. 25). In this combination of traditions, then, Mark tells us beforehand what he will make explicit in the remainder of his Gospel. Jesus, crucified and risen, is the only way to God.

STUDY QUESTION: Is there a "robbers' cave" mentality apparent in some contemporary attitudes about participation in church activities? What would be a correct attitude toward such participation?

Mark 11:27–33
Religious Authorities Challenge Jesus

Some question about the authority that allowed Jesus to act as he had done in the temple was inevitable, and the people who pose it to Jesus represent the groups (chief priests, scribes, elders) that made up the Sanhedrin, the highest Jewish civil and religious court. The question is thus probably to be understood as an interrogation by a deputation from the high court, not as a matter of passing curiosity. That it would have been more appropriately posed during, or immediately after, the purging rather than a day later (vv. 19, 20), is further indication that Mark was responsible for bracketing the story of the temple with that of the fig tree. The collection of five stories of conflict between Jesus and various Jewish religious authorities (cf. 2:1 to 3:6 for a similar group) which this episode begins may originally have been attached directly to the story of the cleansing, showing the reaction of various groups to that act.

The question posed in verse 30 ("from heaven" means "from God"—Jews regularly made that substitution) by Jesus shows how closely Jesus and John were identified. What was said about the authority of the one would be true about the authority of the other. That is the dilemma the question posed for the Sanhedrin deputation. They must have wanted to answer "from human beings," that is, not from God, but fear of the crowd made that answer impossible. Their unwillingness to answer also shows they had not understood the meaning of Jesus' activity in the temple as Mark interpreted it (vv. 22–25), and they were unable to come to Jesus in faith (v. 22). Only those who approach Jesus in faith are able to understand his authority.

STUDY QUESTION: What is there about Jesus' authority that makes it understandable only to those who come to him in faith?

Mark 12:1–12
Jesus Challenges the Temple Authorities

This is the third time Mark identifies what Jesus says as a "parable" (cf. 3:23; 4:2), and the second time it is directed against Jesus' opponents (as in 3:23). There is some question as to whether the parable in its present form can go back to Jesus. Some of the wording in verse 1 is closer to the Greek translation of Isaiah 5:1–2 than to the Hebrew original, and verse 10 is quoted directly from the Greek version of the Old Testament (called the "Septuagint"), something Jesus, whose native language would have been Aramaic, would have been unlikely to do. It points to a later time in the church when Greek had become the common language. The present form of the story also has details that conform it to the history of Israel's relationship to God. As they rejected his prophets (here, the various servants in vv. 2–5), so they rejected his Son (vv. 6–8). Such allegorization of detail drawn from the completed story of Jesus is carried even further in Matthew (21:33–46) and Luke (20:9–19). This points to a history of adapting this particular parable to fit the needs of the later church. Again, the quotation in verse 10 from Psalm 118:22–23, and the idea of Jesus as cornerstone, were popular in early church tradition (Acts 4:11; Rom 9:33; Eph 2:20; 1 Pet 2:6, 7). Finally, verse 9, with its reference to God rejecting Israel and turning to "others," may well reflect the later experience of the church which found its Gospel rejected by the Jewish people as a whole but given a ready hearing by Gentiles. St. Paul engaged in similar reflections on Israel's rejection and the inclusion of Gentiles (Rom 11:17–24). All of this shows the extent to which later tradition contributed to the present shape of the parable.

What form the parable may have had as it came from Jesus, before the experience of the church after his resurrection led to its adaptation for that later time, is difficult to say. Much has been made of the strange, even illogical reaction of the tenants to the owner's rightful claim through his servants to a portion of the harvest. Precedents have been sought in the rebellious attitudes of Jewish peasants toward absentee landlords, in order to qualify this parable as originating with Jesus. Yet aside from the fact that characters in parables do not necessarily act in accordance with "historical precedent" (e.g., the father in Luke 15:22–23; the Samaritan in Luke 10:33–35), in the present form of the parable the tenants represent the rebellious leaders of Israel. Who would claim that rebellion against a loving God is logical?

The activity of the owner of the vineyard is equally strange. Why, knowing the brutal, indeed murderous acts of the tenants against his many servants, would he then send his only son into their hands? But again, in the present story, the owner is God. Who would claim that forgiving love (i.e., grace) is a "logical" response to human rebellion and sin?

Clearly, this parable as Mark presents it is not designed to tell a story of events that could and did happen ordinarily in Roman occupied Palestine. It is a story of the strange, illogical relationship between rebellious Israel and her merciful God, a relationship that will now be shown, in the story of Jesus' passion, at its human illogical, rebellious worst and its divine triumphant, gracious best. In this one story, Mark has presented in capsule form the story of the relationship between God, Israel, and the church, and that is the way we ought to read it. And who can be sure that that is not precisely the way Jesus intended it to be understood originally?

STUDY QUESTION: Why would Mark have thought this was an appropriate place to put this parable?

Mark 12:13–17
What about Taxes?

Apparently sent by the Sanhedrin (on "they" in v. 13, see the note on 11:27), representatives of two Jewish groups come to lay a trap for Jesus. Pharisees sought to take on themselves as laymen priestly rules of purity to fulfill literally Exodus 19:6 ("For me you shall be a kingdom of priests, a holy nation"). Herodians (elsewhere mentioned in Mark only in 3:6) are an unknown group, perhaps supporters of the line of the Roman puppet Herod the Great, or one of his sons. Their compliments are meant to force Jesus, as acknowledged teacher, to answer their trick question. The tax was probably the Roman head tax, whose institution in Palestine in A.D. 6 led to a small revolt (cf. Acts 5:37). It continued to be opposed by zealous Jewish nationalists: How could a people whose king was God pay tribute to any earthly sovereign? The question (v. 14) was designed to show Jesus either a traitor to Rome (don't pay their taxes) or to the Jews (do pay them). The first answer would lose Jesus his freedom, perhaps even his life, the second answer would cost him his popularity.

Jesus, recognizing that intention, asked to see a silver Roman coin, equivalent in value to one twelve-hour day's labor (cf. Matt 20:2, 6, 12). Jesus' answer (v. 17) is more revealing in the Greek, where Jesus asks whose "image" is on the coin. That would immediately have called to his listeners' mind the verse in Genesis (1:26) which says God made human beings in God's "own image." Thus, Jesus says, an item belongs to the one whose image it bears. Coins can go to Caesar, but a human being, bearing the image of God, can only have God as true master.

STUDY QUESTION: Where do we draw the line to determine when demands of the state infringe on a loyalty we can give only to God?

Mark 12:18–27
Riddles on the Resurrection

One after another, Jewish authorities come forth to contest Jesus. This is the only mention of Sadducees in Mark's Gospel. An aristocratic group of priestly families, from whom the high priest was chosen, Sadducees regarded as normative scripture only the first five books of the Old Testament (the "Pentateuch"). Since the only references to resurrection in the Old Testament—and they are scarce indeed—appear in later writings (Isa 26:19; Dan 12:2; perhaps also Isa 25:8; Job 19:25–26; Ps 73:23–24), the Sadducees denied such an idea (cf. Acts 23:6–8; it was a bone of contention between Pharisees who accepted oral tradition and Sadducees who did not). The question they put to Jesus, based on the law of "Levirate marriage" (Deut 25:5–10), was designed to show the absurd consequences of belief in resurrection. Obviously, if (as they thought) Moses had written such a law about marriage, he could not have known of a resurrection when a man and more than one wife would live again. Otherwise, Moses would have foreseen just such a difficulty, and would not have prescribed such a marriage practice.

Jesus' answer is two-fold. The first (vv. 24–25) contests the supposition in the question that the state of the risen will be similar to that of their previous lives in all respects. Since the question depended on such continuity and the resulting absurdity for its force, Jesus' denial of that continuity (the risen, like the angels, live in different relationship to one another than do the presently living) renders the example pointless. Jesus here employs ideas already widespread in certain circles of Judaism (cf. Tob 12:19, where the angel Raphael notes he does not eat).

Jesus' second answer is taken from scripture the Sadducees must acknowledge (Exod 3:6). The logic seems to be that since God says he "is" (not "was") the God of Abraham, Isaac, and Jacob, they must still be alive, perhaps in some risen state. The further statement, recalling the reference to God's power in verse 24, makes clear that the power of the living God is too great to be overcome by death. If God was powerful enough to create life in the beginning, he is powerful enough to recreate it after death. That is the point the Sadducees have missed in their speculative attempts to set limits on God's power.

STUDY QUESTION: Does this passage mean that all speculation about the conditions of life after death is pointless?

Mark 12:28–34
Above all, Love

This is the only story in Mark's Gospel where a scribe has a positive attitude to Jesus. It indicates that, contrary to the usual view, not all orthodox Jews rejected Jesus.

Well-known rabbis were occasionally asked the question here put to Jesus. The ability to state in succinct form the basis of the law was honored as an indication of legal expertise. Jesus' answer is drawn from Jewish scripture. Verses 29–30 are part of a statement of faith every adult Jewish male was expected to recite daily (the "Shema"). The second part of the answer (v. 31) qualifies the first. One cannot love God unless that love is made real toward one's fellow human beings. There is some evidence that these two commands had been combined prior to Jesus, and identified as central to the law. What is important is not simply that Jesus said them, but rather that he incorporated them into his own life, by accepting as fellow human beings people whom others despised (cf. 2:16; 10:14), and by obeying God's will right up to a cross. The scribe's response, especially his added remark about sacrifices (v. 33; he had prophetic precedent, e.g., Isa 1:11; Hos 6:6), shows that he understood the command not as a basis for deducing the remainder of the law as logical extensions, but as a command so important that its observance rendered all other laws superfluous.

However we may want to understand Jesus' final remark about the scribe's relation to God's kingdom (is the kingdom about to come? is it present already? is it where Jesus is?), the stunning fact is that Jesus could make such a statement. Who can really say such a thing except God? Perhaps that is why, after that saying, no one dared to question him any more.

STUDY QUESTION: Where else in Mark's Gospel has Jesus done or said things that could normally be expected only from God?

Mark 12:35–37
A Puzzle about David's Son

This passage represents an unsolved puzzle in interpreting Mark. The clear intention of the verses is simply that the Messiah is not of Davidic descent. Because *David* can say (v. 36): "The Lord [i.e., God] said to *my* Lord [i.e., the Messiah]: Sit . . . ," and because in Jewish custom no one would address his own descendant as "Lord," when David calls the Messiah "Lord," it demonstrates that David could not be speaking to his descendant. Could Mark have thought Jesus was not from David's line? Nowhere in this Gospel is Jesus associated with Bethlehem, the "city of David" (cf. Luke 2:11), nor is Jesus identified as David's son in the entry into Jerusalem (cf. Matt 21:9). Only blind Bartimaeus calls him that, and the title is of no significance for that story (it may only have been another term for "Jew"; cf. Mark 11:10, where apparently any Jew could claim David as "father"). In its present position, the passage continues to demonstrate Jesus' superiority over the religious questions and doctrines of official Judaism, but its meaning is a puzzle in light of the early and consistent New Testament witness to Jesus as David's descendant.

STUDY QUESTION: Some have suggested this passage means Jesus as true Messiah is very different from Jewish expectations expressed in the phrase "son of David." What do you think?

Mark 12:38–44
Spiritual Pride and a Generous Widow

These two stories may have been associated with one another, and with the one preceding them, because of catch-word similarity: scribe (vv. 35, 38) and widow (vv. 40, 42). The fact that the second story (vv. 41–44) presumes routine continuation of temple activities indicates it originated apart from the present context, where, after the temple purging, Jesus would hardly have been allowed to sit undisturbed to watch normal temple activities. As these two stories now stand, however, they report the final episodes of Jesus' public ministry.

Not all scribes are condemned by Jesus (cf. 12:34) in these verses. His words are directed against those characterized by a specious practice of piety that masks an impious reality. "Long robes" were to be worn at prayer and other times of scribal duties (v. 38; for a similar point, cf. Matt 23:5). In the marketplace their only function would be self-glorification. Since the one who was superior waited to receive the greeting of one who was inferior before returning it, pretentious people sought to be greeted first. Piety for show was also condemned in the Judaism contemporary to Jesus' lifetime.

The story of the widow's tiny but generous offering has parallels in both Jewish and pagan writings of Jesus' time. The "treasury" probably refers to the thirteen trumpet-shaped receptacles that were placed around an outer court of the temple (Court of the Israelite Women). The story of one who gave her all is a fitting transition to the story of the passion, where Jesus will give his all, including his life, for us.

STUDY QUESTION: Why would Jesus say that those who pretend to piety will receive harsher judgment than those who do not cover evil deeds with such a cloak (v. 40), since they both do the same things?

Mark 13:1–37
ON EVENTS BEFORE THE END

Mark 13:1–13
Signs of Distress: Tumult and Division
Mark 13 has often been called the "little apocalypse." An apocalypse is a kind of literature designed to comfort readers in a period of great distress by assuring them that even such a period is part of God's plan for history. It also reveals to them ("apocalypse" comes from a Greek word meaning "revelation") what further events must occur before the present time of tribulations comes to an end. What the disciples ask in verse 4 is what an apocalypse seeks to answer. This type of literature was popular in Jewish and early Christian circles. Of the many apocalypses written in that period, two were included in our Bible, Daniel in the Old Testament, and the Apocalypse (Revelation) of John in the New Testament.

This chapter in Mark also serves as Jesus' farewell discourse, a form familiar in the literature of biblical times. Before a famous figure's death, he would give a last speech that contained his final testimony (for Jesus, see also John 14 to 17; for Moses, Deut 31:28 to 32:52; for David, 1 Chr 28:1 to 29:5, to mention only a few). Mark 13 contains the longest speech Jesus gives in Mark, and it concludes the material dealing with the temple.

The first five verses are Mark's introduction to these traditions, and they contain familiar Markan ideas (e.g., private instruction to disciples; cf. 4:10; 7:17; 9:28; 10:10) and language. Although what follows purports to refer to the destruction of the temple (vv. 1–2), its scope is obviously far wider. Perhaps the actual destruction of the temple in Jerusalem when the Romans took the city in A.D. 70 led some Christians to think that that was the sign of the end, and Mark used Jesus' prophecy of the temple's destruction to warn them that this was not the case. That is clearly the point of verses 6–10. Christians are not to let themselves be deceived by statements that the end is near simply because someone announces it in Christ's name (vv. 5–6). The signs of civil strife are preliminary; the final signs will be cosmic, and can hardly be misinterpreted or avoided (cf. vv. 24–27).

Verses 9–13 probably reflect the experience of early Christians who were persecuted for their faith. In fact, Matthew put these verses

into the framework of Jesus' instruction to the disciples as they prepared for their first preaching mission (Matt 10:17–22). Two points are
made about such suffering. One, despite all appearances, such suffering
does not mean that God has deserted them. In critical moments, God's
Spirit will aid them, and help them give appropriate testimony (v. 11).
Two, such testimony is precisely the purpose of that persecution. It
gives Christians a chance to tell of Christ to people they otherwise
would never confront (e.g., governors and kings, v. 9), and helps fulfill
God's plan of having the Gospel proclaimed to all the world (v. 10).

That in such circumstances families will be disrupted (v. 12) should
not be surprising, especially in light of what Jesus said about putting
loyalty to him above all family ties (cf. Matt 10:35–36; Luke 12:52–53).
Yet even this must be borne for the sake of following Jesus (cf. 8:34),
and those who do hold fast to him to the end he will not desert.

STUDY QUESTION: How seriously ought we to take someone
who, claiming the authority of the Bible, or even of Christ, interprets
some events to mean the end of the world is at hand?

Mark 13:14–27
Be Careful of False Interpretations of the Times

These verses present us with a strange tension between descriptions of
events that will let us know when the end will come upon us (vv.
14–20), and a warning that such an interpretation of those events is
deceptive (vv. 21–23). It almost looks as though verses 21–23 want to
warn the reader that any attempt to forecast the events preceding Christ's
second appearance is doomed to failure, even the attempt just recorded.
The fact that verses 14–20 are bracketed by warnings about false Christs
(vv. 5–6, 21–23) strengthens that impression. St. Paul faced similar problems with people who thought they could forecast end times (2 Thess 2).

The events described in verses 14–20 occur in a specific locality,
namely Judea. As with Old Testament prophets, local events are here
understood to have worldwide significance. Perhaps Mark has taken
such a Christian prophetic writing and put it here, bracketed by warnings that the end is in fact not yet at hand.

The meaning of the "disastrous abomination" (or "desolating sacri-
lege," or "abomination of desolation"—a phrase taken from Dan 11:31,

where it referred to a desecration of the Jerusalem Temple in 167 B.C.; cf. also Dan 9:27; 12:11), which in verse 14 is the event that will tell one when to flee, is unknown. Luke interpreted it to mean the fall of Jerusalem (Luke 21:20). If the material in verses 14–20 was already formulated when Mark got it (the reference to the "reader" in v. 14 would imply that), it could refer to the attempt by the Roman emperor Caligula to have his statue erected in the Jerusalem Temple in A.D. 40, something which, had it occurred, Jews would have regarded as a temple desecration. We are not sure, however, to what the phrase refers.

Flat-roofed Palestinian houses are presumed (v. 15) with an outside staircase giving access. The heavier cloak was laid aside for work in the fields (v. 16). The point is that any delay in flight, however trivial, will be fatal, so suddenly does the danger come. Pregnant and nursing women are at a disadvantage in such situations, and winter would mean no food could be found in the wild. The phrase "such distress" (cf. Dan 12:1) perhaps refers to the "messianic woes," in Jewish tradition a period of increasing suffering that would precede rescue by the returning Messiah. Verse 20 assumes that God has a timetable for the duration of the suffering which, if held to, would mean no one could survive to the end (cf. v. 13). God mercifully shortens the period of suffering, however, thus allowing some at least to hold fast to the end.

To think all this lets one predict when Christ will return is wrong, however (vv. 21–22), and those who think that will be deceived (cf. 2 Thess 2:9, where such deception is attributed to Satan). Only after the time of distress is over, and unmistakable cosmic signs occur (vv. 24–25; cf. Isa 13:10; 34:4) will the Son of Man (i.e., Christ) come in an unmistakable way (cf. Dan 7:13). Only then will the angels assemble God's chosen ones to live in God's kingdom.

Mark seems to want to do two things here. One, he wants to make clear that when Christ returns, it will fulfill the many Old Testament prophecies about the end, as shown by the many places the language of these verses reflects Old Testament passages. Two, Mark want to warn his readers not to think they can anticipate when that fulfillment will take place by a cleverly calculated interpretation of certain preliminary events. When that end is at hand, no one will be able to miss it. Before it comes, no one can predict it. The point of these verses is to put us on guard against those who attempt such predictions (v. 23).

STUDY QUESTION: Is it important to know exactly what the "disastrous abomination" is in order to understand the point Mark wants to make in these verses?

Mark 13:28–37
In Uncertain Times, Stay Alert!

We find in this passage the same tension we found in the preceding one. Verses 28–30 presume that certain events foretell the coming end (cf. vv. 14–20), while verses 32–36 say such information is unavailable (cf. vv. 21–23). The problem is heightened by the phrase "these things happening" (or "these things taking place" or "occurring") in verse 29. The phrase cannot refer to the events described in verses 24–27. There the end is not near, it is present. It could best refer to what is described in verses 14–20. Perhaps in their pre-Markan form, verses 14–20 and 28–31 were connected into a kind of apocalyptic guide for reckoning when the end was coming. Mark corrected that view by inserting the qualifications we find in verses 21–23, and especially verse 32.

Verse 28 is similar to other sayings of Jesus (e.g., Luke 12:54–56), where Jesus' own activity is a sign that God's future has cast its shadow on the present through the words and acts of Jesus. But that is a far cry from the kind of apocalyptic reckoning that tries to pinpoint the date of the arrival of that future. Mark in this chapter may be attempting to recover for these and similar words of Jesus, embedded in this prior tradition, a context close to that expressed by Jesus himself. For Jesus, the coming of that future meant: prepare while there is time. Be ready (cf. 1:15). That, of course, is the point Mark is trying to make, especially with verses 33–36, sayings which again reflect other words of Jesus we have (e.g., Luke 12:35–40).

Verses 30 and 31 may also be original words of Jesus, with verse 30 similar to Mark 9:1, and verse 31 applying to Jesus' own words what in another context he applied to words of the law (Matt 5:18). The two verses are apparently linked by catchword association, with "these things" linking verses 29 and 30, and "pass away" linking verses 30 and 31. Perhaps in such a way the pre-Markan tradition formed an apocalyptic "pamphlet" from the words of Jesus.

Whatever the origin of this material may have been, however, what Mark wants to say to us is clear enough. Until Jesus comes—and Mark never doubted that he would—the only appropriate posture for Christians is watchful waiting (vv. 33–37). It can hardly be accidental that he chose just this emphasis to conclude this section. It is apparently the purpose for which Mark composed this whole chapter.

STUDY QUESTION: What kind of circumstances would make such a warning to "stay awake" (i.e., "be alert") appropriate? Jesus' delayed return? Persecution for their faith? Is the warning still appropriate for us?

Mark 14:1–42
THE FINAL ACTS OF JESUS

Mark 14:1–11
Jesus Prepared for the Cross: A Woman and a Traitor

Mark chose to introduce his narrative of Jesus' passion with an account of an anointing of Jesus which he apparently found in his tradition. Both Luke (7:36–50) and John (12:1–8) knew it in somewhat varied form, and put it in different contexts. In characteristic fashion, Mark bracketed his account with another tradition, this one about Jesus' betrayal by Judas. It shows that Mark continued to arrange and shape his traditions in this part of his narrative as he did in the earlier parts.

Simon the leper (v. 3) is mentioned only here in Mark, so we know nothing further about him. Nor is the woman who anointed Jesus named. Only much later was she identified with Mary Magdalene. Her great sacrifice (the cost of the ointment was about a year's wage for a laborer) points to the importance of Jesus. That is emphasized in verse 9, where what she did—rather than who she was—is remembered. What she did was, in an act of prophetic anticipation, to anoint the body of Jesus for burial. It was the only such anointing he would receive. Before his corpse could be anointed later, he had risen from the grave (cf. 16:1–6).

Verse 7 has often been distorted. It does not forbid help to the poor, and it is surely no command to shape an economic system in such a way that some people are held in poverty. Since we cannot anoint the body of Jesus, our responsibility is now to the poor. As so often in Mark, those around Jesus fail to understand the importance of

the events of which they are a part. Here again, they failed to understand this further announcement of Jesus' impending death, preoccupied as they were with their own concerns.

Mark gives no indication of what it was Judas betrayed (v. 11). Perhaps, in light of the authorities' desire not to arouse the wrath of the
crowds with a public arrest (v. 2; cf. 11:32; 12:12), Judas arranged to tell
them when and where they might arrest Jesus in secret, but that is only
guesswork. Nor does Mark give any motivation for Judas's act. That he
did not do it for the money is clear from the fact that payment is mentioned (v. 11) only after Judas has arranged the betrayal (v. 10). Only
later is that motive introduced (Matt 26:15) and then expanded (John
12:4–6). What is clear is that the hour of Jesus' death, so often
announced (3:6; 8:32; 9:31; 10:33–34; 12:12) is now at hand. With
these verses, we begin the climax of Mark's narrative.

STUDY QUESTION: What does Mark want to tell us by combining
these two stories? How do they complement one another? What contrasts are apparent?

Mark 14:12–16
Passover Preparations

These verses, like 11:1–5, presume more frequent visits and wider
acquaintance with Jerusalem by Jesus than the present outline of Mark
indicates. That shows this was again an independent tradition, which
Mark has used to set forward his story of the passion. It is the only passage in Mark that identifies Jesus' last meal with his disciples as a
Passover meal.

The Passover, which celebrates the escape of the Jews from Egyptian bondage (Deut 16:2–3), had early been combined with a second
feast, that of Unleavened Bread. There is some evidence that the day of
preparation that began the festival was also identified as the first day of
Unleavened Bread. The day of preparation, when the Passover lamb
was slaughtered in the temple, was followed by the celebration of the
Passover meal, during which the lamb was eaten. Since Jews reckoned
days to end and begin at sunset, not at midnight as we do, the day of
preparation ended at sunset, and the Passover began. Thus, a lamb sacrificed in the afternoon, before sunset (day of Preparation) would be
eaten that evening, after sunset (Passover). It is this time scheme that is

presumed in these verses, where preparations were made during the day for the Passover meal that evening.

STUDY QUESTION: Are there other places in Mark where the different way of reckoning when days begin and end could lead to confusion among modern readers?

Mark 14:17–31
Eucharist in the Midst of Disciples' Failure

As was the case with 14:1–11, it is apparent that these verses have been assembled by Mark from his traditions. He has again used his familiar bracketing technique, this time bracketing the story of the institution of the Eucharist with traditions about the betrayal of Jesus, both by Judas (vv. 17–21) and by Peter and the other disciples (vv. 27–31). In that way, the saving death of Jesus is placed in starkest contrast to the faithlessness of his closest followers.

The frequent allusions to Old Testament passages (in v. 18 to Ps 41:9; in v. 21 to "scriptures"; in v. 27 to Zech 13:7) show that Jesus' death was not an unfortunate accident, but was part of God's plan for our salvation. Yet that plan cannot be used as an excuse to evade responsibility for one's own acts, as verse 21 makes clear. Within the framework of God's saving plan for humankind, we remain free, responsible people. No plea of historical necessity will allow the disciples, or us, to excuse the betrayal of Jesus.

These verses also present the contrast between what the disciples said and what they would eventually do. While there was as yet only one traitor in the formal sense (vv. 10–11), before this night was out, all would have shown their solidarity with Judas in betraying their Lord (cf. esp. v. 31 with vv. 50, 66–72). The confident assurance that they were not traitors ("Not I, surely," in v. 19), and the brave claims of Peter that they all repeated (vv. 29–31), show up in starkest contrast to their eventual acts.

There is nothing in the description of the meal (vv. 22–24) that would make it anything more than a normal Jewish meal. There is nothing in the description that would compel us to understand it as a Passover celebration, such as reference to the lamb or to the bitter herbs associated with that meal. The repetition of the phrase about eating (v. 22) probably shows that verses 22–25 once circulated independently of the present context. So does the reference to breaking bread, an act that began a meal. It would more properly have been reported in verse 18, if these verses had originated in their present order.

The description of the meal was already at the time of Mark part of the eucharistic liturgy, as 1 Corinthians 11:23–25 shows. Theological reflection on the meaning of this event produced varying descriptions of it in the New Testament (cf. Matt 26:26–29; Luke 22:15–20; 1 Cor 11:23–25; John 6:35–58, in addition to Mark 14:22–25), and continued to bring about changes in subsequent periods of the church's history. Indeed, that process has continued right down to our own day! Similarly, the order in verses 23–24 (first the wine was drunk, only then was the word of institution spoken) has for liturgical and theological reasons been reversed in the church's eucharistic celebration (cf. already Matt 26:27). These verses in Mark, with the implication of drinking blood, would have been all but impossible for Jews like Jesus and the disciples (cf. Lev 17:12; Acts 15:20, 29). They probably reflect the liturgical forms of the Gentile churches. That the shedding of Christ's blood instituted a new covenant would be familiar to Jews, however (cf. Exod 24:5–8), and may reflect an earlier stage of liturgical understanding. Finally, as verse 25 shows, the Eucharist anticipates the return of Christ, when he will preside visibly at the banquet for his followers in God's kingdom.

In all of this, Mark has made it clear enough that faithfulness to Jesus requires more than brave resolve and courageous words. In fact, it requires more than human beings can summon forth. Any true fellowship with Christ therefore depends on God's grace, not on human resolve or strength of purpose. In Mark's view, the Eucharist provides a continual reminder of that fact.

STUDY QUESTION: To what extent do you think Mark intended the disciples to stand for all humanity in their reactions to Jesus? If Peter speaks for them, does he speak for us, too?

Mark 14:32–42
Prayer in Gethsemane: Foreboding and Resolution

This is a difficult passage to evaluate. Despite the assurance of later tradition, we do not know the location of a "Gethsemane." The story itself shows some literary confusion. It has a double introduction in verses 32 and 33–34. In verse 34 the three are told merely to stay

awake, while in verse 38 they are chided for not being awake and praying. Verse 36 simply repeats what we know from verse 35, and if Jesus
prayed at some distance from the disciples who were sleeping, who
heard what he prayed so they could record it? Such evidence makes it
unlikely that we have here purely the record of a historical event. On
the other hand, Jesus' agonized prayer prior to his death is known outside the Gospels (cf. Heb 5:7–8, probably a commentary on just this
event). The word Jesus used to address God ("*Abba*") is also found in
early, nongospel traditions (cf. Rom 8:15; Gal 4:6), and surely goes
back to Jesus himself. No one, Christian or Jew, used this most intimate
address of the little child to its father in reference to almighty God.
Calling God "Dad" is almost as offensive to us as it was to earlier religious people. Such evidence makes it likely that this tradition is based
on a historical event.

   This passage, like so many others in the Gospels, probably therefore
reflects an event in Jesus' life (who would later invent a story that Jesus
was in desperately fearful agony at the prospect of his death?) that has
been altered and reshaped as further theological reflection affected its
telling and retelling.

   Mark has placed this story here to continue the contrast between
brave words from the disciples (v. 31), and their actual cowardly performance (vv. 37–41). The three disciples Jesus took with him are the intimate inner circle in this Gospel (cf. 5:37; 9:2; 13:3). Yet here, their
unreliability is pointedly portrayed. Peter, who had been boldest in his
assertion of unflinching loyalty to Jesus (v. 31a), now cannot brave even
one sleepless hour. James and John, who in easier times had so quickly
asserted that they could and would share Jesus' "cup" (10:38), join Peter
in that sleep. The rejection Jesus would soon experience at the hands of
"sinners" was thus prefigured by his closest friends. If Jesus fulfills God's
will for him, it will not be because he was strengthened by human
companionship. In the end, in his time of searing agony, the Son of
Man was alone.

   Despite that, Jesus withstood the temptation to abandon his God-
willed course, as he had at the outset of his public ministry withstood
temptation by Satan (1:13), and, now prepared, he faced the final climactic events. The hour had come.

STUDY QUESTION: To what extent was Mark speaking to his own
readers, and their situation, through this story of Jesus in Gethsemane?

Mark 14:43 to 15:47
JESUS IN THE HANDS OF RELIGIOUS
AND CIVIL AUTHORITIES

Mark 14:43–52
Arrest and Panic

The Markan form and language of verse 43 show us that Mark continues to adapt individual stories from his traditions in constructing his
narrative. The reference to Jesus teaching daily in the temple (v. 49) is
further evidence of the original independence of these stories from
their present framework. In Mark, Jesus taught in the temple only one
day (11:27–13:1).

The arrest of Jesus was at the behest of the Sanhedrin (v. 43; cf.
11:27). That Jesus' betrayer was "one of the Twelve" is firmly anchored
in the oldest traditions. Given the increasing respect shown the Twelve
in later traditions, it was hardly the invention of a later time. The kiss
with which Judas greeted Jesus was a common form of greeting, particularly among family members (cf. Luke 7:45; Rom 16:16; 1 Cor
16:20; 1 Thess 5:26; 1 Pet 5:14) and was devoid of modern romantic
connotations. The puzzle is why Judas needed to identify Jesus, when
his activities in the temple would have made him familiar to many, and
why it had to be a kiss when a simple gesture would have sufficed. Perhaps it was intended to heighten the drama of the betrayal: it was done
by a friend with a friendly, indeed a family, gesture.

The attempt to defend Jesus (v. 47), though pathetically ineffective,
did catch the imagination of later Christians. By the time Luke got the
story, it was the servant's right ear that had been severed, which Jesus
then healed (22:50–51), and John's tradition added that the servant was
named Malchus, and the swordsman Peter. In the light of the previous
story, with Jesus' resolve to accept his God-willed fate of suffering (cf.
14:36 with 14:41–42), such an armed mob sent to seize him was ludi-
crously unnecessary.

What scripture was fulfilled in these events (v. 49) is not clear,
especially if the arrest itself, which has just occurred, is meant. If the
reference is to the fleeing of the disciples which immediately follows
(v. 50), the reference may be to Zechariah 13:7, to which Jesus had
prophetically referred after the Last Supper with his disciples (see
14:27). The ability of the disciples to carry out their brave resolve is
thus revealed to be nil. This desertion is the last act Mark reports of

them in his Gospel. If they subsequently achieved authority, it was clearly not due to such character traits as bravery or loyalty. Like all humanity, their hope lay solely in God's forgiving grace.

Who the young man was who fled naked (vv. 51–52) we do not know. Neither, apparently, did Luke or Matthew, both of whom simply omitted mention of this. All speculation on his identity is futile. His panicked flight simply emphasizes the total abandonment of Jesus to his enemies.

STUDY QUESTION: This story has little obvious theological reflection incorporated into it. What theological significance do you find in it?

Mark 14:53–65
Jesus Before the Jewish Authorities

Once again, Mark has shaped his narrative by means of bracketing one tradition with another, this time Jesus' "trial" with Peter's denial. Thus, the resolve of Jesus to acknowledge the truth regardless of the consequences (vv. 62–64) is contrasted with Peter's total self-denigration by denying the truth on oath (v. 71). The total abandonment of God's Son is thus displayed in all its painful reality.

An ocean of scholarly ink has been spilled in the attempt to decide whether or not the trial as Mark has recorded it followed Jewish legal precedent, or whether, in their zeal to destroy Jesus, the Sanhedrin trampled their own legal structures into the dust. The problem is insoluble on two grounds. One, the present account in Mark is not the kind of stenographic court report we would need for such an investigation. In its present form, it has been shaped by reflection on Old Testament passages (e.g., v. 61 by Isa 53:7; Ps 38:12–13), and by later theological reflection on the meaning of Jesus' cross and resurrection. Two, we have no way of knowing what constituted normal Jewish legal procedures at this time. Old Testament practices had in many cases been modified, and new practices had developed, but our only written record of them comes from the end of the second century, long after the Sanhedrin passed out of existence as a judicial body, and Jerusalem and the temple had been destroyed. Obviously, Jews in first-century Palestine would not have known, let alone observed, all the idealized legal niceties that were set down almost two centuries later, in their own turn subject to theological reflection on the destruction of Jerusalem and temple.

We can with some confidence conclude, however, that the actual sentence of execution was Roman, not Jewish, since capital punishment under ancient Jewish law was by stoning. Only Romans used the cross, and normally only on non-Roman citizens. In all likelihood, therefore, the Jews at that particular time did not have the right to carry out capital punishment. Hence, the event reflected in verses 53–64 was probably not so much a trial as a kind of preliminary hearing to secure grounds for charging Jesus before Pilate, the Roman official.

Mark presented this nighttime hearing as no more than an attempt to find grounds to justify a verdict long since determined (cf. 3:6; 11:18; 12:12; 14:1 with v. 55). Mark also made clear that the charge against Jesus in regard to the temple was false. Nowhere in Mark did Jesus say *he* would destroy the temple (see 13:2), let alone rebuild it (this latter only in John 2:19). The inability of witnesses to agree on that shows clearly that in Mark's tradition, Jesus faced, and died because of, trumped-up charges.

Jesus' answer to the second question of the high priest is Jesus' only open confession of this sort in Mark, although Jesus characteristically changes the title "Christ" to "Son of Man" (v. 62; cf. 8:29, 31). The answer is based on a combination of Psalm 110:1 and Daniel 7:13, and reflects early Christian confessional language. The point here for Mark is the contrast between who Jesus really is and the way he is being treated. He is sentenced to die for telling the truth and, despite his true identity, he is abused and debased in most cavalier fashion (v. 65). Thus the degradation of God's Son begins, in the name of legal justice and religious rectitude.

STUDY QUESTION: How many contrasts can you find in this passage like the one between Jesus' true reality and the way he is treated? What do they say about the way God confronts people, and the way people respond?

Mark 14:66–72
Peter the Rock
In this story, we stand on the firm ground of history, if not in the details, yet surely in the event here recorded. No one in the early church, where Peter played so important a role (e.g., Acts 2:14–36;

3:4–8; Gal 1:18), would have invented an event like this that cast Peter the "rock" (cf. Mark 3:16; Matt 16:18) in so negative a light.

The details of the story may reflect the storyteller's art. The fact that it would take a second cock-crow to remind Peter of Jesus' prophecy is all but impossible to imagine. In all subsequent accounts, only one crowing is mentioned in Jesus' prediction (Matt 26:34; Luke 22:34; John 13:38) and in the event (Matt 26:75; Luke 22:61; John 18:27). Because roosters were forbidden within Jerusalem, some have suggested that the original reference was to the early morning trumpet call that signaled the fourth watch of the night to the Roman garrison stationed there (that trumpet call was called the "*gallicinium*" in Latin, lit. "cock-crowing").

Bracketing the story of Jesus' trial as it does, this account of Peter's denial of his Lord is intended to contrast the way Jesus met the question directed to him (vv. 61–62) with the way Peter met the question from the servant-girl. If Peter later played a leading role in Christ's church, it was not because he had earned it by his loyalty under fire. It was more likely because he was the first disciple to whom the Risen Lord appeared (1 Cor 15:5; "*Cephas*" in Aramaic, like "*petra*" in Greek, means "rock"), which was understood to mean he had been forgiven (as in John 21:15–17, where the three-fold commission corresponds to the three-fold denial). Peter is thus an apostle by God's forgiving grace, not by his strength of character or moral purity.

STUDY QUESTION: What reasons would have motivated the early Christians to preserve this story about Peter?

Mark 15:1–15
Jesus Before the Roman Authorities
This is no more a stenographic report of court proceedings than was the story of Jesus before the Sanhedrin. There is no hearing of evidence or questioning of witnesses, both of which belonged to normal Roman judicial procedure. Nor is it likely that Pilate, Roman procurator of Palestine in A.D. 26–36 and infamous among his Roman contemporaries for his corruption and cruelty, would have engaged in dialogue with a Jewish mob in an attempt to arrive at a verdict. As throughout his Gospel, Mark is not so much interested in satisfying historical curiosity as he is in pointing to the meaning of the historical

events surrounding Jesus. He tells this story as he tells all the others, to make that meaning clear.

It is evident that, in Mark's view, the Jewish Sanhedrin, not the Roman procurator, was principally responsible for Jesus' death. Not only is the Sanhedrin again identified and its constituent groups individually named (v. 1), but it is also clear from their acts that they are the ones responsible for accusing Jesus (v. 3) and for inciting the crowd to demand his execution (v. 11). Even Pilate is pictured as seeing through their motives (v. 12). Pilate, on the other hand, is portrayed as reluctant to condemn Jesus (vv. 4, 9, 12, 14), and as giving the Jews every opportunity to demand the release of this innocent man. This tendency continued to operate in Christian tradition, putting more and more responsibility on the Jews, rather than the Romans, for Jesus' death (cf. Matt 27:24–27 and Luke 23:13–16 for further development of this tendency). This occurred despite the undeniable fact that it was the Romans who executed Jesus, since it was the Romans, not the Jews, who employed the cross. Thus, in the end, Pilate is also culpable in the execution of a man he thought was innocent of the charges leveled against him.

The account of the release of Barabbas is also told in light of this same tendency. There is no record, Jewish or Roman, of the custom referred to in verse 6. On the other hand, an individual amnesty was always possible, and Pilate, as procurator, could have released any prisoner he chose at any time. Some such amnesty may underlie the tradition about the release of Barabbas. In its present form, however, the narrative is less concerned with Barabbas than with the point that a murderer went free, and the innocent Jesus died, all at the behest of the Jewish mob incited by its leaders. It shows again where early Christians laid the blame.

Underlying this whole account, there are the deepest ironies. Jesus, silent before his accusers, fulfills Old Testament prophecy (Isa 53:7; cf. 1 Pet 2:23), yet Pilate is oblivious to that fact (vv. 4–5). Again, Jesus truly is the king of the Jews, yet not in the political sense Pilate would have meant (v. 2). At that time, any such claim would have been tantamount to rebellion against Rome. So Jesus was killed for what he in fact was, the king of God's chosen people, the Jews, yet king in a way neither Jews nor Pilate imagined. Finally, in the episode concerning Barabbas, the supreme truth about Jesus is portrayed. Although sinless, he dies that sinners may live. Yet neither the Jews, in clamoring for Barabbas's release and Jesus' death, nor Pilate, who ultimately acceded to those requests, understood or intended the event that way.

In each instance, the actors in this historical drama are supremely unaware of the actual meaning of the events in which they participate, and which they cause, events which, for those with eyes to see, tell the true meaning of Jesus. In such a way, says Mark, God fulfills the divine plan, using the acts and decisions of free human beings, even when those acts and decisions intend something quite different. Thus is God sovereign over history, and over our lives, using the free acts of all human beings to fulfill the divine redemptive plan for all of them. That is the supreme irony of the cross, that in this event, despite the intention of the perpetrators, God saves us all.

STUDY QUESTION: Is there any one verse in this passage that best sums up the point Mark is making? Which one would you say it was?

Mark 15:16–20
The Humiliation of the King of the Jews

This event, paralleled in 14:65, shows that both Romans and Jews shared in the derision and brutal humiliation of Jesus. Similar treatment of others in Jesus' time indicates such a scene may well have occurred. Yet again, the point is the utter rejection and degrading of God's Son. The purple robe and crown, the sign of kings, were also awarded for military success and political favor (cf. 1 Macc 10:15–20). A cohort (v. 16) consisted of two hundred to six hundred men. Roman troops were stationed in the fortress of Antonia, adjoining the temple complex on the north, and Pilate, in Jerusalem to keep order during Passover (procurators resided in Caesarea, to the northwest of Jerusalem), may have stayed in that fortress, or perhaps in Herod's palace.

The irony is again evident in this narrative. The soldiers, in spite of themselves, acknowledge both in word (v. 18) and in deed (v. 19b) Jesus' true identity as king of the Jews. All of this once more, unknown to the participants, and surely unintended by them, fulfills scripture (cf. Isa 50:6; 53:3, 5; Ps 22:6).

STUDY QUESTION: Do you think God still accomplishes the divine purposes by using human acts that have no intention of doing that?

Mark 15:21–32
Jesus Crucified and Vilified

Certain characteristics of the style and language of this passage make it likely that Mark assembled it from several traditions, although we can no longer follow the process with any certainty. What is remarkable is the simple, straightforward tone of the narrative, with no attempt to play on our sympathy for Jesus, or to arouse hate against those who destroyed him. Apparently sentimentality has no place in the telling of such a solemn event.

The condemned criminal carried the crossbar ("*patibulum*") of the cross to the place of execution (v. 21), where the upright pole was already set in the ground. No reason is given why in this case Simon of Cyrene (a city in north Africa) was pressed into service. Rufus and Alexander, obviously known to Mark's first readers, are as unknown to us as they were to Matthew and Luke, who omit mention of them. There is a Rufus mentioned in Romans 16:13, but the name was so common (it means "Red") that any identification is precarious. The act of offering the condemned criminal drugged wine to ease the suffering was a kindness practiced by Jews, and was based on Proverbs 31:6. Jesus' refusal may indicate his desire to follow God's will for his suffering to the end. We know neither where Golgotha was located, nor why it was so named. As is usual in such cases, later tradition has filled in the gaps, based perhaps as much on imagination as on any historical facts.

The division of Jesus' clothing (v. 24), a practice otherwise unknown from ancient sources, may reflect the influence of Psalm 22 on the way the crucifixion was narrated (cf. Ps 22:18; cf. also Ps 22:6 with v. 20; Ps 22:16b with v. 25; Ps 22:16a with v. 27; Ps 22:7–8 with v. 29; Ps 22:1 with v. 34). It is no longer possible to determine to what extent details in our story reflect history, and to what extent they reflect the desire to show how this event had been prefigured in the Old Testament. In any case, the parallelism of the actual events to Psalm 22 would have been the original impetus to such correlation.

Recently discovered evidence indicates that the one crucified was at eye-level with passers-by, probably with the body bent in the form of an "S" to keep the feet from touching the ground. The criminal was fastened to the cross by thongs or nails (the latter presumed in John 20:25, although nowhere explicitly stated in any of the Gospels), and death was the result of exhaustion and, more particularly, lack of water.

It was an excruciating death, and one reserved for non-Roman citizens, especially slaves. The one crucified, with a plaque naming the crime (v. 26; cf. 15:2), served as a warning against acts Rome might consider unfriendly.

That others were crucified with Jesus may well be historical (although cf. Ps 22:16a). Their names were apparently unknown to Mark, who does not name them, a gap again remedied by later traditions. As the passion story developed, they came to serve more evident theological purposes (e.g., Luke 23:39–43), where they provide an opportunity for Jesus to show his forgiving love. The words of derision from bystanders, implying that Jesus' failure to save his own life will prove the falsity of all his claims (vv. 30, 31–32a), are particularly ironic in light of God's will for Jesus, and Jesus' own words to his disciples (cf. esp. 8:35). The rejection by passers-by (v. 29), religious officials (v. 31), and even those crucified with him (v. 32) all make clear the utter abandonment of God's Son as he hangs, dying, on the cross.

STUDY QUESTION: What importance do you see in understanding the story of Jesus' crucifixion in light of Psalm 22?

Mark 15:33–39
God's Son Dies

Mark continues to toll the hours (cf. v. 25) as they move relentlessly to the death of God's Son. Mark's Hellenistic readers would recognize in the darkness a portent of the cosmic significance of Jesus' death. With it, the end-time displays its first signs (13:24; cf. Amos 8:9–10).

The cry from the cross (v. 34) is the first verse of Psalm 22. Because it is hard to imagine how anyone who knew enough Aramaic to make sense of the cry would confuse "*Eloi*" ("my God") with "*Eliyah*" ("Elijah"), or how anyone who understood no Aramaic would recognize such a similarity, some have suggested that verse 34 was introduced into the tradition to interpret Jesus' final cry (v. 37) in light of Psalm 22, in which so much of the passion was prefigured (see comments on vv. 21–32). On the other hand, the portent of darkness with its eschatological implications, coupled with the strangled cry from the cross, may have led the bystanders who understood Aramaic to interpret the cry as a summons to Elijah who was expected to return in the last times. However that problem be resolved, in Mark's narrative Jesus' cry shows that now the abandonment of God's Son is complete. Thus did Jesus drain to its dregs his cup of suffering.

If the offer of sour wine (a better translation than "vinegar") was historical, it was perhaps intended as a kindly gesture of refreshment, but in Mark's tradition, it is motivated out of curiosity. If Jesus can be kept alive a little longer, perhaps Elijah will in fact come to save him.

The final two events give further interpretation to Jesus' death. The temple is desecrated (the "veil" protected the inner shrine—the "Holy of Holies"—from religious pollution by the world), bringing to an end Israel's form of worship. The centurion, a Gentile, confesses that Jesus is God's Son (better than "a Son of God"; the Greek is the same as Matt 14:33; 27:43; Luke 1:35), the first time an accurate title is ascribed to Jesus intentionally during the passion events (contrast vv. 9, 18, 26, 32). The fact that a Gentile soldier recognized who Jesus was at the moment of his death shows that it was not until that event that anyone—even his disciples—could truly recognize who he really was. Jesus' death is thus the key to the "messianic secret."

STUDY QUESTION: As the story of Jesus' death was handed on, more and more miraculous events were introduced, a process begun already in Matthew 27:51–53. Why would that have occurred?

Mark 15:40–47
Jesus is Laid in a Tomb

Mark's familiar stylistic device of bracketing one tradition with another is again clear in these verses, where references to the women bracket the account of Jesus' burial. Their importance as witnesses to Jesus' burial is thus underscored, and points to the prominence enjoyed by women in the primitive church, contrary to their lower status in Jewish culture. Although the sons of the second Mary mentioned in verse 40 bear the same names as two of the brothers of Jesus (cf. 6:3), they were common men's names, and it is difficult to imagine that Mark would have identified Jesus' mother in such an ambiguous fashion. Contrary to the account in John (19:26), neither disciple nor relative was present in Mark's account of Jesus' death. This is the first time Mark mentions Mary of Magdala, although there is further information about her in Luke (8:1–3). Such additional information about persons prominent in the

Gospel narratives is typical of the developing tradition, perhaps because those traditions spread beyond people who knew them personally.

It was Jewish custom to bury the dead before sunset (cf. Deut 21:22–23) and, when a person died unattended, burial was often undertaken by pious Jews of some means. Joseph of Arimathaea, who saw to Jesus' burial, was probably not a follower of Jesus, but rather a pious Jew who, like others (e.g., Pharisees, Essenes, Zealots), awaited God's promised reign on earth. His boldness in requesting the body shows the request was a favor, but also provides opportunity for the reader to learn that Jesus was in fact dead (vv. 43–45). His resurrection could therefore not have been merely his revival from the shock of crucifixion. He had died, and his corpse was laid in a tomb. That the embalming was postponed is explained by the fact that the sabbath was at hand (v. 42). Such activity could not be undertaken until the sabbath had passed (cf. 16:1).

The absence in these verses of mention of people who later became prominent in Christian circles gives this account the flavor of historical remembrance. In some such way Jesus, deserted by his family and closest followers, must have received burial.

STUDY QUESTION: In what other accounts in Mark do women play a prominent role?

Mark 16:1–8
ON THE THIRD DAY

Once again, it was the women who attended to Jesus' needs (cf. 15:41). There is a problem in the way they are named, however. If it were not for 15:40, we would read 15:47 as "Mary, the *daughter* of Joset"("Joses" in some translations); 16:1 as "Mary, the *daughter* of James." Perhaps 15:42–47 and 16:1–8 were originally independent traditions, which Mark put together. He then created a continuity between them by means of 15:40, in which those two "Marys" were identified.

The only name that is consistent in those traditions is "Mary Magdalene." That may be more than coincidental. In this earliest account of the empty tomb, it is only women who see it, yet in the Judaism of that day, a woman could not serve in any legal proceeding as a witness. If one had wanted to create a story which, by citing witnesses that the tomb was empty, would have proved that Jesus had risen from the dead, this would not have been the way to go about it (Luke 24:24 and John 20:3–10 later remedy that by having disciples verify that it was empty). Thus the present story may well rest on the historical remembrance that it was Mark Magdalene who first discovered that the tomb was empty (cf. John 20:1).

The reaction of the women (v. 8) further shows that Mark did not think the empty tomb gave rise to a joyous Easter faith, or even underlay Christian proclamation. It is clear that Mark knew that the resurrection was the key to the meaning of Jesus' whole career (cf. 8:31; 9:9, 31; 10:34). The "young man" in the white robe (v. 5), certainly a divine messenger (vv. 6–7), makes it clear that God has now raised Jesus from the dead. Why then this story, in which disobedience and fear still dog the Risen Jesus as they did the earthly Jesus? Perhaps Mark wanted to tell his readers that these momentous events, begun with John the Baptist and the appearance of Jesus (cf. 1:1–9), were still under way. Jesus, now risen, continued to lead his disciples (v. 7) as once he led them to Jerusalem before his death (10:32). If those events were continuing, then suffering, ambiguity, and rejection continue as possibilities for those who follow him (cf. 4:14–19). Only at the last will the harvest come (4:8), only at the last will Jesus return to gather up his own (13:26–27). Until then, Jesus' followers must watch and wait (13:37), knowing that their victorious Lord continues to lead them.

STUDY QUESTION: How does this last passage involve the reader in all the events told in Mark's Gospel?

Mark 16:9–20
EPILOGUE: DEATH COULD NOT HOLD HIM

There are several reason for thinking these verses were not written by the person who wrote the rest of Mark's Gospel. The language is unlike that of the preceding chapters, the passage is absent from some of the best and oldest manuscripts of Mark, and both Jerome and Eusebius, two eminent scholars in the early church, say it was not in their best copies of the New Testament. The passage fits awkwardly into its present context (Mary Magdalene is introduced as though 16:1 were unknown, and 16:3–8 are simply ignored) and presumes information drawn from the other, later New Testament Gospels. It is an amalgam of appearances of Jesus drawn from other Gospel accounts, and other traditions. Perhaps it was originally composed as a summary of the appearances and ascension of the Risen Jesus. At some later point, after both Mark and this passage had been written, someone decided this material could be used to supply the lack of appearance stories in Mark.

The information about Mary Magdalene's earlier history (v. 9) is drawn from Luke 8:1–3, and her meeting with Jesus reflects John 20:14–18. Her report to the disciples (v. 10) reflects John 20:18, and their disbelief (v. 11) reflects Luke 24:11. That Jesus appeared to two followers "in another form" (v. 12) is a comment on Luke 24:16, and explains why they could not recognize him (cf. Luke 24:13–32). Their report to other disciples (v. 13) is also told in Luke 24:33, though the attendant disbelief is not. That unbelief, as verse 14 shows, was a point the author of these verses wanted to emphasize (cf. Matt 28:17b). Jesus' appearance to the assembled disciples (v. 14) reflects Luke 24:36–38 (cf. John 20:19; 1 Cor 15:5), while the detail that they were at table is also reflected in Acts 10:41.

In addition to chiding disbelief in reports that Jesus had risen from the dead, our author wants to show that the outcome of the resurrection is the universal mission of the church. That is clear from verses 15–20, where again he draws on other New Testament traditions. The mission charge (v. 15) is reminiscent of Matthew 28:19 (cf. Acts 1:8), and the resulting division between those who accept the proclamation and those who do not (v. 16) may reflect John 20:23 (cf. Matt 18:18). The accompanying miraculous signs (vv. 17–18) are known in the New Testament (devils: Matt 10:1; Mark 6:7; tongues: Acts 2:4; 1 Cor 12:10; 14:6; snakes: Acts 28:3–6; Luke 10:19; healing: Mark 6:13; Acts 3:1–7; 14:8–10), except for immunity from poison. Such a story is told later of one Justus Barsabas, who was said to have been the disciple not chosen in Acts 1:23 (see Eusebius, *Church History*, III, 39, 9). Jesus' ascension (Acts 1:9) and his being seated at God's right hand are also known in the New Testament (Acts 7:55; Mark 14:62), as are the wondrous signs that accompanied the apostles' preaching (Acts 2:43; 5:12; 6:8; 8:6; 15:12).

If these verses are not Markan, they are nevertheless in the canon, and we can profit from their point. Witness to Jesus, risen from the dead and now with God, remains the unique task of the church, and if, like those earliest followers, we do not always accept or perform as we ought, the Risen Christ continues to challenge us to fulfill the task he has entrusted to his followers.

STUDY QUESTION: What do you think is the most important point these verses are meant to make?

SUGGESTED FURTHER READINGS
ON MARK'S GOSPEL

Paul J. Achtemeier. *Mark* (Proclamation Commentary Series). Second ed., revised and enlarged. Philadelphia: Fortress Press, 1986. Discussion of the theological motifs and emphases of the Gospel, intended to supplement commentaries on Mark.

Patrick J. Flanagan. *The Gospel of Mark Made Easy.* Mahwah, N.J.: Paulist Press, 1997. Contains translation of the text and comments on the verses. Good introduction on relations between Mark, and Luke and Matthew.

John Hargreaves. *A Guide to St. Mark's Gospel.* Revised ed. London: SPCK, 1995. Attempts to bridge the gap between scholars and non-specialists. Contains an introduction, and then a verse-by-verse commentary, along with further study suggestions.

Morna D. Hooker. *The Gospel According to St. Mark* (Black's New Testament Commentaries). London: A. & C. Black, 1991. After an introduction, the author supplies her own translation of the text and provides extensive comments on the verses. A good commentary for the more advanced student.

John J. Kilgallen. *A Brief Commentary on the Gospel of Mark.* Mahwah, N.J.: Paulist Press, 1989. A study, including the RSV text, that proceeds chapter by chapter rather than verses by verse. The advantage is a clearer discussion of the flow of the narrative, rather than comments on individual verses.

Frank J. Matera. *What Are They Saying About Mark?* Mahwah, N.J.: Paulist Press, 1987. A clear discussion of important areas of scholarly discussion of Mark, written in a way the non-specialist can understand. The summaries involve questions of theology as well as method. A good place to start gaining an understanding of current scholarly investigations of this Gospel.

Eduard Schweizer. *The Good News According to Mark,* trans. by D. H. Madvig. Richmond: John Knox Press, 1970. Still one of the best commentaries on Mark in English, it combines solid scholarship with a vibrant faith.

Invitation to Luke

Robert J. Karris, O.F.M.

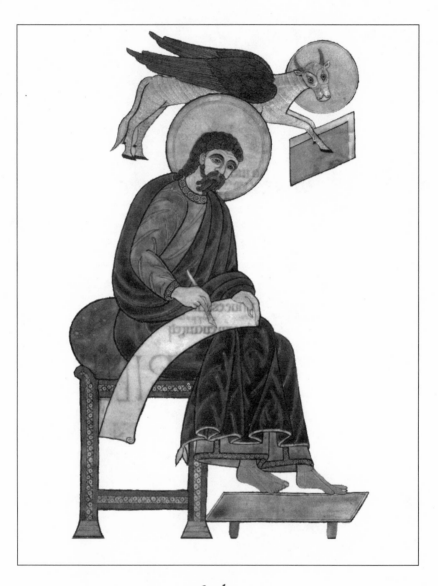

Luke

INTRODUCTION TO LUKE'S GOSPEL

In this introduction I'd like to invite my readers to engage in an exercise of imagination. Visualize with me the situation of Luke and his churches around A.D. 80. The images you conjure up and store in your memory will greatly help you to appreciate the messages Luke addresses to his fellow believers.

Luke's Home As One of Many Missionary Centers

Luke's home is one of many missionary centers or house churches that offer hospitality to guests and that send forth missionaries to Jews and Gentiles. These house churches are often headed by women disciples such as Mary and Martha (Luke 10:38–42) and Lydia (Acts 16). It may be convenient for my readers to imagine contemporary missionary centers. From them the Gospel goes forth and comes into contact and perhaps conflict with different cultures. Important questions begin to pop up all over the place. How much can the Christian message be adapted to a new culture without its being compromised? Can we use the native language and architectural style in liturgy? How can we teach the people that baptismal water should be thicker than tribal blood? How can we continue to preach in a region where the government has imprisoned some of our missionaries because they associated with an outcast group? In other words, we should not imagine Luke writing from some balmy, tranquil island, isolated from the problems of faith and life. Luke's missionary center throbbed with the many problems of making the Christian message alive for different peoples and cultures.

The Trials of Missionary Work

From the little we have said about Luke's home as a missionary center, it is somewhat easy to imagine the ups and downs his house churches

213

experienced. There were surely peaceful and successful missions, but there was also a fair share of turbulent missions. Some of this turbulence is reflected in the new missionary admonitions Jesus gives all his disciples after his Last Supper: "'When I sent you forth without a money bag or a sack or sandals, were you in need of anything?' 'No, nothing,' they replied. He said to them, 'But now one who has a money bag should take it, and likewise a sack, and one who does not have a sword should sell his cloak and buy one'" (Luke 22:35–36). The Acts of the Apostles is replete with the trials of a missionary like Paul: "However, some Jews from Antioch and Iconium arrived and won over the crowds. They stoned Paul and dragged him out of the city, supposing that he was dead. . . . [Paul and Barnabas] strengthened the spirits of the disciples and exhorted them to persevere in the faith, saying, 'It is necessary for us to undergo many hardships to enter the kingdom of God'" (Acts 14:19, 22). Yet amidst all these trials Luke offers his missionaries the consoling words of the Lord Jesus: "Remember, you are not to prepare your defense beforehand, for I myself shall give you a wisdom in speaking that all your adversaries will be powerless to resist or refute" (Luke 21:14–15).

The persecution experienced by Luke's communities was not of the throw-them-to-the-lions type. Its common form was "informal" and consisted of verbal abuse, economic boycotts, and reprisals. "You may have a nice tailor shop going, but we won't buy from you or sell you cloth. Try to make ends meet." "You want your son to learn how to make shoes? Well, we won't take him in as an apprentice."

Luke's Primary Missionary Gospel

Put succinctly, Luke's primary gospel is that God's gracious salvation is for all. It is for Jew, Samaritan, and Gentile. It is for rich and poor, female and male, young and old, well and ill. Luke conveys this gospel in a number of ways. Pride of place goes to Luke's accounts of inclusive table fellowship. In his Gospel Luke, time after time, portrays Jesus as eating with sinners, tax collectors, and Pharisees. At table with his disciples after his resurrection he shares the bread of reconciliation with them. In his Acts of the Apostles Luke thrice narrates how the Lord led Peter to eat at the table of a non-Jew, Cornelius (Acts 10, 11, 15). And Peter, Paul, and James win over conservatively minded Jews to the view that what God has revealed in Peter's eating with Cornelius is the new law of inclusivity (Acts 15).

Another way Luke finds to convey his gospel is his interpretation of the gift of the Spirit upon the 120 men and women gathered in the cenacle on Pentecost. Peter invokes the prophet Joel in his explanation: "'It will come to pass in the last days,' God says, 'that I will pour out a portion of my spirit upon all flesh.... Indeed, upon my servants and my handmaids I will pour out a portion of my spirit in those days, and they shall prophesy'" (Acts 2:17–18). Indeed, God's salvation is not just for one race or for one gender.

It takes very little effort to imagine how readily those with vested interests or with a different understanding of God's revelation would respond to this missionary message of inclusivity. They would not be pleased.

Luke's Missionary Efforts Still Include the Jews

Luke uses the Old Testament extensively to interpret Jesus as the fulfillment of God's promises and to proclaim that God's salvation is for all. See the opening chapters of Luke's Gospel that are full of explicit and implicit Old Testament language and models, such as Luke's comparison of the births of John the Baptist and Jesus with the extraordinary birth of Isaac to Abraham and Sarah or of Samuel to Hannah and Elkanah. And Luke takes very seriously God's universal promise to Abraham that in him all nations, not just those of special, inherited status, will be blessed. It is not incidental that outcast people are linked with Abraham. Jesus heals a woman crippled for eighteen years on the sabbath, declaring her to be "a daughter of Abraham" (Luke 13:16). The lowly and ignored beggar, Lazarus, finds himself in the bosom of Abraham (Luke 16:19–31). And Zacchaeus, the very rich, despised chief tax collector, befriends Jesus who calls him "a descendant of Abraham" (Luke 19:9).

How do Jewish people respond after they have heard this gospel of inclusive salvation from the missionaries of Luke's house churches? Your imagination would not be running wild if you surmise that the vast majority of Luke's Jewish audiences turned their backs on this message. Yet Luke's house churches doggedly continue their mission to God's people. Even when he is under house arrest in Rome, Paul continues to preach to the Jews and has some success (see Acts 28:24).

Luke Writes after the Destruction of Jerusalem

We have often heard from pulpits and read in commentaries that the destruction of Jerusalem and its temple were important events for the

early Christians. Yet I would venture that we have infrequently imagined ourselves back into that situation of A.D. 70. Imagine what would
happen to Americans if Washington, D.C. were destroyed. Where would
American unity, identity, and social security checks come from? Who
would definitively interpret the law without the Supreme Court? Or
imagine the annihilation of the Vatican State; imagine no-trespassing
signs forbidding Roman Catholics from entering the area and under-
taking any reconstruction. What would happen to the papacy? With
their central headquarters destroyed, how would Catholics maintain
unity throughout the world? Who would lead, teach, and instruct
them? No doubt, some self-appointed prophets would arise to trumpet
that such annihilation signaled the end of the world or God's condemnation. The emotions that would pulse through Americans and Roman
Catholics at the mere prospect of Washington, D.C. and Vatican City
being obliterated are somewhat similar, I suggest, to those that coursed
through the members of Luke's community when Jerusalem and its
temple were razed in A.D. 70. It was not as if some far-off city like
Bangkok had been liquidated. One's hometown and the symbol of
one's religious heritage and belonging had been leveled.

God's Fidelity to God's Promises to the Jewish People
The destruction of Jerusalem and its temple may have caused many a
Christian to ask the question: Is God really faithful to the promises
God made? If God is so faithful, why did God let Jerusalem and its
temple—those signs of his presence—be totally destroyed? To these
perplexing questions Luke insists that God has been faithful. Just as in
the past in salvation history when the people defied God's prophets, so
in the present human disobedience does not negate God's promises.
Those Jews who accepted God's fulfillment of his promises in the Messiah, Jesus, form the basis of reconstituted Israel. The destruction of
Jerusalem and its temple is God's judgment on those who failed to
accept the day of God's visitation in Jesus.

Jesus, God's Message of Salvation for All
The points I have mentioned so far come together in the uniquely
beautiful picture that Luke paints of Jesus the Messiah. Like God's
prophets of old, Jesus proclaims God's will. Jesus is the missionary par
excellence who, in fulfillment of God's promises, brings about God's
universal rule of mercy in breaking bread and in healing the sick. He

embraces the marginalized of all stripes with the arms of God's mercy and condemns the evil power of Mammon. As the model servant, Jesus instructs his disciples in the fine art of dying to self to serve others. Jesus' values came into conflict with those in power, and he dies as an innocently suffering righteous person, confident, however, that God will be true to his promises and not abandon him. His hope is not disappointed. And as Risen Lord, he becomes the one in whose name repentance for the forgiveness of sins is preached to all nations.

Luke and Us

We have come to the conclusion of this Introduction. My readers may say that they have found my exercise of imagination interesting, but somewhat quaint. They muse that Luke's situation is light-years away from their contemporary experience. Is it? Today we too face the implications of the fact that God has called and continues to call women to lead house churches. Today we still struggle with the demands of an inclusive Gospel as we seek ways of expanding the guest list for the table of the Lord. Now we not only search the scriptures, Jesus' life, and our experience of God's Spirit and tradition so that we can bring non-Jews to the banquet room and seat them at table. We also search for ways to restore Christians to the table after divorce and remarriage. When fewer and fewer people go to church, we realize that we who do must become missionaries to tell others of our experience of God's goodness toward all. Our global communication networks remind us that the problem of the haves and have-nots has not gone away, not even in such a prosperous country as the USA where more than twenty-five million people live below the poverty level. But there is no need to continue to list analogous situations. We may be taller, heavier, and more expensively dressed than the Christians of Luke's day, but we have the same concerns and quest—the quest to make the inclusive message of Jesus Christ vibrate in our lives in a changed situation.

Luke the Good Pastor

We have imagined ourselves in Luke's situation and glimpsed how similar our situation is. But what did Luke do in his situation? He retold the story of Jesus, adapting the sources of Christian tradition available to him—Mark's Gospel, collections of Jesus' sayings common to that Gospel and Matthew's, and his own church's traditions—to answer the faith questions of his communities. In consoling, guiding, and challeng-

ing them, he is not like some university professor who authors a text-
book that treats all Christian problems from A to Z. He is more like a
good pastor who creatively adapts the Christian message to speak to
the needs of his people. He tells them that just as Jesus showed mercy
to the despised tax collectors of his day, so too must his people extend
mercy to the despised persons they meet. Just as Jesus confronted the
Pharisees of his time for their self-righteous fundamentalism, so too
must his people confront those in their church who equate love of
God and neighbor and even faith in God with the observance of so
many rituals and formulas. It is a sign of the effectiveness of Luke's pas-
toring that his Gospel continues to speak so eloquently today to both
pastors and parishioners after nineteen centuries.

Acknowledgments

In the section on "Suggested Further Readings" I will list those who
have taught me much about Luke's Gospel since this commentary first
appeared. While I maintain the template of my original approach, I
have been happy to add insights from contemporary literary, social, and
feminist studies. These insights have made this a more informed and
inclusive commentary.

Robert J. Karris, O.F.M.

*EDITOR'S NOTE: Unless otherwise indicated, biblical citations are based on the
New American Bible.*

I. LUKE TELLS HIS PURPOSE IN WRITING

Luke 1:1–4

Luke's preface in 1:1–4 is written in the classical Greek form known to us from historians and is one long periodic sentence. Key words for our purposes are: "narrative of the events which have been fulfilled in our midst"; "carefully traced the whole sequence of events from the beginning"; "so that your Excellency may see how reliable the instruction was that you received."

Indeed, Luke's Gospel (and Acts) is a historical narrative. Moreover, it is a salvific narrative, for Luke's narrative has as its purpose to enliven unto salvation the faith of Theophilus and thousands like him. Put in other terms, Luke does not intend to place fact after fact after fact as if he were writing a pedestrian chronicle that strung together statements such as "And then he did this. And after that he said this." He is writing to demonstrate that what he narrates is the accomplishment of God's plan of salvation, especially as revealed in the words and "types" of the Old Testament. Thus, for example, Jesus begins his public ministry by quoting from the prophet Isaiah and saying: "This Scripture *is being fulfilled* in your midst today" (Luke 4:21). If we want to read Luke's Gospel for the Gospel truth, we must recognize the theological and christological ways in which he has "carefully traced the whole sequence of events from the beginning." It will take faith to see that in Jesus Christ God has accomplished God's plan for the salvation of all.

As we have noted in our Introduction, Luke, the skillful pastor, is very much taken up with contemporary issues in his church. He strives by might and main to build up Theophilus's confidence, especially amid the missionary difficulties of proclaiming an inclusive Gospel for

Jews and Gentiles, women and men, rich and poor. And underlying all of Theophilus's questions about the "reliability" of the instruction he received is the fundamental question: Is God indeed merciful and gracious? Is God faithful to God's promises? In the commentary on the rest of the Gospel we will have multiple occasions to see how Luke inspires and assures the members of his house churches that their faith in their Savior, Jesus Christ, is indeed well founded.

STUDY QUESTIONS: Luke seeks to build up faith. In what areas does our faith need shoring up? In our belief that God is good? In our belief that Jesus is the savior of all?

II. JESUS IS THE FULFILLMENT
OF GOD'S PROMISES

Luke 1:5 to 2:52

INTRODUCTION TO LUKE 1:5 TO 2:52

A woman recently shared a priceless discovery with me. As she beamed with happiness at her find, she confided to me that by reading through the first two chapters of Luke's Gospel in one sitting she chanced upon treasure after treasure which she had never known existed. Before she struck it rich in the treasure land of these chapters, she had thought she had a good hold on the meaning of the Christmas story. But now she viewed Mary, the angels, the shepherds, and the infant lying in the manger in the floodlight of the rest of these two chapters. Before you read the commentary on these first chapters, both she and I would highly recommend that you read these two chapters in one sitting. Let the entire sweep of the story fill the horizons of your understanding. You, too, will share the joy of discovering the riches of Luke's story. In the remaining paragraphs of this introduction I will give you some handy hints on what to look for.

As you read through these chapters, you will quickly spy Luke, the consummate artist, at work. He is a master with parallelisms. The annunciation of John the Baptist's birth (1:5–25) is parallel to the annunciation of Jesus' birth (1:26–38). The response of one mother-to-be, Elizabeth (1:39–45) is parallel to the response of the other mother-to-be, Mary (1:46–55). The birth of John the Baptist (1:57–58) is parallel to the birth of Jesus (2:1–20). The circumcision and naming of John the Baptist (1:59–79) are parallel to those of Jesus (2:21). Luke does not deal in parallelisms just to doll up his story. The parallelisms are his vehicles of theological freight as he contrasts John the Baptist with Jesus. In each instance Jesus is greater. For example, John the Baptist "will be great in the sight of the Lord" (1:15), whereas Jesus "will be great and will be called Son of the Most High" (1:32). The door to one of the treasures of meaning in these chapters can be unlocked by reading Luke's parallelisms carefully.

If we ask ourselves about Luke's purpose in these chapters, we are put on the track of uncovering their most valuable treasure. These chapters not only reveal who Jesus is but also show how one must respond to that revelation—in joyful confession. At the very beginning of his Gospel story Luke wants to make it crystal clear to his readers who Jesus is. Jesus is the fulfillment of God's promises in the Old Testament, the Son of God, the universal Savior, the Christ of the Lord, the one who is destined for the fall and rise of many in Israel. The story that unfolds in the remainder of the Gospel is about this Jesus. Mary, Zechariah, Elizabeth, the shepherds, Simeon, and Anna confess their faith in God and joyfully sing the praises of the God who acted in Jesus for humankind's salvation.

There is another side to the coin of Luke's purpose. He uses these chapters as a theological overture to the themes he will orchestrate in the rest of his Gospel and in his Acts of the Apostles. What has happened at Jesus' birth is the result of God's fulfillment of God's promises. As Mary sings in her Magnificat, "God has helped Israel God's servant, remembering God's mercy, *according to the promise* made to our ancestors, to Abraham and to his descendants forever" (1:54–55). The Gospel will end (24:6–7, 25–27, 44–45) and the Acts of the Apostles will begin (1:4) on that very same note of God's fidelity. Zechariah, Mary, the shepherds, Simeon, and Anna are types of those who wait expectantly for God to fulfill God's promise of mercy. Note the description of the prophetess Anna: "[She] spoke about the child to all *who were awaiting the redemption of Jerusalem*" (2:38). This theme is picked up in the Gospel injunctions to pray continually and never lose heart even though God seems to be asleep and disinterested in fulfilling God's promises (see 18:1–8). It is not by chance that the Gospel opens with a scene in the temple (1:5–25; see also 2:22–52) and ends with the disciples "continually in the temple praising God" (24:53), nor that the Acts of the Apostles describes the early Christian community as daily "meeting together in the temple area" (2:46). Jesus and the Christian movement are not born on some desert island, but in the land of God's promises. They are heirs to those promises symbolized by God's presence in the temple. That God's message is readily accepted by the lowly and outcast such as Mary and the shepherds will form a prominent theme in the Gospel, where Jesus is depicted as associating freely with people of that sort (see 15:1–2). Although space prevents us from detailing additional themes, enough has been said to show these two chapters are truly an overture to Luke's Gospel. Keeping in mind the handy hint that Luke's primary purpose in this section is to proclaim who Jesus is, and not to share vignettes from Mary's family album, will help the reader amass treasures of unsurpassed worth.

The last handy hint I proffer is a plea for perseverance in the pursuit of the riches of these chapters, for you are going to encounter one obstacle or another on the way. Perhaps the biggest obstacle is that the traditions that Luke has joined together by means of his artistic parallelisms are not of the same kind. Put another way, the different traditions do not employ the same theological language to express who Jesus is. For example, the traditions behind chapter 2 do not seem to be aware of the annunciation to Mary and her virginal conception. In verses 27, 33, 41, and 48 of chapter 2 we read of Jesus' father and mother. Despite what chapter 1 says about the angel Gabriel's annunciation of Jesus as God's Son, Mary does not understand that Jesus must be about his Father's business (2:50). Although she has been made privy to Jesus' status as Son of God, Mary ponders the meaning of the shepherds' message (2:19) and of the child Jesus' answer (2:51) as if both were new revelations about the nature of her son. In the commentary proper we will help the reader persevere through and overcome these obstacles to unearthing the treasures of these two chapters.

Luke 1:5–38
THE PARALLEL ANNUNCIATIONS

The annunciations of the births of John the Baptist and Jesus follow a stereotype Old Testament pattern about the birth of a notable figure in salvation history. This pattern, evidenced for example in the story of the birth of Isaac to old timers Abraham and Sarah (see Gen 17:1, 3, 15–16, 17, 19), has five points:

1. An angel or God appears (see Luke 1:11 and 1:26);

2. The recipient of the announcement is troubled (see 1:12 and 1:29);

3. Reassurance is given and the birth is announced (see 1:13–17 and 1:30–31);

4. The recipient of the announcement raises an objection (see 1:18 and 1:34);

5. A sign is given to confirm the birth (see 1:19–20 and 1:36–37).

As you study the annunciation to Mary, you will note how closely it corresponds to the biblical pattern except in verses 32–33, 35, and 38, which expand the pattern much as you might develop the basic pattern of a letter or e-mail message to a friend by adding your own personal touch. These verses convey the import of Jesus' and Mary's significance in salvation history. The first expansion, in verses 32–33, clearly resonates with the promise God made to David through the prophet Nathan, a promise which became a cornerstone of messianic expectation: "I will make his [your heir's] royal throne firm forever. I will be a father to him, and he shall be a son to me. . . . Your house and your kingdom shall endure forever before me" (2 Sam 7:13–15, 16). Jesus, of the house of David, is the fulfillment of God's promise to David, his ancient forebear. But Jesus is more, as the second expansion, in verse 35, proclaims. Jesus is Son of God at his conception. The third expansion, in verse 38, highlights Mary as the model of staunch faith. Later on Elizabeth will bless Mary "who believed that what was spoken to [her] by the Lord would be fulfilled" (1:45).

As we mentioned earlier, in the introduction to chapters 1 and 2, the tradition embodied in the annunciation to Mary stands in some tension with traditions in chapter 2. It also stands in tension with other traditions in the New Testament, such as the early creed embodied in Romans 1:3–4, which teaches that Jesus was declared God's Son at his resurrection, and Mark 1:11, which teaches that Jesus was declared God's Son at his baptism. Its teaching of Mary's virginal conception also stands in tension with earlier New Testament writings (e.g., Paul's epistles), which are silent on this vital matter. These tensions do not result from a change in Jesus' nature, as if divine sonship, bestowed on him at his resurrection, somehow became retroactive for his baptism and conception. No, the tensions stem from changes in understanding the reality which was Jesus' from the first. Jesus was Son of God not only at his resurrection and baptism, but also at his conception. Jesus' virginal conception (1:35) relates to this fuller understanding of Jesus and underlines his origin in God.

STUDY QUESTION: This section portrays Jesus' place in God's plan for salvation. How does Jesus figure in our plan for salvation?

Luke 1:39–56
THE TWO MOTHERS-TO-BE

In the rich theological tapestry Luke paints here, more is involved than Mary's generous care of an elderly relative in need. These women come together to engage in prophecy. Elizabeth is filled with the Holy Spirit, knows Mary's condition and its circumstances, and three times proclaims her greatness: How blessed are you because of whom you carry! You, the mother of my Lord, have visited me! You are the true believer! Also, prophetess Elizabeth interprets her son's moving in her womb as the fulfillment of what the angel Gabriel had told her husband about John: he will be a prophet from his mother's womb (1:15). Mary's hymn, the Magnificat (1:46–55), strives mightily to interpret the event of the Son of God's conception by a lowly woman. Jesus, the fulfillment of God's promise of mercy made to father Abraham and mother Sarah and their descendants, serves as a sign of God's fidelity to God's promises. God's action for the lowly handmaid Mary presents a dramatic vision of what salvation is all about. In the end, the lowly will be exalted, and the proud routed.

This section breathes the air of deep faith. As Elizabeth acknowledges, Jesus is her Lord, whose advent she warmly welcomes. John the Baptist gives an advance confession that Jesus is greater than he. Mary is blessed because she has believed what God said to her through the angel Gabriel: she is carrying the Son of God. El Greco correctly interpreted the mind of Luke, his fellow artist, when he painted Mary in the center of his Pentecost canvas. Mary is at the head of that band of female and male believers (Acts 1:14), who wait for the promised Holy Spirit.

STUDY QUESTION: Mary's Magnificat sings of the powerful and lowly. Who are the powerful and lowly of our time? Are we striving to belong to the powerful? To the lowly?

Luke 1:57–80
THE BIRTH, CIRCUMCISION, AND NAMING OF JOHN

Just as Mary's Magnificat interpreted God's gift of Jesus, so too does Zechariah's canticle—the Benedictus (1:68–79)—interpret God's gift to him and to Israel of his son, John.

Luke's introduction to the Benedictus pictures Zechariah, filled with the Holy Spirit and prophesying. As the Messianic Age dawns in the birth of Jesus, God renews his gift of prophecy. His prophets—Elizabeth, Mary, Zechariah, Simeon, and Anna—proclaim the meaning of God's greatest act of mercy—Jesus. The Spirit of prophecy will also characterize the birth of the Christian Church, as detailed in Acts 1 and 2. For example, in his sermon Peter interprets the first Pentecost by appealing to the prophet Joel: "Your sons and your daughters shall prophesy, your young men shall see visions, your old men shall dream dreams" (Acts 2:17).

The Benedictus itself is composed of two stanzas, verses 68–75 and 76–79, and utilizes biblical terms and images. In the first stanza Zechariah blesses God, who, by acting in mercy and fulfilling the promise to Abraham, has visited his people in Jesus. God has determined to come to the rescue of God's people by subduing any force that instills fear in God's people (1:74). In doing this, God intends that God's people serve God in holiness and virtue all their days (1:75).

The second stanza echoes the description of John's role as outlined by the angel Gabriel in 1:16–17. Again God's mercy is emphasized (1:78). The rescue which John will proclaim and defend is not nationalistic sovereignty, but forgiveness of sins, the light of life, and peace.

STUDY QUESTION: Who exactly is John that Luke stops the action of his historical narrative to dedicate a song to him?

Luke 2:1–21
THE BIRTH, CIRCUMCISION, AND NAMING OF JESUS

Its great influence on Christmas crib scenes and on the selection of the Gospel read at Christmas liturgies has imprinted Luke's account of Jesus' birth on the minds and hearts of millions of Christians. Sermon after sermon at Christmas has deepened that imprint. In what follows we will emboss the imprint by pointing out the rich scriptural meditation behind the tradition which Luke preserves in this section. We divide the section into four parts.

Luke 2:1–7
The Setting of Jesus' Birth

While setting the worldwide stage for the angels' revelation, which is the heart of 2:1–21, verses 1–7 make some profound statements of their own about Jesus. Caesar Augustus is mentioned by name in verse 1 and by implication in the next four verses through the words "to enroll," "to be enrolled," "enrollment." Behind the word "enrollment" is the reality of domination: Caesar has vanquished his enemies and now wants to count his subjects and tax them. An ancient inscription praised Caesar Augustus as "a Savior who has made war to cease and who put everything in peaceful order." This same inscription celebrates Augustus's birthday as "the beginning of good news (the gospel) for the whole world." Thus, 2:1–7 sets up the contrast between Lord and Savior Caesar Augustus and Lord and Savior Jesus, and between the good news that each proclaims.

With heavy strokes verse 4 underlines the Davidic origin of Joseph, the father of Jesus (see also 1:27). Whereas in 2:4 the town of David is specified as Bethlehem, it is left unspecified in verse 11 as if the shepherds should straightway know what is meant. This detail in verse 4 is very strange when we recall that in the Old Testament it is Jerusalem—not Bethlehem—that is the city of David. The puzzling nature of this reference invites us to peer behind the scene and spot an interpretation of Jesus' birth which issues from deep reflection upon God's revelation in the Old Testament. One key Old Testament text that figures in this reflection is 1 Samuel 17:12. It informs us that David was from Bethlehem: "David was the son of an Ephrathite named Jesse, who was from Bethlehem in Judah." Since David hailed

from Bethlehem, it could be called his city. But a more important text,
also used by Matthew (see Matt 2:5–6), is a messianic prediction from
the prophet Micah:

> But you, Bethlehem-Ephrathah,
>> too small to be among the clans of Judah,
> From you shall come forth for me
>> one who is to be ruler in Israel....
> Therefore the Lord will give them up, until the time
>> when she who is to give birth has borne....
> He shall stand firm and shepherd his flock
>> by the strength of the LORD,
> in the majestic name of the LORD, his God....
>> He shall be peace. (5:1–4)

Jesus, the Messiah of David's line and longed for by the prophet
Micah, has been born in David's hometown, Bethlehem. The shep-
herding image in the latter part of the quotation from Micah signals
ahead the presence of shepherds at Jesus' birth and also Jesus' role of
feeding his people.

Jesus is explicitly called Mary's firstborn (2:7), so that it will be
patently clear that since he is the firstborn, he is heir to David's throne.

The Old Testament meditation on the meaning of Jesus' birth continues in the latter half of verse 7: "She wrapped him in swaddling
clothes and laid him in a manger, because there was no room for them
in the inn." The "swaddling clothes" allude to King Solomon's wisdom
saying: "In swaddling clothes and with constant care I was nurtured.
For no king has any different origin or birth" (Wisdom 7:4–5). Swaddling clothes do not detract from Jesus' kingly status; even the great
King Solomon, David's son, wore the same garb at his birth. The
manger or feeding trough is vitally important in our passage because it
recurs in verses 12 and 16 as the sign for the shepherds. Jesus, who lies
in a feeding trough, is food for the world. Furthermore, Luke's source
may also be drawing upon Isaiah 1:3: "An ox knows its owner, and an
ass, its master's manger; but Israel does not know, my people has not
understood." The shepherds are representative of God's renewed people. Unlike the people of Isaiah's time, they recognized their master in a
manger. A final scriptural note: Since Luke's tradition in this section
interprets Jesus' birth in Bethlehem so insightfully from the Old Testa-

ment, we should not press "there was no room for them in the inn" too literally and scold the insensitive innkeepers who forced Jesus to be born in the cold outdoors. There is some basis for thinking that a passage such as Jeremiah 14:8 is in view: "O Hope of Israel, O LORD, our savior in time of need! Why should you be a stranger in this land, like a traveler who has stopped but for a night?" Jesus has not come to his people to spend a night at the local Motel 6. He takes up permanent residence among them.

Luke 2:8–14
The Annunciation of Jesus' Birth and Its Meaning
Christian liturgies borrow heavily from Luke's canticles: The church sings his Benedictus at morning prayer, his Magnificat at evening prayer, his Nunc Dimittis at night prayer, and his Gloria at Mass. In their original settings, Luke used these canticles to interpret events in his Infancy Narrative. The Gloria of the angels in 2:14 is his way of telling us how he interprets the birth of Jesus in King David's city of Bethlehem. We give glory and praise to God, for God, through the birth of Davidic Jesus, gives the benefaction of genuine peace on earth to all those whom he graces, even people like the shepherds who are at the bottom of the social and economic ladder. In a real sense, too, 1:52 of Mary's Magnificat is being realized, for the lofty rulers, Caesar Augustus and Quirinius, are put down, and lowly shepherds are exalted.

Luke 2:15–20
The Reactions to Jesus' Revelation
The reactions to the revelation of Jesus are all positive and typical of the responses which Luke desires in his own readers. The shepherds react to what they have witnessed by sharing the message of the angels (2:17). All who hear the shepherd's message are led to further reflection on those events (2:18). Mary ponders what the shepherds have revealed about her son (2:19). The shepherds are the first spokespersons of the customary Lukan reaction of glorifying and praising God for Jesus (2:20). (See those passages where God is praised for a miracle which Jesus performs, e.g., 17:15; also see 23:47, where the centurion praises God for the revelation of God in Jesus' death on the cross.)

Luke 2:21
Jesus' Circumcision and Naming
By means of this verse Luke joins the tradition of 2:1–10 to the one he used earlier in 1:26–38, especially in 1:31. Unlike Matthew 1:21, Luke does not pause to interpret Jesus' name, which means "Savior." The angels had already proclaimed: "For today in the city of David a savior has been born for you who is Messiah and Lord" (2:11).

STUDY QUESTIONS: Are today's equivalents of the shepherds as open as the shepherds of Jesus' time to God's revelation? When are we going to experience the peace that Jesus came to establish?

Luke 2:22–52
JESUS IS FOR ALL PEOPLE

In this section Luke discontinues the parallelisms that have dominated his account so far and sounds the final bars of his theological overture. In his finale he repeats some earlier themes in a new key and introduces some powerful new motifs.

Jesus' parents, like John's (1:6), are described as faithful adherents of God's law (2:22, 23, 27, 39, 41–42). As such, they are open to the revelation of the prophets Simeon and Anna, who give a dual witness to the meaning of Jesus to those who long for the deliverance of Jerusalem (2:38). Jesus, God's Son (1:35), is obedient to his Father's will and goes about his Father's business (2:49). In this theological overture God's opening revelation occurred in the temple (1:5–25); his revelation of his Son's meaning also occurs in the temple on the lips of Simeon (2:29–35) and Jesus himself (2:49). When Jesus enters the temple, he fulfills the messianic promise given by the prophet Malachi: "Lo, I am sending my messenger to prepare the way before me; and suddenly there will come to the temple the LORD whom you seek" (3:1). With Jesus in the temple, the temple itself is stripped of its meaning as a symbol of God's presence. In Jesus, God is really present among God's people.

These final bars introduce two very important new motifs. The Jesus who is so graciously received by the lowly, law-abiding, God-expecting Jewish people depicted in these chapters is also for the non-

Jew. He is universal savior as Simeon proclaims in his Nunc Dimittis: "My eyes have seen your salvation, which you prepared in sight of all the peoples, a light for revelation to the Gentiles, and glory for your people Israel" (2:30–32). But as Savior and Messiah, Jesus' path will not be triumphalistic; he goes the way of suffering (2:34–35). Later on in Luke's Gospel, e.g., 11:53–54 and 15:1–2, we will learn that people do react negatively to Jesus in accordance with Simeon's prediction: "Behold, this child is destined for the fall and rise of many in Israel . . ." (2:34).

These verses form a rousing conclusion to Luke's theological overture or Infancy Narrative and put the reader into the right mind-set to appreciate the story of Jesus which develops in the remainder of the Gospel.

STUDY QUESTION: Make a list of the themes that are sounded in Luke 1:5 to 2:52 and be prepared to note how often they recur in Luke's next twenty-two chapters. Which themes are most appealing to you at this stage of your life? Why?

III. THE ADULT JOHN AND JESUS: JESUS' GALILEAN MINISTRY

Luke 3:1 to 9:50

INTRODUCTION TO LUKE 3:1 TO 9:50

With the melodies of his theological overture of 1:5 to 2:52 still ringing in our ears, Luke brings us to the first movement of his work. Whereas his Infancy Narrative gave top billing to the childhood years of John the Baptist and Jesus, in 3:1 to 4:13 Luke headlines John and Jesus as adults and invites his readers to explore their significance in world and salvation history (3:1–6). In 3:7–20 Luke underlines how John's ministry prepares for Jesus'. By means of his description of the baptism, genealogy, and temptations of Jesus (3:21 to 4:13), Luke gives greater insight into the significance of Jesus whose public ministry in Galilee he will begin detailing in 4:14–30.

The theme of "God's fulfillment of God's promises" dominates this first movement. In his inaugural sermon in Nazareth Jesus preaches that the prophecies of Isaiah will be fulfilled in his ministry: "The Spirit of the Lord is upon me, because he has anointed me to bring glad tidings to the poor. He has sent me to proclaim liberty to captives and recovery of sight to the blind, to let the oppressed go free, and to proclaim a year acceptable to the Lord" (4:18–19). Luke enhances this theme by playing out the many ways in which a gracious God has smiled on God's people in Jesus' preaching and healing. As he befriends sinners and outcasts, eats with them, preaches good news to the poor, and cures the sick, Jesus reveals the goodness of God. Since his message is not a flash in the pan, Jesus gathers male and female disciples and the

Twelve around him to continue his mission. But Jesus' message of God's graciousness to all is about as welcome as a prowler in one's home. Almost from the first hour of his ministry Jesus encounters misunderstanding and opposition (4:28–30). The grumbling of opposition crescendos in chapter 9, where Jesus predicts that there is a cross in his future.

Underneath the music of this first movement one can detect some of Luke's contemporary concerns. A church that marches under the flag of Jesus must welcome sinners, outcasts, and the marginalized if it is to be true to its colors. Opposition will be the church's traveling companion as it preaches and lives the good news of God's graciousness to all. The cross that was in Jesus' future must light the church's way. Christians who are worth their salt will spend lifetimes playing the Jesus game: If you save your life, you lose it; but if you lose it for my sake, you'll gain it (see 9:24).

Luke 3:1–20
THE FEARLESS PREACHER OF GENUINE CONVERSION

Careful reading through this section can nudge one's memory into recalling some of the themes in Luke's theological overture of chapter 1. "The word of God" (3:2) comes to John the prophet (1:76). He gives his people knowledge of God's salvation in Jesus (1:77), a salvation which is for all people (3:6) and not restricted to those who can claim Abraham for their father (3:8). Through his preaching John prepares "a people fit for the Lord" (1:17).

The people who are fit for the Lord are those who go beyond lip service and actually produce the fruits of repentance. In 3:10–14, a passage that is found only in Luke's Gospel and that points ahead to one of his major themes, Luke gives examples of the fruits of repentance as care for and justice to one's fellow human beings. It is important to note who the people are who approach John for the baptism of repentance. It is the lowly and outcast people—and not the religious leaders—who are the people fit for the Lord (see 7:29–30 and the introduction to 19:45 to 23:56). The ability to trace one's lineage back to Abraham does not grant automatic entry into the ranks of God's people.

Despite his status as a fearless preacher and prophet of repentance, John is not the Christ. His preaching prepares the people for Jesus. Jesus, the future judge of all people (3:17), bestows salvation now on Luke's repentant readers through baptism in the Holy Spirit and the fire of Pentecost (3:16; see Acts 1:5 and 2:3–4).

STUDY QUESTION: What are the fruits of repentance asked of us today as a sign that our baptism means something to us?

Luke 3:21–38
JESUS, THOROUGHLY HUMAN AND GOD'S SON

Luke's account of Jesus' baptism and genealogy are packed with clues as to Jesus' significance. But we will have to Marshall our best weather-eye alertness if we are not to miss these clues.

The account of Jesus' baptism (3:21–22) has two main clues: the Holy Spirit, and the declaration from heaven. While at prayer (on prayer in Luke, see the commentary on 11:1–13), Jesus receives the Holy Spirit. As we noted in the commentary on 1:5–38, there is a tension between the account of Jesus' baptism and the account of his virginal conception in 1:35: "The Holy Spirit will come upon you." When we look at these accounts as two sides of the same Lukan coin, we see that this tension is not debilitating but creative. Viewed in conjunction with 1:35, 3:22 does not teach that the completely human Jesus was first adopted by the Holy Spirit to be God's Son at his baptism. What Jesus has been since his conception is now dramatized at the baptism of the adult Jesus. For its part, the baptism account underlines the thoroughly human side of Jesus; Jesus does not sport some sort of nonhuman body because he was virginally conceived. The revelation from heaven illumines Jesus' status from another angle. Endowed with the power of God's Spirit, Jesus must carry out his unique commission as God's Son. Like Israel of old, Jesus is God's Son, the beginning of God's new people, and must gather folk into that people.

Luke's genealogy of Jesus is high theology and should not be read like a list of names in a telephone directory. This clue-studded passage traces Jesus' lineage through the Old Testament back to David and Abraham. Thus, Jesus stands in the line of what God has done for God's people. Jesus' lineage is also traced back to Adam, to show that he has significance not only for the Jewish people but for all peoples. Just as the first Adam was a unique creation of God, so too does the second Adam, Jesus, have a unique origin in God.

STUDY QUESTION: To what extent do the clues of this section contribute to our understanding of Luke's portrait of Jesus?

Luke 4:1–13
JESUS, SON OF GOD,
CONQUERS THE RULER OF THIS WORLD

This section resembles an exquisitely beautiful diamond and the setting which a master craftsman can create for it. By itself the diamond enthralls us with its beauty. Give that same diamond to a master jeweler, and he will fashion a setting for it which will summon our attention to hitherto unseen facets of its glory.

Jesus' three responses to the devil's testing are from Deuteronomy (8:3, 6:13, 6:16) and form the diamond of this section. Deuteronomy 8:2 provides the background for this testing: "Remember how for forty years now the LORD, your God, has directed all your journeying in the desert, so as to test you by affliction and find out whether or not it was your intention to keep the Lord's commandments." Jesus, who embodies the new Israel of God's people, is not like the Israel of old, which failed its testing in the wilderness.

Luke has placed this diamond into a multiply rich setting and thereby enhanced its meaning. When the devil tests Jesus, "If you are the Son of God" (4:3, 9), Luke refers his readers back to Jesus' baptism, where God had declared, "You are my beloved Son" (3:22). Jesus, God's Son, is faithful to his Father and does not fall during his testing as Israel, God's Son, had done. Luke's insertion of the genealogy between Jesus' baptism and his testing reveals another feature of his splendid setting. The genealogy ends with "Adam, the son of God" (3:38). Unlike the first Adam, Jesus, Son of God, emerges victorious from his testing.

The most brilliant features of Luke's setting sparkle in the modifications he has made in the account of Jesus' testing, an account which he has in common with Matthew. Luke underscores the fact that the testing of Jesus is solely the devil's doing (4:1–2). Compare Matthew 4:1, where the Spirit is also involved in Jesus' testing. In verse 6 Luke emphasizes that the devil is lord of the world. Contrast Matthew's more prosaic version (Matthew 4:8). Luke uses these changes to arrange the diamond of Jesus, the new Israel, in a cosmic setting. Jesus' significance lies in his conquest of the ruler of this world.

Master jeweler that he is, Luke adds one final touch to the setting he has fashioned for his diamond. For Luke, Jesus' testing in Jerusalem is the final and climactic testing. After "a time" (4:13) the devil will return to test Jesus in Jerusalem (see 22:3, 53). And in Jerusalem Jesus' severest testing will be threefold as he hangs upon the cross (23:35–39). As Jesus is on the brink of his public ministry, Luke directs our attention to Jerusalem, where God's promises will be ultimately fulfilled.

STUDY QUESTION: Is the tested and victorious Jesus presented in this section a model for Christians? How true is the spiritual tradition which sees in Jesus' three tests the temptations to gluttony, avarice, and pride-filled self-presumption?

Luke 4:14–30
JESUS' VISION OF HIS MINISTRY

Now that he has briefed his readers about the primal significance of Jesus (1:5 to 4:13), Luke turns their attention to Jesus' Galilean ministry (4:14 to 9:50).

Jesus' inaugural sermon in his hometown synagogue (4:16–21) might be likened to a U.S. president's inauguration speech. In that speech the president defines her goals and conveys a vision of what she plans to accomplish during the next four years. Jesus preaches that God's prophecies in Isaiah 61:1–2 and 58:6 are being fulfilled in his ministry; these prophecies define his goals. Isaiah 58:6–7 points to the social dimension of Jesus' ministry: "This, rather, is the fasting that I wish: releasing those bound unjustly, untying the thongs of the yoke; setting free the oppressed, breaking every yoke; sharing your bread with the hungry, sheltering the oppressed and the homeless; clothing the naked when you see them, and not turning your back on your own." And although Jesus' ministry surely has a social dimension, it cannot be equated with mere social action. The Greek word translated by "liberty" and "free" in 4:18 is also used by Luke for *forgiveness* of sins (see, for example, 1:77, 24:47). The liberty and freedom which Jesus brings is liberation from the oppression of sin. Luke goes out of his way in the chapters that follow to show how Jesus' ministry flowed from the vision projected in his inaugural sermon. See the summary passages 4:40–41, 5:15, 6:17–19, and especially 7:20–22.

Like a president's inauguration address, Jesus' inaugural sermon meets with reaction (4:22–30). Or, to change the image, it's like a new president returning to her own hometown and telling her people that they are not going to get any preferential treatment just because she hails from their town. The four years of (presidential) favor are for *all* the nation's poor, captive, blind, and downtrodden. As the examples of Elijah and Elisha show (4:25–27), God's mercy and favor extend beyond the borders of the hometown gang, the chosen people. God's fulfillment of God's promises in Jesus' ministry does not spell immediate bliss for the hometown folk and consummate catastrophe for outsiders. As Mary's Magnificat (1:46–55) proclaimed, reversal of status is the bedfellow of God's fulfillment of God's promises. The self-assured will be humbled, and the humble will be exalted. We also catch a glimpse of a theme that will be developed in Acts: Whereas the majority of God's people refuse to believe in Jesus as Messiah and Lord, the non-Jews receive this message gladly. Finally, we spy the cross of Jesus looming on the horizon. His rejection at Nazareth is the first of many such.

STUDY QUESTION: Must all ministry that prides itself on being Christian espouse Christ's vision of his ministry found in Luke 4:16–21?

Luke 4:31–44
JESUS IS THE WINDOW TO GOD

The key to understanding this section is the phrase, "the kingdom of God" (4:43). This phrase is like the refrain in Martin Luther King, Jr.'s "I Have a Dream" speech. The refrain "I have a dream" sweeps all that goes before and after it into its interpretive train and becomes a meditative rallying point. Throughout his work Luke repeats the refrain "the kingdom of God," to lure his readers away from fixating on individual sayings and deeds of Jesus, so that they can meditate on the significance of Jesus who pronounces these individual sayings and performs these individual deeds. In repeating this refrain, Luke draws upon the Old Testament image of God's kingdom, an image which points to the rule which God exercises and will exercise to establish peace, health, justice, and forgiveness in this world. Caught between foreign Roman domination and the devil's oppressive tactics of sickness and disease, the people of Jesus' time longed for a renewed expression of God's rule on their behalf. What is paramount for Luke is that God's kingdom is no longer just an expectation; God's rule is present in the deeds and teaching of Jesus (see 7:22 and 17:21).

In the section at hand, to "proclaim the Good News of the kingdom of God" (4:43) casts an interpretive net over the two miracles which Jesus works by a mere word (4:31–39). Besides illustrating the authority and effectiveness of Jesus' teaching (4:32, 36), these deeds single out Jesus as the one who brings about God's rule by restoring health to both men (4:33–37) and women (4:38–39). In Jesus' ministry God's rule makes inroads against the devil which holds men and women captive (see 4:18 and 13:16). As Son of God (4:41), Jesus continues his attack on the devil which began in the wilderness (4:1–13). In Jesus, God shows what God's rule is like.

STUDY QUESTION: How is the church and how are its individual members involved in making God's rule present today?

Luke 5:1–11
SIMON PETER, JESUS' DISCIPLE,
BY THE GRACE OF GOD

Luke has drawn much of his material for Jesus' Galilean ministry (4:14 to 9:50) from one of his sources, Mark's Gospel. A comparison of Luke's account of Simon's call with Mark's will help uncover the message of this section. Mark writes: "As [Jesus] passed by the Sea of Galilee, he saw Simon and his brother Andrew casting their nets into the sea; they were fishermen. Jesus said to them, 'Come after me, and I will make you fishers of men.' Then they left their nets and followed him" (1:16–18).

It is obvious that the huge catch of fish (5:4–7) and Simon's reaction to it (5:8–11) lengthen Luke's version. The miracle of the catch of fish is not introduced for its own sake. It's like a story which illustrates a point. Recall the story frequently told about Pope John XXIII. When asked how many people work in the Vatican, the Pope replied, "About half of them." This story illustrates the warm sense of humor which John XXIII possessed.

The story of the huge catch of fish leads into Simon's reaction. In the same way that Jesus' command, "Lower your nets for a catch" (5:4), is effective in the catch of fish, so Jesus' "from now on you will be catching human beings" (5:10) will be effective in Simon's missionary work. Just as the spectacular catch of fish is Jesus' pure gift to Simon, so too is Jesus' commissioning of Simon to be a missionary pure gift. Jesus befriends the sinful Simon (5:8) and enlists him in his corps of kingdom workers.

One final point. By his addition of "left *everything*" (5:11), Luke adds another building block to his theme of poor and rich (see the commentary on 18:15–30). The experience of Jesus' powerful words and deeds in one's life can become a summons to leave all and accept the call to discipleship and mission.

STUDY QUESTION: Are we as open as Simon to Jesus' startling action of calling sinners to be his disciples and missionaries?

Luke 5:12 to 6:11
JESUS EFFECTS GOD'S KINGDOM
WHILE OPPOSITION MOUNTS

In this section Luke follows Mark's sequence most closely (Mark 1:40 to 3:6). In doing so, he crisscrosses many themes and operates on a number of levels.

On one level Luke uses this material to spell out in more detail how Jesus brings about God's kingdom. In fulfillment of God's promises (see 4:18 and 7:22), Jesus cleanses a leper and restores him to community life and worship (5:12–16). When Jesus heals a paralytic, he

scores another knockdown on the devil which holds people captive in
the bonds of sickness. In Jesus, God's rule works for the forgiveness of
sins (5:17–26). Jesus calls the despised toll collector Levi to follow him
and gives most visible expression to God's rule of mercy by supping
with him. As he embraces sinners with arms full of acceptance by eating with them, Jesus images God's kingdom as a banquet (5:27–32; see
Isa 25:6–12). For his part Levi evidences his acceptance of Jesus' forgiveness by his repentance (5:32) in leaving everything (5:28). Jesus'
mission is so God-studded that he has authority over the divine ordi-
nance of the sabbath (6:1–5). His mission of doing good and saving life
is more important than mere sabbath observance (6:6–11).

On another level Luke operates with the theme of opposition. In
effecting God's rule, Jesus brings the unexpected and is harassed by the
Pharisees and scribes who are so sure that their mature way of viewing
God and God's activity is correct that they are unable to bring the new
way of Jesus into focus (5:39). Jesus' claim to forgive sins beckons them
to see Jesus with new eyes, but they continue to use their old categories and cry out, "Blasphemy" (5:21). How can Jesus be from God
and defile himself by eating with sinners (5:30)? Why doesn't Jesus
observe our sabbath regulations (6:2, 7, 11)? The note of opposition,
sounded in 2:34 and 4:16–30, builds up volume in this section and
reaches a high point in 6:11: "But they became enraged and discussed
together what they might do to Jesus."

On still another level Luke's message is addressed to Theophilus
and his kin (1:1–4), who need assurances for their religious faith and
practices amidst opposition from the fundamentalists of their day.
Theophilus and company are in Luke's sights in 5:30 and 33 and 6:2,
where he highlights the disciples and leaves Jesus in the background.
Luke's Christians have been cleansed and forgiven, and must share table
fellowship with sinners despite the popular vote of no confidence
(5:30). They fast, but not frequently (5:33). Following the Lord of the
sabbath, they must allow the norm of love of neighbor to free them
from legalistic tendencies (6:2).

Luke's church is encouraged to continue Jesus' mission, to build its
religious faith and practices on the basis of his words and deeds, and to
withstand the winds of opposition blowing in its day.

STUDY QUESTION: It's easy for us adept second-guessers to repri-
mand the stodgy Pharisees of Jesus' day for failing to follow Jesus. On a

scale of one to ten, do we score higher than they in our befriending of outcasts and sinners?

Luke 6:12–16
THE REBUILDERS OF GOD'S PEOPLE

Prayer. The Twelve. Apostles. To dig behind the meaning of these key words, let's imagine ourselves being challenged by the questions little children ask their parents: "What's that mean?" "Why?" Why did Jesus pray? Why did he choose just twelve? What's an apostle?

As he does so often in his Gospel, Luke spotlights Jesus at prayer (6:12; see the commentary on 11:1–13). The selection of the Twelve is not only Jesus' decision, but also God's will revealed in prayer.

Why just twelve? Wouldn't a hundred do the job more effectively? We can open a door on the significance of the number twelve by recalling that God's people Israel was built upon twelve tribes. Although unity under the twelve tribes dissolved, the twelve-tribe federation continued to serve as a hope-filled model for God's rebuilding of his people. As Paul tells King Agrippa in Acts 26:5–7: "I have lived my life as a Pharisee, the strictest party of our religion. But now I am standing trial because of my hope in the promise [of the resurrection] made by God to our ancestors. Our *twelve tribes* hope to attain to that promise. . . ." Just as the Old Testament Israel was built upon the twelve tribes and their leaders, so the Israel that Jesus constitutes is built upon twelve leaders. The Twelve point beyond themselves to what God is doing through Jesus. God is rebuilding God's people, Israel.

An apostle—the word means "one sent"—represents the one who sends him much as a high-ranking dignitary sent by the president of the United States to a peace conference represents him and is invested with much of his authority. The apostles represent Jesus, the bringer of God's kingdom. In Luke, the apostles also give public testimony to Jesus' significance by witnessing to his earthly life and resurrection. In Peter's guidelines on how to replace Judas and thus fill up the number of twelve apostles, this notion of witness shines through clearly: "Therefore, it is necessary that one of the men who accompanied us the whole time the Lord Jesus came and went among us, beginning from the baptism of John until the day on which he was taken up from us, become with us a witness to his resurrection" (Acts 1:21–22). It is Luke alone who combines the notion of the Twelve with apostle. In 1 Corinthians 15:1–11 Paul shows by his call and mission that he is an apostle, although not a member of the Twelve. And in Romans 16:7 Paul mentions the male apostle Andronicus and the female apostle Junia. The task of the twelve apostles is to represent and witness to Jesus as God's promised Messiah and to rebuild God's people on the foundation of that Jesus.

STUDY QUESTION: We frequently hear and profess in solemn creeds that the church must be apostolic. What does that really mean?

Luke 6:17–26
SETTING THE WORLD'S STANDARDS ON THEIR HEAD

This section begins Luke's Sermon on the Plain (6:17–49), which contains the blueprints for the rebuilding of God's people, Israel.

In verse 20 Luke catches our attention with the refrain, "kingdom of God," and signals to us to meditate once more on Jesus' kingdom ministry. The kingdom of God images the mercy which the king extends to the oppressed, neglected, and poor. This aspect of the kingdom image is front and center stage in this section.

Let's use an example to think ourselves into this aspect of God's rule which Jesus brings. Suppose a pollster phones you and asks what indicators would best describe happiness for you: "Would you equate happiness with being poor, hungry, sorrowful, and being despised by everyone? Or would you equate happiness with abundant money, a well-set table, joy, and being held in high regard by everyone?" No doubt you would choose the last set of indicators. Yet Jesus' beatitudes and woes challenge us to rethink our choice as they turn the world's standards on their head. The kingdom which Jesus brings is a frontal attack on the evil by which people are made economically poor and oppressed. The oppressed and deprived are favored by God, not because they happen to be poor and have no need to repent, but because God the king is merciful. The rich and well-fed also need repentance and must not allow the goods and standards of this world to turn their hands against the poor and God's rule in Jesus.

Luke transmits Jesus' kingdom preaching to his own community. The beatitudes and woes, which were first addressed to the general public of Jesus' day, are now addressed to the "disciples" of Luke's day (6:20). All have already experienced the rule of Jesus the Lord in their own lives. But God's kingdom of justice and mercy has not come in its fullness. Some members of Luke's community are still poor, and are persecuted because of their allegiance to Jesus. These are consoled that, despite signs to the contrary, God's rule will be triumphant in the end. The rich members of Luke's community are warned that wealth is not the be-all and end-all of life. They should not compromise their faith in Jesus to avoid persecution and confiscation of their property. They should befriend their poor and persecuted fellow Christians.

STUDY QUESTION: Is there anything we can do today to promote God's kingdom of mercy and justice in our country, state, city, neighborhood?

Luke 6:27–35
THE LOVE ETHIC OF THE KINGDOM

The love ethic of the kingdom of God is the heart of this section. Jesus preaches the almost-too-good-to-be-true news that the motive force behind God's rule is love. God is not mean and tyrannical. God is kind (6:35); God is a compassionate father (6:36). Those who accept Jesus' message that God is merciful must reflect that same mercy in their own lives. They must love their enemies (6:27, 35). For them the Golden Rule is life's norm: "Do to others as you would have them do to you."

Realizing that Jesus' love ethic is general, Luke applies it to two specific concerns within his community: the persecuted and the possessors. In verses 27–31 the plight of the persecuted is portrayed in graphic detail: They are hated, cursed, maltreated, slapped around, and robbed. Although they are treated so miserably, these Christians are to treat their persecutors as they themselves would like to be treated (6:31). In verses 32–35 Luke applies the love ethic to the possessors within his community. They must cease and desist from the tit-for-tat or reciprocity ethic which is part and parcel of the cultural air they breathe, an ethic that limits their charity to those who have the wherewithal to return the favor. Such self-serving charity must give way to Jesus' love ethic (see the commentary on 14:12–14).

Before we decry Jesus' love ethic as an invitation to joust with a windmill, let's remember that this ethic is addressed to disciples (6:20), to children of the Most High (6:35), to those who have been showered with the transforming love of God's rule and enabled to test the waters of the seemingly impossible.

STUDY QUESTION: Does Luke's application of Jesus' love ethic provide us with guidelines on how we might apply that ethic today?

Luke 6:36–49
THE PROOF OF DISCIPLESHIP IS IN THE DOING

Luke concludes Jesus' Sermon on the Plain with three messages. In 6:36–38 he rounds off the meaning of the love ethic of the kingdom. Disciples must share with one another the mercy they have received from God. To the extent that they show mercy, they will receive mercy from God.

In 6:39–45 the "fully trained" disciples (6:40) are in view. Are these the "apostles" or church leaders? They must not parade around telling everyone else to look into the mirror of the love ethic. While busily telling everyone else that they have a slight bit of cereal on their cheek, they fail to glance into the mirror themselves and see traces of breakfast all over their face. Christians' actions will show whether the love ethic is the center of their lives (6:43–45).

Jesus' love ethic is not to be mouthed, but done (6:46–49). Since Jesus proclaims and brings about God's rule, he can promise that those who lay a foundation on his teaching will escape the catastrophe of the flood. "Lord, Lord" is to be informed with an obedience to Jesus that stems from love, a love whose flame will not die out when persecution rages, when the rich and church leaders give scandal, and when false teachers proclaim that the confession "Lord, Lord" speaks louder than actions done in one's lowly body.

STUDY QUESTION: Jesus' Sermon on the Plain can be described as a pattern for Christian life. Should this pattern be followed rigidly or creatively?

Luke 7:1–17
JESUS, LORD, IS FOR ALL PEOPLE

Now that he has detailed Jesus' kingdom preaching in the Sermon on the Plain (6:17–49), Luke turns to a description of two miracles of Jesus. In doing so, he highlights once more who Jesus is and also sets the stage for John the Baptist's question, "Are you the one who is to come, or should we look for another?" (7:20)

The healing of the centurion's servant (7:1–10) is a strange miracle indeed; the cure is hardly mentioned at all. The emphases within the story fall on the beneficence (7:5) and especially on the faith (7:9) of the centurion. This story signals that a non-Jew is worthy to embrace the benefits issuing from Jesus' kingdom power. It also points toward the Gentile mission. It is not coincidental that the first Gentile convert mentioned in the Acts of the Apostles is a centurion, named Cornelius, who "used to give alms generously to the Jewish people" (Acts 10:2). Cornelius, like the centurion in our story, has faith in Jesus although he has never seen him.

By restoring the only son of the widow of Nain to life (7:11–17), Jesus acts out God's mercy. In Jesus, God is visiting God's people, drawing near to them in their distress (7:16). See 1:68, "Blessed be the Lord, the God of Israel, for he has *visited* God's people and brought them redemption." Jesus may be likened to the prophet Elijah, who through prayer restored a widow's son to life and "gave him to his mother" (7:15; see 1 Kgs 17:23). But Jesus is more. As Lord (7:13), he frees people from death's captivity. Through Jesus "the dead are raised" (7:22).

STUDY QUESTION: What is there about the centurion's faith that merits Jesus' accolade, "I tell you, not even in Israel have I found such faith" (7:9)?

Luke 7:18–35
REVELATION AND REACTION

Let's use "reaction" as the code word by which we can crack open the messages of this section.

In prison John hears about Jesus' preaching and miracles and reacts by sending two disciples to ask him point-blank whether he is the

Messiah. Jesus reacts to John's question by fulfilling, in clear view of John's two witnesses, the prophecy with which he began his public ministry (7:21; see 4:18). John will truly be happy if he rids himself of his opinion that Jesus should be a Messiah in the finest fire-and-brimstone tradition (see 3:17). John the Baptist and Luke's readers are challenged to rethink their image of God and God's Messiah, Jesus. God is merciful, and Jesus embodies that mercy by restoring people to health and by preaching God's mercy to the outcasts of society.

After John's disciples return to their master, Jesus reacts to John's ministry and in doing so reveals more about himself. John is a prophet, and surely no one born of a woman is greater than John, yet he is just the messenger who prepared for God's coming in Jesus (7:27). Although Jesus seemed to be inferior to John because he was baptized by him, he actually is greater than John because he brings God's kingdom (7:28).

The reactions to the revelation of John the Baptist are like the reactions to Jesus' revelation. Whereas the religious leaders of Judaism react negatively to John, all the people and the hated toll collectors react most favorably (7:29–30). John the Baptist and Jesus just couldn't win with the religious leaders. John said, "Let's fast and repent," and they replied that they'd rather eat and drink. Jesus said, "Let's eat and drink and have a party," and they rejoined that they'd rather fast and repent. The people, the toll collectors, and the sinners are open to the revelation of John and Jesus. They form the nucleus of God's renewed people, and by their reactions to John and Jesus they show how truly wise they are.

STUDY QUESTION: Revelation and reaction. Is it possible to become comfortable with a God who loves table fellowship with society's disadvantaged?

Luke 7:36–50
THE WOMAN WHO SHOWED GREAT LOVE TOWARD JESUS

I suppose that most of us have seen a movie which was so powerful that we couldn't grasp its total message in one viewing. We wanted to get a video of it, so that we could see it again and again to spot the things we missed the first time around. This story is like a powerful movie. Before you continue with this commentary, read the story through again. My commentary will show the key scenes in slow motion and allow you to grasp what the story is saying about Jesus, the church, and forgiveness.

The story features prophet Jesus, "friend of toll collectors and sinners" (7:34). Jesus does not share the religious viewpoint which labels mixing with sinners a no-no (7:39). He allows a sinful woman to touch him and to thank him lavishly for forgiving her sins. Note that nowhere does Luke say that this woman was a prostitute. She may have been a "sinner" because her work, for example, of dyeing or midwifery, brought her into frequent contact with unclean Gentiles. Jesus' mercy toward the sinful woman jars the consciousness of Simon and of those at table with him: "Who is this who even forgives sins?" (7:49).

This is the first of three stories in which Jesus dines with a Pharisee (see also 11:37–54 and 14:1–24). Unlike those other accounts, where the Pharisees argue with Jesus about a point of law, here the Pharisee is more concerned about Jesus' mission: How can such a supposedly holy man and prophet associate with sinners? In Luke's eyes the Pharisee is representative of those Christians within his church who haven't experienced great forgiveness and view with some apprehension the church's concern for the general run of humankind who are sinners. Luke reminds these Pharisees that Jesus has revealed God as a God of boundless love. The church should hesitate before rushing in work crews to erect a fence around that mercy.

It is difficult to fathom the rich interrelationships between the words "forgiveness," "love," and "faith" in verses 47–50. On one level, the theological problems of these rich interrelationships are solved by seeing that the woman's acts of love flowed from her belief that Jesus had truly offered her God's mercy and forgiveness on an earlier occasion. On another level, faith saves those who turn from their sins (7:50). They show that they have received forgiveness by their acts of love and thankfulness (7:47).

STUDY QUESTION: Jesus challenged Simon to change his vision of the woman who loved much and of Jesus, the prophet of our merciful God. Do we, too, need corrective lenses, so that we can safely drive along the highway of faith and charity?

Luke 8:1–3
FAITHFUL FEMALE FOLLOWERS OF JESUS

This summary is a literary and theological gem. A summary is a concise
narrative statement that reports an event that went on repeatedly for an
indefinite period of time. Consider the more familiar Lukan summary in
Acts 2:42: The first Christians "devoted themselves to the teaching of the
apostles and to the communal life, to the breaking of bread and to the
prayers." Prayers, breaking of bread, common life, and apostolic teaching
did not occur just once, but were the sum and substance of repeated
daily Christian existence. The summary of Luke 8:1–3 indicates that the
women were not with Jesus just once, but customarily. See, for example,
their presence at the cross and resurrection in Luke 23:49 to 24:11.

A generalization about women in Jesus' time will help us see the
deep theological significance of Jesus' close association with women in
his ministry: In Jewish and Greco-Roman society, women had little
social or religious standing and were marginalized. Against this background it is striking that Jesus, the bringer of God's kingdom, had female
followers. In Jesus, God's rule of love is for both men and women.

This summary resonates with other sections of Luke's work. Besides
Elizabeth, Mary, and Anna (chapters 1 and 2), these other women figure
in Jesus' story: Simon's mother-in-law (4:38–39), the widow at Nain
(7:11–17), a sinner (7:36–50), the woman with the hemorrhage
(8:43–48), Martha and Mary (10:38–42), a crippled woman (13:10–17),
the widow who gives an offering (21:1–4), the women at the crucifixion (23:49, 55), and the women as witnesses to Jesus' resurrection
(24:1–11, 22–23), as well as the women in Jesus' parables of the woman
and the lost coin (15:8–10), and of the widow and the judge (18:1–8).
See also the mention in Acts 1:14 of women and Mary in the Jerusalem
community awaiting the descent of the promised Holy Spirit. A number
of these passages (7:11–17, 7:36–50, 8:1–3, 10:38–42, 13:10–17,
15:8–10, 18:1–8) occur only in Luke's Gospel.

Three key points emerge from Luke's presentation of Jesus' association with women. First, Jesus largely goes against the mores of his time
and associates freely with women, thus manifesting the inclusive nature
of God's kingdom. Second, they are his most faithful followers. Like the
Twelve and the other disciples, they witness to what Jesus says and does
during his earthly ministry; but unlike the twelve apostles, they remain
completely faithful to Jesus when the chips are down (see 23:49, 55).
And they are the first proclaimers of the good news that Jesus is not

dead, but alive (Luke 24:1–11). Finally, indications are that they played an important role in the missionary communities of Luke's time.

STUDY QUESTION: In *Jesus According to a Woman,* Rachel Conrad Wahlberg asks the question: Why has the church been blind to the significance of Jesus' association with women? In your experience has the church been blind?

Luke 8:4–21
THE KINGDOM OF GOD THROUGH MATURE EYES

Imagine yourself asking two people, one aged twenty and the other aged seventy, to read a great piece of literature like *War and Peace.* After they have read the masterpiece, you then ask them to interpret the story for you in terms of their own life experience. I would venture to say that the seventy-year-old would have a richer understanding of the book's message.

The above exercise in imagination sets us on our way to uncovering the meaning of this section. The great piece of literature is "the kingdom of God" which Jesus preaches and brings (see 8:1). The word of God is that God's rule is merciful (8:11). Despite the apparent disaster of rock and thorn, that word will yield a superabundant harvest (8:4–8).

The church, as it beds down with Jesus' message of God's kingdom, can be likened to the seventy-year-old. Since its members have been given knowledge of the secrets of the kingdom of God (8:10), they continue to preach that God's rule is merciful and that Jesus makes God's rule present. They cannot keep the kingdom message hidden under a bed (8:16). The kingdom of God is God's word for them. The experience of age has taught Luke's community that the word, once believed, leads to salvation (8:12). Experience has also advised them that the trials of persecution are going to swoop down on them. The worries and riches and pleasures of this present life are going to gnaw at their faith and erode their membership rolls. The rich harvest of faith is for those who persevere (8:15). Truly, the Christians of Luke's time must take care how they hear God's word (8:18). They will be mothers and brothers to Jesus provided they "hear the word of God and act on it" (8:21).

In powerfully moving words Jesus told the story that God's rule is merciful and that setbacks are only apparent and will not detour that rule from triumphing. Some fifty years after the death of Jesus the church of Luke's time has the rich experience of age to fathom Jesus' story. While its missionary endeavors may meet with rejection and even imprisonment, it, like Paul, continues to proclaim the kingdom of God and to teach the truth about the Lord Jesus Christ to both Jew and Gentile (see Acts 28:31).

STUDY QUESTION: Does this section give us any helpful hints on how we should preach and hear the word of God today—at home and abroad?

Luke 8:22–56
JESUS' DEEDS ARE KEYS TO THE KINGDOM

There are a number of ways of surveying land. One is to size up the overall lay of the land—its terrain, ponds, trees, etc. Another is to make specific probes in some areas for more detailed information about soil content, water level, etc. In our survey of this section we will first take an overall look at the land of these four miracle stories. Then, we'll make some specific probes in the area of Christian mission and faith.

The kingdom of God is God's word (8:11). And it is more. God's rule rescues those perishing (8:22–25), expels demons (8:26–39), cures illness and restores life (8:40–56). But as we have often reflected in this commentary, that kingdom is not some abstract concept soaring in an intellectual stratosphere. God's kingdom is brought about by the historical Jesus of Nazareth. With the storm raging about him, Jesus shows that he has the same power ascribed to God in the Old Testament. As the psalmist confessed: "They cried to the LORD in their distress; from their straits the Lord rescued them. God hushed the storm to a gentle breeze, and the billows of the sea were stilled" (Ps 107:28–29). Jesus not only has power over one or another demon but actually dominates legion and their dwelling place, the abyss (8:31). The Book of Revelation helps us catch the flavor of Jesus' power over the dreadful abyss and its inhabitants when the seer says: "Then I saw an angel come down from heaven, holding in his hand the key to the abyss and a heavy chain. He seized the dragon, the ancient serpent, which is the Devil or Satan, and . . . threw it into the abyss" (Revelation 20:1–3). Jesus also saves people from illness (8:48) and death (8:54–55). The kingdom of God pulses through Jesus' veins with such intensity that his mere commands are enough to restore order to the chaos of nature and to stop demons from harassing humankind with illness (8:25, 31). This broad and sweeping survey shows that at the center of the mysteries of the kingdom of God (8:10) stands Jesus and his kingdom message and deeds.

If we make a specific probe into the story of the Gerasene demoniac (8:26–39), we can spy beneath the surface the future missionary activity of the church. The church will lead people from isolation to community, from chains to liberation, from being naked to being clothed, and from living among the dead to associating with the living. And it is Jesus who effects all these transformations. Indeed, the transformed man is happy to go back home and spread to all and sundry the good news of what God has done for him through Jesus (8:39).

Let's make another probe in our surveying efforts and detect the levels of teaching on the role of faith (8:25, 48, 50). The powers of God's rule, unleashed in Jesus' deeds, do not act in a vacuum. They call for and thrive on faith. Caught in the waves of persecution and tossed by the winds of wealth and pleasures (8:13–14), the disciples must increase their faith in the Jesus who will act to calm their stormy lives (8:22–25). Bumping into Jesus on the street will not save anyone; women and men must have faith that Jesus conveys God's power to cure (8:48). Faith is not a static reality; changed circumstances call for a deepening of that faith (8:50).

STUDY QUESTION: Have you ever experienced some of the transformations experienced by the Gerasene demoniac? Do these four miracle stories contain messages about how we might need to strengthen our faith?

Luke 9:1–9
JESUS, THE TWELVE AS HIS MISSIONARIES, AND THE FUTURE

I use this section as a basis for summarizing Jesus' entire Galilean ministry and do so by using a simple business analogy. When a business firm comes to the end of its fiscal year, it tallies the year's assets and debits and makes forecasts for its future.

In 9:1–50 Jesus completes his Galilean ministry. The instructions on top of the tally sheet for the Jesus firm have one question: "Who is this I hear such reports about?" (9:9; contrast Mark 6:16). The success of Jesus' powerful proclamation of the kingdom of God in word and deed (8:1–56) and of the Twelve's similar proclamation (9:1–6, 10) is the immediate occasion for the question. As Herod tallies Jesus' record, he responds to the question like a curiosity seeker: "Let me see him sometime and then I'll give you a more definite answer" (9:9). Later, in 23:8–11 Herod will indeed see Jesus, but his self-centeredness will blind him to Jesus' significance. The tally of Peter, Jesus' longtime associate, is that he is "the Christ of God" (9:20). God, whose kingdom Jesus brings, voices the authoritative tally: "This is my chosen Son; listen to him" (9:35). But the seemingly dominant forecast in 9:1–50 is that the future of the Jesus firm is bleak. Many don't want its product: "The Son of Man must suffer greatly and be rejected by the elders, the chief priests, and the scribes, and be killed" (9:22). Jesus may be the Messiah of God and God's Son, but he has no long-term staying power.

Although this pessimistic prognostication of the future of the Jesus firm seems to carry the day, it fails to factor in God's action: God will raise up the crucified Jesus on the third day (see 9:22). The Twelve, who form the foundation of God's renewed people, will continue Jesus' kingdom proclamation (9:1–6 and see Acts). Yet the pessimists do have some truth on their side. As the church carries out its missionary work to Jews and Gentiles amidst persecution, it will have to devise new strategies to replace those of the peaceful days in Galilee (9:3; see 22:35–38, the commentary on 10:1–24, and the trials and travails of Paul in Acts).

STUDY QUESTION: From your study, what were the reasons for the successes and failures of Jesus' Galilean ministry? Is it possible for us modern missionaries "to take nothing for the journey" (9:3)?

Luke 9:10–17
JESUS BRINGS SUPERABUNDANT SUSTENANCE

Those of us who lived in Chicago while Richard J. Daley was mayor know that he sometimes answered reporters' questions with a story. When reporters asked him about the trouble a certain political figure had brought down upon his head by a clumsy statement, His Honor proceeded to tell them a story about the large fish he had recently caught while fishing in Lake Michigan. The reporters were annoyed and thought that Daley was evading their question until he meandered to the punch line: "You know, if that fish hadn't opened its mouth, it wouldn't have been caught."

Like reporters, we come to Luke with our question, "Who is this I hear such reports about?" (9:9). Instead of giving us a direct answer in this section, Luke tells us a story. The story answers the question with the refrain "kingdom of God," and with the number twelve (9:12, 17). The kingdom of God, which Jesus brings, gives nourishment for his people much like the manna God gave to his starving people in the desert (see Exod 16:15–16). The Twelve bear witness to the richness of this food, and their helpers, the disciples (9:14, 16), distribute it to the people. In its superabundance of twelve baskets (9:17), it is food for the renewed Israel, built upon the foundation of the Twelve. And the words "he said the blessing over them, broke them, and gave them to the disciples" (9:16) prompt the reader to look beyond this food to the Eucharist, which is for all (9:17; see 22:19 and 24:30; see also "the breaking of bread" in Acts).

Luke has answered our question with a captivating story of God's loving concern for the hungry. Jesus acts out the meaning of God's kingdom by providing nourishment for those in need; he continues to nurture his people through the breaking of the bread in the Eucharist.

STUDY QUESTION: How does Jesus provide sustenance for his followers in this day and age?

Luke 9:18–27
JESUS TEACHES THE TRUTH THAT THE MESSIAH MUST SUFFER

I suppose that most of us have had good teachers who wrote detailed comments on papers we handed in. The teacher counseled that while what we had written was true, it did not go deeply enough into the area under consideration. The teacher gave us pointers on how we could delve deeper into the subject and get a firmer grasp on the truth.

In this section Peter's answer that Jesus is "the Christ of God" (9:20) is indeed true. But it is not the whole truth. Jesus, like a good teacher, instructs Peter on how he can probe more profoundly into the truth. Jesus' role as Messiah of God must include suffering (9:22). This has been destined by God. Or, as the Risen Lord teaches his disciples on the way to Emmaus: "Was it not necessary that the Messiah should suffer these things and enter into his glory?" (24:26). The truth that Jesus is the suffering Messiah of God has vast implications for all who profess it (9:23–25). If their confession of Jesus as the Messiah of God is to make any sense, Jesus' followers must shoulder their cross every day. Dying to one's self-centeredness for the sake of Jesus is the disciple's way of life. It will take disciples a lifetime of commitment to fathom the truth that Jesus is God's suffering Messiah.

Verse 26 gives further insight into this truth by applying it to those who suffer for the faith in Luke's community. Failure to acknowledge Jesus will have dire consequences at the judgment. Verse 27 picks up the refrain "kingdom of God," rounds off this section, and leads into the account of the transfiguration (9:28–36). In Jesus, God has shown the graciousness of his rule. In the transfiguration some will see the glory of God's kingdom reflected in Jesus' person. Some will see God's rule over death manifested in Jesus' glorified body. Some, like Stephen, will experience the graciousness of God's rule as they witness to Jesus the Christ to the point of death (see Acts 7:55–56).

STUDY QUESTION: Is your idea of daily crossbearing for Jesus' sake the same today as it was ten or fifteen years ago?

Luke 9:28–36
THE TRANSFIGURATION DISCLOSES WHO JESUS IS

All of us have disclosed who we are to someone at some time or another. We may have prefaced our intimate remarks with, "Well, I've never told anyone else before...." Or we may have revealed our love for another person by expressing the inexpressible through images: "Your smile is the beacon of my life. Your words cheer my day like a brilliant sunrise."

The transfiguration is a disclosure of who Jesus is. To express the inexpressible, Luke uses imagery drawn from the Old Testament. A verse-by-verse commentary will allow us to ponder the reality being disclosed by these images.

9:28 The startling truth that Jesus is a suffering Messiah (9:18–27) is closely linked to Jesus' disclosure, which occurs on a mountain—a traditional place for revelation/disclosure.

9:29 As Jesus is radiant with the heavenly world, we recall the description of Moses: "As Moses came down from Mount Sinai . . . he did not know that the skin of his face had become radiant while he conversed with the LORD" (Exod 34:29).

9:30–31 The epitomes of God's Old Testament revelation in law and prophetic utterance converse with Jesus, who is going to fulfill all their expectations by his "exodus." Through his death, resurrection, ascension, and gift of the Spirit, Jesus will lead his people in a new exodus from bondage to life.

9:32 Whereas Moses reflected God's glory (Exod 34:29), Jesus' glory is his very own. That is, God's majesty and power are visibly present in Jesus.

9:33 In calling for the erection of three tents, Peter senses the presence of God and wants to capture it. But he misses the point. God's presence is to be found in Jesus' word (see 9:35).

9:34–36 The cloud signifies the presence of God as in Exodus 40:34: "Then the cloud covered the meeting tent, and the glory of the LORD filled the Dwelling." With greater authority than Moses and Elijah, God confirms the truth of what Jesus had announced in 9:18–27. God underlines in words what was disclosed in the transfiguration, while the transfiguration discloses the meaning of the words. The Lord Jesus will be present to his church in his word.

Through the transfiguration Jesus discloses that the cross will not write the final word to the story of his life. "Was it not necessary that the Messiah should suffer these things and enter into his glory?" (24:26).

STUDY QUESTION: What does Jesus' self-disclosure in his transfiguration contribute to our image of him?

Luke 9:37–50
THE TRUTH THAT REVOLUTIONIZES HEART
AND MIND

The truth that Jesus is a suffering and rejected Messiah is not a simple truth like "One plus one equals two," something that can be grasped quickly. It's more like the truth "It is in giving that we receive," which takes a long time, perhaps even a lifetime, to assimilate.

"And all were astonished by the majesty of God" which Jesus manifested in his cure of the demoniac (9:37–43). As they buzzed about the marvels of Jesus' Galilean ministry, "they were all amazed at his every deed" (9:43). But being astonished and amazed only grant waiting room in the lobby of the truth of who Jesus is.

It is easy for the disciples to join ranks with the crowd and play hooky from reflecting more profoundly on Jesus' truth. They are policed back to school by a reminder of Jesus' rejection and cross (9:44). It will take many wrestlings of faith before that truth will dawn on them (9:45). As a matter of fact, they shy away from such a struggle and busily jockey for positions as if they worked for some ruler of this earth. They must learn that a title on their door does not rate them red-carpet treatment. In Jesus' company, greatness is synonymous with being a premier servant of the helpless (9:46–48). They must avoid the discrimination of making ministry their private club (9:49–50).

Jesus' Galilean ministry is over. Luke has presented Jesus as the Messiah of God, whose word and action effects God's rule. The truth that Jesus preached and lived even escaped his disciples. But it abides as a challenge for Luke's readers and all their latter-day kin.

STUDY QUESTION: What images of Jesus did you find most captivating in Luke's presentation of Jesus' Galilean ministry (4:14 to 9:50)? Why did Jesus' Galilean ministry meet with so little success?

IV. THE WAY TO JERUSALEM: INSTRUCTIONS FOR JESUS' FOLLOWERS

Luke 9:51 to 19:44

INTRODUCTION TO LUKE 9:51 TO 19:44

Luke 9:51 opens the door to one of Luke's most signal creations, the narrative of Jesus' journey to Jerusalem (9:51 to 19:44). Around some fifteen references to Jesus' journey, Luke has assembled some of the most beloved texts in all the scriptures, such as the parables of the Good Samaritan and the Prodigal Son. The heading given above for these chapters gives us a preview of the significance of Luke's creation.

In 9:51 to 19:44, Luke plays on the various theological meanings of journey. Jesus' teachings reveal God's way (see 10:21–24). When Jesus visits, the Lord God visits (9:53, 10:1, 19:44; see 7:16). The coming of Jesus brings salvation to those who accept him (19:9).

In depicting Jesus' way as a way to Jerusalem, Luke is not primarily concerned with the historical city Jerusalem. He views Jerusalem as the culmination of God's choicest blessings, as the guardian of God's temple and teaching, as the bridge between the past of God's promises and the present of longed-for fulfillment, as the center of the Jewish religious authorities. Jerusalem is also the site of Jesus' confrontation with and rejection by these authorities—the place of his final teachings, his passion and death. It is also the scene of his resurrection. There the promised Spirit descends upon the 120 men and women gathered in the upper room. From there God continues Jesus' mission to Jews and Gentiles in the Way which is the Christian religion (see Acts 9:2, 18:26, 24:22). Jerusalem illumines all of Jesus' teaching in this section much like the denouement of a story casts light on all the preceding elements. Since the religious authorities reject Jesus in Jerusalem, it seems that Jesus' teachings, all the way from Galilee to Jerusalem (see 23:5), have not revealed God's way. But God does not allow these authorities to spell the end of Jesus' way.

As Jesus goes his way to Jerusalem, his apostles and male and female disciples accompany him. The instructions and warnings which Jesus gives to them about mission, prayer, persecution, the dangers of wealth, etc., are meant for the Christians of Luke's own time—the members of the Way. Jesus' apostles are witnesses of his teaching and will be able to preserve it in the new Way after his resurrection (see Acts 1:21–22). No, the rejection of Jesus by the religious authorities in Jerusalem did not invalidate his teaching. God put God's stamp of approval on Jesus' way by raising him from the dead and by establishing the new Way in Jerusalem. I give one final word about journey as a metaphor for discipleship. Journeying in antiquity was arduous. In 2 Corinthians 11:26 Paul lists as one of his sufferings: "on frequent journeys." He says this almost in the same breath with "I was beaten with rods thrice, once stoned, and thrice shipwrecked."

For the convenience of the reader, I divide Luke's long travel narrative into sections: 9:51 to 13:21, 13:22 to 17:10, and 17:11 to 19:44. The verse which begins each one of these sections explicitly mentions that Jesus is journeying to Jerusalem.

Luke 9:51–62
THE COST OF FOLLOWING JESUS

When Jesus opened his Galilean journey, he suffered rejection (4:16–30). Similarly, he and his disciples encountered rejection on the first leg of their journey to Jerusalem (9:52–56). For his missionary communities Luke shows how Jesus and his traveling disciples are bound to encounter natural and human obstacles on their journeys. Jesus will not allow his disciples to retaliate against acts of inhospitality and thus lives out his own teaching about non-retaliation against enemies (6:27–29, 35).

The three stories of 9:57–62 are streamlined. All attention is centered on Jesus' responses. Since the characters of the would-be disciples are left undeveloped, the Christians of Luke's time and ours can be drawn into the story line and can identify with them. Jesus' sayings themselves are veritable show-stoppers. Jesus does not respond directly to the first person's resolve, but stops him in his tracks to ponder the consequences of that resolve. The reasonable requests of the next two men are bypassed by the admonition to single-mindedness.

Jesus' sayings clearly focus on the overriding importance of following him. Following him is not a task which is added to others like working a second job. Nor does it belong in one compartment of our lives, separated from other aspects of our compartmentalized lives. It is everything. It is a solemn commitment that forces the disciples-to-be to reorder all their other duties. The sharpness of Jesus' sayings jars readers into weighing most seriously their desire to make Jesus' way their way.

STUDY QUESTION: How practical is it to espouse Jesus' method of value clarification and view one's myriad duties and obligations in the light of the one value of following him?

Luke 10:1–24
JESUS' MISSION CONTINUED

Each word in the heading above touches on a key idea in this passage. The mission to be continued is Jesus'. Verses 16, 19, and 21–24 pulsate with some of the most pregnant christological statements in the Gospel. Their vocabulary may not be that of a Karl Rahner or of Chalcedon, but is profound nonetheless. What the people of the Old Testament longed for is present in Jesus' deeds and teaching as Jesus, Son of the Father, reveals God's will and way (10:21–24). As herald of God's kingdom, Jesus overthrows God's enemies, the forces of evil (10:19). When Jesus visits people, the Lord God visits them (10:1, 16). This is the Jesus whose mission is continued.

The perceptive reader will be quick to recall that during Jesus' Galilean ministry there was a mission of the Twelve (9:1–6, 10–11) and to muse, Why this new mission? The answer lies in the richly symbolic number seventy-two. Genesis 10 numbers the nations of the earth at seventy-two. The Christian mission to all the nations of the earth (see

Acts 1:8) is foreshadowed in Jesus' commissioning of the seventy-two. Further, the sending of the seventy-two provides Luke with an opportunity to collect instructions from various sources for the missionaries of his own day (10:2–12). For the most part, these instructions stem from an experience of missionary expansion whose peacefulness enabled Christians to support the missionaries operating in their locale and from their house churches (see 10:4–7).

The seventy-two are not freelance missionaries. They embark on mission under the masthead of Jesus' name and power. "Whoever listens to you listens to me. Whoever rejects you rejects me. And whoever rejects me rejects the one who sent me" (10:16). In Jesus' name the seventy-two subdue the forces of the enemy (10:17).

The missionary work described in this passage is so vital for his church that Luke alludes to it again. During the Last Supper Jesus asks his disciples, "'When I sent you forth without a money bag or a sack or sandals, were you in need of anything?' 'No, nothing,' they replied. He said to them, 'But now... one who does not have a sword should sell his cloak and buy one'" (22:35–36). Luke 10:4 is the obvious referent of Jesus' question. The palpable tension between the two passages reflects different missionary experiences. The instruction of 10:4 originates in peaceful missionary endeavor, whereas 22:35–36 issues from the missionary activity of a church that shares the fate of its persecuted Lord.

STUDY QUESTION: What form should Christian mission assume in a world where the vast majority of people are non-Christian?

Luke 10:25–37
A QUESTION OF LAW:
WHO BELONGS TO THE CHURCH?

This section contains the incomparable parable of the Good Samaritan, but it teaches more than social concern, as in the well-worn news headline "Good Samaritan Comes to the Rescue." Its message is also one about missionary activity among despised people such as the Samaritans, who did not hold sacred the same books of the Bible as the Jews and worshiped God on Mount Gerizim, not on Mount Zion. It is not surprising that Jesus' messengers were not well received in a Samaritan village (9:52–53). And theologically significant for the progress of the Christian mission is the evangelization of Samaria reported in Acts 8.

Luke makes it a habit to interpret his parables by adding introductions or conclusions to them. For example, he creates a special introduction for the three parables of the lost sheep, lost coin, and lost son in chapter 15. In the passage at hand Luke has so artistically added an introduction and conclusion to the parable of the Good Samaritan that the entire passage forms a unity—a controversy story composed of two parallel parts:

1. The lawyer's *question* (10:25)
    Jesus' *counterquestion* (10:26)
    The lawyer's own *answer* (10:27)
    Jesus' *command* (10:28)

2. The lawyer's further *question* (10:29)
    Jesus' *counterquestion* (10:30–36)
    The lawyer's own *answer* (10:37a)
    Jesus' *command* (10:37b)

The passage begins and ends with a question of law. We can specify that question by examining the verses that bracket the parable—verses 29, 36–37.

In verse 29 the lawyer singles out the word "neighbor" from the Old Testament quotations of verse 27. His question is born of controversies over membership in God's covenant people and really means, "Who is a member of God's covenant community and therefore an object of my mercy?" In verse 37a the lawyer is forced by Jesus' parable to answer his own question with "The one who treated him with mercy." Jesus has gotten the upper hand in his controversy with the lawyer and has turned the lawyer's question on its head. In effect, Jesus says, "Don't search for those who are neighbors, but for those who act like a neighbor." The Samaritan, who doesn't belong by birth to God's covenant people, actually acts like a member of that people by being compassionate. Non-Jews, like the Samaritan, can become members of God's covenant people by showing mercy. Jesus' command in the latter part of verse 37 finalizes his victory in the controversy: Jews can lose their membership in God's covenant community if they do not observe the law of mercy.

The parable of the Good Samaritan functions as part of Luke's answer to a gigantic mission problem in his church: What role does the law have in saying who is in or out of the church? Luke's answer is revolutionary: Persons who observe the covenant law of mercy—be they Jews, Samaritans, or Gentiles—are members of God's church (see also what Acts 15 says about the missionary decisions of the First Council of Jerusalem).

STUDY QUESTION: Do missionary churches have to observe the same ecclesiastical laws as established churches? Do we use people's observance of our interpretation of the law as a means of considering them in or out of salvation?

Luke 10:38–42
THE ROLE OF WOMEN IN THE CHURCH'S MISSION

This story exemplifies hospitality offered to the travel-weary Jesus and to those who are missionaries in his name. In the "welcome," which Martha and Mary offer Jesus, they are a positive example of how to receive a missionary (see the "welcome" of 10:8 in Luke's account of the sending of the seventy-two) and counter the negative example of certain Samaritans who would not "welcome" Jesus (9:53).

This story also hints at another role women played in the missionary life of the early church. At the time when Luke's Gospel was written, women were ministers. See, for example, Romans 16:1: "I commend to you Phoebe our sister, who is a minister (Greek: *diakonos*) of the church at Cenchreae." Also at that time, Christians met in the houses of fellow believers. See, for example, 1 Corinthians 16:19: "Aquila and Prisca together with the church at their house send you many greetings." Often the head of the house, male or female, was head of the "house church."

This story belongs to the table-fellowship genre of stories in Luke's Gospel. In each of them Jesus takes people to task and teaches them an important lesson. In the great banquet that Levi throws, Jesus teaches the Pharisees and their scribes the meaning of mercy (5:27–32). In 7:36–50 Jesus teaches Simon the Pharisee the lesson that great love follows gracious forgiveness. In 11:37–54 Jesus excoriates his host and guests for their moral behavior. In 14:1–24 Jesus teaches his Pharisee host and guests the meaning of humility. At the Last Supper Jesus must teach his own disciples the meaning of humble service (22:14–38). Jesus' criticism of Martha's anxiety fits into this genre of table fellowship stories. Her anxiety may well prevent her from hearing the word. See Luke 8:14: "As for the seed that fell among thorns, they are the ones who have heard [the word], but as they go along, they are choked by the *anxieties* and riches and pleasures of life, and they fail to produce mature fruit." Mary, assuming the posture of a disciple at Jesus' feet and being liberated from anxiety, has indeed chosen the better part.

STUDY QUESTION: What anxieties keep us from hearing the word of God today? What role do women have in the missionary endeavors of today's church?

Luke 11:1–13
PRAYER IN THE MIDST OF TRIAL

As we noted in the Introduction, Luke writes his Gospel for Christians who are faced with persecution, especially as they proclaim God's good news on mission. And persecution may create a dual problem, namely, depletion of hope in a God who cares and loss of worldly possessions because of allegiance to Jesus. In this section Luke has masterfully molded three of Jesus' sayings into teaching for these Christians and for ourselves.

For Christians Jesus is the prime example of prayer (11:1; see also 3:21; 5:16; 6:12; 9:18, 28–29; 22:32, 44; 23:34, 46). Jesus is not the example just because he follows a daily prayer regimen and spends a day or night in prayer before major events and decisions. His prayer to his Father enables him to withstand the onslaught of Satan in the midst of the trial of his ministry, betrayal, passion, and death (22:44). As Jesus dies, his prayer, "Father, into your hands I commit my spirit," evidences his complete trust in his gracious Father (23:46).

If the Christians' prayer is to be heard, it must be persistent (11:5–8; see also 18:1–8). Christians must ask, search, and knock (11:9–10). In response to persistent prayer, the heavenly Father will not give worldly goods, which might only create additional problems for the persecuted Christians, but the Holy Spirit, who strengthens in persecution (11:13;

contrast Matthew 7:11). "When they take you before synagogues and before rulers and authorities, do not worry about how or what your defense will be or about what you are to say. For the holy Spirit will teach you at that moment what you should say" (12:11–12).

These commands to imitate Jesus at prayer and to pray persistently could breed despair were it not for the reality behind them. The disciples on Jesus' way experience God as Father because Jesus shares his experience of God-Father with them (11:2). This Father, who cares deeply for Jesus' followers (11:11–13), will not put them to that ultimate test wherein they might fall away (11:4). God is not only imaged as a Father; God is also friend (11:5–8), who cares for Jesus' followers.

STUDY QUESTION: When we pray the Our Father, is our focus more on what God will give us—food, forgiveness, liberation from the ultimate trial—rather than on praising the goodness of God and the realization of God's rule?

Luke 11:14–36
RELENTLESS ADHERENCE TO JESUS

This section contains verses that have puzzled readers for ages—11:24–26 and 11:33–36. The pieces of the puzzle of these verses may fall together if we set them within the larger context of 11:14–36, where Luke has fashioned traditional materials about Jesus' teaching into additional instructions for his church which finds going along Jesus' way rough. After concentrating on specific verses, we will give an overall view of Luke's message.

11:15–16 Not only the religious leaders, the scribes and Pharisees (see 6:11 and 11:53–54), oppose Jesus; ordinary folk join in the fray. Opposition to Christians will issue from leaders and common people. Luke molds a unity out of the different materials in this section by having Jesus answer the opposition of 11:15 in 11:17–28, whereas the objection of 11:16 is first answered in 11:29–36.

11:20–22 These verses stress the signal meaning of Jesus for Christians. Jesus' exorcisms evidence that God acts in and through him, just as

God worked through Moses during the ten plagues of Egypt. See Exodus 8:15, where the phrase "the finger of God" is found in the account of the plagues. Jesus is the stronger one, who has defeated the prince of devils. That Jesus has conquered the evil spirit and that his followers receive the Holy Spirit (11:13) is a tremendous source of consolation and empowerment for Luke's beleaguered church.

11:23–28 In a life-or-death situation, Christians cannot detour from Jesus' way (11:23). Following upon the exorcism of the devil from their lives through conversion (see 8:26–39), they cannot be content merely to sweep and tidy their persons, but they must also welcome Jesus as their permanent house guest. If they try to be neutral, a whole army (the number seven means fullness) of unwelcome guests will descend upon them and take control. Surely, a worse state results (11:24–26). How can Christians adhere to Jesus in such a do-or-die situation where the opposition forces are so numerous and strong? Their strength lies in the Word of God, which they must hear and keep (11:27–28; see also 8:19–21).

11:29–32 This passage builds upon the objection raised in 11:16. No spellbinding sign will be given potential converts. The message preached to them, as it had been to converts before them, is the awesomely simple *Repent*. Jesus, whom the church preaches, is a greater sage than Solomon and a greater prophet than Jonah. The pagan queen of the south and the pagan Ninevites show how one must respond to Jesus. Repentance is continually called for (see 11:23–28).

11:33–36 Verses 34–36 have been added to verse 33, which Luke had previously used in 8:16. The key clause in 11:33 is the uniquely Lukan "but on a lampstand *so that those who enter* might see the light." Contrast the parallel in Matthew 5:15: "Nor do they light a lamp and then put it under a bushel basket; it is set on a lampstand, where it gives light to all *in the house*." Luke's modification of this traditional saying refers to the light of the Christian mission which is to be lit to be seen by those who enter the church—not extinguished at the first muttering of opposition. Luke 11:34–36 follows upon this admonition and stresses the soundness or singleness of the eye (11:34). When the eye is sound, then there is single-minded dedication to the light of the Christian mission. The sound eye results from relentless adherence to Jesus and enables the Christian to view all of reality from the elemental perspective of the Lord Jesus.

Just as Jesus experienced opposition on his way from numerous types of foes, so too will his church. Luke exhorts his fellow Christians to draw strength and consolation from Jesus, who is for them. He also challenges them to see clearly that discipleship involves great risks and single-minded dedication.

STUDY QUESTION: Is the ethic of Christian discipleship really so rigidly either-or that it cannot tolerate an occasional both-and?

Luke 11:37–54
PERSECUTION BECAUSE OF PROPHETIC ATTACKS ON SHAM AND ABUSE OF POWER

The sayings in this story of table fellowship are heavily paralleled in Matthew chapter 23 (see verses 4, 6, 7, 13, 23, 25, 27, 29–31, 34–36). Luke and Matthew have drawn these sayings from a common source. But neither Luke nor Matthew is much interested in preserving these historical records of Jesus the prophet's attacks on religious leaders of his day just for posterity's sake. For his part, Luke adapts these materials to buoy up his church, which faces opposition because it shares in Jesus' prophetic role. We can detect Luke's adaptation especially in verses 37, 41, and 49.

Luke sets this traditional material in the context of a meal with a Pharisee (11:37), a context he employs two other times to give teaching about the law (see 7:36 and 14:1). In 11:41 Luke touches upon one of his prominent themes, that of poor and rich, and gives the startling teaching that cleanliness before God is not achieved by external lustrations but by almsgiving. Proper participation at a meal in the Christian assembly is not governed by rules of handwashing but is open to the needy and those who have aided them (see 16:19–31; Acts 2:42–47 and 4:32–35; contrast Luke 16:14).

Luke's hand is also tipped in 11:49, where he writes "prophets and apostles," which contrasts with Matthew's "prophets and wise men and scribes" (Matt 23:34). Like the prophets of old, Jesus the prophet (see 7:39; 24:19) does not shrink from condemning the sham and corrupt teaching of the powers-that-be. For his efforts, he suffered martyrdom. Christian prophets and apostles, commissioned by Jesus and sharing in his ministry, are experiencing similar treatment in Luke's day.

In the previous sections of this chapter (11:1–13, 14–36) we noted that Luke's purpose is to console and challenge his besieged church. In this section we glimpse one reason why his church may have been under fire. In attacking the abuse of power of their contemporary religious leaders, Luke's church cannot expect a more favorable reception than that accorded Jesus, their prophetic leader on the way (see 11:53–54).

STUDY QUESTION: Are prophetic attacks on governmental corruption and policy unpatriotic? Are prophetic challenges of ecclesiastical policy and law irreligious?

Luke 12:1–12
GOD'S CARE PROVIDES CONSOLATION
FOR HARASSED CHRISTIANS

At first blush this section seems somewhat disjointed; there is no underlying theme. Closer examination, however, will reveal that the section is unified around the theme of consolation for Christians harassed because they own up to their faith in Jesus.

The disciples, the Christians of Luke's day (12:1), are warned that the Christian message cannot be hidden. Its nature demands that it be proclaimed from the rooftops. It will not thrive behind closed doors or in whisperings down darkened corridors (12:3). And when that message is proclaimed, its preachers are apt to encounter opposition. Their natural fear of such harassment is assuaged as they realize that they are Jesus' friends, precious in God's sight (12:4–7). Although their fate may be death for avowing allegiance to Jesus, they are further succored by the assurance that at the judgment Jesus, the Son of Man, will intercede for those who have fearlessly witnessed to him (12:8–9).

Luke 12:10 is a most perplexing verse which seems to mean that those who have rejected Jesus, the Son of Man, are forgiven. They are given a second chance in the preaching of the Christian missionaries who are equipped for their mission by the Holy Spirit (see Acts 1:8). There is no appeal from a second rejection.

Both Jewish and Gentile authorities harass the Christians, who are comforted by the fact that they have the best defense attorney available, the Holy Spirit. See Acts 4:8, where Peter "filled with the holy Spirit," gives a sterling defense of his actions before the Jewish authorities, who, "observing the boldness of Peter and John and perceiving them to be uneducated, ordinary men" (Acts 4:13), were amazed.

The Christians of Luke's day need the encouragement that Paul and Barnabas, both persecuted missionaries, gave their first converts: "It is necessary for us to undergo many hardships to enter the kingdom of God" (Acts 14:22).

STUDY QUESTION: Amidst the sober message this section contains about the consequences of following Jesus, isn't there great consolation in Jesus' statement: "You are worth more than many sparrows" (12:7)?

Luke 12:13–34
THE CHRISTIAN HEART,
TORN BETWEEN GOD AND POSSESSIONS

While the Lukan communities are pressured from the outside by opposition of one sort or another, lifestyle problems agitate it from within. In this section Luke uses Jesus' teachings to answer one of these problems: Do possessions hinder Christians from following Jesus on his way?

Luke fashions a solution to this problem by using verses 15, 21, 31–32, and 33–34 to interpret the traditional parable of verses 16–20. It would seem that the rich man had found security for life in the abundance of his possessions (12:15). Yet as the ending of the parable teaches (12:20), his security procedures had foolishly failed to take God into consideration. Luke 12:21 notes another major flaw in his security plans; he had been so selfishly wrapped up in amassing possessions for himself that he had neglected mercy to the poor. He should have made himself rich by selling some of his possessions, giving them in alms to the poor, and thus amassing treasure in heaven (12:33). The heart follows its treasure like a magnet. If that treasure is God, the Christian heart bypasses other attractions until it rests in God. If the treasure is material possessions, then the heart will chase after the glitter and enjoyment of things that are subject to change without notice and will neglect the needy (12:33–34).

Luke responds further to the problem facing his communities in verses 22–32, whose introductory "Therefore, I tell you" (12:22) links it to the preceding verses 13–21. In the face of the most common human situation imaginable—people scurrying about after necessities (12:30)—Christians are exhorted to put their trust in God, who cares for them (12:31). Such advice is radical and comforting, comforting especially for persecuted Christians who may be deprived of the necessities of life. They should not read opposition as a sign that God has withdrawn from them and gone into serene hiding. They are his beloved "little flock" for whom God cares and to whom God has promised the gift of life (12:32).

Luke's answer to the propertied in his community is general. The propertied must never think that they merit the title Almighty because of their substantial possessions and power. Subject to their creator, they must avoid the conduct of the rich fool like cancer. Further, Christian possessors can never be relieved of their obligation to share their possessions with the poor. Luke stops short of teaching that wealth and its power are evil. Nor does he enjoin well-to-do Christians to sell *all* their possessions and give alms. But he does make it clear that the Christian heart must put its entire trust in God and not in possessions. Propertied Christians are challenged to draw their own conclusions. See Acts 2:42–47 and 4:32–35, especially 4:34–35: "There was no needy person among [the early disciples], for those who owned property or houses would sell them, bring the proceeds of the sale, and put them at the feet of the apostles, and they were distributed to each according to need."

STUDY QUESTION: How possible is it, in our consumerist society, to set our hearts on God alone (see 12:31)?

Luke 12:35–48
WATCHFULNESS MEANS SELFLESS FIDELITY

Luke is not finished interpreting the import of the vitally important parable of the rich fool (12:16–20). In this section he employs additional sayings of Jesus to explicate 12:20: "But God said to him, 'You fool, this night your life will be demanded of you; and the things you have prepared, to whom will they belong?'" The rich fool was not ready for the coming of the Lord; Christians must be. Luke has a double position on when the Lord comes. Here he portrays his coming at the individual's death, and not at the final judgment (see 21:7–36).

If servants are accustomed to going to bed at sundown, they must make superior efforts to fight back sleep and be ready for their master's return at midnight or later (12:35–38). The master graces his watchful servants in an unbelievable manner. He hosts them to a meal and waits on them himself. The Lord, who at the Last Supper calls himself a servant (22:27), goes against societal norms and rewards his faithful followers in a most personal way.

In 12:41 Luke depicts Peter asking a question about the parable of 12:35–38, and in Jesus' response (12:42) changes the "servant" of the parable to someone with more authority, the "steward." By these two modifications of the source he has in common with Matthew (see Matt 24:43–51, especially 24:44–45), Luke teaches that while readiness is an obligation enjoined on all Christians, it weighs most heavily on church leaders, represented by Peter. If these leaders abuse their trust, maltreat church members, and squander the master's possessions in selfish living, their fate will be dire. Their conduct merits exclusion from the faithful and inclusion among the ranks of the nonbelievers (12:46). God has given many good gifts to them and will expect much of them (12:47–48). Church leaders are stewards and not members of some power elite who are entitled to regard God's gifts to them as a free ticket to ignore God and to exalt in their own importance (see further the rich fool's attitudes in 12:16–20).

STUDY QUESTION: Is it hard for us Christians to conceive of our Lord God as one who would assume the role of a lowly servant and wait on us at table (see 12:37)?

Luke 12:49 to 13:9
CONTINUED READINESS
MEANS CONTINUAL REPENTANCE

In this section Luke has garnered materials that detail the response people must give to Jesus, God's messenger. He utilizes these historical records to confront his harassed communities once again with the message of continual readiness for the Lord's return (see 12:35–48). He knows that the flip side of consolation in trial is exhortation to steadfastness. After providing brief comments on individual verses, we conclude with a summary statement.

12:49–50 Jesus applies the judgment terms of fire and water—both fire and water purify—to himself. Jesus brings the purifying fire of judgment in his preaching. Perhaps Luke also thinks of the fire of the Holy Spirit which Jesus sends (see Acts 2:3). Jesus' baptism is the purification of his passion and death (see Mark 10:38–39).

12:54–59 The crowds are quite capable of reading indicators of rain and heat. But they will not lift a finger to evaluate Jesus' preaching (12:54–56). Luke challenges his communities to regard the serious consequences of such noninvolvement (12:57–59).

13:1–9 Jesus rejects the common view that the quantity of one's sufferings evidences the amount of one's guilt (13:2, 4). The Galileans and the eighteen who perished in Jerusalem exemplify the necessity of continual repentance lest death find one unprepared. Perhaps the fig tree planted in the vineyard is Jerusalem (13:6–9; recall that in the Old Testament Israel is frequently likened to God's vineyard, e.g., Isa 5:1–6). The ministry of Jesus and his early communities allowed additional time for Jerusalem to heed Jesus' message.

Luke 12:49 to 13:9 centers on the theme of the necessity of the church's persevering response to Jesus amidst persecution. Luke exhorts his fellow Christians not to become lackluster readers of the signs of the time. They must involve themselves in the consequences of continuing to follow Jesus. Repentance is not something that one does once and forgets (see 17:4 and 9:23). It's like marriage vows, which are pronounced at one particular time, but must be renewed daily if the marriage is not to crumble, especially in times of severe stress.

STUDY QUESTION: Luke's Gospel is rightly hailed as the Gospel of God's mercy and compassion. Does this passage of threats belie that description?

Luke 13:10–21
THE CHURCH'S MISSION WILL SUCCEED

This section is a fitting conclusion to the first portion of Luke's travel narrative (9:51 to 13:21). By joining the story of the healing of a daughter of Abraham (13:10–17) to the twin parables of mustard seed and yeast (13:18–21), Luke has fashioned another message of consolation for his communities on mission who meet opposition. We will comment verse by verse on this rich material.

13:10 This is one of the few miracle stories Luke has used in his travel narrative, which is almost ninety percent teaching material (see 14:1–6, 17:11–19, 18:35–42; consult 11:14 for other miracles). The tag, "miracle story," however, should not blind us to the fact that these miracle stories do not focus solely on Jesus' power but are also vehicles for his teaching. The present miracle story is a case in point. Verses 14–17 recount Jesus' victory in a controversy about the meaning of the sabbath.

13:11–13 The miracle is narrated with a modicum of detail. Jesus is so concerned about the welfare of human life that he takes no precaution against contracting ritual impurity through contact with a woman—a sick one at that. The woman praises God for what God has done for her through Jesus.

13:14–17 The main point here is that the woman, although disadvantaged because of her illness, is a "daughter of Abraham." She is paired with another outcast, Zacchaeus, a despised chief toll collector, who is "a son of Abraham" (19:9). The unfortunate lady of this miracle story has shown faith in Jesus every bit as strong as Abraham's faith in God.

To make his point about who is "a child of Abraham," Jesus often has to oppose religious leaders' understanding of "who's in and who's out" and "what should and what shouldn't be done on the sabbath." For synagogue and sabbath are not just Jewish religious institutions, but can be used as means of erecting boundaries and separating "us" from "them." The controversy of this miracle story occurs because Jesus violates the leader's rules of what "shouldn't be done on the sabbath" in fidelity to his mission of extending the mercy of God's kingdom to the unfortunate.

13:18–19 Since the parable of the mustard seed is joined directly to verse 17 by "Then he said" (13:18), it furthers the message about Jesus' mission. Jesus' and the church's work for the establishment of God's kingdom is like the mustard seed. Proverbially the most insignificant of seeds, this seed attains the prominence of a tree. It may seem that Jesus' ministry and that of the church, small in scope and success, will amount to nothing. The parable warns against drawing this conclusion.

13:20–21 This twin of the first parable communicates the same message of success. Those of us who bake are amazed at the huge amount of flour the woman uses—some 190 cups. Despite its apparent insignificance, a little yeast affects every single particle of the bathtubful of flour. To be sure, Jesus' ministry and that of the church seem to be hardly worth a second glance. That is no reason for despair or inquietude.

Throughout this first part of the travel narrative Luke has been concerned with a church undergoing persecution and has used Jesus' sayings to console and exhort his fellow Christians (see, e.g., 11:1–13, 12:1–12). This section develops the theme of consolation once more. What God has in mind for the ministry of Jesus and the church will come to pass. The church may seem trivial, but, as in the case of the mustard seed and yeast, first appearances are deceptive.

STUDY QUESTION: Luke does not provide timetables or growth charts for the parables of 13:18–21. How is it possible to know when the church is successful in its mission?

Luke 13:22–35
DON'T REST ON YOUR LAURELS

In this section, which begins a new portion of Luke's travel narrative (13:22 to 17:10), Luke unites Jesus' sayings around the theme of Jerusalem (13:22, 33, 34–35).

When Luke was penning his Gospel, Jesus had already met a prophet's fate in Jerusalem (13:33); Jerusalem and its temple had already been destroyed (13:34–35). Christians perceived Jerusalem's destruction

as God's judgment on people who did not try their very best to enter
by the narrow door (13:24), who noised it about that they had connections with Jesus (13:25–27), and who thought that they had been
assured seats at the head table in the heavenly banquet (13:28–29). The
sure bets for first place came in last (13:30). But the destruction of
Jerusalem may not have been God's final word. The last part of verse 35
seems to imply that the Jews will convert at some future date.

Luke's primary concern in this section, however, is not to regale his
community with reasons why Jerusalem failed to respond to Jesus. He
uses the facts of Jesus' unbending demand for repentance (13:23–30)
and of Jerusalem's failure to heed that demand as means of admonish-
ing his own community. Luke's intention is seen especially in verse 23,
where one single individual asks Jesus a question and Luke begins
Jesus' answer with "He said to *them*." Also, the "you" of Jesus' answers in
verses 24–29 is plural, not singular. Jesus is addressing the Christians of
Luke's time. These Christians must not gloat over what happened to
Jerusalem. Luke exhorts them not to rest on their laurels. The shoo-ins
of the other group did not make the winner's circle. The same can happen to you.

STUDY QUESTION: Amidst the strong challenges of this section,
might not we readers take deep solace in what Jesus, the missionary,
says about himself: "How many times I yearned to gather your children
together as a hen gathers her brood under her wings" (13:34)?

Luke 14:1–24
TABLE FELLOWSHIP IN THE CHRISTIAN COMMUNITY

As you glance through this section, you will notice that it consists of
statements Jesus makes while taking a meal with a leading Pharisee (see
7:36–50 and 11:37–54 for two similar occasions). Luke has taken various sayings, spoken by Jesus on different occasions, and has unified
them around a single meal setting. By utilizing the literary form of a
symposium to compose 14:1–24, Luke gives answers to a burning missionary question within his church—who is worthy to share table fellowship? We highlight key points by moving through the section passage by passage. A statement of Luke's purpose concludes our
commentary.

14:1–6 This story, very similar to that of 6:6–11, introduces the entire section and illustrates what Jesus has just said about his ministry in 13:32; he heals as well as casts out demons. The lawyers and the Pharisees are all eyes and seek to catch Jesus out in an error (14:1; see 11:53–54). Jesus gains the ascendancy in the implicit controversy about the meaning of the sabbath. Care for the betterment of human life transcends the Pharisees' interpretation of the sabbath law of rest.

Another meaning may be teased out of 14:1–6. In Luke's Gospel the Pharisees are depicted as greedy and rapacious (see 11:37–44 and 16:14). A person with dropsy or bodily swelling, due to an excess of bodily fluid, is always thirsty. In antiquity a person with dropsy became a symbol for the greedy, who, although filled to excess with money, always thirsted for more. In 14:1–6 Jesus' mercy extends to the man who literally has dropsy. Does it not also extend to the Pharisees who suffer from the dropsy of greed? Will they be as open to Jesus' cure as the man with dropsy was?

14:7–11 Jesus censures the religious leaders for using the occasion of table fellowship to seek plaudits for themselves. At a symposium, one of the major questions was who had more honor than another and therefore deserved a better seat. Such self-serving pride impairs table fellowship and does not impress God (14:11).

14:12–14 The literary form of a symposium also features the guest list. Accentuated are not only those who are invited, but also and especially those who are uninvited. Jesus' instructions on how to make out the invitation list for a feast is revolutionary, especially for Luke's readers. These readers come from a culture that endorses an ethic of reciprocity: by accepting someone's invitation, I commit myself to invite that person at a later time and to provide a feast at least as lavish as the one to which I was invited. In this culture, the poor and unfortunate could never accept such an invitation, for they did not have the financial wherewithal to reciprocate (see 14:15–24). The crippled, the lame, the blind, and the poor, invited to a feast, cannot repay their hosts. God will do that.

14:15–24 When one of those at the table piously notes that those (himself included?) who get to feast at the heavenly banquet will truly be happy, he provides an opening for Jesus' final teaching. There are two major points to the parable of the snubbed invitation. One is the excuses which the invited folk give in verses 18–20. It seems rather incongruous that they would have waited until suppertime to inspect land, try oxen, and set up a new household. Their excuses are lame; they are just too caught up in earthly concerns to heed the invitation. These excuses are typical of the ones that people gave to missionary preaching in Luke's own day. The second major point is that verse 21 repeats verse 13: the poor, the crippled, the blind, and the lame. Those who would seem to be excluded from the banquet because of their social or cultic liabilities actually grace the banquet tables.

Luke explores Jesus' rich image of table fellowship to encourage missionary inclusivity and to admonish the prosperous of his communities. At Jesus' table all peoples are invited whether they have the capability of reciprocating or not. May no one take scandal from Jesus' ways at table (see 15:1–2).

STUDY QUESTION: In what ways can church communities imitate Jesus' inclusive hospitality?

Luke 14:25–35
YOUR YES TO JESUS MUST BE STEADFAST

In this section, Luke gathers sayings of Jesus to exhort his church to steadfast discipleship. After commenting on individual passages, we single out Luke's theme of poor and rich for further discussion.

14:25 The "great crowds" which accompany Jesus represent the multitudes who will join the Christian communities (see the thousands mentioned in Acts 2:41 and 4:4).

14:26–27 The "hating" of 14:26 is a Semitic way of expressing total detachment. To be a steadfast disciple demands much, especially when the prospects of persecution at home and from authorities are so awesome.

14:28–32 These twin parables are sandwiched between the first two discipleship sayings (14:26–27) and the final one (14:33). The point of the parables is wise planning. Weigh the costs before you embark on a project. Otherwise, you will not be able to complete it, will lose honor, and will be shamed by countless jokes.

14:33 This verse must be interpreted in context. Verses 26–27, where the first two "cannot be my disciple" statements occur, suggests a persecution context also for verse 33. This verse builds upon the twin parables of verses 28–32 by highlighting the shame and disgrace of the person who starts something he is unable to finish. Thus, the context indicates that verse 33 does not lay down the unconditional demand that people must sell all their possessions before they can become disciples of Jesus. Rather, it has in view Christian disciples who would allow their possessions to put a halt to their continued walk with Jesus. The situation behind verse 33 may be reflected in another part of the New Testament: "You even joined in the sufferings of those in prison and joyfully accepted the confiscation of your property, knowing that you had a better and lasting possession" (Heb 10:34). Viewed in its context, 14:33 could be paraphrased: "If it's a choice between me and your possessions, you must show your love for me by abandoning all you own."

14:35 The saying about salt describes the fate of the disciple who denies Jesus during persecution.

Luke 14:33 is one of the most important building blocks in Luke's theme of poor and rich. It cannot be dismissed out of hand with the casual remark that it's just another instance of Semitic hyperbole like verse 26. Discipleship is serious business, especially for those who have possessions. Luke advises his prosperous communities that the cost of discipleship has skyrocketed because of persecution. If they want to live as disciples, then they have to pay the price.

STUDY QUESTION: Jesus, like any lover, demands much. Are his demands in this section unreasonable?

Luke 15:1–32
OPEN YOUR HEARTS AND IMITATE GOD'S MERCY

The parable of the Prodigal Son has topped the bestseller lists for centuries. Virtually everyone is familiar with this masterpiece. What follows is a quest for a richer understanding of what is so familiar as to become routine and unimportant. We begin with specific remarks on key verses in chapter 15 and conclude with a panoramic view of the parable in the entire context of the chapter.

General Remarks

15:4 This verse spotlights the apparent recklessness of the shepherd who leaves ninety-nine sheep untended to care the single lost sheep.

15:7 Does God really care for the ninety-nine just? God seems to be all bent on caring for the lost one. An analogy provides an answer: When parents lavish more love on their sick child, that doesn't mean that they love their other children less.

15:8–10 In pairing the story of the shepherd with a story about a woman, is Luke showing forth the inclusivity of Jesus' mission? A rule of thumb may help us get a handle on the troublesome "lost coin" and therefore on the meaning of this parable. This silver coin or drachma was worth a day's wages and should not be visualized by weight, like a dime, but by purchasing power. None but a miser would scour the house for a dime, but most would turn the place upside down to find the equivalent of a day's wages.

15:13 "Where he squandered his inheritance on a life of dissipation." The younger brother's activity should not be interpreted by what his older brother says to their father in verse 30: "swallowed up your property with prostitutes." This is an obvious slur and does not provide unbiased evidence for the kind of sin the younger son committed.

15:19 "Treat me as you would treat one of your hired workers." The younger son has a mistaken view of himself and his father. He really is his father's son and not a paid servant. The father's forgiveness prompts the younger son to throw off the category of the mercenary and to put on the consciousness of being loved as a son.

15:18, 21 "I have sinned against heaven and against you." What was the younger son's sin? He had dissipated his means of caring for his father in case a necessity such as incapacitating illness arose. He had become like a Gentile and for caring for pigs!

15:20 "He ran to his son." The father's conduct is extraordinary and somewhat undignified. One would not expect an elderly oriental father to catch up his garments and run.

15:22 "Quickly bring the finest robe and put it on him; put a ring on his finger and sandals on his feet." The father's forgiveness is acted out. The prodigal is not a hired worker, but wears the trappings of an honored son.

15:29 "I served you." Behind the seemingly innocuous "I served you" lies a misunderstanding. Like his younger brother, the older brother has a mistaken, mercenary view of the man who is his *father*. The younger lad is not a "hired worker" of his father nor is the older lad a "servant" of his father. Both are *sons*. Unless the older lad grasps this fact, he cannot treat the younger lad as his brother. The father's forgiveness is meant to shatter the mercenary outlook of his two sons. The younger son accepts that forgiveness. The parable is open-ended and does not tell us whether the elder son accepted his father as forgiving father and his brother as forgiven brother.

15:30–32 These verses continue the point of verse 29. In responding to his father, the elder son retorts, "But when your son returns." The father addresses his elder son as "my son" and refers to the younger lad as "your brother."

These general remarks have put us on the threshold of a richer understanding of the very familiar parable of the Prodigal Son. They have also hinted that this parable cannot be considered in isolation from its companions in chapter 15. Let us take a panoramic view of the vista which Luke has created by linking this parable with all of chapter 15.

The Parable of the Prodigal Son in Its Context

Since Luke is no curator of museum pieces which he merely dusts off before presenting them to his generation of Christians, we would expect him to hand on the parable of the Prodigal Son in a creatively new way. He does not disappoint our expectations. One feature of his creativity is to combine three, once independent parables into this unit of teaching. Apparently he had prior help as the traditional refrain of "rejoice, lost, found" in verses 6, 9, 23–24, and 32 intimates:

"*Rejoice* with me because I have *found* my *lost* sheep" (15:6).

"*Rejoice* with me because I have *found* the coin that I *lost*" (15:9).

"Then let us *celebrate* with a feast, because this son of mine was dead, and has come to life again; he was *lost,* and has been *found*" (15:23–24).

"But now we must celebrate and *rejoice,* because your brother was dead and has come to life again; he was *lost* and has been *found* (15:32).

This refrain clearly links the three parables together.

While Luke retained this merely literary way of linking the three parables, he added two more substantive connections of his own. First, it is Luke who is responsible for verses 7 and 10, which feature repentant sinners, a prize Lukan theme. Thus, Luke has transformed the meaning of "lost and found" in the first two parables to accord with the meaning of "lost and found" in the third parable. No longer is the object of the search something impersonal—a sheep or coin. Now it is human, and all three parables deal with God's search for the human sinner who repents. Second, Luke introduces the three closely connected parables by means of verses 1 and 2 (see 5:30). Thus, Luke does not allow the three parables to float about anchorless, but addresses them to the complaining Pharisees—people of his own time. This motif of complaining, absent from the twin parables of lost sheep and lost coin, resurfaces in verses 28–30 as the elder son voices his angry disapproval of his father's action. With the motif of complaining, Luke has joined the beginning and the end of chapter 15 together.

Luke's extensive creativity in this chapter results in a message that is beguilingly simple. Jesus' life is the supreme revelation of God's relentlessly merciful love for repentant sinners, who may think of themselves as no more than "hired workers," but in the act of forgiveness experience God as father and themselves as God's children. By means of 15:1–2 Luke confronts the Pharisees of Jesus' time, his time, and our time with this message. We know from the Acts of the Apostles that some Pharisees converted to the Way, but still held onto strict criteria of who could be saved. The Pharisees' objections to the successful missionary work of Paul and Barnabas among the Gentiles leads into the Council of Jerusalem: "But some from the party of the Pharisees who had become believers stood up and said, 'It is necessary to circumcise them and direct them to observe the Mosaic law'" (Acts 15:5). As the rest of Acts 15 shows, the early church did not adopt the opinion of the Pharisees, who wanted to fence in God's mercy. In sum, the members of Luke's church who lobby for severe entrance requirements for sinners are confronted with the threefold tradition of Jesus, revealer of the merciful Father. Their mercenary attitude of "Give them and us our due" must give way to Jesus' attitude of mercy.

STUDY QUESTION: How does the image of God presented in this chapter compare with a commonly held image of God, the heavenly accountant, poised to pounce on the slightest mistake? Are there any rigorists in the contemporary church? Does Jesus' teaching of God's mercy give a blank check to imitate the prodigal son?

Luke 16:1–31
THE POOR ARE MOST WORTHY OF YOUR CONCERN

A popular view is that Jesus champions dishonesty in the parable of the dishonest steward (16:1–13), and this shocks people. Their shock is intensified these days when white-collar crime is so pervasive. I recall the comment I once received after preaching a well-nuanced sermon on this parable, "Nice try, Father, but I still think that Jesus shouldn't have praised dishonesty!" In our commentary on this section we will set the hornets' nest of verses 1–13 within the larger context of all of chapter 16. Within this context we will be able to savor its true meaning and to see how much it contributes to the development of Luke's dominant theme of poor and rich. We divide our comments into two parts, verses 1–13 and verses 14–31.

16:1–13 Countless thousands have had difficulty getting a handle on the understanding of this passage because the economic situation behind the parable is foreign to our culture. The steward was empowered to make legally binding bonds or contracts for his master and was allowed by the customs of the time to make a profit for himself on the deals he made. For example, John Jones would come and make a deal for eighty measures of wheat. He would get the eighty measures of wheat, but his bond or contract would be written to read one hundred. The extra twenty measures of wheat were the steward's legitimate profit. When the very shrewd steward realized that he was going to get the pink slip because of his wastefulness, he moved quickly to forego his profits and issued new bonds. The beneficiaries of his alert thinking would surely reciprocate such largess and welcome him into their homes after his dismissal. On the basis of this economic background, it is plain that the master was not cheated out of anything due him and that the enterprising steward escaped the ordeals of digging and the shame of begging.

Simply put, the point of the parable is that the steward used his money astutely. Stated negatively, the parable does not teach that the master praised his steward because of his dishonesty. The conclusion of the parable is very clear, "And the master commended the dishonest steward *for his astuteness*" (16:8a).

Luke uses the Jesus sayings in verses 16:8b–13 to apply the message of the parable to his own community. Are they as astute in money matters as the steward (16:8b)? They must use their money to give alms and gain the poor as their friends. When the money of those who gave alms runs out at death, they will gain access to heaven (16:9). Christians must remember that money is on loan from God. If they do not use this little loan trustworthily, they will not be trusted with that which really counts—eternal life (16:10–12). Money may not be evil, but it can turn into a god that controls every aspect of one's life. It is very difficult to tightrope the issue of God and money. It's one or the other (16:13). In summary, in verses 8b–13 Luke makes the application of the parable of the astute steward quite specific for his fellow Christians—use your possessions prudently by caring for the poor.

16:14–31 The Pharisees scoff at Jesus' teaching about the use of possessions (16:14). These Pharisees are not the ones whom Jesus encountered during his ministry, but some people in Luke's own community who think that Jesus' message about poor and rich is nonsense. They seem to think that their possessions are a sure sign of God's favor. Since that is the case, why should they give them up for the despicable poor whose very poverty shows the low regard in which God holds them? Jesus condemns the pride of these people who think they have a corner on God's favor (16:15).

On first reading, the one-liners of verses 16–18 do not seem to have anything to do with the theme of poor and rich being developed in chapter 16. There are some connections, however. We have already seen that in verse 15 Jesus rejects the view that wealth is a sign of God's favor. The rich are not privileged in God's sight. Nor are others—not even the poor—excluded from God's kingdom (see the "everyone" of 16:16). Jesus has not abolished the law and the prophets and their teaching about almsgiving (16:17; see the similar phrase, "Moses and the prophets," in 16:29 and 31). Thus, verses 16–17 add pointedly to Luke's theme of poor and rich, for they show that Jesus did not declare almsgiving a nonissue for the rich and powerful.

The first part (16:19–26) of the parable of the rich man and Lazarus does not explore the religious motivations of the two characters. Nor does it say that the rich man was coldhearted toward Lazarus, or that Lazarus was the epitome of patience. It states simply and plainly that their situations were reversed after death. Lazarus enjoys fellowship with Abraham, whereas the rich man is tormented. In verses 27–31 the parable takes on considerable religious coloring. It dawns on the rich man that his conduct toward Lazarus was wrong. He earnestly pleads for help so that his five brothers may repent of similar conduct before it is too late. Abraham reminds the rich man that his brothers have Moses and the prophets, whose teaching on care for the poor is still valid (see 16:17). Let them heed their teaching. If these are shrugged off as nonimportant, even the teachings of the Risen Lord (16:31) will have no impact.

The largely negative teachings of verses 19–31 can be profitably contrasted with the positive instructions of verses 1–13. Verse 9 spotlights the conduct of a rich man who is attentive to the teachings of Moses and the prophets and gives alms to the poor. He is astute; his focus is on eternal life. By contrast, the rich man of verses 19–31 is distracted by the pleasures of this life and neglects to make Lazarus his friend by giving him alms. He needs a radical conversion, because money is the be-all and end-all of his life (16:13).

In chapter 16 Luke adds masterful strokes to his theme of poor and rich and presents a startling message for the possessors of his communities. They must realize that their possessions are on loan from God and have to be used to benefit the poor. Those who think that their possessions are God's unconditional stamp of approval on them and their behavior have their theological heads screwed on wrong.

STUDY QUESTION: How did Lazarus become "a child of Abraham," in the bosom of Abraham? For answers, consult Luke's previous materials, e.g., 3:7–9, 13:16. Religious movements in Third World countries have challenged us members of God's most favored nation to read the parable of the rich man and Lazarus anew. Are the poor in our country and abroad poor because of oppression and exploitation by the rich?

Luke 17:1–10
THE POWER AND NECESSITY OF FAITH

In this section Luke uses Jesus' teaching about the power of faith (17:5–6) as the centerpiece around which he clusters sayings of Jesus. These sayings summarize lessons taught during the second portion of Luke's travel narrative (13:22 to 17:10)—care for the poor, forgiveness, and perseverance during persecution.

It is inevitable that Christians will encounter temptations against faith, even from their fellow believers (17:1–2). Woe to those who, like the rich man of 16:19–31, generate temptations for Christians like Lazarus, "one of these little ones" (17:2).

Christians must ceaselessly share with one another the forgiveness they receive (17:3–4; the symbolic number "seven" means an unlimited number of times). Believers are not restricted to a single, once-for-all-time "I'm sorry, I repent." Their fellow believers must accept their repeated "I'm sorry." Recall the message of chapter 15, "Imitate God's mercy."

The "apostles," speaking for us all, are fully aware of the difficulty created by Jesus' demand to forgive ceaselessly and implore him, "Increase our faith!" (17:5–6). I give this definition of what "faith" means in Luke's Gospel: faith is absolute confidence in God's goodness and in God's ultimate conquest over the power of evil, especially as that conquest is manifested in Jesus the Lord. In this instance, the "apostles" pray for the power to extend the helping hand of forgiveness to mend the fences knocked down by sin.

Luke 17:7 is somewhat strange if it is addressed to the apostles. Were they shepherds and farmers? Might Luke have in mind those who like Paul the apostle labored in missionary "fields" (see 1 Cor 3:5) and like Peter were shepherds of the church (see John 21:15–17 and 1 Pet 5:1–4)? These laborers may have successfully bucked the most powerful waves of persecution, but this does not entitle them to preferential treatment. They are merely servants who are obeying their master and following in his footsteps. Their faith will see them through.

In order to resist the seduction of wealth, to imitate their forgiving Father, and to continue their missionary work, Luke's communities pray to their Lord, "Increase out faith!"

STUDY QUESTION: How do you define faith? How much of your faith is taken up with objective criteria such as the Apostles' Creed? How much is in evidence when we find ourselves in times of trial and confess: "If I didn't have my faith, I would have never survived"?

Luke 17:11–19
SALVATION THROUGH FAITH
AND NOT THROUGH THE MIRACULOUS

This section opens the final portion of Luke's travel narrative (17:11 to 19:44). As is true of the other healings in the travel narrative (see 13:10–17, 14:1–6, 18:35–43), the focus of this story is not on the healing as such (17:11–14), but on Jesus' teaching (17:15–19). This observation is confirmed by the view popularized in sermons that the gist of the story is gratitude, a point first made in the teaching part of the story.

In verses 11–14 Jesus' power to cure—at a distance—is in the forefront, and one is reminded of Jesus' words to the two disciples of John the Baptist: "Go back and tell John what you have seen and heard: the blind see again, the lame walk, *lepers are cleansed...*" (7:22). Jesus is indeed "the one who is to come" (7:20) and restore people to health and active membership in society.

Jesus' teaching dominates 17:15–19. The key words are: praise God (17:15, 18); a Samaritan, this foreigner (17:16, 18); your faith has saved you (17:19). The leper's return shows that he has grasped what Jesus' cure implies: God is operative in Jesus and must be praised (see the centurion's praise of God at Jesus' death in 23:47). The mere experience of the cure did not save. By returning and praising God, the leper gives voice to the faith which saves him. "A Samaritan," "this foreigner" underline the startling and unexpected. If anyone would be expected to return to Jesus to give thanks, it would be a Jew, and not a despised Samaritan. The twofold emphasis given to the ethnic background of the grateful leper directs the reader's attention back to 10:25–37 and the Parable of the Good Samaritan and ahead to the success of the Christian mission among the Samaritans as narrated in Acts 8:1–25.

On one level, the message of this section is gratitude. On a more profound level, however, Luke takes great pains to remind his fellow believers of the nature of salvation. When opposition to their life and mission is most intense, they might yearn for Jesus' miraculous intervention. But the experience of the miraculous is not salvation. Salvation is effected by their continued profession of praise and faith in the Jesus through whom God acts.

STUDY QUESTION: This story gives voice to the Lukan refrain: God's salvation is for all. Do we have trouble accepting this truth, not on a theoretical level, but on the practical level of daily life as we rub shoulders in church with folks from many different lands and races?

Luke 17:20 to 18:8
DON'T ASK "WHEN?" JUST DIE TO SELF

Jesus taught that salvation is present in his teaching and deeds. He also taught that salvation has a future dimension. In this section Luke uses sayings of Jesus to address problems which that future dimension created for his communities, problems such as when will Jesus return in judgment? In what follows, we will comment on this section's passages.

17:20–21 The coming of God's reign is not like the rising of stars which is susceptible to astrologer's observations and plottings. Nor can one track it and yell, "I've found it!" If the Pharisees were open to God's activity, they would know that God is active right among them in Jesus' teachings and deeds, deeds like that of the cleansing of the lepers (17:11–19).

17:22–25 Harassed as they are, believers long for the vindication that the glorious coming of Jesus, the Son of Man, will effect. Some of their number raise their anxiety level by proclaiming that the Son of Man has already come (17:23). Christians are not to go scurrying hither and yon after them like stock investors who change all their plans at the slightest whisper of a "tip." They should not make the same mistake as the Pharisees and try to capture the inside track on God's timetable for the end (see 17:20–21). The Son of Man will come unexpectedly—like lightning. One facet, though, of the coming of the Son of Man is not unexpected: his communities will share his fate of suffering and rejection (17:25).

17:26–30 Comparisons shed additional light on Luke's solution to the problem of the coming of the Son of Man. During the times of Noah and Lot people were engaged in the quotidian human activities of eating, drinking, marrying, and selling. Everything was fine. Why change and repent? Noah and Lot read the situation quite differently. They were prepared for the unexpected judgment. Christians, take note.

17:31–37 Just because two people live together or work side by side is no guarantee that both are prepared for the sudden coming of the Son of Man (17:34–35). The best preparation for Jesus' coming is to lose one's life for the sake of others. In that, is life (17:33). Jesus brushes aside the disciples' snoopy question about the where of his coming with a proverb: Judgment will be as inevitable as the gathering of vultures around a corpse (17:37).

18:1–8 The refrain of "justice" unifies this passage (18:3, 5, 7, 8). Luke uses the parable of the persistent widow, who like the biblical widows Ruth and Tamar takes decisive steps for salvation, to exhort his communities to pray day and night for the Lord's justice. When the Lord delays in coming to do justice for his severely persecuted faithful (18:7), they should not lose heart (18:1). If the self-centered judge granted justice to the courageous widow, how much more will a gracious God grant justice to the beleaguered and steadfast believers of the Son of Man!

Luke's solution to the when of Jesus' coming avoids the deep end of trying to read God's mind and stresses what believers must do to be prepared. As the Christians of Luke's communities wait for the coming of Jesus, they should not chase after rumors that he has already come and change their plans of steadfast adherence to him. Nor should they be lulled into thinking that the assured rhythms of everyday life render the need for repentance obsolete. While yearning and praying to be liberated from persecution by Jesus' coming, they must continue to give of themselves, for that is the only sure way they have of preserving their lives.

STUDY QUESTION: Would Luke's solution to the when of Jesus' coming be enthusiastically welcomed by those who see every earthquake, hurricane, terrorist's bomb, and civil war as a sure sign of the end?

Luke 18:9–14
GOD LOVES SINNERS

This section contains Luke's final contrast between Pharisee and toll collector. We first encountered this pairing in Luke 5:27–32: Levi, a toll collector, has accepted Jesus into his life, and the Pharisees grumble that Jesus is associating with such sinners. Jesus counters their objection by stating that his mission is not "to call the [self-]righteous to repentance but sinners" (5:32). In 7:29–30 Luke describes how the toll collectors gladly accepted John's baptism whereas the Pharisees and scribes rejected God's plan for them. In Luke's introduction to Jesus' parables of lost sheep, lost coin, and lost son we read: "The toll collectors and sinners were all drawing near to listen to [Jesus], but the Pharisees and scribes began to complain, saying, 'This man welcomes sinners and eats with them.'" In sum, the toll collectors acknowledge their sinfulness. The Pharisees complain about Jesus' congress with toll collectors and other sinners, thereby implying that their moral criteria and stature are better than Jesus'.

With the above Lukan background in mind, we readers are not surprised by what we find in 18:9–14. In his prayer the Pharisee emphatically demonstrates how seriously he takes his religion and how many sacrifices he has made to keep his faith alive: abstention from sin, fasting twice weekly, and giving up ten percent of all income. By contrast, the toll collector beats his breast as a sign of remorse and petitions God to have mercy on him, a sinner. In verse 13 Luke uses terminology similar to that used by Paul, especially in Romans and Galatians: God makes sinners right or justifies them. Saints or sinners do not justify themselves before God by their good deeds. Grace is a free gift and is not earned.

Luke asks his communities and his future readers whether they are exalting themselves at the expense of others (18:14) and whether they are among those who, like the Pharisees, are convinced that their behavior has earned them good standing in God's sight and despise all others (18:9).

STUDY QUESTION: As you examine your conscience before God, how many characteristics of the Pharisee and how many characteristics of the toll collector do you find? Is Luke's presentation too black and white?

Luke 18:15–30
VULNERABLE CHILDREN AND POSSESSIONS

Jesus warmly welcomes the little children. He does not set them forth as examples of virtue, for they are not mature enough in life's battles to have won medals of virtue. They are compelling examples of the vulnerable ones in society and of the dependence and trust in God required of disciples. They stand in sharp contrast to the Pharisee who trusted exaltedly in himself (18:9–14). This teaching about dependence and trust in God also anticipates Jesus' sayings about possessions in verses 18–30.

Luke 18:18–23 is a recognition story. Through dialogue or an event, persons recognize something about themselves that they did not know before. For example, a person may boast that he does not use foul language. But put him at a devilishly malfunctioning computer or in traffic that is driven by road rage, and he may recognize himself as the winner of the swear award of the week. The rich aristocrat prides himself on his virtue: I have kept all these commandments from childhood till now. When Jesus asks him to sell all and become his disciple, he recognizes something about himself that he had not known previously—he is attached to his possessions. He cannot say "Yes" to Jesus. Luke's advice to his communities is challenging: Give yourselves this same recognition test; do your possessions stand in the way of your stronger adherence to Jesus?

As the very rich man stands by, Luke uses Jesus' sayings to address further facets of the problem of riches (18:24–27). Riches are a grave hindrance to salvation and are not a sign of God's blessings. God's grace is absolutely necessary for possessors to outdo the feat of a camel passing through the eye of a needle.

After the largely negative admonitions of verses 18–23 and 24–27, Luke now gives positive advice to the well-heeled within his community (18:28–30). These possessors should follow the example of Peter and the first disciples, who left what they had to follow Jesus (18:28). Their example is further clarified in Acts 4:32, 34–35, which describes the ideal early Christian community: "The community of believers was of one heart and mind, and no one claimed that *any of his possessions was his own.* . . . There was no needy person among them, for those who owned property or houses would sell them, bring the proceeds of the sale, and put them at the feet of the apostles, and they were distributed to each according to need." These examples challenge those believers with possessions to look in a brotherly or sisterly way at those in need in the Christian community.

Luke's message, then, to the possessors is basically twofold: detachment from possessions; charity toward those in need.

STUDY QUESTION: Darling children and rich folk. How do we prevent our children, who grow up in a consumer-crazed society, from becoming addicted to "the good life" and blinded to the needy?

Luke 18:31–43
PERSISTENT DISCIPLESHIP

In this section Luke unfurls the final passion prediction of his travel narrative. Jerusalem is not only the goal of pilgrim Jesus. It is also the place where martyrs are killed. By adding "by the prophets" in 18:31,

Luke taps into another rich theme of his: Jesus' death was forewilled by God (see also 9:22; 22:37; 24:25–27, 32, 44–47; Acts 2:22–28; 3:12–26).

In our commentary on Luke's travel narrative we have been observing that the miracles Luke preserves there do not so much underline Jesus' power to heal as serve as vehicles for his teaching. The miracle at hand is no exception. The people inform the blind man that the commotion is caused by the arrival of Jesus the Nazarene. The blind man's faith already surfaces in his confession, "Jesus, Son of David, have pity on me," which goes beyond what the crowd had told him about Jesus. Despite the attempts to silence him, he persists in his faith. In his mercy Jesus performs an act of the Messiah, Son of David, and gives him sight (see Isa 29:18 and Luke 4:18 and 7:22). If the miracle story ended here, Jesus' power to cure would be at center stage. But for the first and only time in all his miracle stories Luke writes that the cured man *follows Jesus.* Jesus opens the eyes of the beggar, who follows him up to Jerusalem. Is more involved here than Jesus' bestowal of physical sight? In 18:18–30 we had a story about the very rich young man who could not bring himself to follow Jesus. In 19:1–10 we will hear the story of the very rich toll collector Zacchaeus who accepts Jesus into his house and life. Both these stories focus on wealth. The blind beggar has no money, but he does have courage, faith, and the resolve to follow Jesus. Is he the one who truly understood God's plan in Jesus (18:31–34) and follows him up to Jerusalem and the cross?

STUDY QUESTION: "Persistent, faithful following of Jesus" is so frequent a Lukan theme that it can roll like jargon from our lips. What ingredients characterize persistent and faithful discipleship? Does the blind beggar give us an example of these ingredients?

Luke 19:1–10
MERCY FOR THE RICH, REPENTANT ZACCHAEUS

As Luke comes to the end of his travel narrative, he uses Jesus' encounter with Zacchaeus as a means of summing up many of Jesus' teachings about possessions and about what constitutes salvation.

Zacchaeus is a chief toll collector and especially hated by the people because of his alleged dishonesty (see v. 7). In 18:9–14 Luke fea-

tured the story of the self-righteous Pharisee and the humble toll collector. Both toll collectors are aware of their need for God's merciful
salvation. In 18:18–30 the very rich official (a Pharisee?) cannot follow
Jesus and enter God's kingdom because he is unwilling to strip himself
of his possessions. In contrast, Zacchaeus willingly gets rid of possessions to accept Jesus. In 18:35–43 the blind beggar knows of his great
need for God's aid and implores Jesus, Son of David, to have mercy on
him. He is saved and sees. Zacchaeus, desirous of seeing Jesus (19:3), is
also saved by Jesus (19:9).

Zacchaeus's inner journey is a model of how salvation works. This
very rich person, despised by his fellow Jews, wants to see Jesus. Jesus
disarmingly draws Zacchaeus to himself as he invites himself to reside
and break bread in Zacchaeus's house (19:5). Zacchaeus willingly and
joyfully allows Jesus to come into his life (19:6). Zacchaeus counters
those who complain about his sinful activities by stating emphatically
his resolve to make restitution with unheard of generosity (not
twofold, but fourfold) and to give one half of his possessions to the
poor (19:8). For his part, Jesus, who has come to seek and save what
was lost, pronounces that Zacchaeus is a son of Abraham and is saved
(19:9–10).

CONCLUSION AND STUDY QUESTION: In 18:18 to 19:10
Luke has presented us with four ways of looking at possessions. The
very rich official cannot separate himself from his possessions
(18:18–23). Peter and his companions have left their possessions to follow Jesus (18:24–30). The blind beggar gains everything from Jesus and
follows him (18:35–43). The very rich toll collector Zacchaeus gives
half of his possessions to the poor (19:1–10) and becomes a member of
God's people, a son of Abraham. What is the common thread that runs
through these stories? Is it that Jesus liberates us from the stranglehold
that the allurement of possessions has on us?

Luke 19:11–27
SHARE GOD'S MESSAGE OR LOSE IT

Jesus' parable of the pounds was not only remembered by the early
Christian communities, but also interpreted for new generations. This

reverent reinterpretation has caused bumps in the smooth road of the parable. One of the biggest bumps is the interweaving of the parable of the rejected king with that of the pounds (see 19:12, 14, 15a, 27).

Luke further reinterprets the parable he inherited from tradition (see Matt 25:14–20 for a similar parable) by decking it out with an introduction (19:11) and by the words "Engage in trade with these" (19:13) and "to learn what they had gained by trading" (19:15). Luke insists that Jesus' role was not to establish an earthly kingdom in Jerusalem (19:11). Rather, after Jesus' death, resurrection, and ascension, the promised Holy Spirit would come upon his disciples in Jerusalem and they would be sent on mission to preach God's kingdom. Note that in the modifications of 19:13 and 19:15 Luke uses economic imagery for the spiritual realities of handing on tradition in mission. Luke 19:27 clearly shows the high stakes in obeying the commands of the rejected, but now victorious king.

Underneath the various layers of reinterpretation, the constant focal point of this parable is the third servant. He is a tragic figure, who is fully cognizant that the money he has belongs to someone who expects a return on his capital, and yet is immobilized at the mere hint of taking a risk and tucks the money away for safekeeping in a piece of linen. Such a servant finds his fears of his master realized as the master strips him of his trust.

The tragic figure in Luke's allegory is not so much an individual as it is Israel or Luke's missionary communities. It is not enough for Israel or the church to strive to preserve what they have received from God. They must turn a profit on the capital entrusted to them as they take that capital out on mission. In his Acts of the Apostles Luke will spend considerable time on this theme, as he narrates in chapters 10 to 15 how God directed that Jesus' Gospel be extended to Gentiles without the necessity that they become Jews through circumcision and observance of the entire law. This God-inspired missionary movement to the Gentiles came about through Peter's baptism of Gentile Cornelius and through the missionary work of Paul and Barnabas among Gentiles. Indeed, Peter "engaged in the trade" of missionary work that the Risen Lord had assigned him and earned profits that we are enjoying today. In brief, those entrusted with God's revelation cannot guard it in a museum or make it windproof to the breath of God's Spirit. They must make that revelation yield dividends by venturing forth with it on mission in changed times and foreign cultures.

STUDY QUESTION: God's revelation cannot be handed on in some antiseptic, ecclesiastical pouch. How can Christians get more deeply involved in the high-risk task of setting forth the meaning of God's revelation for a new generation?

Luke 19:28–44
JESUS IS FOR PEACE

With this Palm Sunday Gospel, Luke concludes his travel narrative and builds upon the rejected-king theme of the preceding section (19:12, 14, 15a, 27). The whole group of disciples hails Jesus as king (19:38), for they acknowledge his miracles as signs of his kingly rule over those enemies of peace—sickness, demons, and death (19:37; see 4:18 and 7:21–22). Contrary to certain Jewish expectations of a messianic conqueror of foreign powers, Jesus' kingly rule is for peace—peace in the comprehensive sense of physical and spiritual wholeness and well-being (19:38, 42)—not for war. As a sign of his peaceful rule, Jesus the King eschews a warhorse and rides on the colt of a lowly donkey. By doing so, he fulfills the prophet Zechariah's prediction of the messianic king: "Rejoice heartily, O daughter Zion, shout for joy, O daughter Jerusalem! See, your king shall come to you; a just savior is he, meek, and riding on an ass, on a colt, the foal of an ass" (Zech 9:9).

Yet Jesus, the peace-bringing king, is rejected. The opposition Jesus encountered during his Galilean ministry and journey to Jerusalem (see, e.g., 11:53–54) reaches its climax here in Jerusalem (19:39, 41–44). In Jerusalem Jesus will continue to prophesy and teach in the face of opposition from the religious powers-that-be (19:45 to 21:38). Although God was present in the peace-effecting teaching and deeds of Jesus the King, such a king did not fit into Jerusalem's plans (19:44).

Besides giving a capsule message on the kingly rule of Messiah-Jesus, Luke has another intention in this section: to contrast the persistent faith of the blind man, now cured, who follows Jesus (18:35–43) with the blindness of the Jerusalem authorities (19:42). Luke asks his fellow Christians whether they will close their eyes to the many manifestations of God's peace they have experienced. The Jewish religious leaders show that such blindness is no respecter of persons.

STUDY QUESTION: This section presents a classic case of the reality of fulfillment conflicting with people's expectations of it. How do we cope when God's action or non-action fails to accord with our hopes and desires?

V. JESUS IN JERUSALEM:
FINAL TEACHING AND REJECTION

Luke 19:45 to 23:56

INTRODUCTION TO LUKE 19:45 TO 23:56

In these chapters Luke's goal is not to provide an exact description of Jesus' last deeds, words, and days. His interest lies elsewhere. He uses the traditions he has inherited to buoy up the faith of his missionary communities. He accomplishes this by bringing to well-rounded conclusions themes he has developed in the course of his Gospel. A preview of these themes will help us spot them when they occur.

The theme of Jesus, the peaceful *king,* culminates in the startling picture of Jesus, the crucified king. "Even the soldiers jeered at him. As they approached to offer him wine they called out, 'If you are King of the Jews, save yourself.' Above him there was an inscription that read, 'This is the King of the Jews'" (23:36–38). Further, to his last breath Jesus continues his *kingly ministry to the sinner* and saves the "good thief," who pleads: "Jesus, remember me when you come into *your kingdom"* (23:42).

Jesus, who taught God's will in Galilee and on his journey to Jerusalem, exercises his kingly rule by *teaching daily in the temple.* "And every day he was teaching in the temple area. The chief priests, the scribes, and the leaders of the people, meanwhile, were seeking to put him to death, but they could find no way to accomplish their purpose because all the people were hanging on his words" (19:47–48). The people flock to hear him while *the religious leaders reject him.*

Through his persecution and rejection by the religious authorities, Jesus continues as God's suffering righteous one, who is *innocent*. Herod and Pilate declare him innocent (23:14–15), and the Roman centurion at the cross, seeing how Jesus died, confident of God's graciousness toward him, exclaims that Jesus was certainly God's innocently suffering righteous one (23:47).

These chapters are especially important for Luke's suffering and innocent missionary communities as they carry out their commission to preach the Gospel to both Jew and Gentile.

Luke 19:45 to 20:19
JESUS, GOD'S PRESENCE AMONG GOD'S PEOPLE

Writing after the faith-rattling destruction of God's temple by the Romans in A.D. 70, Luke faces the problem of the theological significance of that event. In this section he deals with that problem by illuminating Jesus' relationship to the temple and to its demise.

We can get a good clue to what Luke is after if we think ourselves back into the first century A.D. and recall that the temple is not some tourist attraction which lures tens of thousands of gaping camera-toters each year. This magnificent edifice is the place and symbol of God's presence among God's people. It is more. It is the center of the Jewish cult and the goal of the annual religious pilgrimages. In the temple, God's will, revealed in the law, is preserved and taught. In brief, it is the symbolic center of the universe for God's people.

The temple was all this, but a glance through the prophetic books of the Old Testament shows that it was constantly in need of reform. For example, the prophet Jeremiah upbraids the worshipers of his time: "Hear the word of the LORD, all you of Judah who enter these gates to worship the Lord. . . . Reform your ways and your deeds, so that I may remain with you in this place. . . . Are you to steal and murder, commit adultery and perjury. . . go after strange gods that you know not, and yet come to stand before me in this house which bears my name, and say: 'We are safe; we can commit all these abominations again'? Has this house which bears my name become in your eyes *a den of thieves?*" (Jer 7:2–3, 9–11; see Luke 19:46). Prophets who taught after Jeremiah's death announced that the longed-for permanent reform of the temple would occur in the days of the Messiah.

With the above background in mind we can appreciate the fact that nowhere in 19:28–48 does Luke say that Jesus entered Jerusalem. In 19:45 he notes very explicitly that Jesus entered the temple, but does not mention Jerusalem. By means of this subtle change of his source, Mark 11:15, Luke gives prime-time billing to Jesus' actions in the temple. When he casts out the sellers, Jesus performs a messianic act of temple renewal. Further light is shed on this dramatic action from the description of temple renewal found in one of the later prophets, Zechariah: "On that day there shall be no longer be any merchants in the house of the LORD of hosts" (Zech 14:21). Luke builds upon the Old Testament teaching that Jesus is God's renewing presence within the temple.

Jesus' reform of the temple is not restricted to expelling the money-makers. He also reforms it by performing a function that had been neglected—he teaches God's will in the temple (19:47 to 20:1). The implications of these dual acts of reform are not lost on the religious leaders, who question him: "Tell us, by what authority are you doing these things? Or who is the one who gave you this authority?" (20:2). Jesus will not be duped by their intrigue and counters with a question of his own. The Jerusalem religious authorities, the Sanhedrin, reveal the same blindness to God's will as the Galilean Pharisees and lawyers, whose response to God's plan in John the Baptist occurs in Luke 7:29–30. And the people—God's people—are open to Jesus and hang on his every word (20:6).

Luke utilizes a parable, drawn from the real-life Palestinian situation of absentee landowners and rascally defaulting tenants, to cast further light on Jesus' relationship to the temple and to its destruction. Time after time the religious leaders have failed to recognize God's authority in his servants the prophets and have not given fruit to its rightful owner. They even reject the authority of God's final messenger, his dear beloved Son, by throwing him outside the walls of the vineyard and killing him (recall that in Luke's account Jesus is crucified outside the walls of Jerusalem). For rejecting the beloved Son, the tenants will be severely punished, and the vineyard will be given over to others. The people of God, the primary audience of the parable (20:9), do not want this to happen and cry out "God forbid" (20:16). They are not responsible for Jesus' rejection. It is the fault of their religious leaders that the city of Jerusalem and its temple are destroyed. Although the beloved Son is rejected, he will be vindicated by God and become the keystone in God's new building.

Luke employs the events of Jesus' life to comment on the significance of the destruction of God's temple in A.D. 70. Jesus' messianic claims to be God's renewing presence among his people meet with concerted opposition and ultimate rejection from the religious authorities. Because of their continued blindness to God's messengers, these leaders and their temple are rejected. The destruction of God's temple, however, does not spell the end of God's presence among God's people. The people of God who reform their lives and believe in Jesus are a spiritual temple built upon the keystone of the Risen Jesus.

STUDY QUESTION: How can contemporary Christians escape from the temptations of assuming that God's presence among them is a matter of stones and mortar and that they are owners, rather than tenants, of God's gifts to them?

Luke 20:20–44
THE NATURE OF THE MESSIAH-KING, JESUS

In this section Jesus' opponents turn his public teaching in the temple into a press conference and pommel him with loaded questions. These controversies parallel those Jesus had with the Pharisees and the scribes during his Galilean ministry (see 5:17 to 6:11).

Jesus brilliantly parries the question of those who want to paint him into the corner of opposing the Roman occupational forces (20:20–26). The very fact that his questioners have a Roman denarius on their persons indicates that they acknowledge the ruler who issues such coins. Jesus tells them to give those rulers what they require, but not to forget to give God what God is due. Although this passage very clearly shows that Jesus is no revolutionary freedom-fighter, his opponents later use this controversy in their accusations of Jesus before Pilate: "'We found this man misleading our people; he opposes the payment of taxes to Caesar and maintains that he is the Messiah, a king'" (23:2).

Jesus' next opponents are the Sadducees, Jewish aristocrats, who limited God's revelation to the Pentateuch, and did not accept any of

the newer "scriptures" and their teaching of resurrection, such as
Daniel 12:2. For them God's blessings were earthbound: possessions,
long life, and offspring. In Luke's description of Paul's trial before the
Jewish Sanhedrin in Acts 23 we read: "Paul was aware that some were
Sadducees and some Pharisees, so he called out before the Sanhedrin,
'My brothers, I am a Pharisee, the son of Pharisees; I am on trial for
hope in the resurrection of the dead.' When he said this, a dispute
broke out between the Pharisees and Sadducees, and the group became
divided. For the Sadducees say that there is no resurrection or angels or
spirits, while the Pharisees acknowledge all three" (Acts 23:6–8).

The Sadducees' argument against Jesus is based on the Pentateuch
(Deut 25:5–10) and is meant to expose the utter ridiculousness of resurrection belief. In 20:36 Jesus himself appeals to the Pentateuch (Gen
6:2–4) and argues that the children of the resurrection enjoy the same
intimate relationship with God that the angels do. In 20:37–38 Jesus
again appeals to the Pentateuch (Exod 3:6), arguing that God is the
God of the living.

Behind Jesus' phrase in 20:35, "those judged worthy of the resurrection," we catch sight of his vision of God. Resurrection is not inherent in human nature. It is a gracious gift to beloved children from a
very generous God. Through this passage we also glimpse Jesus' trust in
the God who will raise him from the dead.

Jesus' answers reveal the power of his teaching and leave his opponents scurrying for the exits (20:40). It remains for Jesus to clarify the
Davidic nature of the Messiah (20:41–44). The Messiah—Jesus—is
more exalted than King David because he is David's Lord and Master.

In this section Luke underscores some very important aspects of
Jesus' role as Messiah. He is no political revolutionary like the Zealots.
He will not remain in death's grasp, for the God of the living will raise
him up (see Peter's sermon at Pentecost in Acts 2:22–36 for more on
this resurrection belief). He is not merely David's son, but also David's
Lord.

STUDY QUESTION: Days before his death, which he has predicted
thrice, Jesus displays his utmost confidence in God, his Father. Would
Jesus' teaching about the nature of the resurrection have given inspiration to his missionary communities? If so, in what ways?

Luke 20:45 to 21:4
WIDOWS AND LEADERS

We set the religious context for this section by recalling what the Bible says about widows. While some widows may be strong and assertive like Tamar and Judith, widows in Israel were generally among the most vulnerable of the poor, mainly because in a patriarchal society they had been stripped of the protection and economic support of their husbands. God was often described as the protector of widows and orphans, and one of the hallmarks of Jewish kings and religious leaders was care of the poor, the widow, and orphan. Deuteronomy 10:18 describes God as the one "who executes justice for the orphan and the widow." Isaiah 1:23 denounces Israel's princes because "the fatherless they defend not, and the widow's plea does not reach them."

Luke modifies his source, Mark 12:38, by adding that Jesus speaks his warning about the scribes *to his disciples* (20:45). Jesus' disciples, then and now, should not model their leadership on that of the scribes, whose main concern was advertising their importance. As Luke has insisted before (12:41–48) and will insist later on in his Gospel (22:24–27), Christian leadership is for the service of others, not for self-aggrandizement. And leaders must not "devour the houses of widows" (20:47). One of six possible interpretations locates this despicable behavior in the scribes' habit of sponging off the hospitality and generosity of widows and literally eating them out of house and home. The primitive Jerusalem church shows its deep belief in the God of Abraham, Moses, and Jesus by caring for and not taking advantage of the widows among them (see Acts 6:1–7).

The interpretation of what Jesus says about the widow of 21:1–4 is threefold. Jesus may indeed be praising her for her generosity, especially as contrasted to what the rich give from their surplus. Also and in close connection with 20:45–47 he may be condemning a system that instructs a poor widow to give her entire livelihood to religion. Finally, the poor widow, who gives up her whole life (21:4), may prefigure Jesus, who will give up his whole life on the cross.

STUDY QUESTION: What lessons can contemporary church leaders draw from the negative characteristics of the scribes? Why does Luke give space to stories about widows such as Anna (2:36–38), the widow of Nain (7:11–17), the persistent widow (18:1–8), and the widows in the first church (Acts 6:1–7)?

Luke 21:5–38
THE DESTRUCTION OF JERUSALEM
IS NOT THE END OF THE WORLD

This section follows upon Jesus' debates in the temple with the Jewish religious authorities (19:45 to 21:4), who held the temple to be a symbol of God's commitment to them. We get on the wavelength of Luke's presentation by imagining the centrality a city may have in our lives. Longtime residents of a city can become so attached to their city that it becomes the hub of their universe. Move them away, and they become painfully unhappy and disoriented. In this section Luke addresses himself to a situation where members of his community were so attached to the city Jerusalem, God's city, and its temple that these things formed the center of their universe. When that city and its temple were destroyed in A.D. 70, they were distraught and confused and began to think that God had ushered in the end of the world.

An outline of Jesus' discourse will help us home in on Luke's message:

Introduction (21:5–7)
Initial exhortation (21:8–9)
Cosmic disasters (21:10–11)
Things that will occur before the end of the world:
    Christians are persecuted (21:12–19)
    Destruction of Jerusalem (21:20–24)
Cosmic disasters (21:25–33)
Final exhortation (21:34–36)
Conclusion (21:37–38)

The "exhortations" and "cosmic disasters" are parallel and frame the heart of Jesus' discourse: events that will occur before the end of the world, but that are not themselves signs of the end (21:12–24).

Luke 21:8 exhorts believers not to be stampeded by those who declare that the annihilation of Jerusalem is a sure sign that the coming of the Son of Man is imminent (see the commentary on 17:22–25 for more detail on this theme).

Luke begins the description of the cosmic disasters in verses 10–11 and interrupts it in verses 12–24, only to resume it in verses 25–33. Why the interruption? The words "before all this happens" (21:12) are the key to an answer. Before the cosmic disasters—the signs of the end—occur, the events detailed in the interruption will happen.

Into the typical apocalyptic scenarios of the last days, which contain their own emphasis on the human suffering caused by earthquakes, etc., Luke 21:12–19 introduces the suffering that Jesus' disciples will endure because they go on mission to spread his Gospel. Governments will hound them, and families will disown them. In a real sense Jesus' disciples will experience the truth of what Jesus proclaimed earlier: "If any want to become my followers, let them deny themselves and take up their cross daily and follow me" (9:23). In the horrific circumstances of rejection, Jesus will be his disciples' strength: "I myself shall give you a wisdom in speaking that all your adversaries will be powerless to resist or refute" (21:15).

The destruction of Jerusalem and its temple is not a sign of the end of the world (21:20–24). It occurs before the end, whose real signs are listed in verses 25–28. Verse 27, the most important verse in Jesus' entire discourse, occurs here: "And then they will see the Son of Man coming in a cloud with power and great glory." Jesus, proclaiming this discourse on the eve of his condemnation to death, will come as glorious and all-powerful Son of Man. Jesus, the once-rejected one, is victorious over all the powers of evil and controls the future.

Luke uses the parable of the fig tree to assure his readers that the end of the world will surely come (21:29–33). The exhortations of 21:34–36 pick up familiar Lukan themes and conclude the discourse. "Carousing and drunkenness" are the imprint of those servants who lived it up in the absence of their master (12:45). The "anxieties of daily life" recall those folks in the days of Noah and Lot who were totally absorbed in the daily concerns of life (17:26–30). The exhortation to "be vigilant at all times and pray" echoes the parable about the "need to pray always without becoming weary" (18:1–8).

In summary, Luke insists that the destruction of Jerusalem, while traumatic and faith-rattling, is not a sign that the end of the world is around the corner. During the dog days of opposition Christians may be confident that a loving God will not allow a hair of their heads to be lost, for God will preserve their life for eternity. Entanglement in the cares of life will weaken their commitment to the Son of Man, who is going to come at a time determined by God and not by such events as the destruction of Jerusalem and its temple.

STUDY QUESTION: Does this section provide contemporary Christians with any program on how to conduct themselves during the long haul of waiting for the coming of the Son of Man?

Luke 22:1–13
THE DEEPER MEANING OF JESUS' PASSION

In the two scenes of this section we will explore the significance of Luke's modification of his source, Mark.

Luke's addition of verse 3, "Then Satan entered into Judas," sounds the overture to the entire passion account. Satan, whom Jesus had overcome in his temptation in the desert (4:1–13), now attacks Jesus in earnest. Luke also directs his readers' attention beyond a superficial reading of Jesus' passion and crucifixion as the mere work of hostile religious leaders. Luke 22:53 is highly illuminating in this context: Jesus said, "Day after day I was with you in the temple area, and you did not seize me; but this is your hour, *the time for the power of darkness.*"

The second scene (22:7–13) previews the paramount importance of Jesus' farewell meal with his disciples. Three points stand out in Luke's adaptation of Mark. A comparison will uncover Luke's first two points, which are highlighted by italics:

His disciples said to him, "Where do you want us to go and prepare for you to eat the Passover?" (Mark 14:12)

He sent out Peter and John, saying, "Go and make preparations *for us* to eat the Passover." (Luke 22:8)

First, Jesus anticipates his disciples' query and sends two of them. He is in total command of the situation and enters his passion freely and willingly. Second, after he has celebrated a dozen meals earlier in the Gospel, this last meal is a meal "for us." Jesus is not a solitary diner. His last earthly meal—with his disciples—has significance for all Christians. Finally, like Mark, Luke depicts Jesus as a powerful prophet. His predictions are fulfilled to the nth degree (22:13). Such extraordinary power instills confidence in Christians that Jesus' predictions which dominate 22:14–38 (e.g., 22:30) will be fulfilled.

STUDY QUESTION: This section gives top billing to Jesus. Who is this Jesus that his last hours command the total attention of Satan?

Luke 22:14–38
A FAREWELL DISCOURSE
CONVEYS JESUS' PRICELESS LEGACY

When it comes to the events of Holy Week, I would venture to say that all of us—myself included—suffer from the disease of harmonizing-itis. That is, we harmonize the events of those days, selecting bits and pieces from each of the four Gospels to make our collage. For example, our collage might give a position of honor to the footwashing scene from John 13 and have right next to it Luke's crucifixion scene of Jesus' words to the good thief. Unless we diagnose this disease and take steps to combat it, we will miss much of what is uniquely Luke's teaching in this section and in the other parts of his passion account. I would suggest that one of the most effective remedies for harmonizing it is a big dose of active reading. Not just ordinary reading, during which we may tune in and out from time to time, but reading which is disciplined because we repeat in our own words what we think we have read. In the case at hand, this means that we can check the accuracy of what we think we have read by comparing it with the text and by contrasting it with the composite image of the Last Supper which harmonizing has imprinted on our memory. Try this remedy. You'll like it.

If one were to ask what is unique about Luke's Last Supper, the answer would be: It's a series of short speeches. Given by Jesus on the eve of his death, these speeches become his farewell discourse and embody his priceless legacy to his beloved present and future disciples. This legacy consists of the institution of the Eucharist, instructions on how to celebrate the Eucharist worthily, admonitions to church ministers who preside at the community's worship, and exhortations on how to go on mission in ominously changed circumstances. As Jesus speaks, his gaze is fixed on the future.

In Luke's Gospel Jesus thrice has predicted his passion (9:22, 44; 18:31–33). And as he prepares to fulfill these prophecies, he ensures his continued presence with his disciples by means of the legacy of the Eucharist. This legacy is so rich that Luke devotes two accounts to it (22:14–18 and 19–20). These accounts are so streamlined and laced with theological imagery that at first reading their meaning can elude our grasp like mercury. Jesus and his beloved disciples are not eating a frozen pizza dinner or one picked up at a fast-foot emporium like KFC. It's a festive meal, like the ones we celebrate with toasts of wine or speeches to interpret the event. It begins as a Passover meal whose symbolism recalls God's deliverance of the Jews from Egyptian slavery and points forward to God's future deliverance of God's people.

Luke's first account highlights the meal as Jesus' meal with his disciples (see 22:11) and apostles (22:14–15). It is a culmination of those meals which Jesus shared with others as a sign of God's fellowship with them (see the commentary on 5:27–32). In verses 16 and 18 Jesus confidently looks forward to his future where he will enjoy the banquet of heaven. At that time the Passover meal, which he now celebrates, will reach its fulfillment (22:16), for the future deliverance it points to will be present. Until that time, however, the cup which Jesus has blessed and which his disciples and apostles have shared is a pledge of their participation with him at that eternal banquet (22:17). In brief, drinking the cup of the Eucharist is future-oriented, a foretaste of that final sharing with Jesus at the banquet which God has prepared for Jesus' disciples and apostles.

The second account of the Eucharist clashes somewhat with the first. The symbolism of the Passover meal, still present in the first account, recedes into the background. Jesus' legacy is a new meal with its own symbolism. This symbolism emerges in the bread which is broken and the wine which is poured out *for you* and points to the cross where Jesus' life is broken and his blood is poured out *for you*. The Eucharist points to and makes present the power of Jesus' death. A further symbol can be found in the words "new covenant." Covenant means God's pact or contract of love and mercy with God's people. Israel frequently broke its covenant with God and longed for a new and lasting one (see Jer 31:31). The Eucharist makes present God's new relationship with God's people, a relationship effected by Jesus' death.

Now that Luke has depicted Jesus' eucharistic legacy, he adapts the announcement of Judas's betrayal to admonish communicants at the

Lord's Supper. Note that Judas's name is not mentioned in 22:21–23. This is not a slip of Luke's pen. Luke is universalizing the account. The disciples do not question Jesus about betrayal, but one another (contrast Mark 14:19). Luke looks beyond Jesus' Last Supper to his own Lord's Supper and challenges the female and male members of his communities to visualize themselves as Jesus' betrayers. He asks, "Might you betray Jesus?" and suggests community scrutiny as a means of forestalling betrayal of Jesus.

The fracas described in verses 24–27 is extraordinary—a fight at the Last Supper! Luke could have used this dispute in its Markan sequence (Mark 10:41–45) earlier in his Gospel, but he elected to introduce and adapt it here so that he could issue instructions for church ministers who preside at Eucharist. They must remember that the Eucharist makes Jesus the Servant present among his beloved disciples and should not be turned into a power-grabbing charade. Church ministers must not ogle the fashionable leadership styles of their haughty pagan counterparts. Their leadership style must bear the label of Jesus the Servant. Finally, Luke's picture of Jesus eating with disciples who squabble over their greatness fits in ironically with his large theme that Jesus' entire ministry was characterized by his habit of eating with sinners.

Another legacy, which Jesus leaves to the disciples who have stood by him during the fierce opposition he encountered in Galilee, on his journey to Jerusalem, and in Jerusalem itself, is rule or kingdom, even extending to Israel, symbolized by the figure of "twelve tribes" (22:28–30). But the brush of irony also paints these verses, especially verse 28, for only the women disciples stand by Jesus in the ultimate trial of Jesus' death on the cross (see 23:49, 55–56).

Jesus continues his farewell discourse with some stark and consoling words for Peter and the church (22:31–34). The Lord's intercessory prayer is so powerful that Peter's denial is not a loss of his faith in Jesus, but an act of cowardice from which he repents (see 22:61). After the Risen Lord has appeared to and offered reconciliation to Peter (see 24:34), Peter will indeed "strengthen his brothers" (22:32). In the first part of his Acts of the Apostles Luke gives pride of place to Peter, who has become a courageous preacher of the Risen Lord and is instrumental in the spread of the Gospel to Jew and Gentile.

The final speech in this farewell discourse echoes two previous motifs in Luke's account of the Last Supper. Jesus' death is in accord with God's plan as revealed in the scripture (22:37; see 22:22). Luke's missionary communities will suffer opposition and rejection like their Lord (22:35–38; see 22:28). It is not surprising that Jesus' last words in this farewell discourse are ironic: "It is enough!" The disciples at the Last Supper are quite dense and, in this instance, fail to grasp Jesus' message that the model for missionary work he gave in 10:1–12 has to be updated because of new and dangerous circumstances. "A sword" is shorthand for these dangerous circumstances. As 22:49–51 will show dramatically, Jesus prohibits real swords in his ministry.

Luke stamps his account of the Last Supper with the imprint of his communities' concerns. On the eve of his death Jesus does not abandon his beloved disciples, but bestows a precious legacy on them. As they battle various dangers to remain faithful to Jesus, they are assured of his presence among them in the Eucharist.

STUDY QUESTION: How many lessons does Luke teach his communities in 22:14–38? Do these lessons challenge and console us today? Read through the Acts of the Apostles carefully and note how often Luke refers to "the breaking of bread," e.g., Acts 2:46; 20:7. Are the primitive Christian communities celebrating Jesus' gift of the Eucharist in their "breaking of bread"?

Luke 22:39–53
JESUS, STEADFAST IN HIS RESOLVE
TO DO HIS FATHER'S WILL

In this section Luke highlights Jesus' steadfastness and resolve to do his Father's will in the face of his imminent death. There are lessons aplenty for Jesus' disciples when their faith is tested, be it in a situation of persecution or life-threatening illness.

Luke's account of Jesus on the mountain of prayer (22:39–46) has five unique features. First, Luke does not say that Jesus prayed three times as Matthew and Mark do. He centers all attention on Jesus' single prayer: "Not my will, but yours be done" (22:42). Second, he brackets that prayer with the exhortation to all the disciples, "Pray that you may not undergo the test" (22:40, 46). Third, Jesus' "agony" in prayer (22:44) is not the result of being frightened senseless by the prospect of death. The athletic image of "agony" can be likened to that which a weight lifter displays when he tries to lift four hundred pounds. Jesus' "agony" is the marshaling of all his strength and resolve to be obedient to his Father's will and to withstand the test of the crucifixion. Fourth, in his account of Jesus' temptations (4:1–13) Luke does not mention that Jesus was aided by an angel as Matthew and Luke did. In this struggle with "the power of darkness" (22:53; see 22:3) an angel aids Jesus. Fifth, Luke excuses the disciples' failure to watch with Jesus with the strange words, "sleeping from grief." As we all know from hundreds of advertisements from funeral directors and from stories about bereaved relatives, we do not make reasonable decisions when we're caught in the throes of grief. In brief, Jesus at prayer is an example to Luke's communities in its various missionary trials. Their steadfast and resolute prayer will strengthen them as it did Jesus.

Luke 22:47–53 is the unfolding of events set in motion by Judas (22:1–6). Unlike Matthew and Mark, Luke presents Jesus as a teacher who is in supreme command of the situation and is not seized until he ends his teaching (22:53). Since Jesus is not a political messiah, he will not sanction physical violence as a means of escaping from martyrdom—for himself or his followers (22:49–51). Jesus graphically illustrates that his mission is one of peace, not sword-wielding, by healing the servant's ear—the only miracle performed during Jesus' last days in Jerusalem. There is not a single Roman soldier present among those who come to apprehend Jesus. This is an affair between Jewish teachers. Unlike Mark, Luke does not say that Jesus' disciples flee for their lives. The disciples who are present at Jesus' crucifixion are his women disciples who have accompanied him from Galilee (23:49, 55–56; see 8:1–3).

STUDY QUESTION: Go through Luke's previous accounts of Jesus at prayer, e.g., 3:21, 9:29, 11:1–4. How do those accounts relate to Jesus at prayer on the Mount of Olives?

Luke 22:54–71
THE RESOLUTE AND MERCIFUL LORD

This section contrasts Jesus' courageous stand before the full panoply of Jewish authority (22:63–71) with Peter's cowardly performance before such awesome figures as a maidservant (22:54–62). Luke addresses his communities, whose members also deny their relationship with Jesus under trying circumstances.

If you recall, Luke's Last Supper account contained Jesus' assurance to Peter, "But I have prayed that your own faith may not fail" (22:32). To show that Peter's faith did not fail, Luke reinterprets the tradition of Peter's denials and does so in two ways. First, a comparison with Mark 14:66–72 shows the extent to which Luke has weakened the force of Peter's denials. Peter's denials range from the weak "I do not know what you are talking about" (22:60) to the mild "I do not know him" (22:57). Luke omits the vehemently strong denial which Mark has: "But he started calling down curses on himself and swearing, 'I do not know the man of whom you speak'" (Mark 14:71). Second, it is Luke alone who has, "And the Lord turned and looked at Peter" (22:61). The Lord's glance of mercy and forgiveness causes Peter to shed copious tears of repentance. Further, Peter is led to repentance because he "remembered" the Lord's words to him at the Last Supper (22:61). Peter's remembrance is not mere recall, but recollection with deep insight into what the Lord meant. See 24:8 below when the women at the tomb also "remember" Jesus' words and see their profound import. For Luke, Peter is the model for all believers, who under persecution or lesser temptations say that they don't know Jesus, their Lord and "Son of God" (22:70).

Despite the beatings and insults he receives as prophet (22:63–65), Jesus is a rock before his accusers. By couching his answer to the Sanhedrin's question in religious categories, Jesus denies that he is a political messiah. Although they may reject him, God will vindicate him as Son of Man to assume the position of authority, symbolized by "right hand." Remember our common expression, "He's his right hand man." The religious authorities see the implications of Jesus' answer and equate it with "Son of God."

In Luke the Sanhedrin does not accuse Jesus of blasphemy or pronounce a sentence of death. Luke streamlines his account of their "trial" to contrast Jesus resoluteness with Peter's cowardice.

STUDY QUESTION: In the Lithuanian church of St. Anthony in Kennebunkport, Maine, there is a stained glass window of St. Peter. The majestic Peter holds gigantic keys in his hands, and off in the upper left corner there is a cock crowing. Surely this window spoke volumes to Lithuanians persecuted by atheist communists for their faith. Can we, who belong to non-persecuted churches, still draw inspiration from the figure of the repentant Peter?

Luke 23:1–25
JESUS, THE INNOCENT MARTYR

In the general introduction to Luke 19:45 to 23:56 we gave a preview of several key themes in these chapters. The zoom lens of this section focuses on two of those themes: Jesus' innocence, and Jesus' rejection by the religious authorities.

The Sanhedrin is so intent on having Jesus killed that they go as one to plead their case before Pilate. Their accusation is a tissue of lies and innuendo. When and where had Jesus incited the people to revolt against Roman rule? In his discussion about the tribute (20:20–26) had Jesus opposed payment of taxes to Roman authorities? In his trial before the Sanhedrin Jesus had in effect declared that he was not a political messiah or king (22:66–71). Pilate is not taken in by these trumped-up charges and conducts his own scrutiny. He quickly becomes an advocate for the defense: "I find this man not guilty" (23:4). The religious authorities are not rebuffed by this finding and proceed to Plan B of their strategy: Jesus, who comes from Galilee— that hotbed of revolutionary activity—has been radicalizing people all over Palestine with his seditious tongue (23:5). Upon hearing of Jesus' Galilean origin, Pilate seizes the opportunity of obtaining an outside judgment on the case and sends Jesus off to Herod Antipas.

After Jesus returns from Herod, Pilate regathers the Jewish religious authorities and pronounces most solemnly that Jesus is innocent (23:14–15). The force of Pilate's judgment is fully perceived once one realizes the Old Testament background which Luke sees behind it. In Deuteronomy 19:15 two witnesses are required for a declaration of guilt or innocence. In the case at hand, two witnesses, one a pagan and the other a Jew, attest to Jesus' innocence. To cap Luke's argument, it should be noted that Herod was Jesus' enemy (see 13:31). Even an enemy—hardly the person one would expect to give impartial testimony—declares Jesus innocent.

But the religious leaders are not deterred and continue to press for Jesus' death—by crucifixion. They will even tolerate a convicted mur-

derer loose on their streets before they will let the innocent Jesus go
(23:19, 25). Pilate's third declaration of Jesus' innocence falls on deaf
ears (23:22). Under pressure of mob action, he gives in to them. But
Luke makes it clear that Pilate did not deliver a guilty verdict against
Jesus: "The verdict of Pilate was that their demand should be granted.
So he...handed Jesus over to them to deal with as they wished"
(23:24–25). Jesus is innocent. He goes to his death a martyr. Readers
might want to check 2 Maccabees 7 to 8 for stories of Jewish martyrs
suffering miserable deaths for their steadfast faith. Characteristic of
these stories are the following: conflict as the martyr fights against the
power of darkness; the martyr's innocence; mocking of the bystanders;
the martyr's courageous and faith-filled behavior as a model for believers in similar circumstances.

Popular preaching has attuned us to see Luke's purpose written on
the faces of the principal characters in this section: Don't imitate Pilate's
expediency; don't be a thrill-seeking Herod; don't harden your heart as
the religious leaders did. No doubt, such exhortatory displays capture
part of Luke's purpose. Yet Luke's intent runs deeper and on one level is
apologetic. Even though their opponents may charge them with sedition, Christians are no more revolutionary than Jesus, their Lord. And
the Roman officials should and do realize this. See, for example, what
Gallio, Roman Proconsul of Achaia, says to the Jews who accuse missionary Paul of wrongdoing: "If it were a matter of some crime or mali-
cious fraud, I should with reason hear the complaint of you Jews; but
since it is a question of arguments over doctrine and titles and your own
law, see to it yourselves. I do not wish to be a judge of such matters.
And he drove them away from the tribunal" (Acts 18:14–16). See also
Acts 26:31 where the Roman rulers say: "This man [Paul] is doing
nothing that deserves death or imprisonment."

On another deep level Luke taps into a rich theme found in the
Psalms and especially in the Book of Wisdom: Jesus is the innocently
suffering righteous one. Throughout Luke 23 Pilate, Herod, one of
those crucified with Jesus, and the centurion at the cross repeat the
refrain, "Jesus is innocent." On the cross Jesus' last words are from Psalm
31, the psalm of the innocently suffering righteous one who despite
rejection has profound faith in God's loving care. And the Gentile centurion, seeing how Jesus died, pronounces him innocent and righteous.
As the opponents of the innocent, righteous man say in Wisdom 2:18:

"For if the righteous one be the son of God, God will defend him and deliver him from the hand of his foes." And God's response to the innocently suffering righteous Jesus comes in the resurrection which finds loud, earlier echoes in Wisdom 3:1: "But the souls of the righteous are in the hand of God, and no torment shall touch them."

There is a further side to Luke's intent. Earlier in his Gospel (12:11–12 and 21:12–14) Luke consoled his harassed communities with the promise that the Lord would provide their defense attorney. This section goes beyond the trial scene of persecuted believers and conveys a message of stark realism: Although innocent of the charges of sedition, Christians in Luke's communities may be given over to the will of their opponents. As in the case of Jesus the martyr, God will vindicate their innocence.

STUDY QUESTION: How in this section does Luke show Theophilus and us readers "the certainty of the teachings we have received" (Luke 1:4)?

Luke 23:26–56
THE LAST WORDS TELL THE STORY

When I was a boy, the most popular Good Friday devotion was the *Tre Ore* service with its sermons on Jesus' last words. We kids even stopped playing Chicago style softball to attend the service. Although this devotion is largely out of vogue today, it had its finger on the pulse of the Gospel accounts of Jesus' crucifixion. We will center our comments on Jesus' last words—the heart of this section (23:28–31, 34, 43, 46).

Luke provides a theological lead-in for each of Jesus' last words. For his lead-in to Jesus' first word, he adds that unpleasant circumstances forced Simon of Cyrene to bear Jesus' cross and thus makes Simon a model for Christians who find that circumstances place them in Jesus' footsteps (23:26). Jesus' first word is a prophecy, foretelling the destruction of Jerusalem, akin to the one which he uttered as he approached the Holy City for the last time (19:41–44). Because the Jewish religious leaders rejected God's Son and prophet, their temple and Holy City will be devastated. Jesus cautions the women not to be

concerned about him, but about themselves. For if men treat the green
wood—the innocent Jesus—like this, what will happen when it comes
to dry wood—the unrepentant sinners?

Jesus' innocence is the setting for his second word. It is out of theological conviction and not for stylistic variation that Luke separates
Jesus the innocent one from the two criminals: "They crucified him
and the [two] criminals there" (23:33). Jesus' second word is a powerful
summary of his entire mission: "Father, forgive them; they know not
what they are doing" (23:34). It is also the hallmark of Jesus the martyr,
who does not rail against his murderers and lives his own teaching of
"love of enemies" (6:27, 35). Jesus' powerful example was not lost on
later Christian martyrs. In Acts Luke describes the death of the first
Christian martyr Stephen, who is being stoned to death for his profession of faith in Jesus the Messiah: "Then he fell to his knees and cried
out in a loud voice, 'Lord do not hold this sin against them'" (Acts
7:60).

The lead-in to Jesus' third word is long and replete with Lukan
themes (23:35–42). As we have had frequent occasion to note (see, e.g.,
20:16 and 23:48 below), Luke distances the people of God from their
leaders (23:35). It is these leaders who mock and jeer at Jesus while the
people stand by watching. The jeers of the Jewish religious leaders, the
Roman soldiers, and the one criminal resemble Jesus' earlier three
temptations (4:1–13) and ironically contain the genuine Christian message. Jesus is indeed the Christ of God, the Chosen One, the King of
the Jews. He has saved others. But Jesus, faithful to his Father's will to
the end, does not use his power to save his neck. Earlier, Pilate and
Herod had witnessed to Jesus' innocence. Now the "good criminal"
adds his independent witness: "But this man has done nothing criminal" (23:41). The jewel in this rich setting of theological themes follows. It is Jesus' third word, sometimes called "The Gospel within the
Gospel": "Amen, I say to you, today you will be with me in Paradise"
(23:43). Jesus had come to put his arms of mercy around sinners. To the
very last he is true to that kingly vocation. The "good revolutionary" is
promised salvation today, not in some dim future. The words "with
me" and "in Paradise" mean the same thing: The sinner will enjoy
communion with Jesus after his death. The clear implications of Jesus'
promise are that his death and exaltation to glory at the Father's right
hand occur at the same time. Because Jesus will enjoy that blissful state
today, he can promise a share of it to the criminal.

Luke's theological introduction to Jesus' last word zeroes in on the profound significance which Jesus' death has for Jewish worship. The tearing asunder of the veil of the temple (23:45) is just the first stage in the destruction of the temple itself. Entry to God's presence is no longer through the veil of the temple, but through Jesus' death. In calm confidence Jesus utters his last word. He does not die with a curse against God on his lips nor in anguished confusion over his destiny. As one of God's righteous ones who suffer innocently, he serenely commits his life to his Father, in whom he had put all his trust (23:46).

The responses that follow upon Jesus' last words and death interpret their meaning. The centurion, having seen the darkness, the temple curtain rent in two, and how Jesus prayed, gives the response commonly given to Jesus' miracles: He glorified God (23:47; see also, e.g., 7:16; 17:15). In Jesus' death the centurion, a Gentile, has seen God's power at work. The centurion says that Jesus is innocent and righteous (23:47; the Greek word *dikaios* means both "innocent" and "righteous"). Thus, Luke insists again on Jesus' innocence. But at the same time Luke joins the theme of innocence to another he has been developing in his Gospel and will continue to develop in the Acts of the Apostles. And that theme is that Jesus is "the innocently suffering righteous one," who, although persecuted by God's enemies, will be vindicated by God. In Acts 3:14–15, 7:52, and 22:14 Jesus is proclaimed God's Righteous One, who trusted that God will vindicate God's righteous even in their sorest hours. See, for example, Peter's speech in Solomon's Portico of the temple: "The God of Abraham, of Isaac, and of Jacob, the God of our ancestors, has glorified his servant Jesus whom you handed over and denied in Pilate's presence, when he had decided to release him. You denied the Holy and *Righteous One* and asked that a murderer be released to you. The author of life you put to death, but God raised him from the dead" (Acts 3:13–15).

The people of God, who have not abandoned Jesus, beat their breasts as a sign of their repentance (23:48). These repentant people will form the core of Israel, reconstituted after Jesus' death, resurrection, ascension, and gift of the Holy Spirit. After Peter's Pentecost sermon Acts 2:41 says: "Those who accepted his message were baptized, and about three thousand persons were added that day." Jesus' women disciples, who had followed him from Galilee, do not abandon him and remain faithful to the end (23:49, 55–56). These faithful women are eyewitnesses of Jesus' resurrection (24:1–12) and help form the 120 who comprise the new community in Jerusalem (Acts 1 to 2). Finally, Joseph of Arimathea, a member of the Sanhedrin, responds to Jesus, for whose death he had not voted (23:51). The innocent Jesus will not be given a criminal's burial in some pit, but the burial of the innocent in a fresh tomb.

If the last words of any person carry precious freight for their loved ones, how much more those of Jesus the Christ! Perhaps the most important word for members of Luke's missionary communities is Jesus' third: "Amen, I say to you, today you will be with me in Paradise." As they shoulder Jesus' cross daily and may be marched to martyrdom, they are assured that death is not going to triumph over them. God will save them as God saved the innocently suffering Righteous One and martyr Jesus, who represents all of creation subject to the powers of darkness.

STUDY QUESTION: Some scholars have criticized Luke for having a weak theology of the cross, for he generally does not use the language of atonement, that is, "Jesus died to take away our sins." From your study of Luke's passion account (chapters 22 and 23) what would you say about Luke's theology of the cross?

VI. THE END OF THE JESUS STORY IS JUST A BEGINNING

Luke 24:1-53

We come to the end of Luke's Gospel. Accustomed as we are to the events of the first Easter Day, we may miss the startling character of Luke's final chapter. Don't stories of great figures in history, say, an Abraham Lincoln, conclude with a narration of his death? Oh, perhaps there's a word or two about Lincoln's legacy, but then the curtain is drawn. Surprisingly, though, Luke's story does not end with Jesus' death. Jesus is alive! God has resurrected him. I use three images to open the door to Luke's message in chapter 24: the concluding chapter of a book, the execution of the leader of a movement, and a captivatingly beautiful quilt.

Although it was a long time ago, I can still recall the powerful emotions which pulsed through me when I finished reading John Steinbeck's *The Grapes of Wrath*. Its last chapter harnessed all the themes of the book into one overwhelming image, that of a nursing mother suckling a starving adult. This example of the summarizing character of a book's last chapter leads us down the road to appreciating Luke's achievement in chapter 24, where he captures the cascading waters of his themes in a single figure, that of the Risen Lord Jesus.

The Gospel commenced with the priest Zechariah worshiping in the temple. In Luke 2 Jesus' parents find him teaching in that same temple, for he must be about his Father's business. Luke's Gospel hit its story line stride in its central section with Jesus' journey to the temple where he taught authoritatively during the last days of his life. Luke's Gospel ends with Jesus' disciples continually in the temple praising

God and with the blessing of the priest, the Risen Lord Jesus, who has just completed the liturgy of his life (24:50–51). And, for the first and only time in the Gospel, the disciples worship the Risen Lord Jesus (24:52). These same men and women disciples are now poised on the brink of their mission of witnessing to God's Risen Son, Jesus, to the end of the earth (24:48). The two themes of worship and mission cluster around the recapitulating image of the Risen Lord Jesus.

The image of the last chapter of a book provides still another key to chapter 24. Imagine Sherlock Holmes buffs who reach the end of another thriller. As they revel in the mastery by which their hero has put all the pieces of the mystery puzzle together, they look forward to tagging along with him on his next case. Luke, too, leaves his readers leaning forward with keen anticipation to his next volume. In 24:44–53 his story does not trail off with the solution to the murder of Jesus, but points forward to his next book, the Acts of the Apostles, and its story of the missionary work of the church of Jesus the promised Messiah. Jesus' new community will be formed in God's Holy City, Jerusalem, to show that it, as the reconstituted people of God, is heir to God's promises to Israel (24:49). From Jerusalem the Gospel will be preached to all the nations (24:47). The script writer for much of Luke's sequel to his Gospel will be Jesus' Spirit who will guide the new community in its continuation of Jesus' mission (24:49). For more detail on the Spirit's role in Acts, see Luke's account of the descent of the promised Spirit on the 120 men and women in the upper room at Pentecost (Acts 1 and 2). See also Acts 11:15 where Peter describes that it was the Holy Spirit's doing that he went on mission to the Gentile, Cornelius, and had him baptized. The Church Council at Jerusalem issues its decision about a law-free Gospel with the words: "It is the decision of the Holy Spirit and of us . . ." (15:28).

Another image can give us good directions to Luke's message in chapter 24. Recall how frequently governments squelch a movement by arresting or executing its leader. Without its leader the movement loses heart and withers away. Behind Luke's account of the events of that first Easter day we can see the heart going out of Jesus' disciples as they muse: "It's all over now. He's dead. . . . Was he really God's prophet? Maybe our religious leaders were right after all in having him condemned to death?" Although Jesus had predicted his resurrection in 18:31–34, furthest from their minds was any notion that God would vindicate their leader by raising him from the dead. The women's proclamation of the good news that Jesus was alive was met with ridicule. The empty tomb may be a mystery for now, but it can be explained. Just give us time. The Jesus movement thrashes wildly in its death throes. See how easy it is to defuse a movement by liquidating its leader.

The wonder, grandeur, and mystery of Easter is that Jesus has not been liquidated. As God's messengers told the faithful women, Jesus is alive. The Risen Lord has appeared to Simon Peter and offered him reconciliation for his cowardly denial. The two disciples on the way to Emmaus have encountered him in the breaking open of the scriptures and in the breaking of the bread of life. He has appeared to the Eleven and the male and female disciples, shown them his hands and feet, and even eaten a piece of grilled fish. Jesus, the innocently suffering Righteous One and martyr, is not vindicated like an executed criminal whose innocence is later proven by the discovery of new evidence. Whereas that new verdict of innocence will not bring the dead man back to life, God has declared Jesus truly innocent and given him life. He's not a resuscitated corpse like Lazarus, who will die at some future time. Transformed by the power of God, his body is alive with God's life. Yet the disciples are able to identify the Risen Lord with Jesus of Nazareth. Through God's gift of the resurrection Jesus shares God's powers. He has authority to grace his disciples with the largess of the promised Holy Spirit. Because of Jesus those who accept the preaching of his disciples will have their sins forgiven. Jesus is worthy of the worship due to God alone. Yes, Jesus is very much alive. His appearances to his disciples instill new heart and life into them. They aren't sure what God has in store for them, but their Father, who would not let his faithful Son Jesus suffer the corruption of death, is surely to be trusted—no matter how obscure and troubled the future of this Christian missionary movement might be.

A final image will illumine Luke's message from still another angle. A friend of mine has an exquisitely wrought quilt. While the individual pieces are the work of various women, the completed quilt owes its beauty to the consummate skills of the woman artist who sewed the individual pieces together to create the quilt's magnificent array of colors, patterns, and meanings. In many respects Luke 24 resembles that superbly crafted quilt. Other Christians have worked on the traditions which Luke assembled in chapter 24 and described as happening on one single day. In themselves these traditions are of different hues and shapes: the story of the faithful women and the empty tomb (24:1–11),

Peter's visit to the tomb (24:12), the story of the disciples on the way to Emmaus (24:13–33, 35), the announcement that the Lord has risen and appeared to Simon (24:34), the story of Jesus' appearance to the Eleven and men and women disciples (24:36–43). Behind each stands a skilled artist. But it is due to the creative genius of Luke that they form the beautifully moving conclusion to the Third Gospel.

As you run your finger and eye over Luke 24, you can detect one of the weaves that Luke used to create this chapter—fulfillment of promise. And didn't Luke say in his prologue that his intention was to tell "of the events that have been fulfilled among us" (1:1)? I select three passages:

> The angels said to the women: "Why do you seek the living one among the dead? He is not here, but he has been raised. Remember what he said to you while he was still in Galilee, that the Son of Man must be handed over to sinners and be crucified, and rise on the third day." And they remembered his words. (24:5–8)

> "Oh, how foolish you are. How slow of heart to believe all that the prophets spoke. Was it not necessary that the Messiah should suffer these things and enter into his glory?" Then beginning with Moses and all the prophets, he interpreted to them what referred to him in all the scriptures. (24:25–27)

> He said to them, "These are my words that I spoke to you while I was still with you, that everything written about me in the law of Moses and in the prophets and psalms must be ful- filled." Then he opened their minds to understand the scrip- tures. (24:44–45)

Luke joins this theme of fulfillment of promise to another that he weaves through chapter 24. Each story is a story of how disciples moved from perplexity or doubt to faith and joy. Perplexed women, despondent travelers to Emmaus, and dumfounded disciples come to faith and are given the same insight into the mystery of Jesus' death and resurrection: These events are the fulfillment of promise. Foretold in the scriptures long ago, these events have now come to pass. The Risen Lord Jesus is proof positive that God is faithful to what God has promised. God did not let God's innocent and faithful one, Jesus, suffer corruption. With masterful weaving, Luke underlines God's control over the events of salvation and displays God's fidelity to what God has promised. Yet Luke's glance is not so much fixed on the past of God's fidelity as it is on the future of Jesus' church. Contemplating God's fidelity to God's promises to Jesus, Jesus' church can gain confidence in the Father who has promised to be with them as they continue the Messiah's mission in troubled times (24:49).

Besides the issue of God's fidelity, Luke reflects upon other concerns of his missionary communities in his masterful concluding chapter 24. To supply ammunition against those critics who carp that the disciples fabricated the message of Jesus' resurrection, Luke rejoins that the disciples, caught in the vortex of disillusionment, were anything but eager to believe the message themselves. It took the appearances of the Risen Lord and his explanation of God's plan for him in the scriptures to convince them that he was the Risen Messiah. To those Christians who, because of cultural differences, despise the body as unworthy of God's life, Luke insists that the Risen Jesus is not a ghost (24:39). Jesus' full humanity—his earthly body included—has been infused with the new life of the resurrection. Thus, despite the scandal it might cause among his body-scorning readers, Luke must champion the point that the redemption promised to those who follow Jesus is not limited to their spiritual element, but embraces their entire human person. In the artistic story of the disciples on their way to Emmaus, Jesus' homily on the meaning of scripture and his breaking of bread capture the spotlight. While the ascension may mark the end of Jesus' life on earth, it does not spell the absence of the Risen Lord from his church. He is present to them in word and meal. But to recognize his presence, the church must invite him to sup. In response to their hospitality to a stranger, Jesus will become their host and give them life.

Finally and not to be missed in a Gospel that accentuates Jesus' association with all and sundry is Luke's theme of inclusivity. It is the women who have remained faithful to Jesus from their missionary days in Galilee to his death on the cross. And it is they who see into the meaning of Jesus' prophecy of his death and resurrection and thus become the first believers in Jesus' resurrection. But their efforts to proclaim that message to the others, including the Eleven, prove fruitless (see 24:1–11). These women and others are present when the Lord appears for the final time on that first Easter day (24:37–53) and gives his missionary charge. And they will be present, along with Mary, Jesus' mother, in the group of 120 that awaits the coming of the promised Holy Spirit (Acts 1).

STUDY QUESTION: We have come to the end of Luke's Gospel with Jesus' male and female disciples poised to go out on mission. If you were sent on mission with Luke's Gospel as your only resource, what message or messages would you preach and live?

SUGGESTED FURTHER READINGS
ON LUKE'S GOSPEL

Scott Cunningham. *Through Many Tribulations: The Theology of Persecution in Luke-Acts* (Journal for the Study of the New Testament Supplement Series 142). Sheffield: Sheffield Academic Press, 1997. A full-scale, scholarly treatment of this dominant theme in Luke-Acts.

Joseph A. Fitzmyer. *The Gospel According to Luke* (Anchor Bible 28, 28A). Garden City: Doubleday, 1981 and 1985. This study of Luke's use of his predecessors is unparalleled in quality. Meaty and concise interpretations.

Joel B. Green. *The Gospel of Luke* (The New International Commentary on the New Testament). Grand Rapids: Eerdmans, 1997. This is the most comprehensive commentary on Luke's Gospel written from a narratological approach.

Luke Timothy Johnson. *The Gospel of Luke* (Sacra Pagina 3). Collegeville, Minn.: Liturgical Press, 1991. A thorough treatment of Luke's literary artistry and theology with excellent insights for reflection and preaching.

Robert J. Karris. "The Gospel According to Luke," *New Jerome Biblical Commentary*, ed. Raymond E. Brown, Joseph A. Fitzmyer, Roland E. Murphy. Englewood Cliffs: Prentice Hall, 1990, pp. 675–721. Many have found the thematic approach I develop in this commentary beneficial for teaching and preaching.

————. "Missionary Communities: A New Paradigm for the Study of Luke-Acts," *Catholic Biblical Quarterly* 41 (1979) 80–97. This article provides the scholarly underpinning for the approach developed in this brief commentary.

Jerome E. Neyrey, ed. *The Social World of Luke-Acts: Models for Interpretation*. Peabody: Hendrickson, 1991. This collection of essays illumines the Lukan Gospel from an array of social studies, e.g., honor and shame, patron–client relations, meals and table fellowship.

Mark Allan Powell. *Fortress Introduction to the Gospels.* Minneapolis: Fortress Press, 1998. An excellent and highly readable guide to contemporary methodologies used to study the four Gospels plus a very helpful discussion of each Gospel. Pages 85–111 are on Luke's Gospel.

————. *What Are They Saying About Luke?* Mahwah, N.J.: Paulist Press: 1989. This gem of a book situates my "Invitation to Luke" in the various streams of interpretation current in contemporary studies on the Third Gospel.

Barbara E. Reid. *Choosing the Better Part? Women in the Gospel of Luke.* Collegeville, Minn.: Liturgical Press, 1996. A useful study from a feminist perspective on Luke's many stories about women.

Sharon H. Ringe. *Luke* (Westminster Bible Companion). Louisville: Westminster John Knox Press, 1995. Precise, up-to-date commentary from various scholarly perspectives plus paragraphs of golden nuggets for reflection and preaching.

Charles H. Talbert. *Reading Luke: A Literary and Theological Commentary on the Third Gospel.* New York: Crossroad, 1982. This very worthwhile commentary views Luke's Gospel as biography that narrates the deeds and words of Jesus with the intent that they be emulated. Also, Talbert superbly illumines the thematic and narrative interrelationships between Luke's Gospel and Acts.

Invitation to John

George W. MacRae, S.J.
Revised by Daniel J. Harrington, S.J.

John

INTRODUCTION TO JOHN'S GOSPEL

The Fourth Gospel is different. After reading Matthew, Mark, or Luke, one finds in John a strange voice. It begins from a heavenly vantage point and speaks of a divine Word becoming flesh. It depicts a public life of Jesus that lasts several years. In it Jesus does not speak in parables and short sayings but in long, repetitive discourses. His message is not about the kingdom of God breaking into the world, but about himself coming from the Father and returning to him. Is this the same Jesus and the same good news about him?

Reinterpreting the Tradition

To understand the Fourth Gospel we must not try to harmonize it with the others. We must let its own voice speak with all its strangeness. But to do that we will have to compare it constantly with the others. Its author works with a tradition about Jesus that is also found in the other Gospels. In exactly what form he knows this tradition we are not sure. For many years interpreters have debated whether the fourth evangelist made use of Mark or Luke or all three Synoptic Gospels, or whether he used the same traditions about Jesus, in oral or written form, which the other evangelists used. The question is still not settled, but everyone agrees that John's Gospel is basically a reinterpretation of the tradition about Jesus. Since the Synoptic Gospels are virtually our only other witness to this tradition, we must refer to them constantly as we read and study John. For the most part, the closest points of contact will be with Mark and Luke.

The Facts about the Gospel

Some of the most obvious questions to ask about the Fourth Gospel are really unanswerable. Who wrote it? When was it written? Where was it written? For whom was it written? The most direct answer in all cases is that we don't know. And though it is not of primary importance to know such facts about the Gospel, it may be useful to indicate briefly what are the issues.

All four of the Gospels are anonymous, that is, they themselves do not tell us who their authors were. The Fourth Gospel indicates, as we shall see, that "the disciple Jesus loved," who figures prominently in the second half, was responsible for this Gospel, but even he is anonymous. In the second century the names of Matthew, Mark, Luke, and John were attached to the Gospels, and near the end of the century John was identified as the Apostle John. It is unlikely that the Fourth Gospel as we have it was written by an apostle, but it may embody a tradition of interpreting Jesus that originated with an apostle, and of course we can neither prove nor disprove that it was John. For the sake of convenience, we will continue to call the evangelist "John" without making any particular claims about the author.

The Fourth Gospel has been traditionally regarded as the latest of the four, and there is widespread agreement that it was written near the end of the first century A.D. As we shall see in discussing chapter 9 in particular, it presupposes a situation in which there had been a formal breach between the Jewish synagogue and those who believed Jesus was the Messiah. Such a situation most likely developed in the 80s or 90s. The Gospel can't be much later, however, because there is a manuscript fragment of it datable to the early second century. The question of date, like that of author, is bound up with the history of the composition of the Gospel, to which we must turn in a moment.

As for where the Gospel was written, any suggestion would be little more than a guess. Greek was in use throughout the Mediterranean world, and thus the language gives no clue. The question of whom it was written for is more appropriate. Some have thought the Gospel of John was written as a kind of missionary document to convert Jews or pagans to Christianity. Its polemical tone makes this unlikely, however, and much recent scholarly study has focused on the Johannine church as a distinct group of Christians for whom this was "their" Gospel. They are a church that has its roots in Judaism but that has recently been rejected by the Jews. They seem also to be conscious of their own identity vis-à-vis other Christian churches.

The Process of Composition

The student of the Fourth Gospel has to be aware of a complex set of questions about how the Gospel came into being in the form in which we find it in our Bible. There are signs that it has been tampered with, so to speak, in its history, and some awareness of the problems will help us understand it better.

First, there are signs that we may call textual problems, additions to the text of the Gospel made by ancient copyists who aided in spreading the work throughout the church in the early centuries. For example, the moving story of the woman taken in adultery, which has for centuries appeared as John 7:53 to 8:11, is not found in the oldest and best manuscripts of the Gospel and is certainly not an original part of it. The same can be said of John 5:3b–4, which introduces an angel of the Lord into the story of the paralytic at the pool (see the commentary on this passage).

Second, there are indications of additions made to the Gospel before it was circulated, passages which seem secondary but are not absent from any ancient manuscripts. The most widely recognized example is chapter 21, which is added to the Gospel after the formal conclusion at 20:30–31. In content and to some extent in style, this appendix or epilogue is not part of the evangelist's original work, and indeed it does not actually claim to be (see 21:24). Other editorial additions to the text are not so obvious, but recognizing them is important for following the original plan of the book. Two further examples are 12:44–50 and 6:55b–59 (see the commentary on these passages). The presence of such additions to the text indicates that at least one second hand was at work in producing the final form of the Gospel, which is therefore the result of a process of composition. Many think the process consisted of multiple stages from the first formation of Johannine insights into Jesus to the final addition of the appendix.

Third, there are very probably dislocations of passages within the Gospel. One of the greatest of modern commentators on John, Rudolf Bultmann (*The Gospel of John,* German original 1941, English translation 1971), believed that passages throughout the Gospel had been accidentally misplaced, and as a result he completely reorganized the Gospel in his commentary. Most scholars have not followed Bultmann in this respect, since there is a danger of improving upon the evangelist's logic and failing to recognize what the Gospel actually says. Yet,

though we can't explain how it happened, there may be some disloca-
tion of passages. In this commentary we will argue for only one
instance. Chapters 5 and 6 seem on several grounds to be in the wrong
order (see the commentary on 5:1–18).

Sources of the Gospel

John was a reinterpreter of the traditions about Jesus and he certainly
was familiar with much that went into the Synoptic Gospels. He may
even have known one or more of these Gospels themselves. But quite
apart from this issue, there continues to be a great deal of discussion
about other sources used by the evangelist, especially for those parts of
his Gospel which do not have an obvious counterpart in the Synoptics.
The most obvious of these consists of the long discourses of Jesus,
which are characterized by a kind of dualistic language—light and
darkness, above and below, truth and falsehood—and a pattern of talking about Christ ("Christology") as the one who descends from the
Father into the world and reascends to the Father. This sounds like
gnostic language—that of a radically antiworldly religious movement,
prominent in the second century, which had its Christian version but
was generally regarded as heretical. It was again Bultmann who suggested that John took over a collection of pagan gnostic discourses and
adapted them to Jesus. Again, few have accepted this suggestion, but its
merit has been to call our attention to the peculiar character of the discourses. It is more likely that John was simply influenced by the style
and language of revelation literature current in the Greco-Roman
world. John did not intend his work to be gnostic; his emphasis on the
real humanity of Jesus rules that out. But his reinterpretation was tend-
ing toward a position which the Christian gnostics found congenial.

There are clues in the Gospel that suggest another source may have
been used. John 2:11 speaks of "the first of his signs," and 4:54 mentions "the second sign that Jesus did." These passages have led many
interpreters, again including Bultmann, to the view that the evangelist
had a "signs source," a collection of miracle stories about Jesus, which
he incorporated into his Gospel. Some of the stories would have had
their Synoptic counterpart, like the multiplication of the loaves in
6:1–15, and others would have been quite original, like the wine miracle at Cana in 2:1–11. This source, though of course only hypothetical,
is much more likely to have been used. What will be most important

for us, however, is to see how it is used. The Fourth Gospel has a very special attitude toward miracles, which it calls "signs." When they are perceived only as miracles, they do not lead to faith in Jesus. Only when they are seen as signs of God's presence revealed in Jesus can they lead to faith. In the first half of the Gospel especially, the reactions of people to the signs are sharply contrasted with their reactions to the revealing word of Jesus.

Background of the Gospel

We have already mentioned the view of some interpreters that the Fourth Gospel has its background in gnosticism. That view is itself to be rejected, but one can acknowledge that the Gospel is influenced by the kind of religious language that later was recognized as characteristically gnostic. It is much more important to acknowledge that the background of the Gospel is first and foremost the Old Testament. Like most early Christians, the author (or various authors) was thoroughly steeped in Old Testament language and imagery and in a tradition of interpreting it. The modern reader of John, as of the whole New Testament, needs to recognize Old Testament themes, quotations, and allusions to appreciate what is being said. In the commentary we will call attention to a number of these, and the reader should not hesitate to look up the passages.

The situation of the Johannine church, expelled from the synagogue, suggests that the author's background was primarily Jewish, but it is difficult to be more specific about what kind of Judaism. In view of some important similarities with the language of the Dead Sea Scrolls, some have thought of a Judaism directly influenced by the Essenes of Palestine. But this is on other grounds unlikely. The similarities of language show only that the Essenes too were influenced by the Greco-Roman milieu. Wherever John's Jewish roots are to be found, he is quite consciously aware of the Greco-Roman world he lives in. He writes in Greek (though with traces of a Hebrew or an Aramaic background for some traditions) and uses a number of techniques from contemporary classical literature. His choice of symbols and images seems often to be based on their universal appeal to Christians of either Jewish or Gentile background. The world that cradled the early church was a complex one in which many religious currents interacted. The Fourth Gospel is above all a product of that world.

Why Read the Fourth Gospel?

If the Fourth Gospel is so markedly different from the other Gospels, what is its value to the modern Christian? Of course the answer to such a question can be formulated only when one has read and studied the Gospel itself. And it should be formulated in a personal manner by each reader. At the least, one will read John because it is there; it is part of the New Testament and therefore of the Christian heritage. But throughout its history, from the time it was labeled "the spiritual Gospel" in the early third century, it has exercised an enormous appeal. Each reader will have to judge whether that appeal makes worthwhile the effort needed to understand it first of all on its own terms.

Here is one suggestion. The Gospel of John reflects an understanding of God and the world in which everything is drawn in sharp lines. There are radical choices to be made within the framework of opposites in cosmic conflict. But the challenge is always personal, even individual. John serves to remind the Christian that underlying all the legitimate and necessary preoccupations of Christian life, there is the personal, existential attitude of faith, not as a decision to be made once and for all, but as an act that is always present when the believer realizes that God is encountered in the humanity of Jesus.

Study Suggestions

The Fourth Gospel is also distinctive in that it presupposes from the outset that the reader knows the whole story. In a very general way most Christian readers do know it, but John makes many specific allusions to what is to come later. It would be very useful therefore to read the whole Gospel text through quickly at the outset, then to begin studying it passage by passage. And in the study, it would be very helpful to have access to a copy of the whole Bible. There are many references in the following pages, particularly to the Old Testament and to the Synoptic Gospels. For a rewarding study of John one should look them up and compare.

Acknowledgments

The commentator has learned from three sources mainly, and they must be acknowledged if only with a word. First, he has learned from countless great scholars whose work has shed light on the meaning of John. The great commentaries of Bultmann and Raymond E. Brown have been particularly helpful. Second, he has learned from his students, whose interest and enthusiasm for the Gospel have produced valuable insights. Third, he has learned from reading and rereading the text of the Gospel itself. It never seems to fail to unlock more of its own secrets. For the friendly advice of Robert J. Karris, the author expresses his appreciation. And to Dorothy Riehm, who prepared the manuscript with meticulous care, he expresses his thanks.

George W. MacRae, S.J.

EDITOR'S NOTE: Unless otherwise indicated, biblical citations are from the New Revised Standard Version.

I. THE PROLOGUE

John 1:1–18

John 1:1–18
OVERTURE

Interpreters of John are in wide (though not unanimous) agreement that the Gospel begins by fusing a poem or hymn with the story. They disagree equally widely about which verses belong to the hymn, but what is important is the cosmic perspective ("In the beginning," cf. Gen 1:1) with which the author introduces the pre-existent divine Son, the Word. Verses 6–8 and 15 are certainly interpolations in the hymn; in fact, if one began the story with them, the Gospel would begin very much like Mark, and the hymn itself would appear to be the interpolation. The evangelist is clearly joining a timeless theological perspective to the story of Jesus.

The hymn, which may have its origin in a non-Christian poem about a heavenly revealer of God, moves from an assertion of the divine origin of the Word to a witness of the Christian community's faith in him as embodied in Jesus. The movement is from the majestic "In the beginning was the Word" to the personal "we have seen his glory." For a similar hymnic development, see the famous christological hymn in Philippians 2:6–11. No poetic scheme can account for all the verses here in John, since some of them, besides the interpolations mentioned, appear to be explanatory (e.g., 1:13, and perhaps 1:17–18). What holds the poetic structure together, though not with rigorous consistency, is the linking of key words such as "Word," "God," "be," "life," "light," etc.

Whatever the exact literary designation of the Gospel prologue, Rudolf Bultmann and others are no doubt on the mark in calling it an "overture" to the Gospel. It introduces a whole succession of themes that are developed in the chapters that follow: the Word, life, light and darkness, witness, the world, and many others. In verses 11 and 12 there is an outline of the major divisions of the Gospel itself: Chapters 1 to 12 dramatize the coming of Jesus to "his own" and his rejection by most of them, and chapters 13 to 20 detail the effect of his coming on those who do accept him, the disciples, who are privileged to become children of God (see the commentary on 20:17).

Why is Jesus called the Word, especially since he is not called that anywhere else in the Gospel? In fact, in the later history of Christology in the Christian tradition, the title "Word" has played a central role for which the Johannine prologue is the sole witness. Here is the appropriate place to make a general observation: The Fourth Gospel presumes from the beginning that the reader knows the story. To test this insight, one should study the first twelve chapters and then return to the prologue. The reader would then perceive that Jesus is indeed the Word in the sense that his mission is to reveal the Father and even to embody the word of this revelation. In fact, as the Gospel unfolds, it will become clear that there is a decided emphasis on faith in Jesus on the basis of word in contrast to miracle. The readers of the Gospel, for whom the historical activity of Jesus is in the past, have only the word of Gospel proclamation, but it is a major part of the intention of John to declare that this is not a second-best: "Blessed are those who have not seen, and yet have come to believe" (20:29).

Centuries of interpretation of John have recognized that the central focus of the opening passage is on verse 14, the statement of the incarnation. Part of it may be literally rendered, with an explicit allusion to the dwelling of Yahweh among his people in the desert, as "he pitched his tent among us." How we read this verse makes all the difference in the world for understanding Johannine Christology. It is possible, though perhaps less likely, to understand the statement to mean nothing more than that God visited his people. The alternative is to confront the paradox that the eternally pre-existent divine Word actually entered into human, fleshly existence. The implication of the latter understanding, that the human is revelatory of the divine, is more radical, more difficult, and very likely more faithful to the perspective of John.

A few details of interpretation are in order. In verse 1 the text does not unambiguously identify the Word (the Son, Christ) with God but asserts divinity without challenging the monotheism of early Christian faith; the New English Bible very attractively translates "and what God was, the Word was." Second, the division between verses 3 and 4 has from ancient times been problematic. The traditional rendering, most probably under the influence of christological controversies of the fourth century, is "not one thing that came to be had its being but through him." In verses 12–13 it is textually sounder, and in better harmony with Johannine theology, to accept the majority reading of the manuscripts: "to those who believed in his name . . . who were born. . . ." Verse 13 thus refers to those mentioned in verse 12. Finally, the phrase "the only Son" in verse 18 is problematic because the better manuscripts from antiquity say "the only God." One can understand the reluctance of early Christians to call Jesus "God" outrightly, but it may be that Johannine Christology is developed to the point of doing just that (cf. 1:1 and 20:28).

The splendor of the prologue to the Gospel must never be lost in exegetical details. It inaugurates the message of the Gospel on a level unparalleled in the Gospel tradition. In the human, the limited experience of humans, the evangelist sees the divine presence, and perhaps this is his major insight into the story of Jesus. The unfolding of the story will tell.

STUDY QUESTIONS: How can the human be a revelation of the divine? Do we experience such a revelation in our own lives? Would it make a difference if Jesus were only human or "only God"?

II. THE BOOK OF SIGNS

John 1:19 to 12:50

INTRODUCTION TO JOHN 1:19 TO 12:50

Discovering the principles that determine the structure of the Fourth Gospel has long fascinated its interpreters. The problem is not that there are few of them or that they are hard to find, but rather that there are so many and that they interlock in complex patterns. The feast days of the Jewish calendar, Jesus' journeys between Galilee and Jerusalem, his miracles and his discourses, the contexts of his revealing word—these and other principles of structure have been detected.

But there is one arrangement of the Gospel we cannot ignore, and that is the sharp division between chapters 12 and 13. This structures the work in two main parts dealing with Jesus' public ministry, in which he reveals himself to the world at large, and the passion-resurrection story, in which he reveals himself in a new way to his followers. A similar structure, though not rigorously carried out, is found in Mark, where the new section begins at Mark 8:22.

The Book of Signs, as C. H. Dodd has called chapters 1 to 12, is dominated not only by the miracles of Jesus, culminating in the raising of Lazarus from the dead, but also by the discourses of Jesus. Most of these produce conflict with those whom the evangelist calls "the Jews," and the tension mounts in reaction to both discourse and sign until Jesus' death becomes certain.

Running through the Book of Signs are a number of theological issues of great importance for this Gospel. One has to do with the miracles of Jesus, the "signs," which are portrayed as an inadequate basis for faith unless they are properly perceived. True faith in Jesus is a response to his revealing word. Another issue centers around the use of titles to understand the identity of Jesus. In several scenes we will note a progression from recognizing Jesus as the (or a) prophet or as the Messiah to seeing him as the Son of Man or in some other light. Jesus' true identity was of course made known in the prologue, but it is presented as an issue for the characters in the Gospel and it must have been the subject of discussion in the Johannine church as well. The reader of the Book of Signs should be alert to clues about signs, words, and faith, and to the role of christological titles.

John 1:19–34
THE VOICE OF ONE CRYING OUT IN THE WILDERNESS

The opening scenes in the Gospel are clearly set off by the evangelist in four episodes, the last three introduced by the recurring phrase "the next day" (vv. 29, 35, 43). The first two center on John the Baptist and his witness to Jesus; the last two, treated below, focus on the first disciples.

The evangelist's thorough reinterpretation of the traditions about Jesus is quite visible at the outset. To see what he is reinterpreting, the reader might look at Mark 1:1–11, where we find the appearance and ministry of John, his role described in terms of Isaiah 40:3, his "prophecy" of the one to come after him, and his baptism of Jesus. In the Fourth Gospel the baptism of Jesus is alluded to but not actually described. This reticence may be part of a more general tendency in the Gospel to play down the Baptist by not appearing to make Jesus depend on him. Some think there were still followers of the Baptist in touch with the Johannine community and needing to be put in their subordinate place.

John the Baptist plays a very important role, however, as witness to Jesus' identity. Note how the word "witness" is used in verses 19 and 34 (and in Greek in v. 32), framing the scenes. He denies that he is the "Christ"—the Greek term, before it became a name of Jesus, translated "Messiah," as John reminds us in 1:41—or Elijah (see Mal 4:5–6) or the prophet (see Deut 18:15). In thus reinterpreting the theme of speculating on the identity of Jesus (see Mark 6:14–15 and 8:27–28, where some think Jesus is John the Baptist come back to life), the evangelist focuses our attention on Jesus himself, and that is the Baptist's real function (see the commentary on 3:22–36). Witnessing to Jesus is important to this Gospel. Not only does the Baptist do it, but the evangelist himself does also (see for example 19:35).

The theme that binds together all four "days" to the opening of the Gospel is the concentration on the person of Jesus—what is called Johannine Christocentrism—under the rubric of a succession of christological titles. Each of the four "days" introduces its own list of titles, and the cumulative effect is to see a large part of the early church's faith in Jesus laid out before us at the outset of the story.

Besides the titles used negatively about himself in the first scene, the Baptist calls Jesus "the Lamb of God who takes away the sin of the world." The specific background of this unique designation is hard to identify, but it may refer to the role of the suffering servant of God in Isaiah 52:13 to 53:12. To determine exactly what constitutes the world's sin in this Gospel we shall have to be alert to the development of the idea of sin in the following chapters. The Baptist in 1:34 also calls Jesus by the messianic title "the Chosen One of God"; in some of the ancient manuscripts the reading is "the Son of God." In either case, the background of the title is the baptism of Jesus in which God acknowledges his Son-Messiah.

STUDY QUESTION: What kind of witness to the identity of Jesus is the modern Christian called upon to make?

John 1:35–51
WHAT ARE YOU LOOKING FOR?

The third and fourth "days" of the Gospel beginning are closely symmetrical. In each case the first disciple called, Andrew or Philip, is impelled to invite another, Peter or Nathanael, to follow Jesus. A similar dynamic will occur in chapter 4, where the woman at the well undertakes the missionary task of calling the people of her town to believe in Jesus. Discovery of Jesus' identity, even if not yet adequate understanding of him, implies a desire to share the news.

The traditions being reinterpreted here are the "call stories" or accounts of a vocation to discipleship. In Mark 1:16–20 there are two stories of the call of Simon (Peter) and Andrew, and of James and John.

Our evangelist dramatizes such traditional stories in his own way, but his emphasis is still on following, that is, being a disciple of, Jesus. Note the use of the word "follow" in verses 37, 38, 40, 43. The invitation to become a disciple-believer is in the form "Come and see," whether on the lips of Jesus himself or of another disciple. Coupled with the opening words of Jesus in the Gospel—the question "What are you looking for?"—these remarks also serve as an invitation to the Gospel itself, where the revealing word of Jesus is to be found.

The main emphasis of the two stories is still on the person of Jesus and the titles used by early Christians to express their faith in him. Jesus is Rabbi, Messiah, the prophet, Son of God, and King of Israel. It is characteristic of the Christocentrism of this Gospel that Jesus himself is called king instead of being portrayed as preaching about the kingdom of God as in the other Gospels. Nathanael's remarkable confession of faith in Jesus as Messiah is in response to the apparently superhuman insight Jesus displays. The "greater things" that he is about to see include the following incident at Cana and indeed all the signs to come.

The evangelist has added a saying about the Son of Man here to introduce another important christological title. The saying is addressed to a wider audience (plural "you" in Greek) that of course includes the readers of the Gospel. It boldly combines allusions to Jacob's ladder (Gen 28:12) and the heavenly Son of Man (Dan 7:13) to suggest that the heavenly glory of the divine Son will be visible on earth.

STUDY QUESTIONS: What do we seek in approaching Jesus? How does the discovery of his identity affect our lives?

John 2:1–12
THE FIRST OF HIS SIGNS

In presenting Jesus in action for the first time, John gives us a number of clues about how to understand the story. In 2:11 he calls this incident a sign, which in his vocabulary does not simply mean a miracle, as in the traditional phrase "signs and wonders" (4:48), but indicates that one must perceive the meaning of the event in order to understand it. Signs always point beyond themselves. In the same verse he indicates that Jesus "revealed his glory" and in response the disciples "believed in him." Thus the sign is not merely a miracle to arouse astonishment but a manifestation of the divine glory. It is only when a miracle story can be seen this way, as a kind of epiphany of the divine, that it can arouse faith—in the characters in the Gospel or in the readers of it.

There are other clues also. The story itself, on the level of simple narrative, leaves too many questions unanswered, and the setting is implausible. Jesus refers to his "hour," which in the special vocabulary of the Fourth Gospel means the passion-resurrection. It has not come yet but is apparently anticipated here. In this light perhaps we should translate the opening words literally "on the third day" and allow the inevitable connotation of the resurrection to stand. In this Gospel it is precisely the death and resurrection of Jesus which is the ultimate manifestation of Jesus' divine glory, and that is somehow to be seen as anticipated in the miracle of changing water to wine at Cana. The only other appearance of Jesus' mother in the Gospel (19:25–27) links this story with the passion.

We are thus led by the evangelist to read this story on a symbolic level and not merely on a story level. The trouble is that there are so many symbolic allusions in it. For example, contemporaries of the Gospel in the Greco-Roman world would be quite familiar with the manifestation of the god Dionysus in worship and even in miracles involving wine. Whether that background is relevant here is uncertain. There may also be in the mention of the ablution jars an allusion to the inadequacy of Jewish ritual to cope with real human need. But the most plausible area of symbolism—in addition to the reference to the passion—is that of the messianic setting in which the identity of Jesus as Messiah is implied. The occasion is a wedding feast, which, as the parables in Matthew 22:1–14 show, was a messianic occasion. The great abundance of wine provided recalls the imagery of Amos 9:13–14. Most of all, the remark of the steward in verse 10, "You have kept the good wine until now" invites the conclusion that the Messiah is now here.

Jesus' moving to Capernaum as the center of his Galilean ministry is part of the tradition (see Mark 1:21; 2:1), but John has no interest in keeping him there. Hence the rather abrupt statement that he didn't stay long. The remainder of the Book of Signs shows Jesus constantly traveling to and from Jerusalem. Unlike the Synoptic evangelists, John does not confine Jesus' ministry to a single year.

STUDY QUESTIONS: To what extent is an understanding of the Old Testament and its themes a part of the Christian message? What difference does it make to the Christian follower of Jesus?

John 2:13–22
ZEAL FOR YOUR HOUSE

John tells the story of the cleansing of the temple near the beginning of Jesus' ministry; the Synoptic writers connect it with the passion narrative (see, e.g., Mark 11:15–19). But we must remember that they had no choice, since for them Jesus visited Jerusalem only once. It is unlikely that Jesus performed this prophetic gesture twice, and we have no sure way of deciding between John and the other Gospels about the timing of it. For John it establishes the prophetic role of Jesus at the outset and furnishes an opportunity to have him mention his Father for the first time.

The evangelist is still a reinterpreter here. He combines the traditional story with a saying of Jesus about destroying the temple (see Mark 14:58) and with a challenge to Jesus' authority to exercise a prophetic role (see Mark 11:28). The Jews demand a sign—the word is used here in the sense of a proof of authority—as in other contexts they do in the Synoptic tradition (e.g., Mark 8:11–12). If they are meant to understand Jesus as acting like a prophet, their demand for a sign is the classic test of a prophet (see Deut 13:1–21). This scene in the Synoptic tradition is connected with quotations from Isaiah 56:7 and Jeremiah 7:11. John has felt free to cite Psalm 69:9.

The variation in Old Testament passages is an important reminder of how the early Christians turned to their Bible and reinterpreted it in terms of their experience of Jesus and their traditions about him. This procedure is explicitly referred to in verse 22 (and in 12:16, which is a very close parallel). The statement is important for understanding John and indeed all the Gospels. They are all written from the post-Easter perspective of the Christian churches and in the light of Old Testament reinterpretation. John calls this process "remembering," which means something closer to theological reflection than merely recalling. The warrant for this creative activity on the part of evangelists and others is the work of the Paraclete, or Advocate, the Holy Spirit in the community, who will "remind" (literally "cause to remember") the disciples of all that Jesus has said (14:26). It is the same awareness of the Spirit that authorizes the Johannine church to reinterpret the tradition in its own distinctive way.

STUDY QUESTION: Do we approach the Gospels mainly to learn "the facts" about Jesus, or to learn what he means for the lives of his followers?

John 2:23 to 3:21
GOD SO LOVED THE WORLD

The final verses of chapter 2 serve better as an introduction to what follows than a conclusion to the temple story. They contain a sharp criticism of faith that is based merely on seeing the miracles of Jesus. In the Greek of verses 23–24 there is a play on words which we might paraphrase: "many *believed* in his name when they saw the signs that he gave, but Jesus knew them all and did not let himself be *believed* in by them." True faith comes from seeing God's revelation in Jesus, and though that can be seen in the signs if they are understood properly, it comes primarily through Jesus' revealing word. Thus the ambiguity of Nicodemus. He comes to Jesus secretly with a faith, or at least a curiosity, based on signs alone, but he does not seem able to accept the revealing word with which Jesus challenges him.

Actually, the reader doesn't know how Nicodemus turns out. When we meet him again in discussions among Jews (7:50–52) and at the burial of Jesus (19:39, both passages with typical Johannine cross references), we don't know whether he has come fully to be a believer or whether he represents the class of cryptobelievers who are afraid to confess their faith openly (see 12:42–43). But John is not so much interested in the personal history of Nicodemus as in the opportunity to introduce the word of Jesus in action and to present the first of many discourses of Jesus.

The dialogue with Nicodemus, which remains unresolved, is a good example of a favorite technique of this Gospel. Jesus' revealing word is often, because of the very simplicity of his language, ambiguous, and more often than not it provokes misunderstanding. Jesus demands that the would-be believer undergo a spiritual birth, enter on a new life, which the Gospel calls "eternal life," in which the person is turned toward God and is receptive to God's revelation. But he states this in a phrase which in Greek means both "born from above" and "born again." Strictly speaking, Jesus could mean either one here, though "born from above" better fits the thought of the Fourth Gospel. But Nicodemus is not open to the symbolic meaning and stays at the level of incredulity about being born a second time.

The Christian tradition has often understood this passage to refer to baptism, but it is not certain that John intended such a reference. Even the phrase "born of water and Spirit" (3:5) may be using two words for the same thing, since water symbolizes the Spirit in John (see 7:37–39). This Gospel is not unaware of sacramental practice but places very little emphasis on it.

Starting with verse 11, Jesus moves into a discourse and addresses a plural "you." This beautiful and rightly loved passage is typical of the discourses in the Gospel. It emphasizes such Johannine themes as the contrast between the heavenly and the earthly, between light and darkness, eternal life, truth, and the function of Jesus' words as provoking judgment. The judgment which the individual undergoes is for or against Jesus; there is no middle ground.

Since there were no quotation marks in ancient copies of the Gospel, we are unsure whether verses 11–21 are all meant to be spoken by Jesus or whether verses 16–21 are the evangelist's own reflection. The dilemma is instructive, however, for it reminds us that the discourses placed on the lips of Jesus in this Gospel are in the evangelist's own style and they embody his theological reflections on the meaning of Jesus for his people.

Verse 14 contains a remarkably bold allusion to the Old Testament that is found also in some other ancient Jewish and Christian literature. The story is told in Numbers 21:4–9 of how Moses, on Yahweh's instruction, placed a bronze serpent on a pole to save the lives of those afflicted with fatal snake bites. John uses this vivid image to refer to Jesus' death on the cross, which is a source of eternal life for believers. The three references to the lifting up of the Son of Man in John (3:14; 8:28; 12:32–34) are the Johannine counterpart to the three predictions of the passion, also in terms of the Son of Man, in the Synoptic tradition (see Mark 8:31; 9:31; 10:33–34).

STUDY QUESTION: What are the conditions for arriving at true Christian faith?

John 3:22–36
THE FRIEND OF THE BRIDEGROOM

John the Baptist reappears in the Gospel, and again it is to bear witness to Jesus by contrasting his own role as a mere forerunner or herald with that of Jesus as the Messiah. The other Gospels give us no hint that Jesus was once a baptizer like John, and there must have been some discussion of this issue in the community of the Fourth Gospel, since 4:2 places a qualification on 3:22 by confining the baptizing to Jesus' disciples. Perhaps the "correction" is evidence of the stages of composition in John.

From verse 31 on we have the same dilemma we had in the last passage. Who is the speaker? Since no one else is mentioned, one might assume that it is the Baptist who goes on speaking. Yet the verses sound very much like the discourse of Jesus earlier in the chapter—or like the evangelist's reflections. In the complex and probably long process in which the Gospel took shape, this section might have been part of a discourse of Jesus related to 3:11–21. It may be thought appropriate here because it picks up the theme of witnessing, but now it is Jesus who witnesses to the Father.

The radical separation between "above" and "the earth," which some have called Johannine dualism, is expressed in this discourse in strong terms. Only Jesus has bridged the gap, for he is the one who came from heaven to speak God's own words in the world. The consistent pattern of John's Christology is that of the descent and eventual reascent of Jesus; often (as in 3:13) this pattern is particularly associated with the title Son of Man. By speaking God's words in the world, however, that is, by creating faith and conferring eternal life, the Johannine Jesus makes it possible for Christians also to bridge the gap between "above" and "below." The dualism is overcome by faith because Jesus has overcome it in the incarnation.

STUDY QUESTIONS: Does the attitude of John the Baptist suggest any model for the Christian's relationship to Jesus? How does a particular understanding of who Jesus is affect the way a believer behaves?

John 4:1–42
GIVE ME THIS WATER

Because the Fourth Gospel is a more conscious literary reinterpretation than the other Gospels, it does not always lend itself to division into short passages. It will often be the case that we must comment on long sections. But in the beloved story of the woman at the well the evangelist has practiced some of his skillful dramatic techniques, particularly in the way he sandwiches the scene with the disciples between the departure of the woman and the arrival of her fellow townspeople. It is relatively easy, therefore, to organize our comments around the successive scenes of the drama.

Scene 1 (vv. 5–26): Jesus' encounter with the Samaritan woman, which takes the form of a dialogue, is clearly divided into two parts, distinguished both by theme and by style. The first (vv. 7–15) begins with Jesus asking for water and ends with the woman making a similar request. But in between lies a superb example of Johannine ambiguity and misunderstanding. The symbol in question is that of "living water," which can be understood on a natural level as fresh, running water, but symbolically represents God's gift that comes through Jesus-revelation, the Holy Spirit, eternal life. There is no reason to think the woman understands the symbol any better than Nicodemus understood the birth from above, but she remains open to Jesus' word even when she doesn't understand.

In response to the woman's continued interest, Jesus challenges her with a personal word that calls into question her moral life (second part, vv. 16–26). Her response is a classic evasion—a theological discussion of the conflict between Samaritans and Jews over the proper place of worship. Jesus transcends the issue with a short discourse on true worship of the Father. Two things may be singled out from this part of the scene. First, given the obvious antipathy of the Fourth Gospel toward "the Jews," which we shall discuss further below, it is surprising to hear Jesus say "salvation is from the Jews." Yet that is precisely the point: Jesus is a Jew and so are his early followers. The very poignancy of Johannine opposition to "the Jews" arises out of the breach that has arisen between the Johannine church and its Jewish origin. This situation helps to explain the favorable portrayal of willing acceptance of faith in Jesus on the part of the traditional enemies of the Jews, the

Samaritans. The enmity is the sharper because the two groups share much in common.

The second point is the progression of christological titles. The woman first acknowledges Jesus as a prophet (4:19) and then, in response to Jesus' own self-revelation, as the Messiah (vv. 25–26 and 29). But in both cases her faith is based on his extraordinary insight into her life—the equivalent of a "sign." It is only when the townspeople respond to his word that these christological categories are superseded.

Scene 2 (vv. 27–38): The brief discourse of Jesus to the disciples in verses 34–38 is at first sight difficult to understand. The important thing is to be aware that, like many passages in the Gospel, it fuses the two levels of meaning essential to the story: the "historical" level of Jesus and his disciples and the contemporary level of the Christian community of the Gospel. The disciples, representing the community leaders of the evangelist's time, are being invited to share in the work of preaching the Gospel, of confronting people with the revealing word of Jesus—and thus of doing the Father's will. The two proverbs cited are thereby given a new interpretation. In the Fourth Gospel itself the time between the sowing and the harvest has been collapsed (v. 35) and the reaper and sower of the Christian mission (v. 37) rejoice together. This indirect commissioning of the followers of Jesus to carry on his work gets its force from its position within the drama of the Samaritans' faith.

Scene 3 (vv. 39–42): If the woman's faith had been based on Jesus' sign-activity as prophet with divine insight, it is made explicit here that the people go beyond that with a faith-response to his word ("because of his word," v. 41). And in accordance with the degrees of faith reflected in the titles predicated of Jesus, the townspeople go beyond "prophet" and "Messiah" to acknowledge Jesus as "Savior of the world."

The apparent success of Jesus' encounter with the Samaritans stands out in the Book of Signs. In almost all his encounters with Jews from Galilee to the north or Judea to the south, he meets with opposition to some degree. One can speculate whether the favorable response of Samaritans rests on a historical role of Samaritans in early Christianity, but the evidence is too slight to be conclusive. What is more important in this carefully wrought story is the dynamic of coming to faith in response to Jesus' word—and the mission of Jesus' disciples to continue the process.

STUDY QUESTIONS: How does the reaction of the woman at the well differ from that of Nicodemus? What is implied for Christians in Jesus' instruction to the disciples?

John 4:43–54
YOUR SON WILL LIVE

The second sign at Cana in Galilee, which may have stood second in a hypothetical "signs source" used by the evangelist, continues the issue of faith as response to signs or to word. Again both are present. The traditional story which John reinterprets is attested in the source common to Matthew and Luke (see Matt 8:5–13 and Luke 7:1–10). There the focus is not so much on the miracle of healing at a distance but on the faith of the Gentiles as contrasted with the rejection of Jesus by Jews. In the reinterpretation in John, nothing of the Jew-Gentile issue remains.

Instead, the clue to the story lies in verse 48, which is clearly a Johannine insertion, both because it interrupts the narrative and because it is spoken to a plural "you," not just to the court official. The tone is one of mild frustration, and the statement should be compared with the criticism of signs-faith in 2:23–25. Because the situation is so appropriate, Jesus can respond to his petitioner with only a word, but verse 50 makes it explicit that the man believed on the basis of the word. In this instance the miracle, carefully attested in verses 51–53, serves to confirm the power of Jesus' word. Jesus manifests himself as the one who gives life. Belief in the signs of this life-giving power is inadequate only when it focuses on the signs alone and not on the revealing person of their author.

STUDY QUESTION: Why is the Gospel of John critical of faith based on miracles?

John 5:1–18
MY FATHER IS STILL WORKING

In the Introduction to this commentary we discussed the possibility that there are dislocations of passages in the Gospel as we have it. Most of them are hazardous for the commentator, but there is good reason to suggest that chapters 5 and 6 are in the wrong order. The main reason is not so much that transposing these two chapters would straighten out the geographical movements of Jesus between Galilee and Jerusalem. It would of course help, but not completely. More important, if chapter 6 followed chapter 4, it would conclude the main issue of signs, words, and faith; and chapters 5, 7, and the following would address a new issue: the challenge of Jesus' revealing word to the religious institutions of establishment Judaism. There are also internal reasons to think chapter 7 was meant to follow chapter 5 (see 7:23, the issue of the sabbath). Since even modern Bibles do not venture to transpose chapters, we shall deal with them in their traditional order.

Though the "festival of the Jews" (5:1) cannot be identified with certainty—in contrast to the specifically identified feasts of Passover, Tabernacles, and Dedication in other chapters—the issue hinges, somewhat superficially, on the traditional point of sabbath violation. The Gospel tradition has stories of Jesus healing a paralyzed man (e.g., Mark 2:1–12), and it may be one of these that John is reinterpreting here. But there are only minimal literary contacts with the Synoptic tradition.

The setting of this healing miracle—which is not called a sign, unless perhaps it is referred to in 7:31—has fascinated students of the Gospel. Archaeological investigations in Jerusalem have turned up a double pool with five colonnades ("porticoes")—four forming a rectangle, with one running through the middle. And the cryptic Copper Scroll from among the Dead Sea Scrolls has authenticated the name of a pool in Jerusalem as Bethesda (rather than Bethzatha). The setting may have been that of a pagan shrine to the popular healing god Asclepius. At a later time the pool was certainly that, and such a situation is not impossible in first-century Jerusalem. Actually it helps to explain the fact that verses 3b–4, ("waiting for the stirring of the water...whatever disease that person had") look like an attempt to bring a pagan shrine within the Jewish ambit by introducing an angel of the Lord. These verses are almost certainly not part of the original text.

The issue of a violation of sabbath laws against work is somewhat artificial to the story. It serves to stimulate conflict with "the Jews," and it is clear that the miracle itself serves mainly to provide an occasion for a conflict discourse of Jesus. What is most surprising is the abrupt way in which the Jewish resolve to put Jesus to death enters the Gospel. Recall that the reader is expected to know the story and thus not to need a plausible motivation for all the issues raised.

By this time in John "the Jews" are recognized as totally hostile to Jesus, and we must say a word about this term. The Fourth Gospel is not, strictly speaking, anti-Jewish, much less anti-Semitic, though unhappily it may have contributed to Christian anti-Semitism in history. It is not anti-Jewish in any general sense because its opposition to "the Jews," which indeed becomes very fierce in the discourse of chapter 8 and in the passion narrative, reflects the Johannine church's resentment against forced separation from its own background in a Jewish community (see 9:22; 12:42; 16:2). The term "the Jews" is generally equivalent to "the Pharisees," who may have been the leaders of the Jewish communities when the Gospel was written.

STUDY QUESTION: What is the relationship between religious "laws," like the sabbath law, and faith in the Messiah Jesus?

John 5:19–47
THE SON GIVES LIFE TO WHOMEVER HE WISHES

The controversy occasioned by the "giving of life" to the paralytic leads into a long discourse of Jesus that increases tension in its challenge to the Jews. Along the way it develops a number of the typical themes of the discourses in the Fourth Gospel. Like most of these discourses, it is highly repetitive, but powerful in its impact as revealing and challenging word. It is closely linked with its context. The Jews had challenged Jesus' authority to act as he did, and he defended it with an appeal to his Father's activity (5:17). The discourse elaborates on this defense.

In the first section, verses 19–30, Jesus explains the relationship of what he does—that is, how his word functions to provoke judgment—to what the Father does and commissions him to do. Here we meet a trait of the Gospel that occurs in several discourses and sayings of Jesus. It is the placing side by side of basically different perspectives on time and the future, that is, on eschatology. The first part of the section, up to verse 25, which is transitional, refers to the believer possessing eternal life in the present, having already met judgment in hearing Jesus' word. Such a person has already "passed from death to life." This perspective, which is often called realized eschatology, is characteristic of the Gospel of John and occurs throughout. The rest of the section takes up the same theme of Jesus' role, but this time against the background of more traditional, future eschatology which looks to death, judgment, and resurrection in the future. It is possible that the evangelist means to include both perspectives and to assert that Jesus is the focal point of both of them. Many interpreters, however, prefer to see them as evidence of discussion on the subject of eschatology within the Johannine church. Since the Gospel is in other respects the result of a complex process of composition, it may include various stages of theological speculation.

The remainder of the discourse, from verse 31 onward, reintroduces the theme of witness to Jesus and develops it quite systematically. The problem is one of Jewish law: If Jesus bears witness to himself—as he certainly appears to do—his witness is legally invalid. Hence he appeals to a succession of witnesses that corroborate his authority. The list is impressive and very revealing of Johannine theology.

The first witness cited is again John the Baptist (5:31–35), who is spoken of warmly—"a burning and shining lamp"—but still kept in his subordinate place. The second witness is "the works" of Jesus. On the surface this phrase is Jesus' own description of his miracles or "signs." Yet, as will become clearer in succeeding chapters, Jesus' works are the "work" of the Father—singular and plural of key terms like "work," "sin," and "commandment" seem to be interchangeable. And the work of the Father is bringing people to faith. God himself, the Father, is cited as the third witness to Jesus (v. 37). Some think God's witness is merely an introduction to the fourth, the scriptures in which the voice of God is heard, but this point is at least not explicitly made. Since Jesus reveals the Father in himself, God's witness is heard in all he says and does. The scriptures are a witness to Jesus in the sense that the early Christians appealed to them to articulate their faith (see the commentary on 2:22). In typical Johannine irony, the scriptural appeal is effective in the argument with the Jews, because the Bible is their own authority par excellence.

STUDY QUESTION: What are the effective witnesses to Christ in contemporary Christian experience?

John 6:1–15
THIS IS INDEED THE PROPHET

Chapter 6, which as argued above is best considered as an immediate sequel to chapter 4, is a carefully constructed unity, even if one part of it, verses 52–59, is an interpolation. It is possible, however, to comment on it as a succession of smaller units because its structural lines are clear. The overall theme is the identification of Jesus with the bread of life or bread from heaven, and the preoccupation of modern commentators, as well perhaps as ancient ones, is the extent to which this symbol is related to the eucharistic practice of the church.

No one doubts that the popularity of the miracle of the loaves in the early church was connected with the eucharistic interpretation of it. It occurs twice in Mark (see Mark 6:30–44 and 8:1–9) and Matthew and once in Luke, and in all cases it contains the typical language of the eucharistic celebration: Jesus *took* the loaves, *blessed* them (or gave thanks), *broke* them, and *gave* them to the disciples. The Johannine version of the story, though it contains elements that may correspond to the eucharistic practice of the church—for example, the concern about picking up the pieces left over in verse 12—actually minimizes the traditional eucharistic language. Jesus *took* the loaves, and when he had *given thanks,* he *distributed* them. The liturgical formula is broken, and Jesus' contact with the crowd is, in typical Johannine style, not mediated by the disciples.

We cannot conclude that the Fourth Gospel is not interested in the eucharistic understanding of the miracle—nor of course can we speculate on what exactly constituted the miraculous action of Jesus—but we can observe that the traditional eucharistic interpretation is not primary for the evangelist. In the gift of bread Jesus gives himself, of course. Whether this gift is ritualized or not is secondary to the giving itself.

For the Fourth Gospel the christological reaction of the crowd is important. They perceive the event as a sign (v. 14) and in response to it—on a level the evangelist regards as inadequate—they proclaim Jesus to be the eschatological prophet like Moses (note the comparison with Moses in vv. 31–33). Jesus sees the inadequacy of this signs-faith. Though the theme of Jesus as king is central to the Gospel, he is here portrayed as refusing to be made king.

STUDY QUESTIONS: What exactly do we celebrate in the eucharistic worship of the modern church? What gift do we receive in the bread that Jesus provides?

John 6:16–21
DO NOT BE AFRAID

The spectacular miracle of the walking on the water is a part of the Gospel tradition which John is reinterpreting. In the Synoptic tradition it is closely associated with the miracle of the loaves (see Mark 6:45–52), and here the fourth evangelist knows not only the traditions but the sequence of them. Since he is in most instances a creative reinterpreter, the question here is what he intends by the inclusion of this story on which he does not comment formally. It is idle to try to explain away the miracle, for example by translating verse 19 "they saw Jesus walking beside the sea," for the evangelist never tries to shy away from the miraculous tradition about Jesus, even though he is critical of it as a basis for faith.

But we must remember that when miracles are significant for this Gospel, they are manifestations of the divine presence in Jesus. Here the Old Testament comes to mind in the description of God's majestic presence to his creation in Psalm 77:19: "Your way was through the sea, your path, through the mighty waters; yet your footprints were unseen." Since Psalm 78 is the apparent reference in the sequel, it is not improbable that this reference underlies the evangelist's thinking here.

Whether this is really the background of the miracle story or not, there is another reason to regard it as a manifestation of the divine presence in Jesus. That is the use of the expression "It is I," literally "I am," by Jesus at the point of recognition in the story. Some interpreters point out that several of the uses of this otherwise common expression in the Fourth Gospel reflect the Jewish use of "I am" as a name for God (e.g., in Isa 43:25 and elsewhere). We shall see even clearer examples in chapters 8 and 13. If this usage is correctly found here, then Jesus is in a sense identifying himself with God at the moment of his miraculous appearance. Though it is not called a sign in the context, this miracle is a sign in the full Johannine sense.

The function of it in this somewhat complex chapter will become clear only at the end of the chapter. It is not directly alluded to later on. But since the disciples represented by Peter are later on contrasted with the larger group (see vv. 67–69), perhaps we should see a contrast between the two miracles with which the episode begins. The miracle of the loaves elicits a positive response from the crowd but ultimately does not lead to faith. The miracle of the walking on the water is witnessed only by the disciples, and ultimately they confess faith in Jesus. The crowd sees the sign merely as a miracle; the disciples, implicitly perhaps, see their sign as an epiphany of the divine (see 2:11).

STUDY QUESTIONS: We may look for Jesus in moments of distress, but where do we find him? And what do we find in him?

John 6:22–50
I AM THE BREAD OF LIFE

Jesus' miraculous crossing of the lake was for the crowds, in contrast to the disciples, merely a puzzle. Hence the almost too detailed discussion of available boats in verses 22–25.

Verses 26–34 serve as an introduction to the bread-of-life discourse that follows. They contain some important clarifications of Johannine language. For example, verse 26 clearly distinguishes between seeing a sign as such—that is, as a showing forth of the glory of God in Jesus—and seeing it merely as a miracle, in this case implying the satisfaction of having bread to eat.

In view of the importance of "the work(s) of God" in this Gospel, one should translate verses 28–29 literally: "Then they said to him, 'What should we do in order to perform the works of God?' Jesus gave them this answer, 'This is the work of God, that you believe in the one he has sent.'" As we shall continue to observe, "doing God's work" for the Fourth Gospel is a matter of coming to faith, or bringing people to faith. The relation of "works" to "signs" is a close one, but it suggests different levels of understanding of what Jesus is doing and what his followers are to do (see, e.g., 9:4).

The background of the discourse is the story, first told in Exodus 16, of the manna sent by God to feed the Israelites in the desert. Some details of this chapter allude to this story, such as the "complaining," or "murmuring," of the people in verses 41–43, which recalls the plaintive reaction of the Israelites. The quotation in verse 31 which forms the "text" for what follows is not an exact one, but is very likely a reference to Psalm 78:24, a retelling of the Exodus story. Since the context is another demand for a sign (see 2:18), an atmosphere of antagonism is set up—the common feature of the discourses in the Book of Signs—and we are prepared for a sharp contrast to be drawn between Moses and Jesus. Jesus responds in verses 32–33 by offering a different interpretation of the verse from the psalm. The people's request for bread in verse 34 recalls the Samaritan woman's request for water in 4:15, but here the tone is different and the outcome radically in contrast.

The discourse itself, verses 35–50 (actually to v. 51a), is punctuated by Jesus' self-identification with the symbol of bread as a necessity for life (vv. 35, 48, 51a). Only here the symbol is made apparent in that this bread is essential for eternal life. What is it a symbol of? The citation of Isaiah 54:13 in verse 45, which refers to divine teaching, shows that the symbol refers to revelation, as ultimately all the Johannine symbols do. Other features of this discourse are typical of the Gospel: the christological pattern of Jesus' descent from heaven and the placing side by side of different eschatological images, eternal life, and resurrection on the last day.

This discourse is our first introduction to an important device of the Gospel, the use of "I am" sayings with predicates that reflect some of the common images of biblical and even extrabiblical religious language, such as bread, light, life, way, etc. The question for the reader to ask is this: Where should the emphasis be, on the "I" or on the "bread of life"? The answer is not obvious, but it is more in harmony with the Christocentrism of the Gospel to suppose that the symbols are meant to be well known—as indeed they were in the ancient world. In that case Jesus is saying, "What you long for in the religious symbol of the bread of life is to be found in me." The emphasis is on the "I."

STUDY QUESTIONS: What does the christological symbol of bread mean to a modern Christian? How essential is faith in Christ to our lives?

John 6:51–58
MY FLESH IS TRUE FOOD

There is a change of tone, and to a limited extent of language, in these verses, which clearly refer to the eucharistic practice of the Johannine church. Until this point in the chapter, up to verse 51b, the symbol of bread has not been a direct reference to the Eucharist. Now the symbol is reinterpreted in terms of eating the flesh and drinking the blood of Jesus. Unlike the Synoptic Gospels, the Fourth Gospel does not contain an account of the institution of the Eucharist at the Last Supper. But the statement "the bread that I will give for the life of the world is my flesh" is reminiscent of the institution formula in its Lukan form: "This is my body, which is given for you" (Luke 22:19).

The development of this eucharistic interpretation includes some of the same themes as the preceding discourse: the gift of eternal life, the different eschatological perspectives (v. 54), and the background of the Exodus story (v. 58). It is almost as though we have a second version of the bread-of-life discourse, with the focus not on Jesus' identity but on his sacramental presence.

In fact, there are reasons to believe that these verses—probably we should include verse 59 with them—did not stand in an earlier version of the Gospel but were added in order to give prominence to the Eucharist in the context of the symbol of bread, where it is obviously appropriate. The best reason is the sharp inconsistency between the "flesh" here, which is necessary for eternal life, and the "flesh" in verse 63, which "is useless." It is very hard to imagine that these two radically different uses of the word could have been intended to stand side by side without some explanation.

The interpretation of the Eucharist found here is very characteristic of the Gospel of John. It gives no hint of the dimension of a community meal but emphasizes the personal relationship of the communicant with Jesus. Just as the living Father is the source of Jesus' life, so the flesh and blood of Jesus are the source of the communicant's life. In the long discourse of Jesus after the Last Supper, the parallel relationships of the Father and Jesus and of Jesus and his believing disciples will be taken up again, but without reference to the Eucharist.

STUDY QUESTION: Compare the understanding of the Eucharist here with the Last Supper account in Luke 22 and with the instructions of Paul in 1 Corinthians 11.

John 6:59–71
TO WHOM CAN WE GO?

The very different reactions of Jesus' disciples again depict the range of responses to him that we find elsewhere in the Gospel. Some complain, or "murmur," (v. 61) at his words; some (perhaps the same ones) cease being his disciples altogether. Others, the Twelve, for whom Peter is spokesman, confess their faith in him as Messiah, the "Holy One of God." One of them, Judas Iscariot, will ultimately betray Jesus.

These responses, particularly the rejection of Jesus, must be understood on three different levels. First, at an earlier stage of the Gospel when the eucharistic passage was not present, the "difficult teaching" to which many objected was Jesus' statement that he was the bread that came down from heaven. Verse 60 would follow quite naturally immediately after verse 51a. Moreover, Jesus' remarks in verses 62–64 do not take up the issue of eating the flesh but rather the issue of believing in the one who descends from heaven and will reascend. The issue on this level is Christology.

Second, as the text now stands, the "difficult teaching" has become Jesus' statement about the Eucharist. One can readily imagine how even some people attracted to Jesus would balk at his startling emphasis on eating his flesh and drinking his blood. The reader need not, however, try to imagine a historical situation in which Jesus confronted his followers with such a choice. The Eucharist has been made the issue at this level by the process of composition of the Gospel.

Third, we must remember here as in other places that the Gospel addresses the situation of its own time, near the end of the first century, in the Johannine church. That church is aware of some other Christians who have embraced false ideas and thus ceased to be "disciples" of Jesus. It is not easy to decide whether the issue at this level is the eucharistic practice of the church or its christological faith. Perhaps both are at issue, for if one does not understand that the human Jesus is really the divine Son who has come from the Father, then the Eucharist too has become meaningless.

The final scene with the Twelve reminds us again that the evangelist is reinterpreting the tradition about Jesus. For access to the tradition we may turn to Mark 8:27–33, the story of the confession of messianic faith on the part of Peter at Caesarea Philippi. Jesus' question in Mark, "But who do you say that I am?" becomes in John "Do you also wish to go away?" Peter speaks for the disciples in both cases. In Mark, the confession of faith is followed by the first of Jesus' predictions of the passion; John refers to the betrayal by Judas at the same point. Chapter 8 of Mark gives other indications of a common tradition underlying the two Gospels (in the event John did not know Mark directly): These are a multiplication of the loaves, a demand for a sign, a crossing of the lake, and a discussion about bread.

Peter's statement beautifully concludes the long chapter, for the "words of eternal life" sum up a theme that has dominated the whole discourse. The disciples can rise to such a lofty faith because they have witnessed the manifestation of divine glory in the walking on the water.

STUDY QUESTIONS: How does the Eucharist express Christian faith in who Jesus is? Is being a follower of Jesus a necessary consequence of believing in him?

John 7:1–30
HE IS DECEIVING THE CROWD

Chapters 7 and 8 contain a series of discourses of Jesus set in the context of sometimes fierce controversy between Jesus and "the Jews." The place is the temple precincts in Jerusalem, and the time is the early autumn Feast of Tabernacles. We have divided the discourses somewhat arbitrarily into four sections for comment. From a literary point of view, this part of the Gospel leaves something to be desired. It is repetitious, often disjointed, and quite lacking in plausible motivations. But two themes bind it together, and they are central to the dynamic of the Book of Signs. One is the issue of Jesus' identity in relationship to the Father, approached in a variety of ways, and the other is the ever-mounting tension between Jesus and his adversaries. The Gospel is a theological statement. We must beware of reading it on the level of a psychological drama. Were we to do that, the opposition Jesus meets would sometimes appear self-induced. In a way it is, but we must regard the provocation theologically as the encounter produced by the revealing word of God in the world.

We have already mentioned the way in which chapter 7 seems to follow closely on chapter 5 (see the commentary on 5:1–18). The plot to kill Jesus in 7:1, 19, 25 recalls 5:18. The sabbath healing mentioned in 7:23 refers to the paralytic of 5:1–18, and this is Jesus' second direct answer (see 5:17) to the charge of sabbath violation in 5:16. If chapters 5 and 6 are not out of order, then we must suppose the evangelist had additional controversy and discourse material left over, as it were, from chapter 5 which he chose to incorporate here.

The opening scene has puzzled many readers. Jesus refuses to go to Jerusalem for the feast and then goes. But we should hesitate to call Jesus indecisive in the Fourth Gospel. He is anything but that. In antiquity, copyists of the Gospel tried to smooth over the paradoxical behavior of Jesus by the insertion of the word "yet" in verse 8: "I am not yet going to this festival." But the modern interpreter has to wrestle with the more problematic text.

Two main points are made in the first eleven verses. First, Jesus refuses to "come out in the open" on any terms but his own. The device of refusing to go and then going is apparently John's way of making this point, for he depicts a very similar situation in the Lazarus story in chapter 11. Second, the evangelist uses the opportunity to heighten the theme of the rejection of Jesus by "his own" by showing that even Jesus' relatives did not believe in him (v. 5). Here he picks up a motif from the tradition about Jesus, attested in Mark 6:4 and elsewhere, that Jesus' relatives were slow to come to faith in him. The tradition is not implausible and is hardly likely to have been invented by the early Christians, especially in view of the prominence of some of Jesus' "brothers," such as James, in the early church. This note of unbelief is an appropriate introduction to the conflicts in the ensuing chapters.

When Jesus arrives in Jerusalem, the other main theme is introduced in the speculation about Jesus' own person (v. 12). "Deceiving the crowd" was probably a legal offense in Judaism. In any case the charge of being a "deceiver" was part of the Jewish polemic against Jesus and it is reflected in Matthew 27:63. Two questions are raised about Jesus: Where did he get his learning? And how can he be the Messiah if people know where he comes from? Jesus transforms both issues into statements about his relationship to the Father, and it is this which dominates the remainder of the section for the most part.

STUDY QUESTION: How does one distinguish between a genuinely inquiring faith and mere religious curiosity? Does this passage reflect the difference?

John 7:31–52
HE SAID THIS ABOUT THE SPIRIT

As the conflict continues, there are still some who are attracted to faith in Jesus as Messiah (v. 31), but it is a faith based merely on signs and it will not prove durable. Nicodemus, who represented such a faith in 3:2, reappears as the spokesman for a very fair and reasonable position. But there is no indication that he has gone beyond his initial signs-faith.

One of the many examples of Johannine irony in this section is to be found in verse 35. The reaction of the Jews is literalistic: If Jesus is going where we cannot come, can he be going abroad to mingle with Gentiles? The irony is perceptible only to the reader who knows that when this Gospel was written, the Christian mission had brought the message of Jesus to the Jews dispersed among the Gentiles and that the churches were in most cases largely made up of Gentiles.

Verses 37–39 have long occasioned problems for the reader of the Fourth Gospel, but these ought not to obscure the richness of the imagery which John himself interprets for us. The quotation in verse 38 apparently refers to Jesus, and this is in harmony with the Christocentrism of the whole Gospel. When Jesus has been glorified in the passion-resurrection, he will in fact confer the Spirit on his disciples (20:22). This reading seems preferable, but there is another option, and many have taken it. Punctuation is missing from the oldest manuscripts; by adopting a different punctuation, one can translate: "If anyone is thirsty let him come to me and drink. Whoever believes in me, as scripture says, from his breast shall flow fountains of living water." The idea that the believer in turn becomes a source of living water is not foreign to John (see 4:14). The reader should, here as elsewhere, be aware of the options and decide which better fits a total understanding of the Gospel.

As for the "scripture" quoted in verse 38, though it sounds a little like several Old Testament passages dealing with the theme of wisdom (e.g., Prov 18:4), it is not a direct citation from any passage we can identify.

The chapter ends with speculation about the identity of Jesus—which occurs often in John—on the part of the crowd first and then on the part of the Jewish leaders. They cannot agree whether Jesus is the prophet like Moses or the Messiah, or perhaps both at once. As we have seen before and will see again in chapter 8, all such speculation misses the mark. The true identity of Jesus cannot be grasped adequately by categorizing him, even in biblical categories. It can be seen only on his own terms: Jesus is the Son in whom the Father is revealed.

A very old manuscript of John, discovered not long ago, has a reading which makes the end of verse 52 agree with verse 41 and which gets rid of the awkward statement that no prophet comes from Galilee. It inserts an article and reads, "The prophet does not come out of Galilee." Older manuscripts are not always better ones, however, and it may be that this one was smoothing out the difficulties here.

STUDY QUESTION: How do the gift of the Spirit, the revelation of the Father, and eternal life relate to one another in the Fourth Gospel?

John 7:53 to 8:11
NEITHER DO I CONDEMN YOU

As was pointed out in the Introduction, this story is certainly not an original part of the Fourth Gospel. Nevertheless, it is a magnificent story and has rightly been for centuries a prized glimpse of Jesus exercising a wisdom akin to Solomon's and a compassion without parallel. The tone of the story reminds us of Luke, but it probably does not come directly from the Synoptic tradition. Many think it originated in some ancient Gospel, not one of the four in our New Testament, that has not survived. Eventually the story outlived its source and became attached to the Fourth Gospel in some branches of the manuscript tradition. It is hard to say why it was added here, but the introduction to it fits more or less plausibly and the theme of judgment in it is mentioned in 8:15–16.

It is not immediately clear why the question of the scribes and Pharisees constituted a "test" or trap for Jesus. We have to suppose something like the following. The Jewish court has legally convicted the woman and sentenced her to death according to the Mosaic law (see Lev 20:10). But the Roman authorities in Palestine do not permit the Jews to exercise capital punishment. If Jesus advises against execution, he is in conflict with the Mosaic law. If he recommends it, he is in trouble with the Romans.

Jesus skillfully evades the trap by refusing to answer the question. People have speculated endlessly about what Jesus was writing on the ground, as though that would contain a clue to the story. But they may be missing the point. His action is a diversion of attention, meaning simply that he refuses to accept the dilemma thrust upon him, and in fact the trap vanishes as the scribes and Pharisees walk away. It is important to note that Jesus does not condone adultery in this story, nor does he comment on the Mosaic law. What he does is show mercy.

STUDY QUESTIONS: What is distinctive in the behavior of Jesus in this story? How can the modern Christian formulate a position with respect to law, justice, and mercy?

John 8:12–30
I AM THE LIGHT OF THE WORLD

Chapter 8 continues both the themes and the setting of chapter 7; to appreciate the continuity, the reader should reread chapter 7, skip the story of the adulterous woman, and go on to read chapter 8. One of the ceremonies that characterized the Feast of Tabernacles in the Jerusalem temple was the lavish illumination of the outer courtyard. It is perhaps with this in mind that the evangelist introduces a new set of discourses of Jesus with the saying "I am the light of the world." The contrast between walking "in darkness" and having "the light of life" is a good introduction to the sharply drawn contrast between "the Jews" and Jesus that permeates the whole chapter. But the Gospel does not draw out the full implications of Jesus as the light of the world until chapter 9 (see 9:5).

The theme that dominates the whole chapter, with mounting sharpness, is that of fatherhood and sonship. Jesus reveals that God is his Father, beginning with verse 18, and the remaining discourses continue the revelation, which will reach its climax only in chapter 10. In the next section, we will see how the contrast is drawn with the father of Jesus' adversaries.

The first set of discourses and conflict dialogues, verses 13–20, take up again a theme already developed extensively in the discourse of chapter 5, that of witness to Jesus. To understand the contents of the discourses in John, it would help to reread 5:30–47. The evangelist deals with themes somewhat the way a composer deals with thematic elements. He can return to them over and over again, most of the time with variations, occasionally with repetition, and he is not put off by what seem on the surface contradictions. It is the themes that are important. Jesus bears witness to himself (8:18) but also denies it (5:31). With the judgment theme, which we have seen repeatedly in other contexts, Jesus both judges and does not judge (8:15–16; see also, e.g., 3:17 and 5:22). Perhaps in this latter case there are nuances in the word "judge": Jesus does not condemn the world but he does exercise judgment by challenging people to respond to his revealing word with a yes of faith or a no of unbelief (or "sin" in John's sense of the term; see 8:21, 24).

The second part of this collection of discourses, verses 21–30, begins and ends with allusions to Jesus' death, contrasted with dying in sin. The language is indirect: Jesus is "going away" (v. 21) and as Son of Man he will be "lifted up" (v. 28). The death of Jesus, as we shall see, is his return to the Father, the completion and the climax of his mission as revealer. At his death his true identity will be known; he is the one who can appropriate for himself the divine name "I am." The use of this expression without (in Greek) any predicate occurs in 8:24, 28, and 58, and in all cases, though one could make sense of the passages otherwise, the allusion to the name of God is most probable.

The episode ends with the statement that "many believed in him." As we shall see immediately, however, such belief is shallow and does not last long. To appreciate the Fourth Gospel we have to sort out the types of responses to Jesus for which the evangelist can use the word "believe." Ultimately, true faith is belief in Jesus as the one who comes from, reveals in himself, and returns to the Father. The whole Gospel is meant to communicate that.

STUDY QUESTION: The Fourth Gospel (at least in its Greek original) never uses the noun "faith" but only the verb "to believe" or "to have faith." Can you see a reason for this in Johannine theology?

John 8:31–59
THE TRUTH WILL MAKE YOU FREE

The tension that has been growing throughout chapters 5, 7, and 8 now reaches a climax in the vehemence of the argument and in the attempt to kill Jesus. It is a dynamic in which Jesus' revealing word about the Father and his own relationship to him confronts "the Jews" with the real challenge of faith (v. 31). And they fail the test. The use of "word" runs like a thread throughout this section. It occurs in verses 31, 37, 43, 51, 52, and 55. In all cases but the last it is Jesus' word which must be kept, which must be clung to and heard, and which in return will bring the gift of eternal life. Though it is not stated explicitly, the implication of Jesus' whole relationship to the Father is that his revealing word is really God's word which he faithfully keeps (v. 55).

That is why the word can be identified with the truth, and the truth can liberate the slave—one who is in a state of unbelief, of sin—and make him a free child of God (see 1:12). Why should the Jews object to this magisterial promise? They immediately resent the implication that they have been slaves and invoke their descent from the patriarch Abraham. And as the discourse continues, their hostility grows and becomes impenetrable. We have already seen, in the story of the Samaritan woman at the well, that when Jesus' revealing word confronts a person, it must become a personal challenge, it must force the person to examine himself or herself and in the light of that make a response. That is what the Jews refuse to do here. Failure to recognize one's unbelief makes coming to faith impossible.

As the conflict unfolds, the issue of who is whose father dominates. The adversaries appeal to Abraham and then to God as their father. And in the sharpest polemical language yet, Jesus calls the devil their father. In Johannine thought as developed here and elsewhere, the lines are very sharply drawn. The only possible answers to the word are yes or no. To reject it is to reject truth, to be in sin, to be a child of the father of lies. To accept it is to learn the truth, to become free, to be a child of God.

The real issue here and throughout the Gospel is the christological one, and so the theme of God as Jesus' Father is developed here in contrast to the claims of the adversaries. Jesus speaks the Father's word, comes from the Father, is sent by him, receives his glory from him. In fact, he is the pre-existent divine Son who can rightfully invoke the name "I am."

Sometimes the reader of passages like these may be tempted to feel that it is all somehow unfair. "The Jews" in the Gospel don't seem to have a chance, because Jesus neither reasons with them nor tries to persuade them. Instead he confronts them with symbols, with ambiguity, with challenges. We need to recall three things in response to this. First, the evangelist wrote a theological work in the form of a Gospel.

He was more interested in issues than in personalities, and, apart from a few passages, he was not concerned with portraying plausible psychological motivations and reactions. He took the Gospel genre seriously, to be sure, but the Gospel is always proclamation, not merely narrative. Second, the Fourth Gospel was written with a view to its own time and an awareness of what had in fact happened since the time of Jesus. The Jews known to the evangelist had in fact mostly refused to accept Jesus as the Messiah and Son of God, and their rejection was a factual presupposition of the Gospel story. It needed to be recorded, not explained away. And third, there is in the revealing word itself an element of alienness that can only be expressed with a certain ambiguity. It is God speaking in the world of humanity, in human terms of course, but stretching the human beyond itself to an eternal dimension. For this purpose—as to a certain extent in all theological and religious discourse—only symbolic language will do. More important than instant understanding is the willingness to be open to a word from outside ordinary human experience that ultimately reveals latent dimensions of human experience itself. It is a Word made flesh, but at the same time a Word that is with God.

STUDY QUESTION: How does the revealing word of God confront the modern Christian, and how can one be really open to assent to it?

John 9:1–41
NOW I SEE

The literary character of the Gospel changes radically with the introduction of another miracle story. But though all the classic elements of a miracle story are present, it is obvious that this episode is much more than that. Several healings of blind men are to be found in the Synoptic tradition, and it is not possible to say which particular story is being reinterpreted here.

The story is a long one, but it is so carefully constructed that one cannot divide it up for the purposes of commentary. The underlying literary principle is derived from classical drama: it is the so-called law of stage duality, by which a scene is identified as two characters or groups of characters in dialogue on the stage. If we analyze the chapter according to this principle, we find a drama in seven scenes, symmetrically arranged, as follows:

A	1–7	Jesus and the disciples
B	8–12	The blind man and his neighbors
C	13–17	The blind man and the Pharisees
D	18–23	The Pharisees and the parents
C'	24–34	The blind man and the Pharisees
B'	35–38	The blind man and Jesus
A'	39–41	Jesus and the Pharisees

What is the drama about? If the question seems hard to answer, it is only because there are so many plot lines to follow. Let us try to list some of them. First, Jesus performs another sign (v. 16), which characteristically elicits various reactions from those who behold it, ranging from faith on the part of the formerly blind man to rejection on the part of the Pharisees. The sign of giving sight (light) to a man born blind (in perpetual darkness) illustrates in action Jesus' saying "I am the light of the world." Many ancient texts read verse 4 as "*We* must carry out the work of the one who sent me." This seemingly incongruous mixture of pronouns may be quite deliberate. It implies that Jesus is inviting the disciples to join him in the work of the Father (see 4:31–38), which of course is not really performing miracles but bringing people to faith, giving "sight" to the spiritually blind.

Second, there is the issue of sin, which is introduced as a red-herring issue by the disciples in the first scene (v. 2), calling upon the ancient biblical tradition that the sins of the fathers are visited upon the children (see Exod 20:5). The issue returns in the last scene in verse 41 where "sin" is understood in the Johannine sense of unbelief. The Pharisees' reaction to the sign is to solidify their sinful refusal to believe in Jesus. Note also how the issue of sin is ironically raised about both Jesus (v. 24) and the man born blind (v. 34).

Third, there is the issue of christological titles, which progress from prophet in verse 17, to Messiah (Christ) in verse 22, to Son of Man in verse 35. Only the last serves as a basis for real faith on the part of the blind man, because it is Jesus himself who uses it. The formal and almost liturgical response of the man in verse 38 is uncharacteristic of the Fourth Gospel and is probably to be regarded as a later addition arising from the baptismal practice of the church.

Fourth, there is the personal drama of the man born blind. Like the Samaritan woman at the well, he stands out in the Gospel as a real personality, even though he remains nameless. His stubborn defense of the "facts" of his cure leads him along the road to faith in Jesus, though he pays a heavy penalty of ostracism for it. Few subordinate characters in this Gospel emerge with any personal delineation, but this man is surely one of them. In the end he is a model of the Christian believer who suffers for his faith. And the evangelist allows him some intriguingly ironic lines in the play (e.g., v. 27).

Finally, there is the second level of meaning in the drama, which refers not to the time of Jesus but to the events in the Johannine church subsequent to the time of Jesus. The clue here lies in the symmetrical arrangement of scenes which gives prominence to the central scene in which the Pharisees confront the parents of the man born blind. (We will observe a similar structural technique in the Johannine passion narrative.) On the surface, this scene seems to add little to the story, but in reality its prominence must be taken seriously. The parents, who are of course Jews, react out of fear of "the Jews"—already this strange language alerts the reader to the special meaning of "the Jews" for John. The language of verse 22 is highly technical: "the Jews" have formally determined that if anyone acknowledges that Jesus is the Messiah, that person is to be expelled from the synagogue (see also 12:42 and 16:2). It was only very late in the first century A.D. that the Jews had taken such a formal action, and we must infer from this Gospel that such an expulsion had been the fate of the Johannine community. The process is dramatized here in the experience of the man born blind, who in verse 34 is actually expelled. The very poignancy of this expulsion from their Jewish heritage and roots helps to explain the severely negative reaction of the Gospel of John to "the Jews."

Like any good story, this is a rich one precisely because it has multiple story lines and even multiple levels of significance. It deserves to be read and reread with an eye to typical Johannine themes and language.

STUDY QUESTIONS: For the modern Christian, what are the consequences of faith in Jesus? Is some sort of social ostracism an inevitable consequence? If so, why?

John 10:1–21
I AM THE GOOD SHEPHERD

One of the most striking differences between the Jesus of the Synoptic Gospels and the Jesus of the Fourth Gospel is the almost complete absence of parables in the latter. The use of parables is one of the most characteristic features of Jesus' preaching in the Synoptics, and scholars are in broad agreement that parables were historically a mark of Jesus' authentic utterances. This passage in John is the only one where anything like parables are recorded, but even though some translations use the word "parable" for the image of the gate in verse 6, the Greek word *paroimia* is not the ordinary word for "parable" in the Synoptics.

Whatever they should be called, we have here some carefully developed figures of speech which center around two more "I am" sayings with predicates: "I am the gate" and "I am the good shepherd." The two images are quite separate and are used to make quite different points. The first issue, connected with the gate image, is one of access: How does one find access to God, or to life? Through Jesus. The second issue is a christological one which focuses even more directly on the person of Jesus. Jesus is the model shepherd, who in fact lays down his life, in the passion sequence, for the benefit of his flock, both those who believe in him as members of the Johannine community and the "other sheep," who are probably members of other Christian churches.

The background of the shepherd-sheep imagery is of course extensive in the Bible, and though it may require some interpretation for modern Western, urban society, it was of universal significance for the biblical authors. The Old Testament background here may be the familiar language of Psalm 23, "The LORD is my shepherd," where the evangelist would not hesitate to attribute a divine epithet to Jesus or it may be the prophecy of Ezekiel (34:1–31) regarding the shepherds of Israel, whose infidelity is contrasted with Yahweh as his own shepherd and his servant David, whom he will raise up as a model of what a responsible shepherd should be. In the Gospel tradition of the New Testament, which the fourth evangelist is doubtless reinterpreting here, one thinks of the parable of the lost sheep in Luke 15:4–7 and Matthew 18:12–14.

In contrast to the rest of chapter 10, this section has no explicit setting, but it clearly follows on the healing of the blind man in chapter 9, which is referred to in 10:21. Since it concerns the responsibility of religious leaders—and of course the role of Jesus himself—it may well be understood as addressed to the "blind" Pharisees of the preceding episode.

STUDY QUESTION: What are the implications of Jesus' shepherd parables for contemporary religious leadership?

John 10:22–42
THE FATHER AND I ARE ONE

This last encounter between Jesus and "the Jews" has an air of finality about it and brings to a climax the issue of the identity of Jesus. The evangelist places it on another occasion, the December Feast of Dedication or Hanukkah, but nothing in the discourses has any particular reference to that occasion. In fact, the use of the metaphor of sheep (vv. 26–28) connects this passage with the previous one. Several details in the passage remind us of the trial of Jesus before the Jews in the Markan passion tradition (see Mark 14:53–65): for example, the request "If you are the Messiah, tell us plainly" (v. 24), and the charge of blasphemy (v. 33). It is quite possible that John had in mind the trial scene. It is certain that he oriented this passage toward the passion, for it sets up a reason for the arrest and final conviction of Jesus. The next chapter will introduce quite a different reason, the success of Jesus as a result of the raising of Lazarus, but perhaps placing these two motivations side by side is an indication that there was discussion about the issue in the Johannine church.

The main focus is again on who Jesus is, and now, much more explicitly than before, Jesus speaks out. Three statements should be noted in particular. In verse 25 Jesus clearly if indirectly claims to be the Messiah: "I have told you." Then in verse 30 he claims a certain identity with the Father which his adversaries clearly understand to be a claim to divinity. We must be careful not to press this verse too closely, however, as Christians of later centuries did in the controversies about the Trinity. It does not speak either of one person or of one nature. Finally, in verse 36 Jesus speaks of himself as the one who says, "I am God's Son." Throughout the passage Jesus appeals to his doing the works of the Father as evidence to support these claims. Here especially we must give full value to the expression "works": They are the signs, to be sure, but they are also the revealing word of Jesus, both of which are intended to bring about faith.

In verse 34 Jesus quotes Psalm 82:6, attributing it to "your law" as a general name for the whole Old Testament. The argument is a peculiar one, at least to a modern reader. It seems to say that if scripture, which is God's word, can call human beings "gods," then a fortiori it is not blasphemy for Jesus to call himself God's Son. It may be that this kind of argument reflects scriptural debates between Jews and Christians of a later time.

John the Baptist is mentioned for the last time at the end of this chapter, and again it is the quality of his witness to Jesus that is singled out. Even though John did not display the credentials of a prophet, that is, he gave no signs, his testimony to Jesus has proved to be true. We are not told, however, how this happened for the people across the Jordan, but as readers of the Gospel we understand.

STUDY QUESTION: The issue of Jesus' relationship to the Father has come to a conclusion for the Book of Signs. Sum up all the things said about it so far. This will prepare for what the discourse after the Supper has to add to the picture.

John 11:1–44
LET US ALSO GO, THAT WE MAY DIE WITH HIM

There are some reasons to think the evangelist added this powerfully told miracle story to his Gospel at a later stage in its composition. It introduces a completely new line of motivation for the passion (in the following section). "The Jews" in this chapter do not show the same hostility to Jesus as elsewhere in the Gospel. In any case, we may be glad the evangelist included the story, for it is a masterpiece of his art. He may have had in mind to dramatize Jesus' future eschatological saying about those in the tombs hearing his voice and coming out to resurrection (5:28–29). Symbolically, in the presence of Jesus this is shown to be happening already. More probably the evangelist had in mind to foreshadow the resurrection of Jesus himself, as the hour of the passion, death, and resurrection draws close. Several details of the story have their counterpart in chapter 20.

Is the evangelist a reinterpreter of tradition here also? Very likely he is, but it is difficult to specify the method of his reinterpretation. If he knows the traditions of the Synoptics, in this instance of Luke, we can point to a number of passages that may have influenced him in the Lazarus story. First, there are several stories of the raising of the dead by Jesus, and that is a firm part of the tradition about him. We could single out the restoration to life of the son of the widow of Nain in Luke 7:14–17 as an example. But in the Synoptics there is no story which is clearly at the root of John's elaborate story here. Second, for the sisters Martha and Mary one can point to the well-known incident in Luke 10:38–42. The characterization of the two sisters is very close to the picture of them in John 11. Third, there is in Luke the parable of Lazarus and the rich man in heaven and hell (Luke 16:19–31). This is a parable, not a story about actual persons, but John may have been inspired by it. This becomes an intriguing possibility when one recalls that the parable ends with Abraham saying about the rich man's relatives, "If they do not listen to Moses and the prophets, neither will they be convinced even if someone rises from the dead." It is quite possible that all these elements were familiar to John in the composition of the Lazarus story.

We cannot comment on every detail of this story, but we may single out a few parts of it for more explanatory remarks. No "sign" in the Fourth Gospel is as clearly interpreted by the evangelist himself as this one is. The long introduction in verses 1–16 contains a good deal of such interpretation, most of it quite clear in its implications. It offers the evangelist another opportunity to use one of his favorite literary devices, that of ambiguity and misunderstanding. Here the problem centers on the language of death, rest, and sleep. The level on which the sign is to be understood, as in the first sign at Cana (2:1–11), is less that of the miraculous than that of the manifestation of divine glory in Jesus (11:4). Thomas—who will reappear prominently in the context of Jesus' own resurrection—is allowed to speak a fine bit of Johannine irony: "Let us also go, that we may die with him!" (v. 16). The question is, with whom? With Jesus, whose life was threatened in Judea (v. 8), or with Lazarus, who has died (v. 14)? The answer is not obvious, and interpreters have not been unanimous. This is another place at which the reader must decide in light of a general understanding of the Gospel.

Jesus' brief discourse to Martha in verses 25–26 is a famous and deservedly beloved saying. The better attested evidence of the manuscripts should require us to read the beginning of the short discourse this way: "I am the resurrection *and the life.*" This enables us to understand what follows as a comment on each part of the predicate of the "I am" saying. Jesus is the resurrection, an image central to a future eschatological perspective, in the sense that whoever believes in him, even after death, will come to life. And he is the (eternal) life, in a realized eschatological perspective, in the sense that whoever believes in him and possesses eternal life will never die in a definitive sense. The point may be to assert that whatever are the eschatological perspectives of the Christian, Jesus is the basis of them. Martha replies with an impressive christological confession of faith, but her later hesitation at the tomb suggests that even her faith is not yet mature.

The dialogue at the tomb itself (vv. 40–42) is a fine example of how carefully the whole episode is structured. It deals with believing as a proper response to a miracle only if the miracle is perceived as a sign of God's glory. We don't know when Jesus told Martha, "If you believed, you would see the glory of God" (v. 40), but we do know that he has told the reader this explicitly back in verse 4. Similarly, the ending of Jesus' prayer in verse 42, "so that they may believe that you sent me," besides being an excellent statement of the purpose of signs in the Gospel, refers back to Jesus' remark in verse 15.

STUDY QUESTIONS: What kind of eschatological faith or hope should we have as Christians? Does it make any difference to the quality of our lives?

John 11:45–57
EVERYONE WILL BELIEVE IN HIM

The aftermath of the raising of Lazarus offers the evangelist an irresistible occasion to display his command of irony as a literary device. Verse 48 is of course written by and for people who live after the Roman destruction of Jerusalem and its temple in A.D. 70. The implication is that what the Pharisees feared would happen if they let Jesus go on as a messianic pretender—and thus a threat to Roman order—has in fact happened anyway. There may even be irony in the statement that "everyone will believe in him," since Christianity had in fact spread widely before the time this Gospel was written. Even more striking irony—to which the evangelist will refer in a typical cross reference in 18:14—is the "prophecy" of Caiaphas the high priest, "It is better for you to have one man die for the people than to have the whole nation destroyed." For the Christian reader of the Gospel, as indeed for the writer of it, this becomes an unwitting statement of the saving character of Jesus' death. But exactly how Jesus' death was a saving event in the thought of the Fourth Gospel, we must wait to see.

At this point in the Gospel, the die is cast—or perhaps we should say cast again—and the events of the passion narrative are imminent. There remain, however, some additional elements of the tradition to be reinterpreted and some concluding reflections of the evangelist for the first part of his Gospel.

STUDY QUESTIONS: In what sense is Caiaphas a "prophet"? Which of his statements come true?

John 12:1–11
FOR THE DAY OF MY BURIAL

Chapter 12, concluding the Book of Signs, contains a variety of stories, discourses, and reflections, and some of it shows signs of being a collection of materials left over. The first two major incidents are part of the tradition, however, and both are of course reinterpreted.

It is unusually difficult to be precise about just what story John was reinterpreting when he described the anointing of Jesus by Mary of Bethany. In Mark 14:3–9, followed rather closely by Matthew 26:6–13, there is a story of an anointing of Jesus' head by a woman at Bethany. This event just precedes the passion narrative and contains a reference to the burial of Jesus. In Luke 7:36–38 there is a story, unconnected with Bethany or with the passion narrative, in which a woman washes Jesus' feet, dries them with her hair, and anoints them. Two quite separate stories about Jesus underlie these accounts. John knew both, but in exactly what form we are unsure.

What is the point of the story? For John's Gospel, the point is made in verse 7. Mary has performed a symbolic action, almost a prophetic gesture, which calls attention to the death and burial of Jesus. It is not the real anointing of the body for burial; that occurs in 19:39–40. But as a figurative anointing, it serves to keep our attention focused on the climactic events to come. Mary's gesture was an extravagant one, as the dialogue with Judas the betrayer shows, but conventional values do not apply when Jesus' death is in question. The evangelist sets up a contrast between Judas and Mary that makes the reader all the more aware of the coming passion. Verse 8, which could be a misleading principle if it were taken out of its context and generalized, has to be seen as addressed to the same extraordinary situation of the death of Jesus. If we see it as a reply to Judas, we have to remember that he was not really concerned with the poor anyway (v. 6). But this verse is entirely absent in some important ancient manuscripts, and it may have been inserted by some copyist, taking it from Matthew, in order to harmonize the stories.

Verses 9–11 have no counterpart in the tradition but are a link with the motivation for Jesus' death begun in the Lazarus story. We have no other information anywhere on the plot to kill Lazarus too.

STUDY QUESTION: The great saints of every age have done extravagant things to show their love for God. What kind of extravagance makes sense today?

John 12:12–19
THE WORLD HAS GONE AFTER HIM

The entry of Jesus into Jerusalem is often called the "triumphal entry," but in fact that description may be misleading. Actually, in the quotation from Zechariah 9:9, which is important for the evangelist, the word "triumphant" to describe the entering king is omitted. The point of the story is that the crowd publicly acknowledges Jesus as Messiah, "King of Israel" (see 1:49). But this is a christological faith based at best on signs (v. 18), and ultimately it does not last. Given the generally negative assessment of Jesus' public ministry later in chapter 12, we could call this episode a triumphal entry only in an ironic sense. Of course, with his feeling for irony, the evangelist may have perceived it that way too. The final comment of the Pharisees (v. 19) about the "world" running after Jesus is certainly ironical to the readers of the Gospel.

This passage has numerous points in common with the story of the cleansing of the temple (2:13–22), and the reader might have another look at the commentary there before proceeding further. Some interpreters think these two stories were closely connected in the tradition upon which John drew, as indeed they are side by side in Mark 11. Like the earlier story, this one centers around Old Testament passages reinterpreted in the light of Jesus. To the words from Psalm 118:25–26 in verse 13 the evangelist has added the phrase "the King of Israel," thus making the quotation explicitly messianic. All four of the Gospel writers quote this passage, with various modifications. The second quotation (v. 15) is a very abbreviated version of Zechariah 9:9. Only Matthew (21:5) actually quotes this verse, in combination with Isaiah 62:11, but there are hints in all the Gospels to suggest the verse was associated with the entry in the pre-Gospel tradition.

Verse 16 explains the process by which the early Christians used the traditions about Jesus and certain passages of the Old Testament to interpret each other. See the commentary on 2:22. The end of verse 16 has a general application. The point is that what was written about Jesus in the Old Testament was what happened to him in fact, and not only the way the crowd received him into the city.

STUDY QUESTION: The early Christians had no hesitation about reading the Old Testament as written about Christ. How far can we go along with them when we read the Old Testament?

John 12:20–36
WHO IS THIS SON OF MAN?

The "Greeks" who wanted to see Jesus are most probably Gentiles (as in 7:35) who are already attracted to Judaism and therefore have come there for the Passover celebration. They provide an occasion for a discourse of Jesus, but their presence here actually has a good deal more significance than that. On the level of the Gospel—as opposed to that of the history of Jesus—the evangelist is inserting Gentiles, who in his time make up the bulk of the Christian communities, into the Gospel at the crucial moment when "the hour has come."

Jesus' discourse in verses 23–32 makes a series of important statements on the meaning of his death and on discipleship. In most of it traditional sayings of Jesus are being extensively reinterpreted. The "hour" of Jesus (v. 23) in the Johannine vocabulary is the time of the passion, which, also in the Johannine vocabulary, is the "glorification" of Jesus. We have seen that this hour has been spoken of as future, but it could be anticipated when Jesus manifested his glory in signs (see, e.g., the first Cana story, 2:1–11). The coming of the hour will be solemnly announced when the passion narrative begins in 13:1, but here it is proclaimed by Jesus again in an anticipatory manner. It is possible that a similarly special use of the word "hour" was already in the passion tradition, for we find it used twice in Mark's account of the agony in the garden (Mark 14:32–42).

Verse 27 shows us John's reinterpretation of that scene in the garden. With its emphasis on Jesus as divine, the Fourth Gospel does not portray him as praying for deliverance from the impending suffering which he clearly foresees. Instead, he rejects the thought of such a prayer and calls upon God to fulfill the process of glorification, which of course involves Jesus' own death. The divine voice with its solemn utterance lends an awesome supernatural tone to the coming events. The "thunder" is an ancient religious symbol, in the Bible as well as in many other religious traditions, for the voice of God. Though ambiguous in itself, it does not mean here simply that people completely mistook the words for mere thunder.

The solemn tone continues as Jesus places the passion in a cosmic context in which "the ruler of this world," the devil as embodiment of opposition to God, is to be overthrown. The context is also an appropriate one for the third prediction of the passion, the "lifting up" of Jesus. As we know from a cross reference to come in 18:32, this indicates that the "lifting up" means hanging on the cross, a Roman form of execution as opposed to a Jewish execution by stoning, if indeed that was legal. Verse 32 does not mention the Son of Man, which is a firm part of the tradition of the passion predictions, but the question of the crowd in verse 34 serves to bring the prediction into line with the others. To the extent that the fragment of discourse in verses 35–36 may be considered an answer to the question "Who is this Son of Man?" it is a beautiful recapitulation of the light-darkness theme in christological terms. The light and the dark, alternative symbols to the above and the below, the truth and the lie, and other contrasts, align the Son of Man with the world of God appearing in the world of humanity.

STUDY QUESTIONS: In our age, when the value of life is strongly affirmed though not always respected, how shall we understand the saying of Jesus in verse 25? What does it mean to a world that is increasingly less dualistic to speak of "walking in the light" rather than in the darkness?

John 12:37–50
THEY DID NOT BELIEVE IN HIM

There are really two conclusions to the Book of Signs, one a rather negative reflection of the evangelist on the results (vv. 37–43), the other a discourse of Jesus which functions as a summary of his discourses and also has a prominent negative side to it (vv. 44–50). For the negativism of the evangelist's reflections we need to recall the prologue, 1:11: "He came to what was his own and his own people did not accept him." John describes here two classes of people whose response was inadequate. Those who, in spite of the many signs, simply did not come to any kind of faith in Jesus—"the Jews" in the Johannine usage. Second, the cryptobelievers, those who came to a certain level of belief, including some "leading men" among the Jews (Nicodemus among others?), but whose faith was not strong enough to permit them to suffer the consequences, as the man born blind had done. The force of John's scathing description of the latter group is more effective when we realize that the word translated "human glory" in verse 43 is the same as that for "glory" throughout the Gospel. Both groups of people are of course not only characters in the story but contemporaries of the evangelist and his church.

The description of the unbelievers centers around two quotations from Isaiah (53:1; 6:10) which were both used in early Christianity to explain the fact that most Jews had not actually accepted Jesus as Messiah and thus become Christians. The first is also used by Paul in Romans 10:16, and for a purpose similar to John's. The second is used in the other Gospels and in the Acts of the Apostles (see Acts 28:25–27). To see how this theme of fulfillment of prophecy is used, we must recall that the given is the fact that the Jews have not believed. A biblical explanation of the fact is then brought forward. Deterministic as it sounds, the evangelist did not really believe they had no choice in the matter. For the fourth evangelist, Isaiah, like Moses in the law (see 5:46), was writing about the time of Jesus.

The summary discourse of Jesus is, from the point of view of the story, a misfit. In 12:36 Jesus had formally withdrawn, to reappear again in the passion narrative after the introduction to the second part of the Gospel. But here he cries out like a voice from the wings of the stage. The discourse, which is almost totally repetition of discourse themes and phrases used before, is not inappropriate as a summary on the literary level, however. We cannot tell whether the evangelist composed it for this purpose or he simply had it left over from a larger collection of discourses. While the role of Jesus' words in provoking judgment is very prominent in it, the main focus is still on Christology and the relationship of the Son to the Father.

STUDY QUESTIONS: What should be the Christian's attitude toward those who do not enjoy the gift of faith? Do we detect levels of faith in ourselves and in others? Can a contemporary Christian, who deals with the whole Bible, not just with the Fourth Gospel, afford to draw the lines of belief as sharply as John does?

III. The Book of Glory

John 13:1 to 20:31

INTRODUCTION TO JOHN 13:1 TO 20:31

Now that we have become familiar with John's association of the terms "glory" and "glorification" with the death and resurrection of Jesus, it seems appropriate to adopt Raymond E. Brown's name for the second major division of the Gospel. We might recall that though a very formal beginning in chapter 13 marks a new major section, the more important principle of division is the audience Jesus addresses and the consequent tone of his address. From this point on, Jesus' discourses are spoken to the disciples, to those who despite their imperfect understanding of what they have heard and seen, nevertheless have declined to "go away" (6:67). And the content of Jesus' message changes also. It now becomes a message about love—the love of the Father and the Son for each other and of both for the disciples, who are given the new commandment to love each other. And the death of Jesus, which is of course central to any Gospel, is the revelation of a love than which there is none greater (see 15:13).

There are four major sections of the Book of Glory, and in them the reinterpretative hand of the evangelist continues to be prominent. First, there is the account of the Last Supper (13:1–38), which is radically different from its Synoptic counterpart, and therefore presumably from the tradition the evangelist used. Instead of the story of the institution of the Eucharist, which is dominant in the Synoptics, there is a story about footwashing, about which the other Gospels know nothing. Certain other episodes are common to John and the Synoptics, however, as we shall see.

Second, the very long discourse—perhaps better, collection of discourses—which John places after the Supper is an almost completely
original feature of the Fourth Gospel (14:1 to 17:26). At the most this
passage reinterprets some sayings of Jesus from the tradition, but there
are few close ties. It has little or nothing in common with the discourse
of Jesus *before* the passion in the Synoptics (see, e.g., Mark 13). To
understand the Johannine discourse adequately, we must realize that it
is a kind of commentary, in anticipation, on the passion and resurrection narratives. Ideally the student of this Gospel should reread the discourse after reading what follows it. The discourse is often appropriately called Jesus' "farewell discourse." From the point of view of
ancient literature, it has several resemblances to the "testament," the
farewell message and spiritual legacy of a dying religious figure.

Third, the passion narrative itself narrates the events from the arrest
of Jesus to his burial (18:1 to 19:42). We shall note many details of similarity and difference with respect to the Synoptic accounts. The Johannine story accentuates the autonomy of Jesus in the passion. He lays
down his life; it is not just taken from him. In fact, he behaves throughout almost as the architect of the passion, not its victim. He is the Son
of God dying out of love for his friends. The focal point of this section
of the book is obviously the trial before Pilate, which the evangelist has
expanded greatly beyond the rather obscure traditional data and to
which he has devoted some of his most powerful literary talent.

The resurrection stories (20:1–29) include both the empty tomb
and several appearances of the Risen Jesus. But here, as a more detailed
examination will show, there is a great deal of reinterpretation along
the lines of Johannine theology. It is not the resurrection as such that is
important for John, but its value in showing Jesus' fidelity to his
promises to the disciples.

John 13:1–20
SERVANTS ARE NOT GREATER THAN THEIR MASTER

The Book of Glory begins with a very solemn style that is somewhat
unusual for John. Verse 1 in Greek is a single sentence, the end of
which reads: "he loved them to the end." If we understand "to the end"
as "until death," which is a possible meaning of the phrase, then the

statement makes a good introduction to the whole Book of Glory as well as to the Last Supper. It anticipates the interpretation of Jesus' death as an act of love. Love is introduced somewhat abruptly here, but the discourses to follow will explain it fully.

As usual in the Fourth Gospel, the time is indicated in relation to a festival of the Jewish calendar. This time, however, it poses a special problem. In the Synoptic Gospels the Last Supper is not before the Passover but is the festive Passover meal itself, celebrated in the evening after sundown when the feast begins. Even though the Eucharist is not mentioned, the meal here is the same one, as the references to the betrayal by Judas and the prediction of Peter's denials (see next section) show. Are the discrepancies in date reconcilable?

The efforts of interpreters to reconcile them have not proved successful. The most promising suggestion in recent years has centered on evidence that two different Jewish calendars existed in Palestine in Jesus' time, but it has not been shown that Jesus and official Judaism were at variance on this point. Instead of a historical solution, we must seek a theological one. For the Synoptic writers, the Passover symbolism is localized in the Eucharist, which is understood as the Christian Passover celebration. This emphasis necessitates seeing the Last Supper as the Passover and following out the passion chronology accordingly. For John the Eucharist is absent, and the Passover symbolism is applied to Jesus himself, whose death takes place in the afternoon before the Passover meal, at the same time the sacrificial lambs are slaughtered in the temple. It is no longer possible to determine which tradition is historically more accurate. The important thing is that we do not let curiosity about the historicity blind us to the theological symbolism in all the Gospels.

Verses 2–4 also form a single sentence in Greek, combining practical details with a sweeping christological perspective. More than in other accounts of the Last Supper, the betrayal of Jesus by Judas has an overshadowing presence in John. Besides being foretold a number of times in the Book of Signs, as we have seen, it figures prominently here in verses 2, 11, and 18 (where it is interpreted by Ps 41:9), even though it will not be dealt with formally until the next section. The emphasis is all the more remarkable when we realize that in the garden scene Jesus confronts his accusers on his own initiative and there is hardly a role for Judas to play (see 18:2–5). Perhaps the reason for stressing the betrayal is to provide a foil for interpreting Jesus' death as an act of love. Betrayal on the part of a trusted disciple not only contrasts with Jesus' own attitude but makes it all the more powerful.

The footwashing is an act of humility, to be sure—the contrast between the roles of servant and master implies this. But one may question whether humility, which is not mentioned as such, is the main emphasis of the story. Actually, two explanations of the action of Jesus are present in the text. The first, in verses 6–11, demands the disciples' participation in the gesture of Jesus. The Christian tradition has turned to baptism to interpret the event, but not every mention of water is baptismal. Jesus' action may be another prophetic gesture, somehow pointing toward his death, in which his followers must share as beneficiaries of his love for his friends.

The second explanation is in any event clearer (vv. 12–20). In it Jesus defines his authority as Teacher and Lord in terms of performing an act of service, even the menial service associated with the lowest household slave. And he commands his followers to copy his example. The Fourth Gospel has little to say about practical life in the church, but it seems here to convey an important statement about leadership and authority in the church, namely that it is to be exercised in service as Jesus served his disciples. Jesus' ultimate act of service was his death.

The brief discourse at the end of the section provides another occasion for an "I am" saying which lacks any predicate in the context. It suggests that when Jesus is betrayed, that is in his death, his divine identity will appear.

STUDY QUESTION: For centuries the church has interpreted verse 14 literally by celebrating the *mandatum* ("command") on Maundy Thursday, by a liturgical footwashing. How should we evaluate this practice in the light of John's Gospel?

John 13:21–38
AND IT WAS NIGHT

The division between the Last Supper narrative and the farewell discourses is not a neat and clear-cut one. Verses 21–38 are grouped together here because the prediction of Peter's denial at the end of the chapter is traditionally connected with the Last Supper story (see Luke

22:31–34). But the discourses actually begin with 13:33 or even with 13:31.

The story of the departure of Judas mingles the intimacy of the Supper with the cosmic implications of Satan entering into Judas. And with typical Johannine emphasis on the theme of misunderstanding, the other disciples are unaware of the real drama. But unlike the disciples in the Markan account, they do not doubt their own loyalty. The evangelist ends the narrative with consummate dramatic effect by the simple remark "And it was night" (v. 30), which recalls 9:4: "Night is coming when no one can work." In Luke 22:53 Jesus says to those who have come to arrest him: "But this is your hour, and the power of darkness."

The account of the betrayer introduces for the first time the beloved disciple, "the one whom Jesus loved," who enjoys a position close to Jesus at the Supper. An ancient tradition identifies this personage of the Gospel with John the apostle, and one can neither prove nor disprove it. The Gospel itself suggests that this disciple is the authority for the tradition contained in it, if, as is likely, the same person is meant in 19:35. The appendix explicitly states the Johannine church's confidence in his testimony (21:24). Yet some have argued that the beloved disciple is not meant to be a real person but a symbol of the true Johannine believer who is close to Jesus and who testifies to the traditions about him. Perhaps it is not essential to choose between these options. The disciple who was at the root of the peculiarly Johannine understanding of Jesus may indeed have been thought of as a model for the Christian believer.

Jesus gives a "new commandment" of mutual love, about which we shall hear more in the discourses to follow. In view of the fact that the Old Testament had enjoined love of one's neighbor (Lev 19:18, often repeated in the Synoptics and in Paul), one may ask what is "new" about Jesus' commandment. The answer is not obvious, but we may suggest that the newness lies in the analogy with Jesus' own love: "Just as I have loved you, you also should love one another" (v. 34). It is often pointed out that in the Fourth Gospel love is not as demanding or as characteristically Christian as elsewhere in the New Testament. It is only love for one another, not love of neighbor in general, much less love of enemies as in the Sermon on the Mount. Yet if its specificity is that it is love as Jesus loved, then it does have a radical dimension, for Jesus' love was ultimately the laying down of his life (see 15:13). We shall see the same point made repeatedly in the discourses to come, with constant emphasis on the love of the Son and the Father.

The prediction of Peter's denial, with which the reader is familiar from the Synoptic Last Supper accounts, offers the evangelist another opportunity for irony: Peter is willing to "lay down his life for" Jesus— the formula is the same as Jesus uses in 15:13. He will indeed do so, as the appendix reminds us (21:18), but not before he denies Jesus three times.

STUDY QUESTION: The Fourth Gospel offers few details about what Christian love consists of. How should we flesh out this new commandment in practice?

John 14:1–31
IF YOU KNOW ME, YOU WILL KNOW MY FATHER ALSO

The farewell discourses (13:33 to 17:26) are not unified in form or in content, most probably because they consist of various originally distinct portions of discourse. Chapter 14 alerts us to this problem in that it is complete in itself, ending with what appears to be a final remark by Jesus. Yet there are three more chapters of discourse to follow. The result of this collection is a very long section characterized by repetition, variations on the same themes, sometimes even contradiction. But there is an overall unity of themes throughout the chapters, such as the departure and return of Jesus, the sending of the Holy Spirit, the mutual love of Father and Son, the new commandment of love, and others.

What is most distinctive about these discourses, however, is their tone. There is none of the air of confrontation and challenge that marked the discourses of the Book of Signs. Even the use of symbols and misunderstanding is greatly lessened, though Jesus does not speak quite as plainly as the disciples exuberantly exclaim in 16:29. What accounts for the change in tone is that these discourses are addressed to the disciples—and thus to the Christian readers of the Gospel—to help them interpret the death and resurrection of Jesus. It is hard to discover logical patterns that would enable us to divide the discourses into smaller units, and perhaps we are not meant to. We shall comment on them, therefore, in large blocks, calling attention to only some of the recurrent themes. Chapters 14 and 16 have several questions or remarks of the disciples, but these scarcely interrupt the flow of the discourse.

Because the discourses comment on events yet to happen, time is as it were collapsed in them. Present, past, and future are not logically distinct. Verse 25 is a good indication of this, for Jesus speaks as though he had already departed.

The emphasis of the discourse in chapter 14 and indeed of the other chapters also is on the consequences for the disciples of Jesus' return to the Father. But the discourses continue to be christologically oriented, particularly in terms of Jesus' relationship to the Father. Such statements as "If you know me, you will know my Father also" and "Whoever has seen me has seen the Father" (vv. 7, 9) are some of the strongest assertions in the Gospel that Jesus is the revelation of God himself. In Johannine thought it is this primary role of Jesus as revealer which undergirds the exclusive claim of Jesus to be not only the way to the Father but the only way to him (v. 6). Despite the lofty claims of Jesus to be the revelation of the Father, the Fourth Gospel does not simply equate Jesus with God. Jesus and the Father are mutually in each other (v. 11), yet Jesus must go to the Father, "because the Father is greater than I" (v. 28).

One of Jesus' main purposes in this discourse is to instruct the disciples to carry on his mission in the world after his departure to the Father. He tells them that they are to "do the works that I do," and even greater ones (v. 12). Our acquaintance with Johannine vocabulary enables us to translate this task as "to confront the world with the revealing word of God and thus bring people to faith." But the disciples, who lack understanding, are bewildered, and are even about to desert Jesus in his passion, can hardly carry out this mission unaided. Hence Jesus promises them the Holy Spirit of truth who will be with them forever.

Verses 16–17 and 26 are the first two of several passages promising that the Father (or Jesus) will send the Advocate, the Holy Spirit. This designation of the Holy Spirit is unique in the Fourth Gospel (and the First Epistle of John) and obscure in its origin. It may be preferable to use the word "Paraclete," however, which is merely taking over the Greek word used, since such translations as "Advocate" and "Counselor" indicate only limited aspects of what the Paraclete is to do for the church. The most important point to note is that this is another Paraclete (v. 16), implying that Jesus has fulfilled the same role while he was with the disciples. The Holy Spirit, therefore, in this capacity is the continued divine presence assisting the disciples to perform the mission of Jesus in the world. He will remain with them and within them. He will teach them everything and make them remember all that Jesus has said (see the comment on 2:22). The Fourth Gospel itself is thus evidence of the work of the Paraclete in the Johannine church.

STUDY QUESTIONS: What do we learn about God if the ultimate revelation of him is in the human Jesus? How does the Spirit function as a Paraclete (advocate, counselor, instructor) in the church of today?

John 15:1–17
I AM THE TRUE VINE

A new section of the farewell discourses, or perhaps a new discourse in the collection, begins very abruptly with a predicative "I am" saying and introduces a new symbol. We have the feeling that we are suddenly brought into a discussion—about a vine or at least a vineyard, presumably—that has been going on already. That is to say that the extended figure of speech here (compare the use of pastoral imagery in chapter 10) seems to be a commentary on something—a parable? a metaphor?—but we cannot say on what. The technique is allegorical: Jesus identifies the vine, the vinedresser, the branches, the dead branches, and (implicitly) the fruit.

Symbolism involving vines and vineyards can be found extensively in the Old Testament (e.g., Isa 5:1–7; Ezek 17; Ps 80:8–16; etc.) and in some parables in the Gospel tradition (e.g., Mark 12:1–11, etc.), but it can also be found in pagan religious traditions. No specific background for John's imagery here has been convincingly demonstrated, and perhaps we should regard the vine symbol on a par with many of the other Johannine symbols such as water, bread, light, and the rest. They are chosen because their value as religious symbols is widespread—perhaps, in the experience of the evangelist, universal. Biblical backgrounds are not excluded, but are not exclusive either.

For some interpreters, ancient and modern, the vine symbol has eucharistic significance, suggested partly by the connection between the farewell discourses and the Last Supper account. In the Markan account of the Supper Jesus says, "I will never again drink of the fruit of the vine until that day when I drink it new in the kingdom of God" (Mark 14:25). But the image in John 15 does not mention wine, only the vine, the branches, and the fruit, and John displays no interest in the Eucharist at the Last Supper.

Similarly, we should be hesitant to speak of imagery of the church here. There is no hint of the collective relationship of the branches to the vine, but rather of the individual, personal relationship of the disciples to Jesus as the source of their life. Such an emphasis is characteristic of the Fourth Gospel and should neither be subordinated nor preferred to other images of Christian life in the New Testament. They all have their contribution to make to Christian theology and self-understanding.

All questions of background aside, the passage is an eloquent expression of the relationship of the believer to Christ and of the meaning of the commandment of love. Here the commandment is rooted in the mutual love of Father and Son and the mutual love of Jesus and the disciples. The theme of mutuality, or reciprocity, of love has its almost mystical counterpart in the notion of mutual indwelling of Father, Son, and disciples. Love of Christians for one another is for John but a reflection of love at much deeper levels.

STUDY QUESTION: Obviously Christian faith and love cannot be merely an individual matter. How then should one express the importance of individual relationship to Christ in a modern, socially oriented church?

John 15:18 to 16:4a
THEY HATED ME WITHOUT A CAUSE

The theme of this section of the discourse is that of incomprehension, opposition, and finally persecution on the part of "the world." And throughout, the analogy is drawn between the way the world has treated, and in the passion will treat, Jesus and the way it will treat the believers in Jesus. The statement of 13:16 that "servants are not greater than their master" is reinterpreted here to mean that if the master was not exempt from persecution, neither will the servants be (v. 20).

The Fourth Gospel uses the word "world" with great frequency and in its own distinctive but not quite uniform way. It does not mean simply material creation as opposed to spiritual reality. If it is proper to speak of dualism in John, it is not a gnostic type of dualism. For John, the world means the world of people, something close to the term "humankind." Jesus' mission is to be Savior of the world (4:42) and light of the world (8:12) because the Father loved the world (3:16). But in a majority of cases in the Gospel, and increasingly in the latter half of it, "the world" is used in a pejorative sense for those who reject faith in Jesus, who oppose and persecute him and his followers. The world in this sense is dominated by Satan, "the ruler of this world" (14:30), and Jesus must conquer it (16:33). Especially in the prayer of Jesus in chapter 17 the lines are drawn sharply between the disciples of Jesus and the world.

The Johannine church experiences opposition from outside itself and defines its experience in the radically opposing poles of God vs. world. It is clear from verse 25, which cites Psalm 35:19 or 69:4, that "the world" for this church is virtually equivalent to "the Jews." The opening verses of chapter 16 remind us for a third time that what is at issue is expulsion of the Christians from the synagogue. Jesus' words predict not only such an expulsion but even the killing of Christians. It is hard to say whether there actually was such violent persecution of Christians in the experience of the Johannine community, but they are encouraged to be prepared for it.

The Paraclete is mentioned in this discourse also (15:26–27), and this time his role is to bear witness to Jesus in the presence of a hostile world, as Jesus himself did in the polemical discourses of the Book of Signs. Actually the witnessing function is to be that of the disciples, but it is the Spirit who will empower them to carry it out.

This discourse also ends with a note of finality in the first half of 16:4, but another discourse follows with no new introduction.

STUDY QUESTIONS: How does the modern Christian experience the world? Is it necessary, or even proper, for modern Christians to adopt the Johannine attitude toward the world?

John 16:4b–33
YOUR PAIN WILL TURN INTO JOY

A new discourse or fragment of discourse begins with the second half of verse 4. It covers much of the same ground as chapter 14 does but with a different development of the themes and with some different emphases. Evidence that this is a separate treatment of the themes may be found at the outset when Jesus comments that no one asks where he is going (v. 5). Actually Peter has asked this in so many words (13:36) as has Thomas in a less direct manner (14:5). The contradiction is less glaring if we suppose this is another version of the earlier farewell discourse.

It is somewhat startling to hear Jesus say, "It is to your advantage that I go away" (v. 7), but the sequel explains the remark. In order for the disciples to carry out their mission, they must be aided by the Paraclete, and Jesus has promised to send the Paraclete only when he himself departs. The last discussion of the Paraclete (vv. 7–15) is the most extensive. It portrays the Spirit in the two major roles connected with the designation Paraclete: a juridical role over the world (see 15:26–27) and an instructional role with regard to the church (see 14:26).

Verses 8–11 are in general clear but are very difficult to understand in detail. The Paraclete will deal with three major issues of Jesus' own preaching throughout the Gospel. Sin is understood as refusal to believe. "Righteousness"—the expression is not found elsewhere in John—is understood as Jesus fulfilling the revelation of his true identity by keeping his promise to return to the Father; the return is thus a kind of guarantee of the truth of his revelation. Judgment is understood as the decisive condemnation—expressed here in cosmic terms—of those who reject the revealing word. Though the Paraclete's role, to be exercised of course by the Johannine church and by the Gospel itself, is to convict the world of these things, we must suppose it is before a court of Christians. John does not predict a major change of heart on the part of the world.

Verses 12–15 reiterate the role of the Spirit in leading the disciples to understand Jesus and his message. Even though Jesus says he has more to say, we need not suppose the Paraclete is going to add to Jesus' word. It is a matter of understanding, as is shown by such verses as 2:22; 12:16; and 14:26.

Beginning with verse 16, Jesus speaks of his death and resurrection and uses the beautiful and powerful simile of the woman giving birth (v. 21) to contrast his followers' pain and joy. We will note, when considering the resurrection appearance of Jesus to the disciples, how many of the themes of the discourses, such as joy and peace, reappear there. Once pain is turned into joy—that is, once the disciples realize that Jesus has indeed returned to the Father—they may have full confidence in the Father's love (v. 27) and trust in his bounty.

One of the most difficult issues for the reader of the farewell discourses—as apparently for the disciples as they are portrayed hearing them—is to keep straight the language of Jesus' coming and going. On the one hand, his death is his return to the Father; on the other, his resurrection is in some sense a return to the disciples, though in this chapter the language used is exclusively that of "seeing" Jesus. Some interpreters think there is also in the discourses mention of Jesus' second coming at the end of time, the parousia (e.g., 14:3), but even in this instance it is possible to think of the resurrection appearances. Jesus does come to the disciples after the resurrection. From then on, guided to the truth by the Paraclete and enjoying the gift of eternal life, their relationship to Jesus and the Father is as described in the farewell discourses.

The conclusion to the present discourse (vv. 29–33) contains both a confession of faith on the part of the disciples and a prediction of their abandoning Jesus in the passion. Are the two compatible? Once again Jesus questions the adequacy of their faith. They believe that Jesus came from God; only after the death and resurrection, the glorification of Jesus, will they be able to believe that he has returned to the Father. True christological faith in the Fourth Gospel involves believing both movements of the pattern of Christology, descent and reascent.

STUDY QUESTIONS: According to John, what is the basis for confidence in prayer? How is joy compatible with the suffering promised in the previous section?

John 17:1–26
THAT THEY MAY ALL BE ONE

The farewell discourses end, as is fitting for a testament, with a majestic prayer of Jesus, which takes up again some of the themes that pervade the earlier discourses. The chapter is deservedly a favorite because of the admirable poetic simplicity of its language and because it portrays Jesus' ultimate concern not only for his disciples but for Christians of the future. Traditionally it has been called the priestly or high-priestly prayer of Jesus, because it is a prayer of intercession for others. The model is Jesus the high priest of the Epistle to the Hebrews who intercedes for the people (e.g., Heb 7:25). But even though verses 17–19 use the language of "sanctification," which is sometimes used in the context of sacrifice, we should hesitate to attribute to the Fourth Gospel a Christology of priesthood.

The prayer is so carefully composed that one would expect to find a careful structure in it, but there is little agreement on what that structure is. We comment on it here by dividing simply according to the persons or groups prayed for.

Verses 1–5 are a prayer for Jesus himself, that God will crown the work Jesus has undertaken at his command, that is, glorify Jesus. The perspective is still that of the passion-resurrection both future and past. Jesus has finished the work, though he has not yet returned to the Father. Jesus also prays that he may confer the gift of eternal life, which is here defined as knowing God and Jesus.

Verses 6–19 center on the disciples, for whom Jesus prays explicitly from verse 9 on. The petitions of the prayer are that God will keep the disciples faithful to himself as Jesus has done thus far, and that God will protect them in a hostile world. The phrase "as we are one" at the end of verse 11 is missing in some important ancient manuscripts and translations of John and probably does not belong here. The unity of the disciples has never been in question in the Gospel.

Verses 20–23 are an explicit prayer for the Christians of the evangelist's own time, who have come to faith through the word, the preaching, of the disciples. In their case Jesus prays emphatically for their unity, which will indicate to the world that Jesus' mission was really from God. The basis of Christian unity for John is the unity of Father and Son and the mutual relationship of Jesus and believers, and thus that unity can be a public sign of God's love for Jesus and Jesus' love for his followers.

Verses 24–26 conclude the prayer with a petition for continued union between Jesus and his followers even after he returns to the Father. Again the relationship is defined as one of love and indwelling.

STUDY QUESTIONS: In what respects can Jesus' prayer serve as a model of Christian prayer? How important to contemporary Christians is, or should be, unity among them? What kind of unity is desirable?

John 18:1–27
WHY DO YOU STRIKE ME?

After the very long interlude of the farewell discourses, the Gospel returns to the events of the passion narrative and moves swiftly toward its conclusion. In doing so it once again takes up traditional material, and the process of reinterpretation again becomes more obvious. But this is another instance where it is not easy to determine exactly what John's source is. His narrative has many points in common with Mark, but it also has a whole succession of Lukan parallels precisely where Luke differs from Mark and is widely thought to be using a separate passion story. Thus we cannot be sure whether John has an independent source for the passion or he selectively follows the same sources as the Synoptic writers do. It is still helpful in highlighting John's special emphases, however, to compare John with the Synoptics.

Even in the material covered in this section, from the garden scene to the interrogation before the Jewish authorities, there are some notable differences. For example, the moving story of the agony of Jesus in the garden is omitted (see comment on 12:27), no doubt in the interests of presenting Jesus as firmly in command of the decisive events. Yet a trace of the tradition remains in Jesus' remark to Peter in verse 11, "Am I not to drink the cup that the Father has given me?" Also, the Jewish interrogation of Jesus takes place not before the reigning high priest, Caiaphas, nor before the Jewish council but before the somewhat shadowy figure of Annas (v. 13). If John knew of another interrogation before Caiaphas (v. 24) he is silent about it. The minimizing of the Jewish legal or quasi-legal processes is part of the evangelist's purpose to focus on the trial before Pilate (next section). In addition to substantial differences such as these, there are numerous variations of detail in John's narrative, many of them easily explained by his overall understanding of Jesus and the passion. The reader would be helped by reading the Markan passion story (Mark 14:32 to 15:47) before proceeding further with John.

In the story of the arrest of Jesus in the garden, Jesus plays a dominant role—anything but that of a helpless victim—even to the point of reducing the betrayal on Judas's part to merely pointing out where the garden was. Contrast the dramatic image of the Judas kiss in the Synoptics (see especially Luke 22:47–48). The dominance of Jesus over the whole scene comes in his use of another "I am" statement (v. 5) connoting the divine presence, before which everyone falls to the ground powerless. Not all agree that the "I am" is so significant here—it could of course mean simply "I am Jesus the Nazarene"—but one should compare 13:19, where the context alludes to the betrayal. Cross references are typical of this Gospel, whether explicit or not. Verse 9 explicitly refers to 17:12, though it interprets it somewhat less spiritually.

Peter's triple denial of Jesus is woven together with the interrogation before the Jewish authorities, as it is also in Mark, though not in precisely the same way. The "other disciple" who witnesses the interrogation is generally thought to be the "beloved disciple," who is at the origin of the Johannine traditions. The power of this complex scene speaks for itself in John as in all the Gospels.

STUDY QUESTION: Betrayal of Jesus or denial of him are still not uncommon reactions of Christians under stress. What can we learn from this unhappy aspect of the passion story?

John 18:28 to 19:16a
MY KINGDOM IS NOT FROM THIS WORLD

The trial of Jesus before Pilate is clearly the centerpiece of the Johannine passion narrative. It brings the theme of judgment that has pervaded the Gospel to a climax with fine dramatic power and the most irony in the Gospel. It is easy to see that the evangelist wants to highlight it. First, he has greatly expanded the brief dialogue between Jesus and Pilate into two substantial scenes. Second, with complete disregard for the historical situation, he has displaced the mocking and scourging of Jesus, which should follow the trial as part of the punishment, and put it in the center of the trial. Third, he has again used the technique of the stage to structure the whole incident. The result is very similar to the dramatic structure of chapter 9, but the organizing principle is the frequent change of scene from outside Pilate's official chambers, the Praetorium, to inside and back again. The device is explained, not implausibly, by the Jews' reluctance to incur ritual defilement (18:28). If we note the words indicating going out and going in, we observe the following structure:

A	28–32	Outside	The charge: Jesus must die
B	33–38a	Inside	Interrogation: kingship
C	38b–40	Outside	Declaration of innocence; Barabbas
D	1–3	(Inside)	Mocking of the king
C'	4–8	Outside	Declaration of innocence; Ecce homo
B'	9–12	Inside	Interrogation: power
A'	13–16a	Outside	The verdict: Jesus will die

Of course, John is not a script writer and hence not concerned with stage directions. But he uses dramatic technique very effectively in his narrative. The scenes he portrays have a certain symmetrical structure which enhances the development of plot while giving some prominence to the central scene. In fact, the theme of kingship plays a dominant role in the passage, occurring in every scene but the first. Only in the central scene does anyone actually acknowledge Jesus' kingship. There, with consummate dramatic irony, soldiers hail Jesus as king in a moment of utter human degradation.

An effective drama has more than one plot. Sometimes, as here, all the characters have their own. We can comment briefly on this passage by following the various plots in summary fashion. The careful reader will note many more details that cannot be mentioned here.

Pilate's drama is that of a representative of "the world," in the Johannine sense, who tries to avoid getting involved with the revealing word of God in Jesus and finds that neutrality is not possible. His job is to judge, and though he seeks to evade it, not even formally pronouncing a verdict or a sentence, he cannot. In the process he undergoes judgment himself, as everyone does in the presence of Jesus. Note how the term "hand over" is used in the passage; it is the term used for the betrayal on the part of Judas and had become almost a technical term in Christian circles. The Jews "hand over" Jesus to Pilate (18:30), and Pilate and Jesus both discuss this action (18:35 and 36, "handed over"). In the second interrogation scene Jesus declares that the "greater sin" is that of the one who hands him over (19:11). Finally, trapped by his

refusal to judge, Pilate himself "handed him over to them to be crucified" (19:16).

"The Jews" are of course by this time in the Gospel resolutely
opposed to accepting Jesus as the Messiah-King. They are the antago-
nists of the play whose mounting, almost frenzied opposition to Jesus
leads them to an ultimate denial of the very religious values they seek to
protect. They are portrayed as concerned with ritual purity (18:28) and
the law (19:7) but motivated by their rejection of Jesus' revelation of
God in himself (19:7). And in the end they deny the messianic hopes
they sought to defend: "We have no king but the emperor" (19:15).

Jesus' drama lies in the irony of the situation. As the reader knows,
he really is the Messiah-King, but his is not a kingdom of this world
but a kingdom of truth (18:36–37). He is on trial, but in reality he is
the judge, whose word provokes judgment wherever it is heard. Pilate
taunts Jesus' adversaries by displaying him as a mock king and—perhaps with another bit of theological irony—calling attention to his
humanity: "Here is the man" (19:5). The final scene can be read somewhat differently: "Pilate . . . brought Jesus outside and sat him on the
judge's bench" (19:13). In this reading (which is grammatically quite
possible), Pilate again taunts the Jews, and the sight elicits their horrify-
ing cry. But unwittingly he places Jesus in the role of judge before
whom the Jews condemn themselves by denying their messianic hope,
and Pilate condemns himself by becoming a betrayer. And the
inevitable result also takes place: Jesus will be crucified.

STUDY QUESTIONS: Why can't "the world," like Pilate, remain
indifferent to the revealing word of God? Are there even situations in
which the stubborn defense of religious positions leads to an implicit
denial of them? Why does John in this story subtly and perhaps ironically emphasize the humanity of Jesus?

John 19:16b–42
THEY WILL LOOK ON THE ONE
WHOM THEY HAVE PIERCED

The remainder of the Johannine passion narrative, basically the crucifixion, death, and burial of Jesus, is a mixture of elements of the com-

mon Gospel tradition, all reinterpreted, and incidents peculiar to the
Fourth Gospel. Sometimes even the order in which things are mentioned is quite different (within the limitations of the story, of
course). It is possible that the evangelist is adapting them to a literary
structure here, but it is less easy to detect one.

What should strike the reader most of all is the sharp difference in
the tone of the narrative when compared with any of the Synoptics.
In John there is a distinct air of majesty, of serenity, and of course of
finality about the whole Golgotha scene. The chilling details of this
scene in the Synoptic tradition, such as the mockery of the crowds,
the darkness, the rending of the temple veil, are as it were systematically eliminated. Jesus dies, not with a loud cry as in the Synoptics, but
with a decisive comment on his fulfilling his divine mission, "It is finished" (v. 30). Jesus is still not the victim so much as the Son of God
who lays down his life. He commands the scene. Even Simon of
Cyrene, who is pressed into service to carry the cross in the Synoptics,
is eliminated, and Jesus carries his own cross. The fourth evangelist
offers us a wholly different side of the story of the cross.

In this part of the passion tradition in all the Gospels, we become
aware of how important Psalm 22 was to Christian reflection on the
story (the reader should turn to Psalm 22 to see the force of this
remark). We may even say that the interpretation of the psalm (and
other Old Testament passages) was so inextricably bound up with the
traditions about what happened at the cross that there was mutual influence in the Gospel accounts. For example, all mention that the soldiers
cast lots for Jesus' garments in accordance with Psalm 22:18—and with
the custom at Roman executions—but John develops the story fully to
illustrate the two lines of the psalm which he quotes (vv. 23–24). Jesus'
remark "I am thirsty," though it is not an exact quotation, may refer to
Psalm 69:21: "For my thirst they gave me vinegar to drink," but it also
illustrates Psalm 22:15. The Markan passion places on the lips of Jesus
the opening words of Psalm 22: "My God, my God, why have you for-
saken me?" Here, for reasons readily recognizable, John does not make
use of this verse of the psalm. For other examples of Old Testament
influence, see the use of Exodus 12:46 in verse 36, giving to the death
of Jesus the symbolism of the Passover lamb sacrificed on the same day,
and the use of Zechariah 12:10 to interpret the piercing of Jesus' side.

Numerous details of this part of chapter 19 are peculiar to John or
are highly developed from mere hints in the tradition. Let us mention

but a few of them. From the tradition that there were women present at the crucifixion (see, e.g., Mark 15:40) the evangelist has developed the beautiful scene in verses 25–27. It is much more than an exemplary act of filial piety on Jesus' part: To the beloved disciple, who represents the Johannine church, Jesus entrusts his mother and a new way of Christian life is about to begin.

The account of the piercing of Jesus' side and the flow of blood and water is unique to John and has always been puzzling to his readers (as 1 John 5:6–8 shows). Much of the Christian tradition has seen the sacraments of Eucharist and baptism symbolized here. We should be cautious about such an identification in this Gospel, however, though it is not impossible. We cannot help recalling 7:37–39 here with its image of the water, symbolizing the Spirit, flowing from Jesus' body once he has been glorified. His glorification, his return to the Father, takes place when he has shed his blood, like the Passover lamb, in death. The solemn insistence of verse 35 on the trustworthiness of this account—which may well be a later addition to the text (see 21:24)—draws attention to its importance.

Finally, we may note the burial scene. John identifies the traditional Joseph of Arimathea as a secret believer and associates with him Nicodemus, who we already suspect is one. We know from 12:42–43 what he thinks of such people. The question here is whether he intends the burial scene to mean that Joseph and Nicodemus both come out into the open with their faith in Jesus, providing an example for others in the evangelist's own time. This seems likely, for their action was a very public one. Their preparation of the body for burial has the effect of removing the reason for the women going to the tomb on Easter morning. As we shall see presently, such a reason is not mentioned in the next chapter.

STUDY QUESTIONS: When sentimentality (not true emotion!) is set aside, how should a Christian react to the cross of Christ? Is it mere rhetoric to see in the death of Jesus a source of new life?

John 20:1–18
"I HAVE SEEN THE LORD"

The first major division of the final chapter of the Gospel actually contains two separate stories—the second one, the appearance of Jesus to

Mary of Magdala, a masterpiece of Johannine art. But they are so intri-
cately woven together that we must deal with them under one heading. First, however, a general word about the Gospel traditions concerning the resurrection is in order. There are two types of such
traditions: stories of the empty tomb in all the Gospels, and stories of
appearances of the Risen Jesus in Matthew, Luke, John, Acts, and 1
Corinthians 15:5–8. The tradition with which John was working, we
must suppose, contained a story of the women at the empty tomb (see
Mark 16: 1–8) and one or more stories of appearances to the disciples
(see Luke 24:36–49). In this passage, John has described an empty-
tomb visit on the part of Peter and the beloved disciple, which may be
an expansion of the tradition, and has transformed an empty-tomb
story involving Mary into a dramatic appearance story. Let us concentrate on a few details of each.

The byplay between Peter, acknowledged leader of the church at
large, and the beloved disciple, authority of the Johannine church, must
be significant, though it is hard to specify with confidence (vv. 3–10).
The beloved disciple clearly has the edge, in speed and in insight, but
he defers to Peter. Perhaps the Johannine church yields something to
the larger Christian movement while at the same time claiming its own
spiritual prerogatives. For the details regarding the burial cloths, contrast 11:44.

The real issue is that the beloved disciple "saw and believed." It is
not actually said that Peter did not believe, and we need not pursue an
unexpressed contrast. But what did the beloved disciple believe? Verse 9
says that "as yet they did not understand the scripture, that he must rise
from the dead." So presumably the disciples did not understand that
Jesus had risen. In light of other statements in the Gospel (see, e.g., the
comment on 16:30), we may suppose he believed that Jesus had indeed
returned to the Father, as he had promised. This is what constitutes
true christological faith in the Fourth Gospel. Thus the resurrection as
such is not (yet) the object of faith.

It is typical of the Fourth Gospel to alter the story of a group of
women at the tomb so that an individual is involved. Mary experiences
perplexity at the empty tomb, concluding that the body has been
removed. We should note that the empty tomb of itself proves nothing
about the resurrection; a gardener or anyone else could have removed
the body. In the Synoptic tradition the empty tomb has to be interpreted by a revelation: One or more angels must reveal that it means
Jesus has risen from the dead. In John the angels, part of the tradition,

are present, but they serve no revealing purpose since the empty-tomb story has become an appearance story, and Jesus can speak for himself.

The evangelist uses very effectively the ancient literary device of the recognition scene, and no comment can add to its moving power. But why does Jesus say, "Do not hold on to me" (v. 17)? Among many and quite diverse suggestions one commends itself: Jesus is warning Mary not to try to hold on to the Jesus she knew, for he is returning to the Father, as he said he would. To cling to the earthly Jesus would be tantamount to a faith based merely on signs, and that is not enough.

What is the Easter message to be relayed to the disciples? In the Synoptic tradition it is of course "He is risen." But nowhere in John 20 is that message mentioned. Instead, the message is that Mary had seen the Lord (v. 18; see also v. 25). The focus is not on the resurrection itself but on the visual evidence that Jesus has not vanished in death but is returning to the Father as he promised: "Say to them, 'I am ascending to my Father'" (v. 17). The really striking point, however, is in the expression, used for the first time here "my Father and your Father, my God and your God." The Father is, now that Jesus has completed the cycle of his revealing work, the Father of his followers. In other words, they can now become children of God. The assertion of the prologue (1:12) has been fulfilled: "To all who received him, who believed in his name, he gave power to become children of God."

STUDY QUESTIONS: Is the resurrection of Jesus a matter of faith or of reason? How essential for the modern Christian is the empty-tomb tradition? Another way of putting this question is: What is the relationship between our view of human nature and our Christian faith in resurrection?

John 20:19–31
BLESSED ARE THOSE WHO HAVE NOT SEEN

The last two appearances of the Risen Jesus in the main body of the Fourth Gospel also serve to make specific points besides demonstrating to the disciples that Jesus is risen. The latter purpose as such is not actually mentioned at all. Both times the disciples are in rooms with closed doors; yet Jesus "came" to them and showed the identifying marks of his crucified body. Jesus has now ascended to the Father—the ascension as a distinct episode is Lukan, not Johannine—and can come to the disciples to let them *see* him as he promised (see 16:16 and the comment there). It is really Jesus, but the Fourth Gospel (unlike 1 Cor 15) has no speculation about the nature of a risen body.

The first appearance to the disciples echoes many themes from the farewell discourses which have the cumulative effect of showing that what Jesus has promised proves to be fulfilled. We list some of these themes here with sample references to the discourses:

Jesus came: 14:18

Peace be with you: 14:27; 16:33

filled with joy: 15:11; 16:20–22

they saw the Lord: 16:16–19

I am sending you: 17:18

receive the Holy Spirit: 14:16–17, 26

sin: 15:22–24; 16:8–9

In the Gospel traditions the resurrection appearance of Jesus to the disciples regularly contained the element of commissioning them to undertake the task of evangelizing (see Matt 28:18–20; Luke 24:47; Acts 1:8). In John the commission is in terms of forgiving or retaining sins (v. 23). In view of its close affinity to Matthew 16:19 and 18:18, this saying must have originally referred to the practice of early Christian churches. But does John mean simply to reaffirm that practice, which otherwise is not hinted at in his Gospel? Given the context of the saying as a postresurrection commissioning of the disciples, and given the special Johannine use of "sin" as rejection of belief in Jesus (singular and plural are interchangeable, 8:21–24), we may suppose Jesus is referring here to the general mission of his followers to share in his work of confronting people with the revealing word to provoke faith or rejection ("sin").

"Doubting Thomas" has long been a fixed part of our vocabulary. But it may be that mere doubt is not a good description of his role when we see him in the light of Johannine thought. In his statement in verse 25 he does not just doubt, he refuses to believe. In demanding physical contact with Jesus he actually sets up the conditions for a faith based merely on signs. He becomes one of those whom Jesus had referred to when he said: "Unless you see signs and wonders you will not believe" (4:48). Yet when Jesus confronts him, it is not said that he wants any longer to fulfill his conditions, that is, he does not have to actually touch Jesus. Instead, he sees him and responds to his word with a very lofty confession of christological faith, the most explicit attribution of divinity to Jesus in the Gospel. Thus Thomas is more than a doubter, and we should translate Jesus' command to him, "Do not doubt but believe" (v. 27).

Thomas has another function, however. He is one who must see in order to believe. Seeing Jesus is of course not unimportant, since the disciples' experience is the witness at the root of the Gospel. But the Gospel is addressed to a generation of Christians who have not seen Jesus and must rely on the word of the Gospel itself. Thus the story of Thomas provides a setting for Jesus' final words, which are stated solemnly in the form of a beatitude: "Blessed are those who have not seen and yet have come to believe" (v. 29).

Verses 30–31 are a formal conclusion to the Gospel which, because it mentions "signs," has often been thought of as originally a conclusion to a collection of miracle stories used in the Johannine community. Whether that is so or not, the evangelist has used it to conclude the Gospel, and it does so appropriately. Note that it places the emphasis on why the Gospel was written, not why the events happened. But on reflection the two are not distinct. Aided by the Spirit of truth, the evangelist has written to do what Jesus' revealing word was meant to do: to elicit faith and thus make eternal life possible.

STUDY QUESTIONS: What implications for Christian life does faith in Jesus as risen have? In what sense would John agree with Paul that "if Christ has not been raised, then our proclamation has been in vain and your faith has been in vain" (1 Cor 15:14)?

IV. Appendix

John 21:1–25

John 21:1–25
FEED MY SHEEP

We have already indicated briefly in the Introduction why chapter 21 cannot be regarded as an original part of the Fourth Gospel. It should not for that reason be treated lightly, however. It has a narrative power not unlike that of the Gospel itself, though it introduces a number of puzzles for the reader. The chapter consists basically of a third resurrection appearance of Jesus to a group of disciples (v. 14). More precisely, it contains a miraculous catch of fish coupled with a recognition of the Risen Jesus (vv. 1–8), a meal with Jesus (vv. 9–14), a commissioning of Peter to be responsible for the church (vv. 15–17), a prediction of Peter's martyrdom (vv. 18–19), a discussion about the implied death of the beloved disciple (vv. 20–23), and a new conclusion to the Gospel (vv. 24–25). What is hardest to fathom in all this is what really holds it together and why it was appended to the completed Gospel. Some of these issues have implications for the life of the Johannine community and its relationship to the larger Christian church, of which Peter is seen as the leader or representative, and in that consideration may lie a reason for the chapter.

In verse 24 the Johannine community speaks in the plural "we" about the beloved disciple as author of the Gospel. Though the verse implies that he wrote what precedes immediately, it is nevertheless uncertain whether the same evangelist wrote both the Gospel and the appendix. Verses 20–23 make sense only if the beloved disciple has already died. But whoever wrote the appendix was also an interpreter of earlier traditions. For the miraculous catch of fish, he knew a story similar to that in Luke 5:1–11, which has many points in common with John 21. In Luke the story is a vocation story, calling Peter to become a fisherman of people (compare the "follow me" in 21:19), but it may originally have been a resurrection appearance transformed into something else by Luke. Possibly the author of chapter 21 also knew the tradition of a resurrection appearance to Peter (see Luke 24:34; 1 Cor 15:5).

Traditional interpretation has seen a number of symbolisms in details of this chapter. In verse 7, for example, the fact that the beloved disciple is first to recognize the Risen Jesus suggests the superior spiritual insight of the Johannine church (see 20:8). The precise number of fish, 153, is so unusual as to be significant (v. 11), and guessing its meaning has always been tantalizing. For many it suggests the inclusiveness of the church. The meal of bread and fish (v. 13) reminds us of the multiplication of the loaves and is often taken as a eucharistic meal. The three-part dialogue of Jesus with Peter (vv. 15–17) corresponds to Peter's triple denial, though we must note that it is the reader who makes this point, not the writer.

The second conclusion is at least to some extent imitative of the first. By its use of hyperbole, it is much less impressive than its model.

STUDY QUESTIONS: What might the various stories in the appendix say to the church today? How do they link discipleship to Jesus' death and resurrection?

SUGGESTED FURTHER READINGS
ON JOHN'S GOSPEL

John Ashton. *Understanding the Fourth Gospel.* Oxford–New York: Oxford University Press, 1992. An elegant investigation of the genesis of John's Gospel in relation to contemporary Judaism, and of revelation as its central idea.

————, ed. *The Interpretation of John.* Expanded ed. Edinburgh: T & T Clark, 1997. Fourteen classic essays on various aspects of Johannine interpretation and theology.

Raymond E. Brown. *The Community of the Beloved Disciple.* New York: Paulist Press, 1979. A fascinating attempt at charting the history of the community in which John's Gospel was written.

————. *The Gospel According to John* (The Anchor Bible). 2 Vols. Garden City, N.Y.: Doubleday, 1966, 1970. A scholarly yet readable reference commentary that has stood up well over the years.

Rudolf Bultmann. *The Gospel of John, A Commentary.* Oxford: Blackwell, 1971. A groundbreaking work, still valuable for its theological insights.

R. Alan Culpepper and C. Clifton Black, eds. *Exploring the Gospel of John.* Louisville: Westminster/John Knox, 1996. Twenty articles provide an accurate snapshot of current Johannine research.

Stanley B. Marrow. *The Gospel of John.* Mahwah, N.J.: Paulist Press, 1995. A lively theological tour of John's Gospel, with an emphasis on its significance and spirituality.

Francis J. Moloney. *The Gospel of John* (Sacra Pagina). Collegeville, Minn.: Liturgical Press, 1998. This narrative-critical exposition of John's Gospel brings to light the theology of the Evangelist and its significance for people today.

Rudolf Schnackenburg. *The Gospel According to St. John.* New York: Crossroad, 1968–82. A mammoth reference commentary that presents fairly the views of other scholars as well as a rich exposition of the text.

Dwight Moody Smith. *The Theology of the Gospel of John* (New Testament Theology). Cambridge, UK–New York: Cambridge University Press, 1995. The "dean" of modern Johannine studies deals with the setting and sources of the Gospel, the themes of Johannine theology, and some issues raised by Johannine theology.